CW00370600

This book surveys two hundred years of German economic thought, from the *Staatwissenschaften* of the eighteenth century to National Socialism and the Social Market in the twentieth. Whereas Classical Economics, from Smith, through Ricardo, to Marx and Mill, laid emphasis upon value, distribution and production as the theoretical core of economic reasoning, the emphasis among German economists was placed on human need and order. This contrast of the variety of human need with the processual orderliness of economic organisation has been a constant preoccupation of German writers on economic affairs since the early eighteenth century. What form of rationality guides this process? What mechanisms ensure that the rational choices of households and individuals will translate into a rational economic system capable of meeting their wants and needs? These essays demonstrate that there are different solutions to this problem of order, and that different strategies can be devised.

IDEAS IN CONTEXT

STRATEGIES OF ECONOMIC ORDER

IDEAS IN CONTEXT

Edited by QUENTIN SKINNER *General Editor*
Series editors
LORRAINE DASTON, WOLF LEPENIES, RICHARD RORTY
and J. B. SCHNEEWIND

The books in this series will discuss the emergence of intellectual traditions and of related new disciplines. The procedures, aims and vocabularies that were generated will be set in the context of the alternatives available within the contemporary frameworks of ideas and institutions. Through detailed studies of the evolution of such traditions, and their modification by different audiences, it is hoped that a new picture will form of the development of ideas in their concrete contexts. By this means, artificial distinctions between the history of philosophy, of the various sciences, of society and politics, and of literature may be seen to dissolve.

The series is published with the support of the Exxon Foundation.

A list of books in the series will be found at the end of the volume.

STRATEGIES OF ECONOMIC ORDER

German economic discourse, 1750–1950

KEITH TRIBE

Keele University

CAMBRIDGE
UNIVERSITY PRESS

Published by the Press Syndicate of the University of Cambridge
The Pitt Building, Trumpington Street, Cambridge CB2 1RP
40 West 20th Street, New York, NY 10011-4211, USA
10 Stamford Road, Oakleigh, Victoria 3166, Australia

First published 1995

Printed in Great Britain at the University Press, Cambridge

A catalogue record for this book is available from the British Library

Library of Congress cataloguing in publication data
Tribe, Keith.
Strategies of economic order: German economic discourse,
1750–1950/Keith Tribe.
p.   cm.–(Ideas in context)
Includes bibliographical references and index.
ISBN 0 521 46291 6
1. Economics–Germany–History.   2. Economics–Philosophy.
I. Title.   II. Series.
HB107.A2t76   1995
330'.0943–dc20   94-5623   CIP

ISBN 0 521 46291 6 hardback

SE

Contents

vii

Acknowledgements

The first essay in this collection is based upon a paper presented to a seminar in the Research Centre, King's College, Cambridge in January 1981; it was later published in revised form in the *Journal of Modern History*; the version published here has been further revised. Chapter 2 is based upon a paper first drafted in 1982; an abbreviated version later appeared in *Manchester School* (1988). The version published here returns to the original draft and title, and has been considerably extended and revised. Chapter 6, on Neumann's *Behemoth*, is derived from an essay written for a Humboldt Stiftung Conference on the Frankfurt School in 1984, and published in A. Honneth, A. Wellmer (eds.) *Die Frankfurter Schule und die Folgen* (Berlin 1986) in the original German; this too has been substantially altered and extended in the translation and rewriting. The remaining chapters are all new, so far as their publication history goes; they are based upon papers presented to seminars and conferences in Cambridge, London, Manchester, Birmingham, Durham, Bielefeld, Freiburg i. Br., Florence, and Cambridge (Mass.).

During the period that I gathered materials and discussed the issues raised below I have been greatly assisted by many individuals and institutions. Foremost among the latter are the Alexander von Humboldt Stiftung, whose financial support made it possible for me to begin serious investigations of German economics; and the Max Planck Institut für Geschichte, Göttingen, whose Director, Rudolf Vierhaus, was unfailingly generous in his hospitality. The research for Chapter 4, linked to my current research into commercial and economic education in Britain, was facilitated by a research grant from the Economic and Social Research Council. All quotations from foreign-language sources are of course my own translation.

Personal thanks are due to a variety of friends and colleagues who have provided welcome hospitality and/or criticism. As always here my greatest debt is to Doris and Jürgen Rudolph, who have for many years been a constant source of hospitality and good humour. But for them, I would never have been able to pursue my interest in German economics; their friendship over the years has sustained me through some bleak periods, both personal and academic.

I am also indebted in a number of ways to my colleagues in the Economics Department at Keele. Although I do not generally have the opportunity of teaching my 'specialism' (there is a strictly limited demand for undergraduate courses on cameralism, after all), I have profited in many ways from membership of the most constructive and friendly economics department known to me.

Hans Bödeker and Diethelm Klippel were extremely liberal in supplying me with xeroxes of obscure material, both from the German inter-library loan system and from the resources of their own institutions. It is their efforts on my behalf that I have to thank for many of the sources used in the chapter on German business education. Thanks are also due to Akira Hayashima, Wilhelm Hennis, Istvan Hont, Peter Intelmann, Ellen Kennedy, David Kettler, Reinhart Koselleck, David Lindenfeld, Monika Maron, Stefan Speck, Grahame Thompson, and Richard Whitley.

Most of the work for this book was completed after I married, gained a family, and ended the life of a bachelor: in my case, one which primarily involved lengthy sojourns in the reading rooms of various German university libraries and an obsession with Ducati motorcycles. Domestic bliss is incompatible with such behaviour, and I am grateful to Lin for the firm but generous manner in which she has guided me to this basic insight. This book is, therefore, dedicated to her.

CHAPTER I

Introduction: From Cameralism to Ordoliberalism

Goya's 'The Dream of Reason brings forth Monsters' was originally sketched in 1797[1] and forms part of the *Capriccio* cycle of engravings, first published in 1799. The cycle was conceived as a denunciation of human error and viciousness, and motivated by enthusiastic support for the enlightened ideals of the French Revolution. The individual works in the series are characterised by a contrast between light and shade, reason and madness, enlightenment and reaction, freedom and servitude. Goya added a short comment to this aquatint version:[2] 'Imagination deserted by reason creates impossible, useless thoughts. United with reason, imagination is the mother of all art and the source of all its beauty.'[3] Reason, left to work alone, creates monsters; while imagination unalloyed by the power of reason gives rise to futile ideas. This fundamental dialectic lies at the heart of the Enlightenment; and it remains with us today, embedded in our elementary thoughts and argument.

Wilhelm Hennis brought my attention to Goya's engraving after reading an earlier version of Chapter 6, prompted by Neurath's conception of economic organisation based upon natural calculation. As I argue in that chapter, Neurath's vision is of a rationalistic, transparent world in which human need and the goods required for its satisfaction can be calculated *in natura*, without the intervention of monetary forms of calculation which, by virtue of their abstraction, conceal the material nature of choices made. The relentlessness with which Neurath – a liberal, genial man and in every respect an enlightened scholar – pursued his vision of perfectibility and rational choice leads us from Max Weber's insight into the irrational aspects of rational behaviour to George Orwell's vision of the world in the year

---

[1] This version is in the Prado, Madrid.
[2] It can be found in the Neue Kunsthalle, Hamburg.
[3] Cited in *The Complete Etchings of Goya*, Crown Publishers, New York 1943.

I

1984. For when, in the closing passages of his *Protestant Ethic*, Max Weber conjures up a vision of a future inhabited by soulless technicians, he writes without evident irony of these *letzten Menschen* of human development. Mastering the world with perfected rational calculation, these are in Weber's sense 'ultimate beings'; but we might also here recall that the original title for Orwell's vision of civilisation's future was *The Last Man in Europe*; and it is not inappropriate to regard Winston Smith's Oceania as a fitting realisation of Weber's vision.

Goya's counterpoint of reason and imagination crystallises this ambiguity at the heart of Enlightenment rationalism, in which the increasing rationalisation of the world serves not necessarily liberty and welfare, but, potentially, bureaucratisation and servitude. This thought underlies many of the essays collected here, but there is more to it than a sceptical view of Enlightenment conceptions of progress and rationalism. Although nowhere explicitly argued in the following, the founding assumption of these studies of German economic discourse is that our modern intellectual world remains ensnared within the antinomies of a perspective first minted in the eighteenth century, but whose form we no longer fully understand. The process of intellectual rationalisation and secularisation that was set in train in the second half of the eighteenth century seems to have left that century far behind; but this world is at once close and distant. Close, in that we derive from a number of eighteenth-century writers a fundamental view of society as rational and perfectible; distant, in that a major effort has to be made if we are to understand quite how they conceived human rationality and its consequences.

To suggest that we should be sceptical of an association of progress with rationalism by no means involves a rejection of the values of liberty and equality with which, in the eighteenth century, they were linked. Instead, it involves a rejection of the idea that the application of rationalistic techniques suffices to realise these values in a reorganised world. The progressive rationalisation of the modern world has not brought about the universal welfare of socialism, nor the *doux commerce* of the free market, nor democratic equality. It has brought about fragmentation, irrationality, disorder, inequality, and subjection; a world in which conceptions like pauperism, political corruption, and vanity too often seem a better guide to our understanding than those 'modern' discourses of social policy, political science and cultural sociology.

It is usual to chart the intellectual distance travelled since the eighteenth century by the creation of a cumulative chronology of theoretical progress – in economics, statistics, mathematics, physics, biology, and chemistry, for example. The technical development of these disciplines, as they became during the nineteenth century, has advanced so far that these early origins are mostly of professional interest only to historians, not to scientists. The manner in which this chronology is constructed is further obscured by the habitual application of a twentieth-century theoretical apparatus to the writings of previous centuries: this is the familiar complaint concerning the prevalence of anachronistic retrospective histories, but it is a complaint that bears repetition. When in the essays below some aspect seems to have a curiously modern ring, this is not an effect produced by a discursive *trompe-l'oeil*, which has inserted familiar categories amongst unfamiliar material. It is rather, I hope, the consequence of employing a historical method which strives to understand past discourses in their proper context, rather than forcibly conscript them through the application of anachronistic categories to be our contemporaries. The reconstruction of past writings in this fashion enables us to see them afresh. Their inherent modernity becomes more evident. They are no longer arranged in a steady progression of scientific achievement from distant rudimentariness to modern truths; they become part of the history of our present, rather than of our past.

The essays presented here are indeed ordered in a rough chronology reaching from the 1720s to the 1940s, but there is no strict progression in their content. Instead, a degree of symmetry continually re-emerges linking the eighteenth to the twentieth century. This is evident in the development of Cameralism in the eighteenth century, and the emergence of *Betriebswirtschaftslehre* in the twentieth, both of which involve the development, within an academic setting, of a new discipline aimed at the training of economic administrators. The account of the work of Friedrich List, and the role played by his involvement in American economic debates, has a clear connection with the discussion of European integration in Chapter 9. One aim of Chapter 4 is to downgrade the significance of a so-called Historical School as a category with any real meaning in our understanding of German economics from the mid-nineteenth to the mid-twentieth century.

The principle by which the subjects for analysis have been selected is governed by the same idea. The essays are drawn up around a history of German economic discourse, but do not seek to define it substantively. No effort is made at achieving a degree of comprehensiveness, indeed the idea that one could write such a comprehensive history is itself highly questionable. On the other hand, it has to be said that the principle of selection has not been governed by the usual criteria of 'influence' or 'originality'. There is in the following, for example, no systematic discussion of the Historical School, Younger or Older; no exposition of Austrian economics; nor of the social question articulated by von Stein and Schäffle. It is not as though we were already awash with studies of these topics; important as they are for an understanding of the genesis of the social sciences, the number of useful articles, let along monographs, dedicated to such themes can be counted on the fingers of one hand. No deliberate attempt is made here to provide insight into the more obvious *lacunae* in existing commentary upon German economics. Instead, these essays present economic argument as it surfaces in the work of popularisation, dissemination, pedagogy, projects for rational economies, and the rhetoric of economic reorganisation and reconstruction. They are intended to invite reflection upon the various guises in which the condition of economic order can be posited and implemented, and the function of rationalism in the creation of this order. The constant concern below is the conditions under which economic order can be installed, manufactured, maintained, restored: to delineate the conditions under which the endless variety of everyday economic activity can be conceived as an orderly, rather than as a disorderly, process. German economics has implicitly turned upon the question of order since the eighteenth century, and these essays serve to highlight the diversity of possible resolutions to the paradoxes created by the ever-extending scope and variety of human needs.

   This contrast of the variety of human need, on the one hand, with the processual orderliness of economic organisation, on the other, has been a constant preoccupation of German writers on economic affairs since the early eighteenth century. What form of rationality guides this process? What mechanisms ensure that the rational choices of households and individuals will translate into a rational economic system capable of meeting their wants and needs? There are different solutions to this problem of order, different strategies that can be conceptualised. A constant feature is however an inherent belief in the capacity of the economic agent to arrive at rational decisions; decisions, that is, whose foreseen consequences correspond with the perceived grounds for choice. Seen from this perspective, the contrast between market and plan, between economic liberty and state guidance, becomes of secondary importance. Liberals who argue that the capacity of the free individual to make rational choices is only impaired by state action in fact share substantial common ground with advocates of state intervention and planning. For such advocates likewise subscribe to belief in the inherent rationality of the economic agent; indeed, that the potential for rational calculation and purposive action is so great that it is considered possible to formalise the conditions under which welfare is maximised, and then deliberately create an optimal allocation of resources. Here, the line separating neo-classicism from Bolshevism suddenly becomes less distinct than we are accustomed to think.

This brings us back to the linkage of reason and imagination that Goya made. The distance between aspiration and achievement that typifies modern economic discourse is one which is determined by the degree to which rational argument diverges from imaginative insight. The steady progression since the 1950s of economic discourse towards ever-more abstract models of economic action is a more general manifestation of the same phenomenon. In an effort to make sense of an increasingly fragmented and complex world, ever-greater degrees of rational abstraction are applied, seeking to make the world 'reasonable', susceptible to reason. In some respects, this *is* the history of economics: the elaboration of new techniques for the understanding of economic life which succeed only by strictly restricting and delimiting that which can be rationally appraised. One paradoxical consequence of this process is that what, for a non-specialist, would be assumed to be the central concern of modern economic analysis – markets and their mechanisms – is addressed only in a disjointed and fragmented fashion. This is a serious deficiency for those in Eastern European economies anxious to learn how a market economy works; the only prudent and sensible response here is, 'not exactly like the textbooks', which is of course neither a very helpful, nor impressive, answer.

The last three essays in the collection take up rather more directly the question of modernisation and rationality in a twentieth-century context. During this century Germany has given the world both National Socialism and the Social Market Economy, the poles, it would appear, of a politico-economic continuum reaching from servitude to liberty. This neat polarisation is placed in question. Chapter 7 reviews the intellectual instrumentarium with which Franz

Neumann sought to come to terms with the phenomenon of National Socialism, and argues that the ambiguity of his conclusions is primarily dictated by the limitations of his conceptual apparatus. In the following essay the accepted intellectual foundations of the Social Market economy are placed in question. The final essay in this closing trilogy then proposes a recalibration of the relationship between the Social Market and National Socialism. Rather than treating the Social Market as an awakening from the nightmare of National Socialist Germany, continuities are emphasised. Recent historical work in this area has begun to consider the modernising aspects of National Socialism. It is now at least arguable that one of the reasons for the rapid economic recovery of Germany after the war was the comparative modernity of the social structure created during the period of National Socialism. This extended into areas such as health and social welfare, infrastructure, vocational training, urban planning, and schooling – the building-blocks of the modern European economy.

Such an approach involves a significant change of perspective from that of Franz Neumann, whose *Behemoth* remains, however, the most systematic attempt to make sense of the disorderly organisation of National Socialist Germany through the application of established conceptions of rationality and legitimacy. A new vision of National Socialism as a moment of modernity has brought criticism from historians steeped in the assumptions of 1960s political science, who automatically assume that 'modernisation' and 'development' are positively charged, 'progressive' forces. There is however nothing inherently 'progressive' about 'modernisation'. One need only reflect, to take a mundane but relevant example, upon the urban wildernesses and slums created during the 1960s in the name of 'development' to appreciate the force of this point. The deliberate, rational reorganisation of the world can create order or disorder; in the name of rational calculation the most irrational consequences can ensue. 'Modernisation' can have grim consequences, and this is an important lesson to be learned from the experience of National Socialism.

This is of course a time of economic reorganisation and reconstruction, and the tenets of modern economics have not so far been an overwhelming success when confronted with the collapse of state socialist economies, or the problems of global indebtedness, or of poverty in the midst of plenty. There are no easy solutions to these problems, nor can any be found ready-made by delving into the archive of superseded economic theories. But if we are to respond constructively to the social and economic problems of the world, some considerable effort of imagination is needed, an effort that can perhaps be stimulated by reflection on the discarded histories of modern certitudes.

CHAPTER 2

Cameralism and the science of government

> To the important and relevant question: Which are the two
> most secure and important foundations for making people,
> *Reich* and *Land* happy? the wise and courageous monarch
> Cyrus made, in all his experience and power, the following
> response: *Eine auserlesene Armee und eine gute Wirthschafft
> der Unterthanen.*[1]

In 1727 Friedrich Wilhelm I decreed that a chair for 'Oeconomie,
Policey and Kammer-Sachen' be established at the University of
Halle; shortly after, a further chair was founded at the University of
Frankfurt on the Oder. This marked the formal inauguration of
courses of study for future state officials, and hence of the formation of
'Kameral- und Polizeiwissenschaften'. In the previous century a
series of texts had appeared – among them von Seckendorff's *Teutscher
Fürsten-Stat* (1656), Becher's *Politische Discurs* (1668) and von
Schröder's *Fürstliche Schatz- und Rentenkammer* (1686) – which were
composed for the rulers of the Protestant states of the Holy Roman
Empire. These seventeenth-century advisory tracts set up a relationship between the interests of a ruler and the welfare of his subjects,
arguing that if a ruler wished to secure his power, then he should first
attend to the welfare of his subjects. In the early eighteenth century
this idea was transferred to the lectureroom, and made the basis of the
new cameralistic sciences. However, this shift from Court to lectureroom brought with it a number of other changes, not least of which was

---

[1] J. P. von Ludewig, *Die, von Sr. Königlichen Majestät, unserm allergnädigstem Könige/ auf Dero
Universität Halle, am 14. Iulii 1727 Neu angerichtete Profession, in Oeconomie, Policey und Kammer-
Sachen*, Halle 1727, p. 1. Cyrus' answer which, von Ludewig notes, struck Socrates as good
sense, could be rendered as: 'an excellent army and well-fed subjects'. But this is only the
loosest of translations – literally it would read 'a good economy of subjects'. *Wirthschaft* could
be accurately translated in this context as subsistence, happiness or wealth; the importance of
these variations is discussed below.

the conversion of general issues of rulership and economic welfare into
the regularities of pedagogic discourse.

Gasser, appointed to the new chair at Halle, was trained in law and
experienced in administration; his appointment in 1721 to the Law
Faculty at Halle and to the Board of Mines was a political reward for
work on the royal domains in Cleves. The chief responsibility of a
university professor was to deliver a course of lectures on the subject
covered by the post held. In German universities, such lectures took
the form of exegesis and critique of an assigned textbook, and it was
usual for professors to write a text suited to this purpose; but for the
first two years Gasser read lectures on Seckendorff's *Teutscher Fürsten
Stat*, before in 1729 producing his own *Einleitung zu den Oeconomischen
Politischen und Cameralwissenschaften*.[2] This might pass without
comment if it were not for the hiatus that exists between the text of
Seckendorff to which Gasser originally lectured, and the textbook
that he then went on to produce for the same course: for while
Seckendorff presents a compendium of the tasks of proper government on the part of the ruler of a seventeenth-century German
principality, Gasser writes exclusively of the business of agriculture
and the revenues that arise from it. It can of course be argued that this
concern with agricultural administration addresses the *financing* of a
principality's objectives, but it does neglect entirely the issues which
Seckendorff, Becher, and Schröder regarded as central: namely, the
nature of such objectives and techniques of government appropriate
to them.

Gasser's textbook covers in quick succession the practical work of
domains and estates: the maintenance of buildings, projects for the
laying out of meadows, for the development of cattle herds, and
discussion of various taxes and duties. He presents in this manner the
business of administration as it confronted the officials of the *Kammer*.[3]
And if we turn to the text produced somewhat later by Dithmar,

---

[2] W. Kähler, 'Die Einleitung des staatswissenschaftlichen Unterrichts an der Universität
Halle', in H.Paasche (ed.), *Festgabe für Johannes Conrad*, Sammlung nationalökonomischer
und statistischer Abhandlungen, Bd. 20, Gustav Fischer, Jena 1898, p. 131.

[3] Derived from the Greek and Latin *camera*, as *Kammer* or *Cammer*, and initially signifying the
palace or apartment of the Prince, later the place from which the domains were administered.
As Pasquale Pasquino has pointed out in a seminar paper 'L'"Utopia" praticabile. Governo
ed economia nel cameralismo tedesco del settocento' (presented at the Feltrinelli Foundation
in 1980) *Kammermusik*, 'chamber music', comes from the same root, designating court as
opposed to church or sacred music.

appointed to the chair in Frankfurt on the Oder, we find a definition
of the field of this new cameralistic science: '*Cameral-Wissenschaft*
concerns itself with the means of raising revenues for the *Landes-Fürst*,
their general improvement and utilisation in the maintenance of the
commonweal [*gemeinen Wesens*] so that every year a surplus remains.'[4]
Dithmar does present under this rubric material organised in a
manner comparable to Gasser, but confines his coverage of the
material to the final section of a book which also includes discussion of
Oeconomie and *Polizei*. In his usage, therefore, 'Cameralism' does not
represent the entire scope of administrative practice, as is implied by
Gasser: he places it alongside the other two domains, while Gasser, the
title of his book notwithstanding,[5] simply ignores them. Furthermore,
it seems that in some respects Cameralism has no independent subject
matter, simply dealing with material and issues also included within
the domain of *Oeconomie* and *Polizei*. There is therefore some difficulty
here in determining the scope and limits of 'Cameral-Wissenschaft',
or in establishing the nature of the relationship between the 'Cameral-
und Staatswissenschaften'. Subsequent commentaries have tended to
obscure this problem by treating Cameralism as if it were a variant of
mercantilism, hence a form of economic discourse that is considered a
predecessor to a truly scientific economics;[6] although it is the familiar-
ity of the concept of 'mercantilism' which recommends it here, not its
clarity or utility. Ordering unfamiliar images or figures through the
imposition of more familiar, but inappropriate, classificatory devices
simply translates what we do not know into that which we think we

[4] J. C. Dithmar, *Einleitung in die Oeconomische Policey und Cameralwissenschaften*, New edn,
Frankfurt a. O. 1745, p. 225.
[5] The reference in Gasser's title to 'politische Wissenschaft' should be read as 'Polizeiwissenschaft', as in Dithmar. This point is discussed below.
[6] Although it must be said that Albion Small's *The Cameralists* (University of Chicago Press,
Chicago 1909) can still be read with benefit. Louise Sommer's entry in the first edition of the
Encyclopedia of the Social Sciences on Cameralism characterises it as primarily a *political* discourse
while at the same time calling it the 'German and Austrian variety of mercantilism' (vol. III, p.
159). Associated with absolutism, state intervention, and centralisation, its theoretical
foundation is stated to be Pufendorf's doctrine of natural right as developed by Thomasius
and Wolff; but according to Sommer it never developed any independent and systematic
structure (p. 160). Cf. H. J. Braun, 'Economic Theory and Policy in Germany 1750–1800',
Journal of European Economic History, vol. 4 (1975), pp. 301–22; and M. Walker, 'Rights and
Functions: The Social Categories of Eighteenth-Century German Jurists and Cameralists',
Journal of Modern History, vol. 50 (1978), pp. 234–51. See also P. Schiera's *Dall'Arte di Governo
alle Scienze dello Stato*, Giuffrè, Milan 1968, which seeks to link cameralistic writings directly to
the development of Prussian economic administration and the construction of the State; and
my *Governing Economy. The Reformation of German Economic Discourse 1750–1840*, Cambridge
University Press, Cambridge 1988.

do. As an approach to historical understanding this route has very little to recommend it. Instead, we should avoid hasty generalisation and consider the manner in which both Gasser and Dithmar seemingly maintain a distinction between the *Oeconomische-*, *Polizei-*, and *Kameralwissenschaften*, a distinction which is today hard to discern either in terms of content or of boundaries.

Jutta Brückner first drew attention to this problem in her discussion of the ambiguity in the title of Dithmar's book – for entitled as it is, *Einleitung in die Oeconomische Policei und Cameral-Wissenschaften*, it is not clear whether *Oeconomische* refers to *Policei*, or to *Wissenschaften*. If the latter is the case, then by modern grammatical standards the adjective fails to agree with its noun; if the former, then it fails the test of modern orthography, for it should not begin with a capital letter. However, eighteenth-century standards were looser and more irregular than those that developed in the early nineteenth century; and we are here seeking to understand a text in its proper context, not apply modern conventions. We can make use of this ambiguity to question the nature of the distinction being made between *Oeconomie* as the promotion of individual happiness, and *Polizei* as the promotion of general happiness – both of which then merge into a *Cameralwissenschaft* which is extended to cover the promotion of 'gute Polizei'.[7] The definitions provided by Dithmar might appear to clarify this:

Oeconomic science or the art of house-economy and husbandry [Haus-Wirthschaffts- und Haushaltungs-Kunst] concerns itself with the manner in which, as a result of rightful industry in town and country, sustenance and wealth can contribute to the promotion of happiness.... The science of Polizei deals with Polizei affairs, although what is included among the latter is a subject of debate, some including only food, drink and clothing, others extending and contrasting it to the Judiciary.[8]

Notwithstanding the lack of clarity in the second definition, a lack of clarity which is, as we shall see below, inherent to the category of *Polizei* and thus resistant to clarification, it might appear that a distinction could now be made after the following fashion: Cameralism is principally concerned with the administration of a state; *Oeconomie* relates this activity of administration materially to the objective of happiness; and *Polizei* concerns itself with the general condition of order prevailing in the state.

[7] J. Brückner, *Staatswissenschaften, Kameralismus und Naturrecht*, C. H. Beck, Munich 1977, p. 72.
[8] Dithmar, *Einleitung*, pp. 2, 5.

This neat separation is however only effective on the basis of modern conceptions of economy and polity, conceptions not yet current in the eighteenth century. Since, roughly speaking, the end of that century, concepts such as wealth, liberty, need, and happiness (that is, satisfaction) have become linked in a chain of meaning which is founded upon the economy as constitutive moment. The texts which have been introduced above, on the other hand, move in a discursive order which could be characterised as politico-ethical, in part Aristotelian; but as we shall see, this was itself coming under attack. Accordingly, this latter conception of the polity is not one of a zone of action, nor of a kind of relation between subjects, but rather embraces the whole state through the medium of regulation. In turn, this process of regulation cannot be conceived in terms of state intervention in the economy, for state and economy have no independent existence – or put another way, they are the same thing. As noted by Dithmar above, *Polizei* represents a nonjuridical form of regulation, a form of order not based upon the law. *Polizei* orders the realm of the ruler according to the objectives of 'peace and happiness'; 'politics' is something that takes place between states or between the subjects of different states – at this time it is not applied to the internal organisation of states.[9]

The promotion of good order and happiness within the state bears however on objects which are also treated under the rubric of Cameralism and *Oeconomie*, such that, for instance, Dithmar selects as the first specific task of *Polizei* the promotion of the populousness of a state.[10] Proceeding then in turn to religious matters and education, later chapters return to cattle, meadows, mills, and breweries, while dealing with such objects under the rubric of *Polizei*. The same objects can be found under the heading of *Cameralwissenschaft*, and also under *Oeconomie* – as if wherever the discourse takes its point of departure, it constantly reverts to a preoccupation with the ordering of productive activity.

This problem is perhaps best approached by returning to the foundation of these new disciplines, and considering in greater detail

[9] The problems of 'state and 'politics' that arise here are touched on below, but crucial for this line of argument is Otto Brunner's *Land und Herrschaft*, Wissenschaftliche Buchgesellschaft, Darmstadt 1973 (originally published 1939); although concerned with an earlier period, this book laid the basis for a complete reappraisal of 'absolutist politics'. See my remarks on Brunner's approach in 'The *Geschichtliche Grundbegriffe* Project: From History of Ideas to Conceptual History', *Comparative Studies in Society and History*, vol. 31 (1989), p. 182.
[10] Dithmar, *Einleitung*, p. 136.

the literature which delineated the requirements of formal university teaching for future state officials, rather than the education of a prince, as can be found for instance in Chapter 6 of Julius Bernhard von Rohr's *Einleitung zur Staats-Klugheit*.[11] Two such works appeared in 1716, one of them also by von Rohr, in which he called for the establishment of a 'Professori Oeconomicae' in the universities. He foresaw two possible objections: first, that no suitable candidates could be found; but second and more importantly, that the subject matter was already covered by the Professori Moralium, that is, within the Aristotelian trinity of politics, ethics, and oeconomy.[12] Von Rohr suggested that present teaching in this area was insufficient for a thorough grounding in the subject. Another writer, Sincerus, was in his tract more forthright: the customary Aristotelian teaching was quite inappropriate to the task of instructing officials, since Aristotle himself had obscured the useful elements in Xenophon's treatment of the household, and rendered it into an ethics.[13]

Von Ludewig, chancellor of the University of Halle, took up this theme in his address to the Prussian Monarch on the foundation of the new chair in 1727:

Professors of *Oeconomie* were not certain whether ears of corn were to be found on trees or in the fields. For their teacher [Aristotle] deals in his oeconomic books almost exclusively with the ethics (*Sitten-Lehre*) of a patriarch (*Hausvater*); housewife; children and servants of the house. What happens in the fields, meadows, ponds, woods, gardens or relates to planting; how to treat cattle in their stalls; how to increase manure; how to brew and sell corn; the tasks of a husbandman on every day of the year; what reserves to lay by and how to stock a store room; how to properly organise kitchen and cellar; what to keep and what to distribute: not a word of this appears in Aristotle.[14]

The proposal that a new academic discipline be created thus involved a deliberate break with established Aristotelian doctrine which united an Oeconomics with an Ethics; although it must be noted that during the eighteenth century Cameralism and *Polizei* were taught almost exclusively within the philosophy, and not law, faculties. The point of departure of this caesura is clear enough in Ludewig: instead of treating the doctrine of the household as the basis of an ethical

[11] Leipzig, 1718.
[12] J. B. von Rohr, *Compendieuse Haußhaltungs-Bibliothek*, Leipzig 1716.
[13] A. Sincerus [pseud. Christoph Heinrich Amthor], *Project der Oeconomie in Form einer Wissenschaft*, 2nd edn, Frankfurt 1717, Zuschrift. Amthor, professor of law at the University of Kiel, sought to provide a systematisation of *Oeconomie* as a precondition for its teaching by specialist professors.　　[14] Ludewig, *Profession*, pp. 142–3.

doctrine, it was to be given a new content, which focused on techniques and objects of administration.

The textbook nominated by Ludewig in his address as the most useful for this new teaching was not Sincerus' *Project*, but rather Florinus' *Oeconomus prudens et legalis*. As already noted, the actual appointee opted for Seckendorff.[15] Nevertheless, Ludewig's suggestion introduces the same hiatus that exists between Gasser's textbook and Seckendorff's *Fürsten-Stat*, since the text bearing the name of Florinus is firmly within the tradition of *Hausväterliteratur*, addressing the head of a household, not a prince, nor even the latter's officials.[16] *Oeconomus prudens* does include the kind of material that Ludewig called for – although the first book, 'On the General Foundations for the Conduct of the Household', addresses the Christian rights and duties of the various component members of the household. With the second book however, dealing with the preparations necessary for the running of the household, the technical aspect comes to the fore in the shape of architectural drawings, since the initial task turns out to be 'first build your house'. Having established the buildings, surveyed the fields and outlined the qualities of the different seasons, the way is opened for details of the sowing, manuring, and harvesting of various crops, the care of gardens and woods, the treatment of farm animals, the keeping of bees and silkworms, and the stocking of ponds, concluding with a 'home doctor' section and a cookbook. The organisation and administration of productive activity are thus placed in the context of a household, a context which Gasser in his *Einleitung* largely displaced in favour of *domain* administration. In Florinus we can see at work the redefinition of *Oeconomie*, based upon the institution of the household, as an exposition of techniques of administration and objects of activity, which once articulated in this manner can be extended to the administration of state domains.

When Florinus chose to characterise the nature of this new

[15] *Ibid.*, p. 160.
[16] The classic study of *Hausväterliteratur* is Otto Brunner's *Adeliges Landleben und Europäischer Geist*, Otto Müller, Salzburg 1949, Chapter 4. A more extensive treatment is to be found in J. Hoffmann's *Die Hausväterliteratur und die Predigten über den christlichen Hausstand*, Julius Beltz, Weinheim 1959. Florinus' text was perhaps the most massive and elaborate work in the tradition, running to over 1,400 pages in the 1702 edition, liberally illustrated with engravings, and in the judgment of Haushofer forms the highpoint of this literature (*Neue Deutsche Biographie*, Bd. 5, p. 225). The authorship of this text, and its process of construction, remains somewhat mysterious. Franz Philipp Florinus was a Protestant priest, at one time librarian to Christian August van Sulzbach; but the text appears to be the product of collective work. See H. Haushofer, 'Das Problem des Florinus', *Zeitschrift für Agrargeschichte and Agrarsoziologie*, Jg. 30 (1982), pp. 168–75.

Hausväterliteratur in which the emphasis was on the organisation of productive activity, he wrote as follows:

Everybody knows full well/ that the art of householding/ which is also called *Wirthschaft*/ is nothing but a proper and orderly organisation/ which the *Haus-Vatter* has to observe in temporal and material goods and means of subsistence: and is in this form also called *Oeconomia*/ which is constructed from two Greek words/ *Haus*/ and Law or Order (*Gesetz oder Ordnung*)/.[17]

With this form of definition we can finally return to Cyrus' epigrammatic remarks reported by von Ludewig at the beginning of his address to the Prussian king on the foundation of the first chair in Cameralism. The first point arises out of the form of the question – it is assumed that the ultimate objective of government is making people, *Reich* and *Land*, 'happy'.[18] In response, Cyrus suggests that this ultimate objective can be gained by the possession of 'eine auserlesene Armee und eine gute Wirthschafft der Unterthanen', which means rather more than 'an excellent army and well-fed subjects'. As can be seen in the citation from Florinus, *Wirtschaft* could be synonymous with householding and thence with *Oeconomie*, but this would render Cyrus as saying 'a good householding', which reads rather curiously, although apparently accurately. The puzzle is solved by emphasising *Wirt* in its sense of a host, or an innkeeper, *Wirtschaft* then not being just the act of being hospitable but also the objects provided.[19] The act of providing these objects and services can thus be assessed qualitatively: the *Wirtschaft* of a household could be good or bad, depending on the food and board there provided. In modern German, *Wirtschaft* principally signifies the economy as a domain characterised by particular kinds of activity, but this clearly demarcated domain is unknown territory in the early eighteenth century.[20] *Oeconomie* had a more general connotation, thanks to its usage by Aristotle and

---

[17] The 1719 edition referred to by von Ludewig was somewhat different to that of 1702, since it focused more on the prince and his court than on the patriarch and his household. This revision itself represents the kind of shift which is described here, although rather curiously the 1702 text is more nearly the one called for by von Ludewig, and is therefore the one outlined above.

[18] That is, *glücklich* – there is no satisfactory translation for this; 'content' would imply a finitude to wants that is not here relevant.

[19] Grimm, *Deutsches Wörterbuch*, Bd. 14/2, cols. 661ff., esp. 670–2.

[20] In Southern Germany the term *Wirtschaft* is still used to denote a restaurant, so that one could still be understood if one spoke of being well or ill *bewirtschaftet*. If an English speaker reflects on the manner that English usage of 'economy' can be extended to being 'economical with the truth', then this highlights the clear distinction between English and German concepts of economy. One might render this English usage intelligible to a German speaker by using the term *ökonomisch*, but might well not be properly understood if *wirtschaftlich* were used.

Xenophon, but one which was tied quite strictly to agricultural activity in the household, classically opposed to chrematistics or money-getting.

This constellation of concepts is illuminated by consideration of a more obscure term, which can be found in Schröder and von Rohr: the use of the word *menage* or *menagieren*: 'If the territorial ruler is to better *menagieren* the loyalty of his subjects then it is good to follow the counsel of Aristotle, and in the giving of judgments to himself announce the happy and good, while leaving the penalties and rejections to his servants.'[21]

And turning to von Schröder: 'The *menagie* of the territorial ruler's revenues consists in the proper distribution of expenditures and also the extension and increase of the same, that is in two words, in *distribuendo et augmentando*.'[22] Clearly we are dealing with an idea of *management* here, with respect to political administration in the first case and economic in the second – and from the point of view of the modern French *ménage*[23] this is not any surprise. In the eighteenth century this meaning was current in the German language, except that it was more closely tied to the subsistence of the household than to the organisation of the household itself; it could also be used to refer to the provisioning of troops.[24] Understood in this fashion, the term then begins to approximate the meaning of *Wirtschaft* as noted above.

Finally, if we turn to the English word 'manage', which derives from the same French roots as the German *menagieren*, we discover that it is in fact composed of two parts, *mannège* and *ménage*.[25] The first denotes 'leading' in the sense of a horse and its trainer; the second to use carefully, to husband. The aural resemblance of these two words has blended both senses into the modern usage of 'manage'. It might also be noted that modern German has not derived any linguistically independent term for the economic sense of this usage, and has thus introduced the anglicism *das Management* to denote the activity of

---

[21] Von Rohr, *Einleitung zur Staats-Klugheit*, p. 42.
[22] W. von Schröder, *Fürstliche Schatz- und Rentkammer*, Königsberg 1752, p. 11 (first published in 1686). Von Rohr in his *Staats-Klugheit* repeats this formulation word-for-word in his Chapter 4 entitled 'Von dem Oeconomie Wesen' (p. 96).
[23] Translated as 'householding', 'household' as *ménagement*.
[24] *Deutsches Fremdwörterbuch*, Bd. 2, Berlin 1942, p. 100.
[25] *New English Dictionary on Historical Principles*, VI, Part 2 (1908), p. 104. Two examples given there are pertinent to this discussion: 'Lorenso I commit into your hands, The husbandry and mannage of my house', 1596, *Merchant of Venice*, III: IV, 25. 'For the mennage of a Family, I know it better than any Lady in Sicily', 1673, Dryden, *Marriage à la Mode*, I: i.

organising enterprises. The closest German equivalent, *Betriebsleitung* (literally 'the conduct or leadership of an enterprise'), denotes the formal exercise of leadership but does not carry the normative connotation of husbandry and parsimony typical in English usage.

But aside from this modern perspective, it could be suggested that the employment of *menagieren* by Schröder and von Rohr represents a way of identifying the organisational tasks of a ruler while at the same time avoiding the classical language of 'householding' associated with *Oeconomie* and *Wirtschaft*. This usage disappears by the mid-eighteenth century, with the clear rejection of the Aristotelian association of an ethics with *Oeconomie*, the tendency to associate the latter with agricultural production, and the formation of a new content for the concept of *Wirtschaft*, which becomes a generic term for productive rather than subsistence activity, and is consequently no longer synonymous with *Oeconomie*.[26] A general treatment of economic processes independent of the classical household can then develop in the guise of a *Wirtschaftslehre*, which appears however under the name *Nationalökonomie* in the first few years of the nineteenth century.

Returning to the discourse on government of the later seventeenth century, it is now possible to evaluate the nature and importance of *Cammerwesen*. One of the functions performed by the Aristotelian influence on German political writings was to deny the pertinence of Machiavellian doctrine, which was generally thought to propose that government be based upon deception and swindling. This is a constant theme through to Frederick the Great's famous diatribe *Anti-Machiavel*; writers would castigate the unchristian nature of a Machiavellian politics, but in so doing reiterate the importance of the relation of ruler and ruled. If the ruler is to be strong, runs the argument, he needs a strong army; but this is useless without sufficient revenues to support it, for without 'money in the box', as von Schröder points out, no successful wars can be fought. Fiscal exploitation of the ruler's subjects will eventually result in the erosion of the base on which the revenues are raised. Instead, the argument runs, if the ruler first makes his people wealthy and content (or happy), his revenues will surely steadily increase. At the same time the relation of ruler to ruled will be secured in terms of a mutual economic interest, rather than in a relationship of political opportunism as is the case with Machiavelli.

---

[26] The process of this separation is outlined by H. L. Stoltenberg, *Geschichte der deutschen Gruppwissenschaft (Soziologie)*, Hans Buske Verlag, Leipzig 1937, p. 207, n. 6.

The governmental fabric of this state ruled according to this *Modell*[27] is that of the *Cammer* and its objects. Pasquale Pasquino has correctly summarised the problem facing Seckendorff's text as that of the rational foundation of the *res publica* and the legitimacy of the new powers of the sovereign, Cameralism assuming its place as a theory of the exercise of this power. The preoccupation of *Teutscher Fürsten-Stat* is not with the 'thinkability' and legitimacy of monarchial authority, but rather with its *constructibility*.[28] The formation of a *Cameralwissenschaft* in the early eighteenth century was in effect the culmination of this imperative.

Cameralism is therefore a concept that serves to draw together certain techniques of government available to the ruler of the eighteenth-century German state, techniques which both stabilise and increase his powers. As such it is not confined to the interiority of this state, an interiority which is both established and maintained in the essentially domestic activity of *Polizei*; it also directs itself to the production and circulation of goods which can be exchanged with those of other principalities. Here the watchword is: keep money at home – that is, do everything to augment the productive activities of the ruler's subjects, in this way paving the way for their enhanced happiness and the ruler's income. Depending on the goods concerned, such advantage might be located in their production domestically, their purchase abroad or their transshipment and finishing off. Significantly the texts which discuss such matters appear indifferent to the means by which this end is attained: agricultural and urban production, skilled and unskilled labour, domains and estates, trading and manufacturing, all are potential sources of welfare and no one source is privileged over another. Typical for this form of argument is the manner in which description of domainal administration can move, without any sense of a hiatus, to discussion of the regulation of trade, the nature of urban trades, and the promotion of exports.

This is of particular importance if we consider for a moment the manner in which cameralistic writings are affected by their categorisation in terms of mercantilism, that is, with respect to a particular view of trade and policy. It is no accident that Eli Heckscher,

---

[27] So described by von Seckendorff, *Teutscher Fürsten-Stat*, 'Inhalt und Disposition des gantzen Tractats', Frankfurt a. M., 1656.

[28] Pasquino, p. 6. 'A ruler must not only think of the expansion of his *Cammer-Gut* and *dominii*/but must also be able to be a happy and good ruler....'; Seckendorff, *Additiones* to 5th edn of *Teutscher Fürsten Staat*, Frankfurt a. M., 1678, p. 25. Cf. here also G. Marchet, *Studien über die Entwicklung der Verwaltungslehre in Deutschland*, R. Oldenbourg, Munich 1885, pp. 31 ff.

investigating economic policy and trading relations in the creation of wealth,[29] found great difficulty in bringing the German literature into his framework. His consequent focus on the maritime trading nations of England, France, and Holland leaves little space for the massive German literature, apart from some addenda and comments on prominent writers such as Becher.

It is quite clear to Heckscher that tolls, weights and measures, guilds, corporations, capital, and coinage are economic phenomena; argument to the contrary in the German and Austrian secondary literature that he cites is accordingly ignored, for example Zielen-ziger's insistence that insofar as mercantilism is a theory it is a political, and not an economic, theory.[30] Most notably, the difficulty already outlined in distinguishing *Polizei-* from *Cameralwissenschaft* never arises, for the term *Polizei* is nowhere mentioned, despite constant reference in the secondary texts to which he refers. Heckscher also regards wealth as an inherently economic phenome-non, obscuring the important point that a primary form of wealth for a ruler consisted in the good order of his subject population. Heckscher's work quickly achieved canonical status among historians and economists unacquainted with the wider continental literature upon which he drew; but the clarity and intelligibility of his analytical approach derived from twentieth-century economic analysis, a con-ceptual apparatus that did not, and could not, exist in the eighteenth. Some kind of sense can always, of course, be made of eighteenth-century writers through the imposition of modern concepts and categories; but this advances our understanding of historical discourse very little, since we make sense of the past in terms of a present configured in a different conceptual language. How then, can we describe the classifications and distinctions made by Dithmar and Gasser?

Cameralism can be generally defined as a set of discourses related to the maintenance of land and people which, if it turns to questions of trade, necessarily evaluates the benefits and drawbacks of relations with other states. *Polizei* on the other hand is confined to internal

---

[29] *Mercantilism*, 2nd edn, George Allen and Unwin, London 1955; this book unfortunately revived the ailing fortunes of a form of classification initiated by Adam Smith, later reinterpreted by Schmoller into a policy for state formation, but which by the early twentieth century was encountering increasingly critical comments from scholars – see my discussion of this and related issues in 'Mercantilism and the Economics of State Formation', in Lars Magnusson (ed.), *Mercantilism*, Kluwer, Dordrecht 1993, pp. 175–86.

[30] K. Zielenziger, *Die alten deutschen Kameralisten*, Gustav Fischer, Jena 1914, p. 52.

order, although an element of the maintenance of this good order and happiness necessarily involves evaluation of the internal consequences of objects treated by Cameralism. Or perhaps we can say: Cameralism assembles the objects which *Polizei* then orders for the good of the state and its subjects. Both of these belong in the eighteenth century to a *Politik*, as is clear from Johann Georg Sulzer's *Kurzer Begriff aller Wissenschaften*:

Staatswissenschaft, or *Politik*, contains the theory of the happiness of entire states or civil societies, and demonstrates the means by which it can be attained. Out of the nature and intentions of a civil state it derives the best form of government and basic laws. Since, however, most forms of government arise by chance rather than being deduced from the fundamental principles of *Politik*, it investigates, in the light of general theory, the advantages and disadvantages of each form of government.[31]

'Entire states or civil societies', and the later apparent hybrid 'civil state' are not confusions, but significant pointers to the set of categories within which this discourse of government moves. For this state is not an entity distinct from society, or a political order present within the social body. It is *synonymous* with this social body: *Staat* and *bürgerliche Gesellschaft* are alternative ways of designating the same political order, governed according to rules of prudence by a ruler. Government in turn meant regulation, in particular, aiding those who were unable to help themselves – so that administration must intervene, regulate, help, protect, order, and restrict.[32] Norms of activity were specified to the smallest detail through the workings of *Polizei*; only through the effective operation of such a work of regulation could happiness be achieved. This objective of the state, its justification for existence, was not something that was naturally created out of human action in society, for the summing of human interaction revealed no regularity, just a chaotic repetition – harmony within the state was therefore a condition which was to be permanently and deliberately under construction, an ever-extending and never-ending task.

This is evident in the description which von Berg composed at the beginning of the nineteenth century, in a systematisation that ran to seven volumes in all:

Policey is like a well-intentioned genius who carefully levels the way for those committed to his care; cleans the air that they breathe; secures the villages

---

[31] J. G. Sulzer, *Kurzer Begriff aller Wissenschaften*, 2nd edn, Leipzig 1759, pp. 180–1.
[32] Cf. Marchet, *Verwaltungslehre*, p. 50.

and holdings in which they dwell and the streets along which they walk; protects the fields that they cultivate, secures their homes against fire and flood and they themselves against illness, poverty, ignorance, superstition and immorality; who, even if he cannot prevent all accidents, seeks however to diminish and ease their consequences and offers refuge in time of need to every pauper, casualty or person in need. Its watchful eye is ubiquitous; its helping hand is ever-ready, and we are invisibly surrounded by its unceasing care.[33]

While *Polizei* constituted a programme of total regulation, it was at the same time nonjuridical, seeking not to adjudicate the legality of completed actions, but rather attempting to define the conditions of good order and public safety in advance. The future becomes calculable in terms of a potentially exhaustive set of situations whose outcomes can be weighed and regulated. This in effect abolishes the distinction of present from future in terms of the couple knowable/ unknowable, for instead, both present and future are established in a finitude of decrees, actions, and agents. Furthermore, this orientation itself generates the requirement that information on such actions and agents be systematically gathered and collated. Accordingly, in the mid-eighteenth century texts began to appear with directions on the collection of such material, of which von Justi's *Grundfeste zu der Macht und Gluckseeligkeit der Staaten*[34] is one example. This programme was then in effect self-sustaining, or self-regulating; actual transgressions of its rules represented a system-failure rather than transgressions as such. Such problems could be dealt with administratively, or alternatively assigned to legal processes which addressed themselves to the regulation of past actions.

The elaboration of *Polizeiordnungen* and the *Polizeiwissenschaft* to which they gave rise was not the consequence of the rise of a centralising state, gathering powers to a central instance and securing that power through the creation of an apparatus of control and administration. Quite the reverse: it expanded autonomously, locally, as a result of its own activity generating further objects of regulation, promoting the actual lack of finality within a postulated finitude of assigned objectives. This tension between postulated closure and actual infinity formed the basis for the extension of regulation and literature – writers on the subject constantly sought to define its limits as a means of creating some kind of mechanism of closure. It had no unitary origin and no clear boundary as an

[33] G. H. von Berg, *Handbuch des Teutschen Policeyrechts*, Bd. i, 2nd edn, Gebrüder Hahn, Hanover 1802, pp. 1–2.   [34] Königsberg and Leipzig, 2 vols., 1760–61.

instrument of government, but it permeated the state and gave it form. Only through its activity could the highest goal of the state, general happiness and security, be realised – or as von Justi stated in his *Grundriß einer Guten Regierung*, 'The common happiness of the whole society is accordingly the ultimate end of the civil constitution.'[35]

Von Justi played a major part in the systematisation of Cameralism and *Polizeiwissenschaft*, along with the Austrian, von Sonnenfels, whose *Grundsätze* were reprinted repeatedly, the last time being in 1819. The work of Sonnenfels was also summarised in the form of coursebooks by other authors,[36] diffusing the basic structure and argument of the *Grundsätze* throughout Central Europe during the later eighteenth century. In this limited sense his writing was more influential than that of Justi, despite its derivative nature.[37]

The *Grundsätze* appeared in three volumes, beginning in 1765; they dealt respectively with *Polizei*, commerce, and finance. In the first volume we find the general theoretical principles established, which deduce the existence of the state from the natural order of men in society, that is, in families, which must associate for the furtherance of their individual welfare through the furtherance of a common good. This common good does however require revenue for its maintenance; the measures necessary for the foundation of welfare and its promotion are to be found systematised in the form of a science, *Staatswissenschaft*, the 'science of government'.[38]

The extent to which the three areas referred to in the title are in fact discrete, and if so, their mode of relation to one another, emerges when von Sonnenfels seeks to codify his terms of reference:

Polizeiwissenschaft is concerned with the principles according to which *internal security* is founded and maintained. *Handlungswissenschaft* is the teaching concerned with the *multiplication of the means of subsistence* through the most advantageous use of what the earth and labour can produce. Finally *Finanzwissenschaft* shows the most advantageous manner in which the *revenues of the state* should be raised. German writers define *Polizei, Handlung* and *Finanz* also under the heading *Staatswirthschaft* or call them the *oeconomic* sciences. The last two are also referred to as the *Kameralwissenschaften*, from

[35] J. H. G. von Justi, *Grundriß einer Guten Regierung*, Frankfurt 1759, p. 5.
[36] Cf. K.-H. Osterloh, *Joseph von Sonnenfels und die österreiche Reformbewegung im Zeitalter des aufgeklärten Absolutismus*, Matthiesen Verlag, Lübeck 1970, esp. p. 37.
[37] Justi was certainly the more original of the two, although the comparison is invidious: Sonnenfels gained his professorial post in Vienna without demonstrating any prior expertise in the subject, and his proposals of the time suggest that his knowledge of the *Staatswissenschaften* was scanty. See my *Governing Economy*, pp. 79–80.
[38] Joseph von Sonnenfels, *Grundsätze der Polizey, Handlung, und Finanz*, Bd. I, 5th edn Vienna 1787 p. 16.

the *Kammer* of the rulers from where the affairs which they are concerned with are customarily administered.[39]

While these divisions are maintained in the course of the three volumes, there is a persistent tendency, visible in the final statement above, to conceive of them as different aspects of the same set of principles. For example, one of the leading principles of *Finanzwissenschaft* proves to be that the manner in which revenues are raised should not disturb internal order; it is thus governed by the same imperative which the work of *Polizei* is designed to uphold, that internal order must be created and maintained.

Von Sonnenfels conceives *Polizei* primarily as an instrument for the advancement of a secure moral order – the task of promoting 'good morals' through religion, education, and the sciences.[40] This delineates a form of social morality, the ideal state of equilibrium which laws, regulations, and decrees enjoin and promote, the freedom of subjects resulting from their complete identification with the objectives of welfare, security, and the common good. In part, these objectives are to be realised through the elimination of the power, hitherto enjoyed by *Stände* and family, to oppose the will of the state. Such power is thought to derive from the accumulation of wealth in the hands of the *Stände* and prominent families. Freedom of commerce is endangered by such power, being defined as 'the condition in which we have nothing to fear as a result of our actions'. Such liberty is not unlimited, but constrained by social duties; and this distinguishes commercial liberty from unconfined independence, and the freedom of arbitrary action.[41] Freedom of the subject is subordinated to the dictates of the common good; thus under the rubric of the safety of persons, suicide, abortion, and child murder are banned on the grounds that they diminish the size of the population, not from any conception of individual morality or ethics. This line of argument is pursued with some consequence, extending to the proposal that disfigured or crippled persons, likely to shock pregnant women and thereby perhaps give rise to miscarriages, be removed from public places.[42]

Concern with the person as a component of a population, rather than as a moral entity, is evident from further regulatory measures, involving the safety of public places, the regulation of health, the control of food and drink, and the general care of the poor. These

[39] *Ibid.*, Bd. I, pp. 20–1.   [40] *Ibid.*, Bd. I, p. 74.
[41] *Ibid.*, Bd. I, p. 217.   [42] *Ibid.*, Bd. I, p. 277.

regulations cluster around the person, but do not presuppose any
innate capacity for self-regulation. The social body is an aggregate of
persons who require, for the achievement of order, welfare and
harmony, a constant work of regulation. Social morality does not
arise spontaneously, but must needs be constructed by a deliberate
work of regulation. In a society conceived in these terms, there are no
laws of motion inhering in the regularities of autonomous economic
activity; without regulation the social order would stagnate or
collapse, consequent upon an insufficiency of good government.

The second volume apparently recapitulates some of the subject
matter of the first, but from a distinct point of view: the various
activities of the population are considered· with respect to their
contribution to the objective of commerce, that is, the increase of
population. Commerce is here treated as the delineation of a number
of regions of activity which might, or might not, be conducive to the
promotion of the common good. Agriculture, manufacture, external
trade, land-borne and water-borne cargoes, coinage, credit – all are
considered in turn. However, von Sonnenfels remarks when dealing
with agriculture that he will only deal with tillage and cattle, 'and
these only from the *political* aspect, not in the practical application,
which is dealt with by the so-called *Oekonomie*.'[43] In the discussion of
manufacture criticisms of Physiocratic doctrines are made; the manner in which different types of manufacturing are appraised at times
recalls the approach of Adam Smith. And this is not entirely
coincidental: for Smith's *Wealth of Nations* does after all direct itself to
the productive capacities of a population, and, like Sonnenfels'
Grundsätze, discusses at length the fiscal policy of a well-run state.

Nonetheless, while von Sonnenfels cites Smith's discussion of the
division of labour in his section on manufactures,[44] there is little
common ground shared by the two texts. For in Smith, society is
endowed with a basic mechanism which generates movement, and
the 'natural system of liberty' is designed to permit this mechanism to
function with as little disturbance as possible. In the *Grundsätze* there is
no motion that is not the outcome of proper government; without
proper government, there follows only decline and disorder.

The distance separating the cameralistic sciences from the new
Smithian political economy has often been introduced as a major
component in the explanation of the rapid demise of the older,
German tradition. Once the new science was disseminated in Europe,
so the argument runs, it displaced former discourses on wealth and

---

[43] *Ibid.*, Bd. II, p. 34.   [44] *Ibid.*, Bd. II, p. 219.

happiness, replacing them with political economy. Furthermore, once this had occurred, the older body of concepts and principles became quite simply unintelligible. From a high point in mid-century, marked by the textbooks of von Sonnenfels and von Justi, Cameralism and *Polizeiwissenschaft* had by the 1790s entered terminal decline; by the first decade of the nineteenth century they were facing heavy criticism from a competing system of political and economic theory; and by the 1820s Cameralism had disappeared in all but name. This chronology is conventionally attributed to the impact of Smithian doctrines, the first such detailed account being provided by Roscher in 1867,[45] who established themes later taken up in several monographs and dissertations of the 1920s and 1930s.

While there is a rough correspondence between the rates at which Smithian ideas became popular and the older doctrines declined, it is dangerous to suppose that this coincidence indicates that the demise of the one is entirely the result of the rise of the other. As we saw earlier, shifts were taking place in the categories of Cameralism in the early part of the eighteenth century which, when combined with developments in practical philosophy and natural jurisprudence, render appreciation of such developments a quite complex matter. It can be said with some degree of certainty that when Smith's *Wealth of Nations* was first translated into German (in 1776 and 1778, and as two parts) there was very little response.[46] As Hufeland wrote in 1807, 'In Germany the name of Smith is often invoked; but only the literature of the last few years shows clear evidence that he has been read and completely understood.'[47] He goes on to instance the citation of *Wealth of Nations* by Johann Georg Büsch in 1780, who subsequently admitted in the second edition of his book (*Abhandlung von dem Geldumlauf*) that he had not read Smith very carefully; and the only instance of some deeper understanding that Hufeland can find before 1796 is the work of Theodor Schmalz, a convinced Physiocrat.

[45] W. Roscher, 'Die Ein- und Durchführung des Adam Smith'schen Systems in Deutschland', *Berichte über die Verhandlungen der königlich sächsischen Gesellschaft der Wissenschaften zu Leipzig*, Bd. 19 (1867), pp. 1–74.

[46] H. Maier's authoritative account of the early history of the Staatswissenschaften, *Die ältere deutsche Staats- und Verwaltungslehre*, 2nd edn, C. H. Beck, Munich 1980, commits an interesting error in stating that Christian Garve's translation of *Wealth of Nations* (1794–96) was the first translation – interesting because this obscures the point made here, that *Wealth of Nations* was quickly available in German translation, but then widely ignored. Maier's chronology of the demise of Cameralism is faulty in part because he fails to deal with the 'grey area' of 1770–90 (or, say, from von Sonnenfels to Sartorius) and then proceeds to imply that Rau's *Kameralwissenschaft* of 1823 is cameralistic in the eighteenth-century sense, which it is not. These and other points are covered in my *Governing Economy*, Chapters 7, 8.

[47] G. Hufeland, *Neue Grundlegung der Staatswirthschaftskunst*, Bd. 1, Gießen 1807, Vorrede.

The first review of *Wealth of Nations* appeared in March 1777 and was of the English edition; it did however establish many of the judgments that were to be repeated in the following twenty years – it was a 'political investigation', rather repetitious and unclear in places, and associated with the 'French School', that is, with Physiocracy.[48] A review of the first part of the German translation which appeared later in that same year went further, and concluded that the first three books of *Wealth of Nations* demonstrate how the fluctuations in the level of rent are an index of wealth, proceeding elsewhere to render Smith's terminology into that of the Physiocrats.[49] A later review in the same journal, of the second part of the *Wealth of Nations*, noted Smith's rejection of the Physiocratic position, but suggests that this is achieved merely by logomachy and that he does after all basically agrees with the 'Agricultural School'.[50] The handful of reviews that *Wealth of Nations* received up to the 1790s represents the most extensive treatment of its ideas in the German language. The textbook literature of the period refers only very occasionally to it in passing, and when it does so it commonly treats Smith's inspiration as fundamentally Physiocratic. There are several reasons for this, perhaps here the most important being that the German Physiocrats constituted the only substantial alternative to Cameralism, and so the distance between cameralistic forms of argument and those of *Wealth of Nations* were registered in terms of the distance separating Cameralism from Physiocracy.

It was only following the second translation of *Wealth of Nations* by Garve and Dörrien that serious discussion can be found in textbooks and treatises, and the first substantial treatment is to be found in the lectures of Sartorius at the University of Göttingen.[51] Roscher[52]

---

48 Anon. [J. G. H. Feder], Review of Adam Smith, *An Inquiry into the Nature and Causes of the Wealth of Nations*, *Göttingische Anzeigen von gelehrten Sachen*, 1. Bd. 30. St. (10 March 1777), pp. 234–5. For a thorough account of the Smith reception see my *Governing Economy*, Chapter 7.

49 'Px', Review of Smith, *Untersuchung der Natur und Ursachen von Nationalreichthumern*, Bd. I, *Allgemeine deutsche Bibliothek*, Bd. 31, 2. Th. (1777), pp. 588–9.

50 Review of Smith, *Untersuchungen der Natur und Ursachen von Nationalreichthum*, Bd. II, *Allgemeine deutsche Bibliothek*, Bd. 38, l. Th. (1779), p. 300.

51 It is sometimes suggested that Johann Friedrich Schiller's original translation was inferior to that of Garve and Dörrien and that this therefore accounts at least in part for the delayed reception. Comparison of the two translations with the original reveals however no such substantial deficiencies; and indeed Garve noted in his introduction that, having read *Wealth of Nations* in the original only after having first read Schiller's translation, he discovered nothing substantive that had been hitherto concealed from him by the translation – C. Garve, 'Vorrede des Uebersetzers' to A. Smith, *Untersuchung über die Natur und die Ursachen des Nationalreichtums*, Bd. I, Breslau 1794, p. IV.

52 W. Roscher, *Geschichte der National-Oekonomik in Deutschland*, R. Oldenbourg, Munich 1874, p. 615.

describes the *Handbuch* that Sartorius produced in 1796 as a summary of *Wealth of Nations*, but as a summary it has important features. Firstly, Sartorius reduces the sometimes rambling text of *Wealth of Nations* to sets of theses and propositions, but in so doing he obscures the historical form in which Smith's argument develops. The fact that the *Handbuch* is only 234 pages long does perhaps make drastic simplification inevitable, but there is a second, more obvious, feature of Sartorius' exposition. The *Handbuch* is divided into two parts, in which Part I deals with Books I and II of *Wealth of Nations*, and Part II with Books III, IV, and V. Instead, however, of beginning Part II with a summary of Smith's Book III, Sartorius first interjects a discussion of the nature of *Staatswirthschaft* which is his own gloss on Smith, and corresponds to no passage written by the latter. Book III of *Wealth of Nations* is then reduced to a set of principles (this the most 'historical' of the part of the book). The greatest and most significant divergence comes in the treatment of Smith's Book V, marked by a shift from précis to commentary, where the expenses and revenues of the state are assessed with respect to a specific objective of the state, 'the security of all native persons and rightfully established law'.[53] This places the various institutions that appear in *Wealth of Nations* with respect to a *Staatszweck* which is proper to *Polizeiwissenschaft*, and is not clearly in evidence in Smith's text.

The revised second edition of Sartorius' text which appeared in 1806 did in fact confine itself to précis – the treatment of Book III is shifted to Part I and the language of *Staatszweck* disappears. This only serves to emphasize the manner in which the first edition represents a form of accommodation between two programmes of government whose contradictory demands become clearer in subsequent attempts to write 'according to Adam Smith'.

One of the first instances of this is Lueder's *Ueber Nationalindustrie und Staatswirthschaft. Nach Adam Smith bearbeitet*, which saw in *Wealth of Nations* a system which could reveal the eternal laws of man's existence, if only the confusion resulting from Smith's method of presentation could be removed.[54] It was also necessary to add a third book left out of the original, 'On Nature', divided into two parts: 'How Nature affects the Accumulation of Capital' and 'How Nature

---

[53] G. Sartorius, *Handbuch der Staatswirthschaft zum Gebrauche bey akademischen Vorlesungen, nach Adam Smith's Grundsätzen ausgearbeitet*, Berlin 1796, p. 153.

[54] Berlin, 1800, p. xiii. Lueder had studied at Göttingen, and at the time this text appeared was a councillor to the court of the Duke of Brunswick. In 1810 he became professor of philosophy at Göttingen.

Affects the Market'. The three volumes of this work are considerably
more extended than *Wealth of Nations*, as the text develops, becoming
more diffuse and finally abandoning any pretence of a commentary
on Smith. It is nevertheless noteworthy that in Book V, 'Internal
Security Harmed and Destroyed by Rulers Themselves', the discussion of security and abuse of power, standard problems within later
Polizeiwissenschaft, is carried on without any mention of *Polizei* or its
writers; instead the points of reference are established with names
such as Hume, Steuart, Hufeland, Smith, and Kant. The significance
of Lueder's volumes lies not so much in their repetition or acceptance
of propositions to be found in *Wealth of Nations*, but rather in the way
that the association with Smith serves to block references in the
narrative to the established writings of *Staatswissenschaft*, utilising
instead a combination of historical and practical philosophy.

Another example of the reception of *Wealth of Nations* can be found
in Weber's *Systematisches Handbuch der Staatswirthschaft*, Bd. I. At first
sight this appears to offer a paraphrase of the Introduction to *Wealth
of Nations*, arguing that the property of a state consisted not only of
goods and chattels but of the skills of its inhabitants, which combine to
meet the needs of the state and its citizens:

The condition under which this is possible is the application and use of the
property of the state; and this can only take place through the labour of the
citizen, ie., through the expenditure of effort which the citizen must make in
the utilisation of property. Labour is the immediate fund of all the income of
a nation and thereby also all the income of the state, and represents the only
resource on which the state can draw. The condition, or the real value of the
entire national income constitutes national wealth; whose different levels are
dependent upon the various degrees of development and completeness of the
labour of the nation. The surest foundation for *national wealth*, its highest
development and most advantageous use must be the goal of the internal
administration of the state, and thus of the science concerned with this task,
which is the object of our study here.[55]

The language of 'national wealth', labour, and income used here
draws on that of Smith, but the 'goal of the internal administration of
the state' turns out to be not the programme of minimal government
and self-regulation of the economy that appears in *Wealth of Nations*,
but rather that of regulation and *Polizei*. Only through the action of
this latter programme will the most advantageous development of

---

[55] F. B. Weber, *Systematisches Handbuch der Staatswirthschaft*, Bd. I, Abt. I, Berlin 1804, p. 4. At this
  time Weber was professor for *Oeconomie und Cameralwissenschaft* at Frankfurt a. O.

national wealth take place, argues Weber. His use of 'labour', while drawing on Smith, is also closer to the conception of 'population' to be found in Sonnenfels or Justi.

Appreciation of *Wealth of Nations* and its doctrines by the reforming discipline of economic science is uneven and ambiguous in the first two decades of the nineteenth century; examples introduced here could be replaced by several others, without affecting the general line of argument. Palyi's conclusion that the German reception of Smith involved first an uncritical acceptance, followed by a relapse into Cameralism in the 1820s, is false and misleading. As we have seen, first *Wealth of Nations* was ignored, and then the adoption of certain Smithian formulations was conditioned by the established forms of argument then prevailing.[56] That which went under the label of Cameralism in the 1820s was significantly different from the doctrines of the eighteenth century, not least because state and society had ceased to be synonyms, *Polizei* had become a state apparatus separate from considerations of welfare and happiness, and the principal training for state officials had became the law. The development of *Nationalökonomie* in the first half of the nineteenth century did not owe its theoretical basis to Smithianism; but the rupture with cameralistic traditions that it brought about created the space in which a new *Nationalökonomie* could become established.

Those commentaries which treat *Wealth of Nations* as a constitutive moment in the birth of German economic liberalism[57] neglect the real unevennesses in the text which allegedly had such great impact – unevennesses which did for instance lead to Smith's being classed as a Physiocrat for over two decades, or even as a *Staatswissenschaftler*. These were not the result of misunderstanding, but rather the outcome of the confrontation of two distinct programmes of government: for one, civil society is an entity permanently under construction through the work of *Polizei*, and synonymous with the state; for the other, civil society is an entity detached from the state, with an autonomous and inherent capacity for self-regulation and subject only to a framework of law emanating from the state. One of the first key statements of the 'liberal economy' that articulates the implications of this detachment of civil society from the state is to be found

56 M. Palyi, 'The Introduction of Adam Smith on the Continent', in *Adam Smith 1776–1926*, Augustus M. Kelley, New York 1966, p. 215.
57 For example, C. W. Hasek, *The Introduction of Adam Smith's Doctrines into Germany*, Faculty of Political Science, Columbia University, New York 1925, Chapter 3.

in Kant's 'On the Saying, That may be so in Theory, but not in Practice' from 1793 – here we are presented with the freedom of each member of society to seek his own happiness (no one can be forced to be happy); equality between the members of society; and their independence as citizens within the common weal.[58]

How is civil society so constituted to be regulated, in the absence of the structure of decrees, prohibitions, and recommendations that characterised the society postulated by Cameralism and *Polizeiwissenschaft*? Not by the action of the state, for the laws which it is to lay down are constitutional in character; no longer is it to be concerned with the promotion of welfare, or with the morality of its citizenry. Instead, civil society is discovered to possess its own laws, laws of motion which regulate its development via the interactions of the agents constituting it. The citizenry, free and equal as proposed by Kant, form a mass of calculating agents with specific interests and needs, whose interactions promote a harmonious social order independent of their particular powers. Henceforth, it is economic activity that is to be constitutive of social order.[59]

Within this framework *Wealth of Nations* appears to offer an exemplary solution, presenting a model order in which equilibrium emerges from among a mass of conflicting interests and demands. Dreitzel has dubbed this programme a 'Utopia' – economic society as a harmonious, self-equilibrating system that requires only to be liberated from arbitrary interference.[60] In this ideal world each is independent, within a differentiated structure; and independence requires only that the individual has access to the resources needed for purposeful and sustaining activity, and is in addition provided with a guarantee that this independence will not be arbitrarily restricted. An economy of mutuality is to govern this order, where wealth and happiness are the autonomous product of social relations, rather than being an objective whose substance is authoritatively decreed. This new economic order thus possesses its own laws; these laws are no longer issued by a monarch, but are the 'laws of motion' inhering in civil society. Cameralism set out to locate the objects which were to be the material for the exercise of prudence in the government of a state;

58 I. Kant, 'Über den Gemeinspruch: Das Mag in der Theorie richtig sein, taugt aber nicht für die Praxis', *Werke*, Bd. VIII, Walter de Gruyter, Berlin 1968, p. 290.
59 This argument has been advanced by Dora Fabian in her dissertation *Staat, Gesellschaft, Wirtschaft in ihren Beziehung zueinander*, Gießen 1928, pp. 98–9.
60 H. Dreitzel, 'Ideen, Ideologien, Wissenschaften: Zum politischen Denken in Deutschland in der Frühen Neuzeit', *Neue Politische Literatur*, Jg. 25 (1980), p. 12.

the new science of economics is, instead, concerned with the discovery of those laws which regulate the interactions of economic agents.

But as Kant might have said, that may be all right in theory; the practice was lacking, however, in the execution. The society of economic equals was to prove a chimera, spawning the Social Question and the Social Movement. The contradictions of the order which emerged from this system of government became in turn the domain of a new science of administration developed by Lorenz von Stein.[61] The State, instead of simply laying down the law, intervened to restore order, regulating conditions of work, standards of living, standards of behaviour. Whereas *Polizei* encountered its limit in the apparent inexhaustibility of the objects that could be regulated, the new liberalism encountered its limit in the perpetual invasion of that which it had expelled, the State; or more exactly, it encountered its limit in the distinction which it had constructed between the self-regulating order of society and the law-making instance of the State. Once this new conceptual configuration had installed itself, the regularities of the older *Staatswissenschaften* became obscure, archaic, and irrelevant. Our modern perspective was thereby endowed with a beguiling comprehensiveness, for what it could not recognise it simply treated as of no importance. But this is, of course, an ocular fault. The apparent universality of our modern perspective turns out to be a product of the manner in which it is foreshortened; it recognises only itself. One route out of this circularity is to seek an understanding of anterior conceptual orders; such as that shared by Gasser, Dithmar, von Rohr, Justi and Sonnenfels. If we are even partially successful in so doing, then our perspective will be extended, not only with respect to antecedant regularities, but in the range and scope of modern economic categories involving wealth, welfare, and regulation.

[61] See P. Pasquino, 'Introduction to Lorenz von Stein', *Economy and Society*, vol. 10 (1981), pp. 1–6.

CHAPTER 3

Die Vernunft des List. *National economy and the critique of cosmopolitical economy*

> His object is to transplant economic theory
> (*Staatswirtschaftslehre*) from the lecture hall to the office, and in
> this he succeeds admirably. Such a book, making the most
> important parts of economics common property and
> illuminating austere thought processes with striking
> illustrations in a readable, conversational style, cannot fail also
> in Germany to find a larger public.[1]

So wrote Friedrich List to the publisher J.G. Cotta in 1822, offering to translate Louis Say's *Considerations sur l'industrie et la législation*, a book which presented a series of readable summaries of recent economic treatises.[2] Nothing came of this particular proposal to translate Say; but the project of rendering economic principles accessible to a wider popular audience was one which List later made his own. Unlike Louis Say, however, he eschewed straightforward summary of the principles advanced by contemporary economic writers. Instead, he developed a systematic critique of economic orthodoxies, a critique that turned on his contention that the intellectual legacy of Adam Smith was marked by an artificial divorce of politics from economics. As a consequence, he suggested, political distinctions and national interests failed to find a place in a doctrinal system that assumed a world ruled by general, universally valid economic laws. The 'School', as he dubbed the heirs of Adam Smith, therefore practised a

---

[1] List to Cotta, 1 May 1822; *Schriften*, vol. 8, p. 215. I have used throughout the 10 volume edition of List's work, *Schriften/ Reden/ Briefe*, Verlag von Reimar Hobbing, Berlin 1927–35; cited below as *Schriften*.

[2] J.-P. Aillaud, Paris 1822. Apart from introductory and concluding remarks, Say's book dealt with: Dupont de Nemours, *Physiocratie*; Smith, *Recherches* (87 pp.); Canard, *Principes d'Économie politique*; Lauderdale, *Recherches*; Ganilh, *Théorie de l'Économie politique*; Ricardo, *Principes* (96 pp.); Malthus, *Principes* (56 pp.); J.-B. Say, *Traité* (32 pp.); de Tracy, *Commentaire sur l'Esprit des lois*; Saint-Chemans, *Du système d'impot*. The summaries of Smith, Ricardo, Malthus and Say occupy almost three-quarters of the book.

32

Cosmopolitical Economy, rather than a true Political Economy which recognised the exigencies of national interests and political forces.[3]

List's most accessible critique of prevailing economic orthodoxies was presented in *The National System of Political Economy*,[4] a book which is however in many respects a compendium of themes repeatedly broached in numerous articles and essays written over the previous two decades. This is a reflection of the fact that List's chief occupation and source of income from the time of his exile from his native Württemberg in 1825 was journalism. Editor of a succession of journals and newspapers, he frequently expatiated upon his favourite themes: in the Pennsylvanian *Readinger Adler* from 1826–30, in the *Eisenbahnjournal* from 1835–37, and in the *Zollvereinsblatt* from 1843, among others. This occupational imperative accounts for both the repetitive nature of his writing and its unscholarly character, features which create difficulties for the unwary reader today, and which have marked the literature of commentary that has grown up around it.

List was no simple populariser of prevailing orthodoxies; instead, he systematically criticised those principles that commanded general contemporary support. Although we would today regard his critique of Smith's *Wealth of Nations* as superficial and misleading, this critique does nonetheless possess a general coherence that transcends its flawed detail, and it is to this level of coherence that we should address our attention. Moreover, as a populariser, List owed little to his German contemporaries – for a 'famous German economist' List drew very lightly upon recognisable German intellectual traditions. It is not simply that, as a journalist, List had not studied German economists of the 1820s and 1830s very deeply; rather, there is no sign that he owes anything at all to the literature of *Nationalökonomie* as it

---

[3] The term *Kosmopolit*, a person with no fixed home, first emerged in mid-eighteenth-century Germany associated with *Weltbürger*, thereby counterposed to *Patriot* (see W. Feldman, 'Modewörter des 18. Jahrhunderts. 2. Teil', *Zeitschrift für deutsche Wortforschung*, Bd. 6 (1942), pp. 346–7). The OED gives examples of 'cosmopolitan' as an adjective only from 1844, which is an American instance; the first English case given is from J. S. Mill writing in 1848 about capital. In the American edition of *National System*, *kosmopolitische* was translated as 'cosmopolite', which the OED suggests is a nineteenth-century revival of a seventeenth-century term (vol. II, p. 1032).

[4] *Das nationale System der politischen Oekonomie*, Bd. I *Der internationale Handel, die Handelspolitik und der deutsche Zollverein*. Published in 1841, no further volumes appeared. The first English translation was published in the United States (J. B. Lippincot and Co., Philadelphia 1856, introduction by S. Colwell. Both Lippincot and Colwell were prominent representatives of Philadelphia's Careyite business community). It was not published in Britain until 1885.

developed from the early 1800s.[5] His sweeping characterisation of post-Smithian political economy as 'cosmopolitical' stands at the beginning of a long tradition of popular economic writing that deliberately sets itself in opposition to the assumptions and policy implications of a prevailing theoretical tradition; but there is no obvious German source for this stance. The name of Adam Müller is the one most frequently cited by those seeking to talk up List's Germanic filiations; but although there are indeed echoes of Müller's cultural criticism in List's work, there was nothing in Müller's critique of political economy that could sustain the kind of critical programme that List developed. Given that List's talent lay in popularising the ideas of others, proper identification of his sources could well turn out to throw new light on his work. Where, then, can we find the rational source of this critical programme?

At the time that List wrote to Cotta in 1822 suggesting a translation of Louis Say's compendium, he had only a very general acquaintance with political economy, despite the fact that this postdates his brief career as a professor and as a protagonist of a German customs' union. His first serious engagement with the principles of political economy occurred during his stay in the United States. Furthermore, his sojourn in the United States coincided with the initiation of an American debate over free trade and protection. The terms in which this debate was conducted were distinctly 'post-Smithian' in character. In the *Wealth of Nations* the advantages of a natural system of liberty were counterposed to regimes of mercantile regulation which limit the prospects for economic growth. Insofar as an international economic order is considered, this was conceived in terms of the benefits of a division of labour, later elaborated by Ricardo in his *Principles of Political Economy and Taxation* in terms of the theory of comparative advantage.

Ricardo had used the example of trade between Portugal and England in wine and wool to demonstrate the advantages to each of a 'system of perfectly free commerce'.[6] This system, he went on

---

[5] Thus for example although List distinguished three component parts of political economy in his *Outlines of American Political Economy, Schriften*, Bd. 2 p. 101, this tripartite distinction is based upon a differentiation of the substance of political economy that contests the derivation of 'National Economy' by Fulda, Soden, and other German economists of the period. See below.

[6] David Ricardo, *On the Principles of Political Economy and Taxation*, Works and Correspondence, vol. I, Cambridge University Press, Cambridge 1951, p. 133.

by increasing the general mass of productions, ... diffuses general benefit, and binds together by one common tie of interest and intercourse, the universal society of nations throughout the civilized world. It is this principle which determines that wine shall be made in France and Portugal, that corn shall be grown in America and Poland, and that hardware and other goods shall be manufactured in England.[7]

But what would happen if America wished to manufacture the 'hardware and other goods' that is here the prerogative of England? The harmonious distribution of economic activities envisaged by Ricardo relates to the international order of the eighteenth century, and presupposes but one industrial power, Great Britain. The problems of industrial development in the context of a developing international economy, the problems faced by the United States in the 1820s, and subsequently by other European economies in the course of the century, are not addressed by these principles of comparative advantage. These principles presuppose an inter-national economic order in which natural endowments provide the chief supports of national advantages, a supposition still valid in the eighteenth century, but not in the nineteenth. Once the process of industrialisation had begun, this harmonious distribution of econ-omic activity between national economies was disrupted. This first became apparent in the relationship of the United States to European commercial nations, and it was in this American context that List elaborated his conception of economic protection based upon the 'infant industries' thesis. It was likewise in this context that he developed a conception of national economic growth within an international order.

List's critique of 'cosmopolitical economy' originated from Ameri-can economic debates, not those of Germany. When subsequently imported into the Germany of the 1830s these principles could then form a coherent basis for the elaboration of a conception of national economic development accessible to popular understanding. As a journalist, List was not concerned with scholarly debate; he had in view a broader public interested in the interaction of economic affairs and politics. Roscher, reviewing the *National System* in 1842, recog-nised this point. He objected to the way in which 'the School' was treated as an Aunt Sally, and first suggested that 'However correct these observations are in general, the errors which characterise the

[7] Ricardo, *Principles*, p. 134.

whole book of Herr List are clearly displayed – the principles themselves are one-sided, and there is a marshalling of evidence whose apparent force is directed primarily at readers with superficial knowledge'.[8] He then went on, however, to suggest that, while as a theoretical work the text was faulty, it should rather be judged in terms of its practical intent. List was the theorist of the greater *Zollverein*, the book was a party manifesto, suggested Roscher; the *National System* consciously established and argued from a position with which a diversity of political tendencies could agree, emphasising the development of material welfare, German unity, and national power.[9] Indeed, List subsequently became honoured as a major contributor to the Unification of 1871, but as Schmoller later recognised, List was 'an agitator and no Professor';[10] while Menger in an article celebrating the centenary of List's birth made clear that it was the nationalism of List's principles that lived on, rather than any specific theoretical heritage.[11] In 1934 the centenary of the founding of the *Zollverein* was widely celebrated, and in this context List was reincarnated as a theorist of the new National Socialist order, a reconstitution to which the conservative editors of the critical edition of List's work could merely uneasily assent.[12] List's writing has been readily adopted by diverse nationalist currents, a resource for Liberal as well as National Socialist sentiments; even the historical association of the *Zollverein* with the European Community has led to a revival of List as the original theorist of European unity.[13]

The work of Friedrich List was therefore, even in his own times, primarily viewed as economic journalism in support of the cause of

[8] W. Roscher, Review of List, *Das nationale System der politischen Ökonomie, Göttingische gelehrte Anzeigen*, Bd. 1, St. 118 (1842), pp. 1182.
[9] *Ibid.*, St. 121, pp. l2l4–16.
[10] G. Schmoller, 'Friedrich List', in his *Zur Litteraturgeschichte der Staats- und Sozialwissenschaften*, Duncker und Humblot, Berlin 1888, p. 103.
[11] C. Menger, 'Friedrich List', in his *Gesammelte Werke*, Bd. 3, 2nd edn, J. C. B. Mohr (Paul Siebeck), Tübingen 1970, pp. 247–57.
[12] During the period 1933–45 a number of publications appeared devoted to the theme of List's contribution to the National Socialist *Volksstaat*, among which the following statement from the introduction to a selection of List's writing is quite typical: 'The growth of a people does not occur in leaps, everything has to develop according to its own laws, in which the farthest deviation remains the path to the final goal. List's economic attempts from the middle, Bismarck's political consolidation from above – all this had to collapse before, on the basis of a new and solid foundation, Adolf Hitler completed *volkspolitisch* the construction of the Great German Reich from below.' H. Voss, 'Einleitung' to F. List, *Kräfte und Mächte*, Wilhelm Langewiesche-Brandt, Ebenhausen bei München 1942.
[13] See for example E. N. Roussakis, *Friedrich List, the Zollverein and the Uniting of Europe*, College of Europe, Bruges 1968.

national economic development. The fact that his writing took the form of a critique of orthodoxies without any evident European precedent has been for the most part overlooked by commentators intent on recruiting List to later national economic causes, or alternatively demonstrating his theoretical failings. The absence of rigorous argument and the prevalence of tenuously supported generalisations in List's writings render them peculiarly susceptible to such processes of reconstruction. The manner in which these texts should be read today is therefore a problem. How are they to be analysed without either, on the one hand, overestimating their consistency and rigour, treating List as if he were an 'original thinker'; or, on the other, colluding with their evident superficiality and satisfying ourselves with bland generalisations equally applicable to large numbers of List's contemporaries?

The former approach was, for example, the one adopted by the editors of the collected writings in the 1920s and 1930s. Here much editorial effort is expended establishing sources, emphasising originality and demonstrating parallelisms, as if List were a writer whose intellectual sources have to be laboriously reconstructed, so that we might gain insight into the nature of his achievement. With List, this approach is reduced for the most part to identifying the book from which he borrowed a particular idea; more a work of inventory than intellectual history. The tedious and scholastic way in which List's editors go about this mundane task tends to obscure the nature of the intellectual resources mobilised by List, since they adopt a literalistic view of his writings: they comb through all the sources that he cites, while ignoring possible sources that he does not.

There is an alternative temptation, to dismiss the writings of List on the grounds that they are popular or ephemeral, that his principles do not stand rigorous examination. It is perhaps for this reason that most of the List commentary exhausts itself with the question of originality, concluding either that List was little better than a plagiarist of this or that writer, or on the other hand laboriously vindicating him from such charges. This trend set in very early, well before the editorial work of the 1920s; for example, Marx's recently published draft article on List falls squarely into this category.[14] The fact remains that List's work was taken seriously in the 1840s by major German

---

[14] K. Marx, 'Draft of an Article on Friedrich List's Book *Das Nationale System der politischen Ökonomie*', Marx, Engels, *Collected Works*, vol. IV, Lawrence and Wishart, London 1975, pp. 265–93.

economists of the stature of Rau and Hildebrand,[15] and his work
continues to attract a level of attention far beyond that given to his
more scholarly and original contemporaries. The dreary nature of the
secondary literature and the tedious repetition of List's own writing
should not be permitted to obstruct appraisal of its rational basis. For
indeed there is such a rational basis: the American writings on
political economy that List encountered in the mid-1820s. Once we
focus attention squarely upon this American tradition of political
economy we can gain new insights into the substance of List's
economic critique, while at the same time taking proper account of his
journalistic preoccupations.

These preoccupations are lent emphasis by one project that went
beyond journalism, that of Rotteck and Welcker's *Staatslexikon*. List
had first proposed this idea for a reference work in alphabetical form
covering the entire *Staatsleben* in 1831, suggesting as a model the
Konversationslexikon begun in 1796 by Löbel, and taken over in 1806 by
Brockhaus. Rotteck and Welcker, two well-known liberal academics,
agreed in 1833 to assist List in this enterprise, and in September 1833
Welcker wrote to List of their aims in the following terms:

> We believe (and also understand your earlier suggestions in this way) that
> this work should not be for the satisfaction of real scholars or even the merely
> 'curious', but that it should serve to extend the wealth of practical political
> knowledge and experience among the great class of administrators and
> educated citizenry, providing them through its alphabetical arrangement
> with assistance in their political activities.[16]

Similar sentiments were expressed by List in a draft prospectus for the
Staatslexikon, emphasising the importance of a knowledge of the
Staatswissenschaften for the industrialist, the landowner, and the representative of the public at whatever level.[17] Early nineteenth-century
German liberalism was strongly associated with culture and education, and the development of liberal politics as an essentially discursive activity created a space in which journalism became a major form

---

[15] K. H. Rau, Review of *Nationales System* in *Archiv der politischen Oekonomie und Polizeiwissenschaft*,
Bd. 5 (1843), pp. 252–97, 349–412; B. Hildebrand, *Die Nationalökonomie der Gegenwart und
Zukunft*, Literarische Anstalt (J. Rütten), Frankfurt a. M., 1848, pp. 58–97.

[16] Cited in H. Zehnter, *Das Staatslexikon von Rotteck und Welcker*, Gustav Fischer, Jena 1929, p. 11,
n. 4. This book appeared as Heft 3 of the *List Studien*. It must be noted that one of the many
points of disagreement that arose between List and his fellow editors related to List's belief in
the merit of politically committed yet scholarly articles, while Rotteck and Welcker pursued
an editorial policy in which political polemic excluded all non-liberal positions.

[17] Zehnter, *Das Staatslexikon*, p. 109.

of political activity.[18] It was after all in this context that the familiar figure of Karl Marx began his journalistic career as editor of the *Rheinische Zeitung*; and Marx spoke for himself, as well as for List, when he argued that, since the bourgeoisie did not possess state power, it must clothe its attempt to attain such power in the language of proposals for reform and the strengthening of the structure of the state.[19] List's later engagement with railway development went to the heart of the symbolism of the new order, and his promotion of economic protection presupposed the formation of a liberal state whose objectives were henceforth formulated in the language of economic, rather than political, power. From this perspective, the contemporary significance attached to List's writings becomes more understandable, and this provides us with an avenue through which we can gain deeper insight into his work.

It is simplest to begin by ordering List's extensive literary activity and projects according to his varied career, since so much of his writing was prompted by immediate commitments. Unfortunately, as with many an inveterate self-publicist, important points in an otherwise public career remain shrouded in obscurity, and due care has to be observed when imputing intentions to action and writing. Accounts that List gave of his career at a dinner in his honour in Pennsylvania in 1827, and in a foreword to the *National System*, are in places quite unreliable; while on the other hand the extensive surviving correspondence and archival material sheds no useful light on critical moments of his life. It is for this reason that much of the painstaking editorial work on the *Schriften* is to so little effect. Relying heavily on the material in the Reutlingen archives, the editors failed to formulate problems or employ evidence not immediately supported by these archival resources. No clear intellectual or political motivation can for instance be established, on the basis of archival evidence, for his involvement with the *Deutsche Handels- und Gewerbsverein* which he helped found in 1819, and which formed the focus of his economic agitation in the following two years. This is a rather serious obscurity, given that this represents his main contribution to the foundation of the *Zollverein*. However, since the archives do not illuminate this question, the editors simply register this lacuna and move on; they do not attempt to resolve this problem by turning to

---

[18] J. J. Sheehan, *German Liberalism in the Nineteenth Century*, University of Chicago Press, Chicago 1978, Chapter 1.   [19] Marx, Review of List in *Collected Works*, vol. IV, p. 274.

other sources. Many preconceptions about who List was, and what he represents, turn out to be questionable; but the archives and writings provide no direct resolution to these conundrums. Some attention to his biography will permit us to understand the limitations of many preconceptions, and quite why it is that American Political Economy has been so greatly neglected in assessments of his work.

List was born in the Württemberg town of Reutlingen in 1789.[20] At the age of fifteen he left school and worked for a short time in his father's tannery, before entering the state administration as a clerk. From November 1810 he was employed in Ulm, moving on in 1811 to the Actuaries' Office in Tübingen. Here he took the opportunity of attending the occasional university lecture, for in 1798 provision had been made for the training of young administrators and clerks by the foundation of a chair of Cameralistic Sciences. List never formally registered for this course of study, however; during this period he concentrated on legal studies. He surrendered his government post in 1813, but then failed to take the final examination for lawyers; he sat, and passed, the Actuarial Examination in 1814 instead. The following years were spent in various posts in state administration, none of them especially significant for the processes of reform that preceded and developed with the defeat of Napoleon. Little interest was shown by List in the consequences of the peace of 1815, apart from those aspects which bore directly on the conduct of administration. His involvement with the contemporary movement for reform was confined to the joint establishment of a journal, the *Württembergisches Archiv* of 1816 and 1817; his contributions dealt only with issues bearing directly on administrative reform.

The *Archiv* had initially been associated with a wider project for a scientific association aimed at improving the training and education of state administrators, and in 1817 this project re-emerged in a proposal that List made for the reorganisation of teaching at Tübingen. What he suggested was that the Law Faculty should be

---

[20] In fact debate begins on his exact date of birth and his name. With respect to the first, the date usually given, 6 August, is actually the date of his baptism, since birthdates were not recorded at that time; cf. P. Gehring, *Friedrich List*, J. C. B. Mohr (Paul Siebeck), Tübingen 1964, p. 4. As to the name: most assume that he was called Georg Friedrich (cf. M. E. Hirst, *Life of Friedrich List and Selections from his Writings*, Smith, Elder and Co., London 1902, p. 2); Gehring states on the other hand that his name was Daniel Friedrich (op. cit., p. 8). W. O. Henderson's book on List (*Friedrich List*, Frank Cass, London 1983), also gives more biographical information, but continues the tradition established by List's editors of studiously repeating what is to be found in the archives, while failing to raise important issues that cannot be resolved simply by direct reference to the existing archives.

expanded and divided into two sections, one dealing with state administration, and one with the law.[21] Instead, after some discussion between the university and the Ministry of Interior, a fifth faculty was created: of *Staatswirthschaft*, with List as Professor of Administrative Practice. While it was not at the time unusual for state officials with no formal university education to be appointed to such positions, it must be borne in mind that List, as one-time 'University Professor', had a non-academic background and was not appointed to teach economics, even as then understood.

What he actually did teach remains quite unclear. List was supposed to begin lecturing in January 1818, but his activities clearly gave rise to some disquiet since by May of the same year he was required to make an official report to the king. He later claimed to have preached free trade in these lectures, but this cannot be substantiated and is certainly not reflected in any of the surviving writings.[22] He also claimed to have studied the effects of the Continental System at this time, and arrived at the conclusion that free trade only worked under conditions of total reciprocity. The recognition of this principle, he contended, then led to the distinction of political from cosmopolitical economy, and to the idea of a German unity based on a customs union and protective tariffs. This version of his intellectual development would naturally imply that it was during his tenure of the Tübingen chair that he formed many of his most important ideas; that is, before his exile and (significantly) before his first practical involvement in commercial agitation. There is however no trace of such a neat progression from theory to practice to be found in the pre-1819 writings. He also later claimed to have studied the writings of Rousseau, Say, Smith, and other political economists during the Tübingen period; but his writings likewise betray no such influence, directly or indirectly. List's wider interests were at this time involved with political reform in Württemberg, and his writings and speeches of the period indicate that whatever economics he might know, it was commonplace and derivative of popular literature.[23]

In April 1819 there came a second request for information on List

[21] 'Gutachten über die Errichtung einer staatswirtschaftlichen Fakultät', *Schriften*, Bd. 1.1, p. 345. A more detailed account of the background to the formation of the Tübingen faculty can be found in my *Governing Economy*, Cambridge University Press, Cambridge 1988, pp. 178–80.
[22] 'Vorrede' to *Das Nationale System der politischen Oekonomie*, *Schriften*, Bd. 6, pp. 7–8.
[23] As can be judged for instance from his second speech to the Württemberg Assembly on financial reform, 18 December 1820: *Schriften*, Bd. 1.1 p. 334.

from Stuttgart, since he had failed to appear to teach in Tübingen at the beginning of the summer semester. As it transpired he was in Frankfurt, founding the *Verein* – but no one, including his wife, seemed to have any idea of his movements and activities. Having established above that he was not led into commercial agitation by any prior theoretical discovery of the errors of political economy, it now transpires that the inauguration of his agitation on behalf of internal free trade and a customs' union was so little premeditated that even his closest colleagues and family knew nothing of it.[24] When the authorities discovered that, instead of carrying out his teaching duties, List was busily engaged in the organisation of a commercial pressure group, they immediately and unceremoniously sacked him. Thus a short-lived and quite undistinguished academic career was brought to an abrupt end.

Whatever the personal background, List's presence at the Frankfurt Fair was instrumental in founding the first association of businessman aimed at the promotion of a customs union. First a petition to the German *Bund* was made, and then the *Verein* was established with the express purpose of extending the agitation. List spent the next year travelling the German Courts with various delegations and delivering petitions aimed at furthering economic unity, the most elaborated petition being that delivered to the Kaiser in Vienna in March 1820. The objective of abolishing internal duties is here clearly stated to be the fostering of German national unity, and allusions are made to the erroneousness of the Smithian principle of buying and selling in the most favourable markets regardless of the effects on domestic manufacture.[25] This principle was to become one of the main targets in List's protectionist criticisms of Smith, opposing national interest to cosmopolitan theory, but there is no wider consideration of political economy in his arguments of the time.

List had also become editor of the paper of the Verein, the *Organ für den deutschen Handels- und Fabrikenstand*, continuing in this post until January 1821 when the effects of his political activities in Württem-

---

[24] 'List had travelled from Tübingen – on academic business to Göttingen he wrote to the King; on private business, he wrote in the *National System*, to visit Görres in Koblenz, says J. M. Elch.' H.-P. Olshausen, *Friedrich List und der deutsche Handels- und Gewerbsverein*, Gustav Fischer, Jena 1935, p. 15. Olshausen, typifying the National Socialist inflection of List, adds: 'List had completed the tasks set him by his restricted fatherland, the Great Fatherland of the Germans now drew him under its influence' (p. 16). The first archival trace of List's new role comes in a letter to his wife dated 20 April 1819, in which he announces that he has been appointed organiser. [25] *Schriften*, Bd. 1.2, pp. 538–9.

berg intervened. In 1820 he had been appointed to the Chamber of Deputies by his native town, one of his first moves being to propose a reform of the constitution; this led swiftly to proceedings being initiated against him by the state administration, his expulsion from the Assembly following in 1821. He was tried and sentenced in April 1822 to ten months' imprisonment and a fine; his response was flight into exile. Returning some time later under the mistaken impression that the authorities had lost interest in him, he was arrested and imprisoned, and then on his release permanently exiled with his family.

While evading execution of his sentence List had visited London and then Paris, where he met Lafayette and received an invitation to visit the United States. In part because of this contact, List decided on his release to emigrate to the United States; and in June 1825 he duly arrived in New York.[26] By chance, this coincided with a tour that Lafayette was making of the United States, and List lost no time in becoming a member of the entourage, staying with Lafayette's party for three months. He gained in this way immediate and personal access to a wide range of prominent American politicians sympathetic to the Northern, industrial interest; for it was precisely at this time that a distinction was emerging between this Northern interest, and a Southern, free-trade agricultural tendency. This emergent polarisation turned on tariffs and the slavery question, and the economic debates that the former issue engendered were to become crucial for List's subsequent writings.

After a brief and unsuccessful attempt at farming, List moved to Reading, Pennsylvania where he became the editor of the German-language newspaper, the *Readinger Adler*. He also made contact with business circles in Philadelphia, and it was suggested that he write a popular pamphlet in favour of protection. Accordingly, following the Harrisburg Convention of July–August 1827 promoting protectionist measures, he published a series of letters (in English) critical of free trade doctrine, under the general title *Outlines of American Political Economy*. These letters were very well received, being reprinted in several newspapers; and in November 1827 a dinner was given in his honour by the Pennsylvania Society for the Promotion of Manufactures and Mechanic Arts. The Pennsylvania Society also requested that he write a textbook on political economy for schools, but this

---

[26] See W. Notz, 'Frederick List in America', *American Economic Review*, vol. 16 (1926), pp. 249–65; and his Introduction 'Friedrich List in Amerika', *Schriften*, Bd. 2, pp. 3–61.

project was never completed.[27] The later years of List's stay were occupied with journalism, and with his entrepreneurial activities in mining and railway development. Although he became a naturalised American subject in 1830, he returned to Germany in 1832 with the provisional title of American Consul to Baden, later becoming American Consul in Leipzig in 1834 for a term of three years.

What was the importance of this American period in List's life? When List left Germany for the United States, he was a liberal politician with a background in state administration, who had agitated for a customs union as the basis of national unity, but with only the vaguest ideas of economic development. His arrival in the United States coincided with the development of theoretical and policy arguments associated with protection – arguments which were underlined by the disputed assumption of the presidency by John Quincy Adams (National Republican) in 1825, and his replacement by the Democrat Jackson in 1828. The basic elements of List's 'post-Smithian' economics were shaped in the period 1825–28, and not before; and his emphasis on internal communications as a means of national unity can also be dated from this time. Any direct contribution that he made to the formation of the *Zollverein* fell in the period 1819–21; for although the *Zollverein* was not formed until 1834, two years after his return to Germany, he played no significant further agitational part in its promotion.

It is misleading to think of List as a German economist, for he learnt his economics in the United States from writers embroiled in American economic controversies. It was in this climate that a conception of the 'School' of Smith and his followers could develop in terms of a polarity between free trade and protection, a polarity which of course was as Roscher remarked one-sided, or one dimensional. But while in Germany such a characterisation seemed a polemical distortion, in the United States commercial and industrial interests had by the mid-1820s been formed along precisely these lines. 'Liberalism' in the German *Vormärz* was associated with political freedoms, and did not presuppose any particular allegiance to economic programmes or principles.[28] Having aligned his arguments according to American controversies in which such a relationship between economic principles and policy did exist, List then transferred them to the European

[27] 'Fragment of the *American Economist*', *Schriften*, Bd. 2, pp. 173–5.
[28] See Rudolph Vierhaus, 'Liberalismus', in O. Brunner, W. Conze, and R. Koselleck (eds.), *Geschichtliche Grundbegriffe*, Bd. 3, Klett-Cotta, Stuttgart 1982, pp. 760–2.

context and elaborated them into a general analysis of economic development.

Although commentators have discussed the general impact of American controversies on List's later writings, little effort has been made to elaborate the consequences in detail. In fact, of the three writers who most often appear in List commentary as 'sources' for his ideas – Müller, Hamilton, and Raymond – two are American.[29] Furthermore, while there are very strong grounds for supposing that much of what passes for List's economics is taken from Hamilton and Raymond, commentators have generally overestimated the potential inspiration supplied by Adam Müller, the only plausible German candidate. Once due allowance is made for this practice, then List's economics appear even more 'American' in inspiration. What then is the basis for the identification of Müller as the sole German nominee among those writers who form List's intellectual heritage?

The charge that List had plagiarised Adam Müller's *Elemente der Staatskunst* was first made in 1842.[30] Now part of the difficulty here is that Adam Müller was never an especially lucid writer, the most marked quality of his work being a romantic blend of cultural criticism and reaction, out of touch with the contemporary *Staatswissenschaften*.[31] The *Elemente der Staatskunst* had been delivered as a series of public lectures given during the winter of 1808–9 in Dresden to officials and diplomats, and the book articulates an organic conception of state activity at odds with contemporary political and economic thought, which laid emphasis on human need and autonomous economic activity in the context of civil society, not the state.[32] Insofar as Brüggeman is able to identify specific filiations linking the work of List to Müller, this is done by pointing to organic conceptions of the state and national unity, and the occurrence of the term 'productive forces' in the writings of both Müller and List. As was soon noted by Bruno Hildebrand,[33] this does not amount to a very strong argument; while conceding that Müller and List shared an opposition to Adam

[29] A review of the various arguments can be found in Eheberg's 'Historische und kritische Einleitung' to the 7th edn of the *National System*, J. G. Cotta, Stuttgart 1883, pp. 144–53.
[30] K. H. Brüggemann, *Dr. Lists nationales System der politischen Ökonomie*, W. Cornelius, Berlin 1842, pp. 31ff.
[31] Roscher noted that Müller's reaction to Smith was not unthinking, but was marred by a lack of system – 'Die romantische Schule der Nationalökonomik in Deutschland', *Zeitschrift für die gesamte Staatswissenschaft*, Bd. 26 (1870), pp. 77–8.
[32] Adam Müller, *Die Elemente der Staatskunst*, 3 Bde., Berlin 1809; reprinted in 2 vols., edited by J. Baxa, Gustav Fischer, Jena 1922. See my comments on Müller in *Governing Economy*, p. 175.
[33] Hildebrand, *Nationalökonomie*, pp. 61–2.

Smith in both general and particular aspects, he also emphasised that each arrived at different conclusions. During the 1920s the charge of plagiarism was revived, and Sommer responded to renewed suggestions that the term 'productive forces' was taken, unacknowledged, from Müller.[34] Sommer indicated that List, in replying to Brüggemann's criticism, claimed that it was only after writing the *National System* that he had leafed through the *Elemente der Staatskunst*. As it happens, this claim is supported by evidence in the Reutlingen archives, which contain some notes of books to be read dating from the autumn or winter of 1842, among which is Müller's *Elemente*.[35]

Although we seem to have here documentary vindication of List, Sommer's argument is irrelevant. Evidence of this kind is valid where a writer adheres to the usual standards and conventions of scholarship; but List's own literary practices were never of this nature. The general theses advanced in Müller's lectures were widely known by the 1820s, and given the fact that List taught in the new faculty at Tübingen, it seems highly unlikely that he would be entirely unfamiliar with such themes. Then, as now, books of this kind are more often cited in discussion than closely studied, and so the 'proof' advanced by Sommer is no certain evidence that List was unfamiliar with Müller's principal arguments. More damaging to the contention that List plagiarised from Müller is detailed consideration of relevant American writings in political economy, where intellectual filiations can be readily identified, both in terminology and in policy strategies, without resort to forced speculation. Since List's first serious engagement with political economy occurred in the United States, this does seem a more pertinent context.

Sommer does not appear to have been very familiar with American political economy, going so far as to suggest that Chaptal's *De l'industrie française*[36] was of far greater significance for List than the writings of Daniel Raymond, the American political economist.[37] One can only suppose that Sommer never saw a copy of Raymond's

[34] A. Sommer, 'Friedrich List und Adam Müller', *Weltwirtschaftliches Archiv*, Bd. 25, Heft 2 (1927), pp. 345–76; responding to J. Baxa, 'Der Ursprung von Friedrich Lists Theorie der produktiven Kräfte', *Zeitschrift für Volkswirtschaft und Sozialpolitik*, N. F. Bd. 3 (1923), pp. 153ff. There was in the early 1920s a conservative revival of Adam Müller's writing, and Baxa edited several collections related to this.   [35] Sommer in *Schriften*, Bd. 4, p. 54, n. l2.
[36] 2 vols., A.-A. Renouard, Paris 1819.
[37] Sommer explores the influence of respectively Chaptal, Dupin, and Ferrier at tedious length in his 'Einleitung zum natürlichen System', *Schriften*, Bd. 4, pp. 54–9. The case for Chaptal and Ferrier had first been advanced by E. Ladenthin, *Zur Entwickelung der nationalökonomischen Ansichten Fr. Lists von 1820–1825*, Verlagsbuchhandlung Carl Konegen, Vienna 1912.

treatise on political economy. Chaptal's text is little more than a description of the contemporary French economy, as is Dupin's *Forces productives et commerciales de la France*,[38] which Sommer claims had the greatest influence on List after 1827. Sommer also considers Ferrier's *Du gouvernement considéré dans ses rapports avec le commerce*,[39] but concludes by doubting whether List ever read the text.[40] None of these French authors developed a general critique of political economy, nor did they argue for a particular policy regime in the way that List did. The source of List's economic arguments is to be found not in Germany, nor in France, but in the United States of the 1820s.

The importance of American political economy for List has been put forcefully by Seligman in his survey of the development of American economics, where he states that

It was from Raymond that List derived his theory of nationalism, just as it was from his experience of the United States, as disclosed during his American stay, that List deduced his conclusions on railroads and on the customs union which he later developed with such vigour on his return to his own country. Raymond, however, employed but few arguments that are not already found in Hamilton's report on manufactures; so that Hamilton may well be called the spiritual father of Friedrich List.[41]

Sommer notes that List only mentions Raymond's *Elements of Political Economy* once directly, in a letter to his wife from Paris in 1838, asking her to look out some books and bring them with her.[42] This established that List possessed a copy of the text, but, Sommer continues, no direct evidence concerning acquaintance with the book can be traced in any of his published writing. This tenaciously literalist approach on the part of Sommer as an editor of List's writing is worthy but misconceived, for while it might well be true that List had not actually read Raymond's book when he wrote *Outlines*, the

---

[38] 2 vols., Bachelier, Paris 1827.   [39] 3rd edn, Pelicier, Paris 1822.

[40] Marx on the other hand was convinced otherwise: 'The book by Ferrier, sous inspecteur des douanes under Napoleon, *Du gouvernement considéré dans ses rapports avec le commerce*, Paris 1805, is the work from which Herr List copied. In List's book there is not a single basic idea that has not been stated, and better stated, in Ferrier's book'. 'Draft of an Article', p. 290.

[41] E. R. A. Seligman, 'Economics in the United States: An Historical Sketch', *Essays in Economics*, Macmillan, New York 1925, pp. 134–5. The remark concerning the customs' union is exaggerated; a more appropriate factor would be protection as government policy. Meuser upholds the originality of List's work and his independence from Raymond by the curious device of citing extensively from List, while failing to cite Raymond at all: E. Meuser, 'List oder Raymond?', *Zeitschrift für die gesamte Staatswissenschaft*, Bd. 69 (1913), pp. 104–15.

[42] F. List to Karoline List, 28 January 1838, *Schriften*, Bd. 8, Letter 426, p. 504. The title appears in a list of books including Cooper's *Political Economy*, Carey's *Political Economy*, *Niles Weekly Register*, as well as German economic writings from Lotz, Lueder, and Jakob.

arguments are in many respects clearly similar in substance and purpose. The question is: why should this be so?

Whereas with Müller there is but the vaguest terminological resonance in List's writing, List was in the *Outlines* making common cause with Raymond in constructing a critique of a system of political economy identified with the *Wealth of Nations*. Raymond's text appeared twice before 1827, but only 1,250 copies in all were printed;[43] nevertheless, it was the first systematic treatise on political economy to originate in the United States, and it was recognised as such. It seems entirely legitimate to assume that List would, faced with the task of writing his first work in political economy (and in English at that), turn to recent American literature for guidance. It is in the *Outlines* that we can first see the general framework of economic argument that List was to develop over the next fifteen years; and this framework rested upon arguments over the proper economic strategy for the new republic of the United States of America.

During the eighteenth century there had developed in America a view of Britain that regarded corruption and degeneracy as necessary corollaries of industrial economic development. Jefferson, in his *Notes on the State of Virginia*, proposed upon this basis a general conception of economic development in which moral virtue could only be preserved by a society formed by independent husbandmen. An expanding population in America could simply occupy more land, augmenting the number of independent farmers; in Europe on the other hand there was a shortage of land, and occupations had to be found for the consequent surplus population in manufactures.[44] American demand for finer goods should be met not by the development of domestic manufacture, but rather by imports. In contrast to the contemporary European emphasis on the benefits of domestic manufacture, Jefferson and others argued for the import of manufactured goods, on the grounds that virtue could only be maintained through the pursuit of agricultural production, and that industrial development was necessarily corrupting. It was not possible to postpone such development permanently; but America was uniquely privileged, through its possession of unsettled lands, to defer the social consequences of industrial economic development.

[43] Two editions of Raymond, the first entitled *Thoughts on Political Economy* and the second revised edition *The Elements of Political Economy* (2 vols.), were published in Baltimore in 1820 and 1823 respectively.

[44] See D. R. McCoy, *The Elusive Republic*, University of North Carolina Press, Chapel Hill 1980, Chapter 1.

The War of Independence was in part at least based on a dissatisfaction with Britain's refusal to recognise the growing significance of America in world trade, and in the course of the Revolution the aspiration arose for a reorganisation of international trade and the displacement of Britain as its dominant power. Hamilton, the first Secretary of the Treasury, perceived however that the outcome of such a position would be commercial war with Britain, and since the funding of the debt required trade with Britain, he rejected the agrarian arguments of Jefferson and Madison. It might be noted at this point that these agrarian arguments were in fact in agreement with those advanced by Smith in Book 3 of the *Wealth of Nations* concerning natural and unnatural forms of social and economic development; and this agrarianism could be held to be 'Smithian' in other respects as well – particularly in the relation of trade to the international division of labour.

Hamilton's rejection of the classical agrarian arguments in his *Report on the Subject of Manufactures* of 1791 did involve the foundation of 'protectionist' as opposed to 'free trade' arguments, but this did not mean that principles established in the *Wealth of Nations* were thereby necessarily rejected. It was only in the nineteenth century that the *Wealth of Nations* became viewed as an uncompromising treatise on the virtues of free trade, to the detriment of Smith's more general conceptions of liberty and exchange; and it was this process of reinterpretation of Smith that lent force to the charge of 'cosmopolitanism'. Hamilton drew directly and extensively on the *Wealth of Nations* for his arguments, and his principal objective – to demonstrate that only on the basis of a flourishing manufacturing industry can a nation increase its wealth – employs a form of reasoning drawn directly from Smith.

First he uses Smith's arguments against the Physiocratic evaluation of agriculture and manufacture,[45] and then Smith's argument that manufacturing is inherently more amenable to enhancement of productivity than agriculture.[46] The *Report* argues that the development of agriculture and manufacture must be joint, but with

---

[45] This appears as a straight paraphrase of Smith: Hamilton, *The Report on the Subject of Manufactures*, *Papers of Alexander Hamilton*, vol. x, Columbia University Press, New York 1966, p. 237. Hamilton's practice of paraphrase rather than direct citation means that the reliance of his text on the *Wealth of Nations* is not immediately apparent. E. G. Bourne's article 'Alexander Hamilton and Adam Smith', *Quarterly Journal of Economics*, vol. 8 (1894), pp. 328–44 was the first exhaustive demonstration of the reliance of Hamilton upon Smith.

[46] *Report*, pp. 247–9.

manufacture taking the leading position in stimulating their mutual
development and thereby increasing domestic demand for raw
produce. Only in this way, suggests Hamilton, will the 'productive
powers' of labour be augmented.[47]

But unless manufacture in the United States were protected, the
competition of established manufacturing nations in Europe would
endanger such a process of indigenous joint development. Hamilton
agrees that the 'system of perfect liberty' is desirable and that, if it
prevailed, then agricultural specialisation would not be entirely
undesirable for the United States. In the contemporary world,
however, perfect liberty did not prevail, and the United States was in
danger of being forced into unsuitable specialisation: 'In such a
position of things, the United States cannot exchange with Europe on
equal terms; and the want of reciprocity would render them the
victim of a system, which should induce them to confine their views to
Agriculture and refrain from Manufactures.'[48] The issue over which
Hamilton departs from the principles of Smith, according to which a
nation should buy in the cheapest market and sell in the dearest,
irrespective of the national composition of output,[49] coincides exactly
with the manner in which List first approached the problem; for it was
exactly on this point some thirty years later that List made his first
criticism of Smith.[50] The argument that Hamilton then went on to
develop, and which became the basis of protectionist doctrine,
suggested that the only means that a nation like the United States had
available to secure the eventual benefits of joint development of
agriculture and manufacture was a system of protective tariffs –
protecting the young American manufacturers from the advantages
their European counterparts enjoyed by virtue of their maturity.[51]

[47] Hamilton, *Report*, p. 251. List's usage of 'productive powers' in *Outlines* (*Schriften*, Bd. 2, pp. 116–7) follows that of Hamilton; it was then translated into German by List as *Produktivkräfte* (i.e. productive forces). See his letter to Ernst Weber, 2 October 1828, *Schriften*, Bd. 3.1, p. 116.   [48] *Report*, p. 263.
[49] This is qualified in *Wealth of Nations* with respect to the requirement of defence. But the argument is important, for Smith suggests that any system of restriction which encourages domestic production of goods that could be purchased cheaper abroad is damaging, both in the short and in the long run.
[50] List raised this in the 'Denkschrift' to the Kaiser of 1820, *Schriften*, Bd. 1.2, p. 538. It is restated in relation to the question of harmony between agriculture and manufacture in 'Inwiefern ist der Grundbesitzer und also vorzüglich der grossbegüterte Adel bei einem Prohibitivsystem interessiert?', *Schriften*, Bd. 1.2, p. 585.
[51] 'The superiority antecedently enjoyed by nations, who have preoccupied and perfected a branch of industry, constitutes a more formidable obstacle, than either of those, which have been mentioned, to the introduction of the same branch into a country, in which it did not before exist. To maintain between the recent establishments of one country and the long

By 1820 a strong protectionist lobby had become established in the United States, roughly associated with the industrialising North as opposed to the agricultural South; although the Northwest was also developing as an agricultural region, and the mercantile interests of Boston were more closely associated with the free-trading sentiments of the South. The close of the European Wars in 1815 initiated a new era in international trade in which the question of commercial competition between Europe and America was sharpened, although the agricultural exports from the South (cotton, rice, and tobacco) were naturally not seriously affected. This led to a number of controversies over tariffs, at the same time as political economy was becoming established as an academic discipline. Naturally enough, this academic discourse was shaped by contemporary controversy, and it was this discourse which List took up when writing *Outlines*.

List had certainly read Alexander Hamilton: the Pennsylvania Society reprinted the *Report* in 1824 and 1827, and as Notz observed, List's citation of Hamilton in his 'Observations on the Report of the Committee of Ways and Means' (1828) corresponds exactly to the passages printed in heavy type in the Pennsylvania Society edition of Hamilton's *Report*.[52] In any case, by the 1820s the themes broached in Hamilton's *Report* were familiar to both proponents and opponents of protection. The discipline of Political Economy as an indigenous product was however quite new; only in 1817, with the introduction of teaching of political economy at Harvard, can it be said that it gained a foothold in North America, followed by its introduction at Columbia in 1818 and Princeton in 1819.[53] By 1827 it was being taught in thirteen other colleges, and in part this was a reflection of a growing secularisation of higher education. The texts most often used in teaching were European reprints, principally of Say and Mrs Marcet.[54]

O'Connor identifies three principal antagonists to the clerical school which had initially dominated the colleges of the Northeast: first, the Southern republicanism represented in the sponsorship by Jefferson of Destutt de Tracy's *Treatise on Political Economy*, published

---

matured establishments of another country, a competition upon equal terms, both as to quality and price, is in most cases impracticable.' Hamilton, *Report*, p. 268. This is of course the original 'infant industries' argument.   [52] *Schriften*, Bd. 2, p. 55.

[53] M. J. L. O'Connor, *Origins of Academic Economics in the United States*, Columbia University Press, New York 1944, p. 100; and E. V. Wills, 'Political Economy in the Early American College Curriculum', *South Atlantic Quarterly*, vol. 24 (1925), pp. 131–53.

[54] O'Connor, *Origins of Academic Economics*, pp. 111–5.

in Georgetown, 1818; the protectionist tendency centring on Matthew Carey and best exemplified by Raymond's text; and in the Southern reaction to Jefferson after his death, exemplified by the work of Thomas Cooper at Columbia, South Carolina from 1820–34. The second and third had become the most significant forces by 1827, such that the first indigenous textbooks written in opposition to clerical teaching came from the pens of Daniel Raymond and Thomas Cooper. It was the latter's *Lectures on the Elements of Political Economy*, published in 1826, which List was asked by his protectionist friends in Philadelphia to critically review. That in so doing he adopted many of the arguments already made by Daniel Raymond was unsurprising, given that Raymond provided a ready-made alternative.

Raymond's treatise placed Smith's *Wealth of Nations* in an adversary position, and so the form taken by his argument is distinct from that followed by Hamilton. Much of Raymond's argument is sustained by a diffuse hostility to the principles advanced in the *Wealth of Nations*, and as Neill has suggested, this perhaps accounted for its poor reception – too liberal for the protectionists and too protectionist for the liberals, Raymond compounded this by his opposition to banks *and* slavery.[55] Remarks made by Raymond in the preface to the first edition indicate that he was aware of the folly of his position, but he remained unrepentant.[56]

Although Raymond acknowledges Hamilton's *Report* in his Preface, he correctly notes that the latter had produced a work less general than the one now presented to the public. If we are to identify a specific source for Raymond's arguments against Smith, it can be found in the work of Lauderdale, cited frequently in both editions of the treatise. This is particularly notable in his statements on the nature of national wealth, which he seeks to distinguish sharply from individual wealth. The latter is 'The possession of property, for the use of which, the owner can obtain a quantity of the necessaries and

[55] C. P. Neill, *Daniel Raymond. An Early Chapter in the History of Economic Theory in the United States*, Johns Hopkins University Studies in Historical and Political Sciences 15th series, vol. 16, Johns Hopkins University Press, Baltimore 1897, pp. 23–4.
[56] 'The best excuse I can allege for publishing, is, that it pleases me to do so, and one feels a sort of satisfaction in doing as he pleases, without consulting any one. If I have done wrong, the public will of course punish me as I deserve. If it shall please the public to read what I have written, well; if not, although not quite so well, it will, perhaps, be well enough, as the neglect of the public may teach me a good lesson, but will neither make me the worse or the better man; and philosophers tell us, it is the part of wisdom to disregard public opinion; which is a very consoling doctrine to an author who has written a book that nobody will read.' *Thoughts on Political Economy*, Fielding Lucas Jun., Baltimore 1820, p. ii.

comforts of life';[57] national wealth is on the other hand 'a capacity for acquiring the necessaries and comforts of life'.[58] Failure to grasp this fundamental distinction, suggests Raymond, results in the Smithian error of seeing accumulation as a result of thriftiness, rather than as a development of resources at a national level. For the nation is conceived in his text as an entity distinct from an aggregate of persons; it is as he says a 'unity, and possesses all the properties of unity'.[59] Hence public economy and private economy are distinct, and the public economy of a nation cannot be properly assessed by decomposing it into constituent parts. The national unity is the object of national policy, it cannot be guided by the resultant of a number of divergent interests:

It is the duty of legislators, to foresee the public evil consequences of any particular policy, and guard against them. Private citizens can only be expected to be wise for themselves – it is not their duty to look after the public interests – they are not the conservators of national wealth. This belongs to the department of legislation.[60]

As in Hamilton, the public interest is best served by an adequate balance of agriculture and manufacture – maintenance of a proper balance is the duty of the government, encouraging or protecting where necessary.[61]

Neill has worked through Raymond's treatise and established those passages which bear comparison with various later writings of List, describing the outcome as a number of 'coincidences'.[62] A comparison with the more popular writings of Carey reveals a uniformity of the arguments with which the case for protection was established at this time, together with the perceived effects of a failure to protect

---

[57] D. Raymond, The *Elements of Political Economy*, Vol. 1, F. Lucas Jun. and E. J. Coale, Baltimore 1823, p. 36.   [58] *Ibid.*, p. 47.   [59] *Ibid.*, p. 35.   [60] *Ibid.*, pp. 220–1.
[61] *Ibid.*, pp. 218–19.
[62] Neill, *Daniel Raymond*, p. 57. His conclusion is worth noting in full: 'Raymond and List, alike, reject the economic system of the school of Adam Smith, on the ground that it is individual economy, not public, or political, economy; they both deny the assumed harmony of interests between the individual and society; they both insist on the recognition of nations as organic unities; they both make political economy the science which regards the interest of the nation, as such, rather than the interest of the individual or the race; they both reject value, denying it any place in a true theory of political economy; they both make national wealth to consist, not in commodities, as also does private wealth, but in 'capacity', or 'productive power'; they both accordingly reject Smith's classification of productive and unproductive labor; they both reject his arguments for the international division of labour and free trade; they both advocate, in opposition to this, the harmonious development in each nation of agricultural and manufacturing interests; and they both repudiate laissez faire, and look to the government to conserve and develop national wealth.' (pp. 56–7).

emergent manufactures. Carey included in his *Essays on Political Economy* a balance of the advantages to national industry of policies of protection and free trade; nineteen benificent outcomes of protection are set against thirty-one increasingly doleful outcomes of free trade.[63] We might reasonably infer that these arguments were, by the mid-1820s, well established and familiar. Cooper had opposed protectionist arguments in his *Lectures*; List had been asked to write in reply to Cooper, and so it was entirely natural that in so doing he should articulate the prevailing critique of free trade.

'I confine my exertions ... solely to the refutation of the theory of Adam Smith and Co. the fundamental errors of which have not yet been understood so clearly as they ought to be' stated List at the beginning of the first Letter to Ingersoll, printed in the *National Gazette* in August 1827.[64] Cooper's arguments are referred to at once, citing a passage where Cooper describes as 'ignorance' the attempt to support an industry through duties when the goods may be purchased cheaper elsewhere. As was noted above, this Smithian principle, here abrasively articulated by Cooper, was the target of List's first general objection to Smith's political economy. The better to demonstrate the error of this view, List divides the component part of political economy into three: individual economy; national economy; and Economy of Mankind. List then suggests that Smith, whilst entitling his book the *Wealth of Nations*, had failed to deal properly with national economy, the second of the three component parts of political economy: 'his book is a mere treatise on the question: How the economy of the individuals and of mankind would stand, if the human race were not separated into nations, but united by a general law and by an equal culture of mankind?'[65] The economic principles of individuals and of mankind are of a general nature, as distinct from the specific conditions guiding national economy: consequently, argues List, the concern of national economy is to direct the economy of individuals and restrict the economy of mankind for the purposes of

---

[63] M. Carey, *Essays on Political Economy*, H. C. Carey and I. Lea, Philadelphia 1822. Here we find under protection 'Industry fostered and prosperous'; whereas free trade is associated with the following litany of woe: '7. Decay of national industry; 8. Workmen discharged; 9. Poor rates augmented; 10. Increase of idleness, pauperism and guilt; 11. Soup houses; 12. Manufacturing establishments in ruins; 13. Manufactures bankrupt; 14. Merchants and traders following in their train ... ' – concluding with '31. Alienation from a government regardless of the suffering of its citizens.'

[64] *Schriften*, Bd. 2, p. 99. The twelve letters to C. J. Ingersoll in Philadelphia were published from August to November in the *National Gazette* and then published as *Outlines of American Political Economy*, Philadelphia 1827.   [65] *Schriften*, Bd. 2, p. 101.

countering foreign power, or enhancing domestic power.[66] The increase of national wealth is the object of national economy alone; for the economy of individuals and their interests has no necessarily beneficial consequence for the nation,[67] while the economy of mankind looks to a common humanity existing in a state of perpetual peace: 'The object of individual economy is merely to obtain the necessities and comforts of life.[68] The object of the economy of mankind, or, to express it more properly, of cosmopolitical economy, is to secure to the whole human race the greatest quantity of the necessities and comforts of life.'[69] *Contra* Adam Smith and Dr Cooper, argues List, national economy aims to increase not simply wealth, but power, and hence its principles go beyond the economy to the political.[70] The objective of national policy is to enhance national power and wealth by ensuring that agriculture, commerce, and manufactures exist in a state of harmony. Insofar as this harmony cannot be established by the free activities of individuals, then the government has a duty to promote the wealth and power of a nation, 'placing the manufacturer by the side of the farmer' as Jefferson had proposed.[71]

Political Economy was redefined by List in terms of his conception of national economy: 'Every nation must follow its own course in developing its productive powers; or, in other words, every nation has its particular *Political Economy*'.[72] This was not to be confused with Cosmopolitical Economy, which simply became a weapon for older manufacturing countries seeking to prevent the emergence of newer ones. American Political Economy should focus on its own wants and

---

[66] List's use of 'national economy' here has no relation to contemporary German usage. Fulda, who taught at Tübingen when List was a student, distinguished three component parts of economics: private, national and state. 'National Economy' here is defined as the laws and principles of economics, whose founder was Adam Smith – *Grundsätze der ökonomisch-politischen Kameralwissenschaften*, Tübingen 1816, p. 199. *Nationalökonomie* as a compendium of abstract principles and laws was elaborated likewise by Jakob and Soden, among others – see my *Governing Economy*, pp. 170–5. However, List's comment in *Outlines* that Soden was 'the most celebrated German author in political economy' (*Schriften*, Bd. 2, p. 111) is proof, if such were needed, of his shaky grasp of the *Staatswissenschaften*.

[67] This is directed against Thomas Cooper, whose definition of Political Economy runs: 'Political Economy treats of the sources and acquisition of wealth: of its prudent distribution: of its consumption: and its accumulation. A nation like an individual, must practice and promote industry, and frugality, if the individuals who compose it, would live safely and comfortably at home, and be respected abroad.' *Lectures on the Elements of Political Economy*, Columbia 1826, p. 1.

[68] This echoes Raymond's definition of individual wealth, *Elements*, p. 36.

[69] *Schriften*, Bd. 2, p. 103.   [70] *Ibid.*, p. 105.   [71] *Ibid.*, p. 123.

[72] *Ibid.*, p. 124.

resources; this would also lend domestic manufactures an ascendancy over the products of those overseas competitors who did not enjoy the monopoly of an interior market.[73] Pursuit of free trade would merely further English, rather than American, economic objectives; and this applied not only to American manufacturers, but also to American producers of grain and cotton.[74]

The fact that the main protagonists of cosmopolitical economics based their analysis on the case of England enabled List to argue that it was in Britain's interest to foster free trade as a doctrinal principle, since this was the means by which Britain could ensure world domination:

English national economy has for its object to manufacture for the whole world, to monopolize all manufacturing power, even at the expense of the lives of the citizens, to keep the world and especially her colonies in a state of infancy and vassalage by political management as well as by the superiority of her capital, her skill and her navy. American economy has for its object to bring into harmony the three branches of industry, without which no national industry can attain perfection. It has for its object to supply its own wants, by its own materials and its own industry – to people an unsettled country – to attract foreign population, foreign capital and skill – to increase its power and its means of defence, in order to secure the independence and future growth of the nation. It has for its objects lastly to be free and independent and powerful, and to let everyone else enjoy freedom, power and wealth as he please. English national economy is predominant; American national economy aspires only to become independent.[75]

The great objective then was not the accumulation of capital,[76] but the enhancement of a nation's productive powers, conceived as national assets.

Here it is worth pointing out that this mode of argument is new for List. In 1820 he had argued that the system of liberty in imports and exports was not necessarily beneficial to individual countries; he had also made some remarks about complementarity between agriculture and manufacturing. But the dominant form in which he expressed his argument in favour of the abolition of internal tariffs and the establishment of a common customs frontier among the German states drew upon a politico-administrative discourse. The fortunes of the German nation were to be enhanced by the reorganisation of

---

[73] *Ibid.*, p. 135.   [74] *Ibid.*, pp. 146–7.   [75] *Ibid.*, p. 108.
[76] 'Greater part of the productive power consists in the intellectual and social conditions of the individuals, which I call capital of mind', *Schriften*, Bd. 2, p. 119.

economic administration; examples from other nations were added solely for the purpose of illustration.

Confrontation with Cooper's *Lectures* forced List into a reconstruction of this position, and this reconstruction drew upon the language of American political economy. It is striking that *Lectures* opens with a list of twenty-five maxims[77] that could, argued Cooper, be shown to be false on the basis of political economy. Many of these 'falsehoods' actually directly anticipate the exact arguments advanced by List concerning commerce, wealth, taxation and the role of agriculture and manufacture in national economic development. Among them we find the following 'confutable maxim': 'That every infant manufacture ought to be brought to maturity at the expense of the consumers; and at whatever cost; for the benefit of posterity.'[78] List's own principles of national economy were articulated in counterpoint to Cooper's views; and it was through this systematic process of rebuttal that he developed economic arguments for national development.

Common to arguments for and against protection and free trade in the United States was an understanding of the relation between economic development and national welfare within a federal political structure. There was a sufficient degree of similarity between the internal conflicts of the United States and those of the German states during the early part of the nineteenth century to render plausible the intellectual extension that List went on to make, identifying economic integration with economic development. Hitherto List had couched his arguments for a customs' union in administrative terms; the established theoretical positions which List encountered on his arrival in the United States made it natural to recast these arguments in the terminology of contemporary political economy – hence the formulation of national economy as a tendency opposed to cosmopolitical economy. The result is the construction of an argument which presupposes that economic forces in the contemporary international order operate upon a terrain divided into distinct national entities. The principles of cosmopolitical economy are not therefore held to be wrong in themselves; the error of a cosmopolitical economics is to suppose that economic forces are unmodified by the diversity of national interests, by the forces of international politics.

This point was elaborated in the Prize Essay that List composed in

---

[77] Cooper, *Lectures*, pp. 16–18.   [78] *Ibid.*, p. 17.

1837. The essay was written in response to a competition in which the question, set by Dupin, inquired: When a nation proposes to establish commercial freedom or to modify its customs legislation, what facts must it take into consideration for conciliating in the fairest fashion the interests of national producers on the one side, and the mass of consumers on the other? List knew that Dupin was to be one of the judges, and was thus keen to write an essay which would summarise principles that, he believed, were shared with Dupin.

In his Prize Essay List argued that any development from a largely agricultural society to one based on manufacturing must of necessity be a gradual and evolutionary process. In this he concurs with arguments advanced by Adam Smith in Book III of the *Wealth of Nations*. For this evolutionary development to occur naturally, however, a situation of eternal peace would have to obtain; humanity would have to be subordinated to one set of laws and, as Say had indicated, a global republic would have to exist.[79] But, List continued, the world was divided into a number of nations which were both sovereign bodies charged with the maintenance of their independence and the development of their properties, and also members of human society working as far as possible for a common prosperity. The economic universality potential within this system was expressed by free trade, but the free and equal development of the world economy could not be furthered by unilateral declarations of free trade, nor by its imposition regardless of the level of development of individual nations. Without a manufacturing capacity the basis of national independence was insecure;[80] protective tariffs were thus necessary to ensure that each nation could follow the true path of economic evolution and secure a proper balance of agriculture and industry.

Having introduced the argument on English domination already familiar from *Outlines*, together with its consequent arrangement of the world into colonies and metropolitan powers, List sketched a series of developmental stages which characterised the natural course of economic development. The first is the primitive evolution of the forces of production in agriculture from hunting and gathering to settled farming (Chapter 9); the introduction of foreign trade into a relatively stagnant agrarian state marks the beginning of the second stage, during which domestic manufacture begins to develop

---

[79] *Le Système Naturel d'Economie Politique, Schriften*, Bd. 4, p. 178. This has now been translated by Henderson as *The Natural System of Political Economy*, Frank Cass, London 1983.
[80] *Schriften*, Bd. 4, p. 184.

(Chapter 10); the third stage sees the equilibriation of manufacture and agriculture in the nation, with control of the domestic market being won by manufacture (Chapter 11); the fourth stage is marked by the import of raw materials and the export of manufactured goods, stimulating further domestic agriculture (Chapter 18); and finally a less distinct fifth stage is sketched, where prohibitions and tariffs eventually disappear and the system of perfect liberty can emerge (Chapter 25):

Here we are also cosmopolitans, but our cosmopolitanism rests on a sound basis, on nationality. Even in the system presented here we arrive at a point where the system of commercial liberty is the most advantageous one for a nation, and not the system of restrictions; but we arrive at this point by a completely different route to that of Smith and Say. We are citizens of the state before we are citizens of the world.[81]

In some respects we have come full circle back to Hamilton, who used Smith to construct his general principles and then differed on the question of protection for contemporary policy. List always argued that Smith's principles were fine for a world without economic frontiers and existing in a state of eternal peace – if such a world could be created, then the system of natural liberty would hold sway. Premature introduction of such a system would on the other hand condemn the world to English, or at best European, domination. Only the national economic perspective could provide a secure foundation for a process of joint world development; and this would progress on a similar basis to the ideal relation of agriculture and manufacture within a nation, dividing the world into a temperate manufacturing zone, and a hot agricultural zone.

Elaboration of this conception of an emergent international economic order is taken further in the 'Introduction' to the *National System*, where it becomes a theory of the civilizing process:

Civilisation, the political development (*Ausbildung*) and power of nations are principally determined by their economic circumstances, and vice versa. The more a nation's economy is complete and developed, the more civilised and powerful is that nation; the more its civilisation and power increases, so much the higher will its political development be able to rise.[82]

Nations which are at a much lower level of culture than the advanced manufacturing nations best develop themselves initially through free

---

[81] *Ibid.*, p. 396. Cf. Henderson's translation, p. 122, which modifies the original considerably.
[82] *Schriften*, Bd. 6, p. 49. The emphasis on the 'civilising' role of railways – 'genuine machines of welfare and individual development' was suggested in the *Staats-Lexikon*, Bd. 4, p. 657.

trade with their economic superiors. Protection is here relevant only at the point at which free trade begins to limit the market for domestic manufacture. On the other hand, for countries such as England free trade is also the most favourable option, since its power is advanced through the promotion of cosmopolitan principles.[83]

The *National System* is organised into four parts, covering a historical account of the development of particular nations, the elaboration of his basic principles, an outline of the diverse economic systems, and a sketch of the development of policy. It should also be recalled that the *National System* was intended as the first of a series of volumes, although the subtitle – 'International Trade, Trade Policy and the Zollverein' – is hardly descriptive of the content as represented by its four component parts.

Book 1 contains individual chapters on European states, the Hansa, and North America; forced into the paradigm of stages, they are dominated by the theme of what England has become. Although there is later in the text an extended attempt to specify the structure of a 'normal nation', in the descriptive passages this plays no role. Thus, as Sommer correctly indicates, the history of Italy is organised around the principle that it 'failed to become England'.[84] Much of the material that appears in this first book is re-ordered from the *Système Naturel*, and adds little to the arguments already advanced there.

In Book 2 List begins to elaborate his doctrine through a confrontation with the errors of the cosmopolitan school. First, it is argued that Quesnay and the Physiocrats are the originators of the school through their agrarian universalism, proceeding directly from the particular circumstances of France to a general theory of economic development. In the criticism of Smith and Say a more general argument is developed, concerning the nature of productive forces and the function of the division of labour.

Against the classical theory of value, List sets his theory of productive forces (Chapter 12). The principal feature of classical thinking, suggests List, is to associate wealth with material accumulation of capital, and this finds its clearest expression in the arguments on productive and unproductive labour. The theory of productive forces on the other hand perceives these to consist in material as well as immaterial objects and qualities – notably skills, intellectual and moral faculties are emphasised as indispensable elements of national wealth. Say did recognise the existence of immaterial goods, states

[83] *Schriften*, Bd. 6 pp. 54–6.   [84] Sommer, *Friedrich Lists System*, p. 98.

List, but these are held to be productive only insofar as they possess exchange value, and not because they create productive forces.[85]

With respect to the notion of the division of labour as elaborated in the *Wealth of Nations*, List suggested that concentration on the division of tasks and operations was permitted to obscure the increased interdependence that this generated. Had Smith emphasised this aspect more strongly, it is suggested, he would have been able to develop the comments on social labour which he makes in this context. Furthermore, in his exposition of the benefits of the division of labour Smith restricted his view to the division of labour within the individual enterprise, instead of examining the relation of agriculture and manufacturing at the level of the entire 'Ökonomie der Nation'.[86]

This then leads into a specification of this economy through an enumeration of the characteristics of the 'normal nation'. The nation stands between the individual, with its private economy, and mankind, with its cosmopolitan economy. In its 'normal' state it possesses

a common language and literature, a substantial territory possessed of a multitude of natural resources, and a large population. Agriculture, manufactures, trade and shipping are equally developed; arts and sciences, educational institutions and general culture exist at the same level as material production. Constitution, laws and institutions guarantee its members a high degree of freedom and security, promote religiosity, morality and welfare, in a word have the welfare of the citizen as their goal. It possesses adequate power on sea and land for the defence of its independence and autonomy, together with its foreign trade. It possesses the power to affect the culture of less developed nations, and with the surplus of its population, along with its intellectual and material capitals, it can found colonies and create new nations.[87]

For all List's criticisms of Smith, this conception of a 'normal' course of economic development, for nation and world economy alike, is not far distant from the principles which are advanced in Book III of *Wealth of Nations*. Like Smith, List was concerned that the distortions arising from evolution along a non-optimal path would restrict, or even confound, the potential for development which each nation had. The difference between the policy agendas of Smith and List amounts to the difference between the international economic orders of the eighteenth and the nineteenth centuries. In the eighteenth century trade on the basis of natural resources and population dictated the

[85] *Schriften*, Bd. 6, p. 181.   [86] *Ibid.*, p. 188.

[87] *Ibid.*, p. 210. The two later books – Book 3, which deals with the systems of economic doctrine, and Book 4, which deals with policy – add little to the text as a whole.

structure of the international economy. In the course of the nineteenth century this structure was altered by the diffusion of successive
technological changes in production and distribution. National
welfare, and competition between national economies, became
increasingly dependent upon access to and utilisation of new technological processes.

The first of many such technologies was that of the railway and
steam locomotive. List's imagination was seized by the implications of
railway technology for internal economic development. Important in
this was not a simple fascination with the technology of rail transport,
but an insight into the implications of a network of railway lines. List
himself stated that his interest in railways dated from a visit to
England in 1824. As Henderson points out, this is scarcely plausible,
since the only railway that he could have encountered at this time was
the horse-drawn Wandsworth–Croydon line, scarcely the harbinger
of a modern railway network as conceived by List in the 1830s.[88] In
America, List had been involved in the construction of a railway line,
but this was simply a substitute for a canal. On his return to Germany,
List became American Consul in Leipzig.[89] Here he became involved
with a group of projectors promoting railway development, and he
soon articulated the arguments for such development in terms of
economic space and its structure, becoming one of the first of many
railway ideologues. He also quickly fell out with his associates, one of
the more constant features of List's public career.

The first literary trace of List's interest in railway development
appears in a letter supporting a campaign for railway, rather than
canal, development in Bavaria. List wrote to von Baader that 'It
cannot escape the wise and powerful Bavarian government that with
the invention of the railways it is provided with a significant means of
providing for its interior all the advantages of coastal states.'[90] While
the railway line that List had been connected with in Pennsylvania
merely linked two points – a coalfield and a concentration of
consumers – his writing in the 1830s was to be characterised by a
concern with the interior market as a geographical space structured
by a rail network. Many commentators have noted that the view of

---

[88] Henderson, *Friedrich List*, p. 124.
[89] This appointment was for political services rendered in support of Andrew Jackson's
presidential campaign; although this is itself a curiosity, given the National Republican
theoretico-political position laid down in *Outlines*, for Jackson was a Democrat.
[90] Letter 1 September 1828, later published in *Mitteilungen aus Nordamerika*, Hamburg 1829;
Schriften, Bd. 3.1, p. 84.

the future railway system outlined in his essay on the Leipzig–Dresden railway in 1833 closely resembles the German network that did eventually emerge; none have however gone on to consider why this should be the case.[91] For List, railways were a powerful means for the creation of interior unity; it was not a matter of simply connecting one city with another, but of creating a network and so lending structure to enlarged markets. In his earlier writings he had been given to employing military metaphors to express economic ideas – war and peace, fortifications, defence and security – and it is in fact in an article on the military use of railways that one of the clearest statements on the spatial significance of the railway is to be found: 'The needs of industry and communication will compel the railway systems of the larger Continental nations to assume the form of a network, concentrating on the interior principal points and radiating from the centre to the frontiers ...'[92] The creation of a customs union involved the homogenisation of internal space, a space which was then delimited by the establishment of a common economic frontier. Having created this 'empty economic space', empty that is of the previous political and geographical boundaries, the railway network functioned to lend this space a structure which had economic implications.

Price, in his account of the formation of the Zollverein, suggests that such ideas are not to be found in List's writings in the early 1820s, which addressed themselves to the issues of tariff reform and the possibilities of a customs' union. His arguments for common frontiers and tariffs were not accompanied by any clear conception of the extent of economic unification, nor of its detailed organisation.[93] It should, however, be remembered that during List's early agitation on behalf of a customs' union railway technology was very primitive, as the English example above demonstrates. Not until the later 1820s was steam technology successfully added to iron rails and rolling stock, mechanising the railway and substantially increasing speeds. This new means of transport was, according to List, a means of making man 'an eternally happy, wealthy and complete being',

[91] The map of the German rail network can be found appended to the pamphlet 'Über ein sächsisches Eisenbahnsystem als Grundlage eines allgemeinen deutschen Eisenbahnsystems und insbesondere über die Anlegung einer Eisenbahn von Leipzig nach Dresden', *Schriften*, Bd. 3.1, pp. 155–95. A survey of the railway literature can be found in Henderson, *Friedrich List*, Chapter 3.
[92] 'Deutschlands Eisenbahnsystem in militärischen Beziehung', *Schriften*, Bd. 3.1, p. 264. This article was printed in the *Eisenbahn-Journal* in 1836.
[93] A. H. Price, *The Evolution of the Zollverein*, University of Michigan Press, Ann Arbor 1949, p. 36.

widening the impact of the action of the individual to an area which potentially included the whole of humanity.[94]

List's original pamphlet of 1833 on the financial and engineering aspects of the Leipzig project was followed in 1834 by a more general essay in which the social consequences of railway development were more boldly spelled out:

> If one can travel in a few hours from one town to another, without difficulty and at insignificant cost, then both become *one* community: Leipzig becomes the suburb of Dresden, and Dresden that of Leipzig. ... Science and art, trade and industry, social and family life, every relationship and activity will gain by this connection. ... Since the time that Germany has possessed the internal freedom of traffic indispensable to its industrial welfare, it only required in addition cheaper and faster means of transport for it to advance to the level of the earth's most industrious nations.[95]

These ideas were repeated in a number of essays and articles over the next few years without further development. Such repetition of basic ideas was typical of List, but this does not diminish the importance of his insight. He perceived that the revolution in transportation that the railway brought with it would have profound social and economic consequences. The free movement of persons and goods within a nation would intensify economic relationships, providing a material framework for economic progress and market development.

List's railway writings have obvious economic implications, but they are neither explicitly linked to, nor derived from, principles advanced in *Outlines*, his Prize Essay or, more importantly, the *National System*. Nevertheless, the basic theses advanced do complement the conception of economic development and national economic integration expounded in these writings. List's emphasis on the centrality of 'productive forces', as opposed to the cosmopolitan theory of value, directed attention to the material structure of a national economy. This was not all. The critique of 'cosmopolitical theory' that he mounted meant that this conception of material economic structure was articulated in terms of a theoretical system absent from the descriptive writings of Dupin or Chaptal. His confrontation in the later 1820s with American debates on economic policy, framed as they were in the terminology of political economy,

---

[94] F. List, 'Eisenbahnen und Canäle, Dampfboote und Dampfwagentransport', in Rotteck and Welcker, *Staats-Lexikon*, Bd. 4, pp. 659–60.

[95] 'Aufruf an unsere Mitbürger in Sachsen die Anlage einer Eisenbahn zwischen Dresden und Leipzig betreffend', *Schriften*, Bd. 3.1, pp. 207–9.

provided the rational core for his analysis of national and international economic development. The clear alternatives in policy and theory provided by the texts of Cooper and Raymond had no counterpart in Europe until much later in the century.

Ironic indeed, then, that List's economic conceptions of protectionism and customs' unions, which derive directly from the United States of the 1820s, should come to be so closely associated with the *Zollverein*. Throughout the nineteenth century the United States remained protectionist, and relatively uninvolved in the growth of international trade. The domestic dynamism of American economic development was nonetheless clearly linked to a process of political integration, driven on towards the end of the century by the activities of big business and finance houses. Similar forces were operating in the European economy, most notably in the unification of Germany. But, despite the increasing degree of economic interdependence between nations, it was not until the mid-twentieth century that deliberate effort was made to further European integration as a political objective. In the late 1940s, the American Government sought, through the medium of the Marshall Plan, to impel the Western European states towards the formation of a United States of Europe; a phrase now fallen into disrepute, and employed only by those hostile to the extension of powers embodied by the European Union. But in adopting the strategy of a customs' union, and creating a general system of economic protectionism, the Treaty of Rome had simply adopted a strategy of economic integration already successfully implemented in the early years of the new American federal republic. The political success of this republic rested not a little on the economic bonds which linked its member states to a central federal government: a system of federal taxation instituted by Alexander Hamilton, and a single currency. When opponents of European political integration argue that the aims of the Community should go no further than an economic free-trade area, then they are rehearsing an argument already lost by the early 1800s in the American context. Friedrich List was, after all, an American citizen; and we can perhaps better understand the dynamics of European integration, if we first understand the genesis and sources of the arguments used by academics, politicians, and journalists in seeking to come to terms with this process.

CHAPTER 4

Historical Economics, the Methodenstreit, and the economics of Max Weber

It is generally supposed that 'German economics' in the later nineteenth century was synonymous with 'the German School of Historical Economics', a school whose most prominent headmaster was Gustav von Schmoller. Through this school there passed two generations of German economists. The first of these can be dated from Wilhelm Roscher's manifesto statement of 1843, and by all accounts includes just two other members: Bruno Hildebrand and Karl Knies. Schmoller was the leader of the Younger Historical School, the academic successor of the first group, and that with which Max Weber expressly associated himself. Historical Economics as an intellectual enterprise clashed dramatically with the new marginal economics of Carl Menger in the 1870s, providing the occasion for the 'debate on method' which was only indirectly resolved by the progressive international shift of academic economics away from a descriptive and inductive method towards theoretical and analytical argument. Conveniently for this understanding of German economics, the new economics that clashed with the Historical School was 'Austrian' in provenance, so that the conflict between historical and theoretical economics could be conveniently represented by a national, as well as an intellectual, boundary.

It is fair to say that, despite the evident crudities of this characterisation, it does reflect central elements of the image of German economics carried abroad by American and British students during the 1870s and 1880s. This image subsequently hardened into a received wisdom that proved resistant to further modification; and the lack of a reliable and systematic survey of the actual complexity of the international development of economics around the turn of the century has led to a situation where, for want of an alternative story, even German scholars today believe this version of events.[1] Viewed more critically, on the other hand, it can be questioned whether many of the products of this school pass muster as either good history or good economics. Certainly a great deal of the writings of Schmoller, for example, leaves much to be desired by the standards of contemporary analytical argument, and the conception of history that the school promoted is one that appears today simplistic and dated. In such circumstances, any attempt at a rational reconstruction of the 'Historical School of Economics' threatens to degenerate into a listing of persona, organisations, and books that bears a striking resemblance to the principal methodological failings of the school itself.[2]

The problem thus becomes: is it possible to arrive at a systematic understanding of an object so diffuse as the 'Historical School'? Certainly, this was a label that united the majority of German economists in their self-understanding, but it can be doubted whether direct interrogation of this object would today yield very much more than vague generalisations. By contrast, a more worthwhile exercise would be to emphasise the ever-shifting heterogeneity of economic argument, rather than concentrating attention on 'Schools' and theoretical traditions, adherents to which turn out, on closer inspection, to share little of substance. The pursuit of generalisations at a high level of aggregation hinders, rather than helps, our understanding of the development of economic discourse. Too often effort is devoted to gathering together contemporaries under some convenient label, seeking to minimise or ignore inconvenient differences. A more useful attitude of mind is to accept heterogeneity as a natural, rather than a pathological, condition; we should accept it for the insights that it can give us, rather than seek to abolish it. Such an attitude will

---

[1] Entirely representative of this is the entry 'German Historical School' by F. Schinzinger in J. Eatwell, M. Milgate and P. Newman (eds.), *The New Palgrave Dictionary of Economics*, vol. II, Macmillan Press, London 1987, pp. 516–18. Elsewhere it is usual to encounter the new economics treated as synonymous with marginal utility analysis and hence counterposed to historical economics – M. Schön, for example ('Gustav Schmoller and Max Weber', in W. J. Mommsen and J. Osterhammel (eds.), *Max Weber and his Contemporaries*, Allen and Unwin, London 1987, p. 60), states that Weber's lecture outline of 1898 'is largely oriented towards the theory of marginal utility', which is quite inaccurate; cf. Osterhammel on Schumpeter in the same collection, pp. 108–10.

[2] An example of this is D. Krüger, *Nationalökonomen im wilhelminischen Deutschland*, Vandenhoeck und Ruprecht, Göttingen 1983, which contains a great deal of material but little discernible argument. Schumpeter's *History of Economic Analysis* (Allen and Unwin, London 1954, pp. 850ff.) provides a better outline than most, as does J. K. Ingram, *History of Political Economy*, 2nd edn, Adam and Charles Black, London 1907, Chapter 6 (first published 1885).

also assist our understanding of those forces generating areas of common agreement, as well as points of conflict; not forgetting the equally important areas in which divergence of interest leads to simple mutual indifference. Not only can we then identify sources for the dynamism of economic discourse, it also becomes easier to deal with the fact that no 'School' ever speaks with one voice all the time.

The strategy adopted below is as follows: first of all, the foundations of historical economics as expressed in the work of Wilhelm Roscher and others will be briefly considered. This will then be contrasted with the manner in which Carl Menger developed his economic principles, making possible in turn an appreciation of the chief points at issue in the *Methodenstreit*. Although in all appearance the result of this clash was a standoff, by the 1890s a further generational shift within the 'Younger' School was taking place that was to play an important part in the waning influence of historical economics within the German economics profession. Max Weber, appointed to a chair of economics in Freiburg in 1893, and then successor to Knies at Heidelberg in 1896, is a representative of this new generation. His brief career as a university professor was followed by a longer one as an editor, alongside two other economists, of the major social science periodical in late Wilhelminian Germany, the *Archiv für Sozialwissenschaft und Sozialpolitik*. Placing Weber in the tradition of German economics in this way serves both to clarify aspects of this tradition, as well illuminate Weber's own understanding of his relation to German economics from Roscher onward. As his essay 'Roscher and Knies and the Logical Problems of Historical Economics' demonstrates, his methodological critique of historicism took the form of a close reading of the writings of Roscher, and of his economics teacher, Knies.

Roscher's *Grundriß*[3] of 1843 is still today generally recognised as the charter for a new historical economics, although as I have argued elsewhere it is in important respects continuous with prevailing forms of economic argument in the Germany of the 1830s and 1840s.[4] Roscher did present his programme as a new departure, aligned with the method adopted in jurisprudence by Savigny and Eichhorn, and distanced from the economics of the school of Ricardo. We should note straightaway that an option between historical and abstract

---

[3] *Grundriß zu Vorlesungen über die Staatswirthschaft. Nach geschichtlicher Methode*, Dieterische Buchhandlung, Göttingen 1843.
[4] See my *Governing Economy. The Reformation of German Economic Discourse 1750–1840*, Cambridge University Press, Cambridge 1988, pp. 205f.

method stated in this manner is a curiosity; the appeal to the Historical School of Law is understandable, but the association of an alternative, abstract method with the name of Ricardo introduces a figure of little contemporary significance in Germany. Ricardo's work was known in Germany, and his *Principles of Political Economy and Taxation* had been translated twice;[5] but it would be wrong to infer that Ricardianism had any influence at the time in Germany.[6] Roscher's invocation of historical jurisprudence as a methodological guide involves a shift of emphasis, rather than a radical departure, in contemporary economic discourse. His use of Ricardo's name serves only to disguise this degree of real continuity, implying that a viable theoretical alternative actually existed. On the contrary: Roscher's option for historicism did not require either an explicit or an implicit rejection of a prevailing and acknowledged alternative.

Furthermore, in calling upon the names of Savigny and Eichhorn, Roscher invoked a form of historicism that was internally incoherent. Savigny's historical jurisprudence presupposed the existence of a 'national spirit' arising out of immanent principles, and was actually quite impervious to the relativisation of legal relations through the study of social and economic conditions.[7] Although invoking Savigny's historicism, Roscher did not in fact adopt this presumption of national spirit, but instead supposed the existence of basic economic laws that could be inferred from the study of masses of historical facts. The consequent difficulty of identifying essential elements in the midst of a mass of phenomena impelled Roscher to call for systematic economic comparison of all recorded peoples one with another, a form of total history of economic life different in character to the methodological imperatives of the Historical School of Law.[8] As his lecture outline suggested, the project was to 'Summarise as a developmental law that which was common to the diverse development of peoples'.[9] Much later, Gustav Cohn noted in his obituary notice for Roscher

---

[5] Translated as *Die Grundsätze der politischen Oekonomie* (Weimar 1821) and *Grundsätze der Volkswirthschaft und der Besteuerung* (Leipzig 1837).

[6] Marx for example, who by 1847 in the *Philosophy of Poverty* was a full-blown Ricardian, had in his first economic writings of 1843 and 1844 shown little interest in the work of Ricardo, treating instead James Mill and Adam Smith as the leading proponents of Classical Political Economy. Marx's long-lasting admiration for Ricardo was a product of his reading in exile, and owed nothing to the intellectual environment that he left behind in Germany.

[7] See for a critique of the Historical School of Law E.-W. Böckenförde, 'Die Historische Rechtsschule und das Problem der Geschichtlichkeit des Rechts', in his *Staat, Gesellschaft, Freiheit*, Suhrkamp Verlag, Frankfurt 1976, pp. 9–41.   [8] Roscher, *Grundriß*, p. v.

[9] Roscher, *Grundriß*, p. 2, §1, 'Methode der Staatswissenschaften überhaupt'.

that this programme, while challenging and superficially attractive, was one too diffuse to form a working guide for successful research; and, insofar as a historical 'method' can be identified at work in the writings of the school, this is to be found in general programmatic statements, rather than systematic principles embedded in its products.[10]

This project for the identification of laws of development from study of the economic activity of historically existing peoples required a common working definition of economic activity, and in this aspect of his work Roscher drew directly upon his contemporaries and predecessors. In his programme, Roscher defined goods as objects that can be used for the satisfaction of human wants, the range of such objects extending with the advance of civilisation. 'Economic goods' are defined as things, personal services and relationships; 'economic action' is defined as all ongoing activity for the maintenance, increase, and use of property.[11] *Nationalökonomie*, argued Roscher, was

the anatomy and physiology of economic life. It was concerned with the study of the natural laws according to which peoples satisfied their material wants: the needs of food and clothing, lodging and firewood, of the sexual drive etc.; above all those natural laws by which these needs affect the state and are in turn influenced by the state.[12]

This conception of economic action arising from the process by which humans satisfy their wants and needs, and in so doing constitute a realm of goods out of a world of objects, is continuous with the standard definition of economic action that had emerged at the turn of the century in Germany. Roscher's articulation of such a conception was, by the 1840s, entirely conventional.

When therefore the first volume of Roscher's textbook *System der Volkswirthschaft* appeared in 1854, the introduction to its 'Basic Concepts' started with a definition of goods in terms of the satisfaction of human needs:

Goods are all those things which are recognised as being useful to the satisfaction of human needs. To this extent one might say: if the human being can just as little create as destroy the substance of goods; if in addition their form only partly depends on his labour: so it is his spirit (Geist), his conception of means and ends, that makes them goods as such.[13]

---

[10] G. Cohn, 'Wilhelm Roscher', *Economic Journal*, vol. 4 (1894), p. 559.
[11] Roscher, *Grundriß*, pp. 2–4, §§ 2–4.
[12] W. Roscher, 'Der gegenwärtige Zustand der wissenschaftlichen Nationalökonomie', *Deutsche Vierteljahrsschrift*, Bd. 1, H. 1 (1849), pp. 180–1.
[13] W. Roscher, *System der Volkswirthschaft*, Bd. 1, J. G. Cotta, Stuttgart 1854, p. 1, §1.

Roscher does underscore the heritage of this *topos* by a reference to Hufeland's *Neue Grundlegung der Staatswirthschaftskunst*. This reference deserves some attention, for Hufeland was a conscious proponent of Smithianism who, in the preface of his book, rehearsed the place of Smith in the various systems of economic thought and the rate of his reception in Germany.[14] Roscher's historicism did not, as we might anticipate, lead him to oppose on principle Smithian and Ricardian economics; he was on the contrary open to their use wherever relevant. But this openness to doctrines subsequently assumed to be in conflict with historicist argument makes it even more difficult to identify with any clarity the actual substance of Roscher's methodological position. Roscher displays the same kind of pragmatic openness that we find in Rau's *Lehrbuch*, in which material from opposing theoretical camps is integrated into a general description of economic activity. Schmoller likewise emphasised the importance of Karl Heinrich Rau for Roscher, arguing that Roscher's *System der Volkswirthschaft*, intended as a supplement, not a replacement, for Rau's *Lehrbuch*, adopted the latter's tripartite scheme, form of argument, and style.[15]

A similar difficulty exists with the principal text of Bruno Hildebrand, who is customarily associated with Roscher as an early progenitor of historical economics. His *Nationalökonomie der Gegenwart und Zukunft*[16] takes the form of a history of economic doctrines from Smith to Proudhon. This was intended as the first part of a project that would redirect *Nationalökonomie* into a doctrine of the economic laws of development of peoples, bringing about a reform of economic understanding analogous to that which had recently occurred in philology.[17] Hildebrand applies no standard test to the work of Smith, Ricardo, List, and Müller; instead, after providing a summary of their principles, he conducts an immanent critique. The Smithian system is accused of pretending to a generality that it does not possess, it being rather an expression of the prevailing money economy;[18] while Müller's economic analysis is held to derive from a conception of individual and state that dates from classical antiquity.[19] These and

[14] Bd. 1, Gießen 1807, 'Vorrede'.
[15] The text was published in five volumes from 1854–86. G. Schmoller, 'Wilhelm Roscher (1888)', *Zur Litteraturgeschichte der Staats- und Sozialwissenschaften*, Duncker und Humblot, Leipzig 1888, p. 154.   [16] Frankfurt a. M. 1848.
[17] The second phase of this project, dealing with the method of *Nationalökonomie*, was never published.   [18] Hildebrand, *Nationalökonomie, p. 29.*
[19] Hildebrand, *Nationalökonomie*, p. 52.

other judgements betray the presence of some kind of critical analytical scheme, but the analytical criteria are never explicitly articulated. Furthermore, in his project to reform *Nationalökonomie*, Hildebrand did not succeed in penetrating beyond his initial review of the existing doctrinal framework supporting existing economic understanding; in no respect do we gain sight of a doctrine elaborating the economic laws of development of peoples. Here once more we find that a gulf separates the historicist project from the actual writings of those who most prominently espoused its aims.

This problem is again evident if we compare the economic writings of historical economists with those produced by a figure not normally considered a member of the Historical School: Lorenz von Stein, Professor for Staatswissenschaft und *Nationalökonomie* in Vienna from 1855 to 1888.[20] Stein was described by Schmoller in 1866 as 'perhaps the last remnant of speculative philosophy in the domain of Staatswissenschaft',[21] but this should not obscure the fact that the 'theory of goods' as the object of human activity that he develops in his *System* is entirely compatible with the work of Roscher and others. While embedded in a different language, the emphasis on the world of goods and needs is entirely familiar. Society, argues Stein, begins where the natural fact of the possession of goods becomes a fact of personal life and begins to dominate the social order and its development:

> Insofar as goods here appear as the foundation of the personal order, of the domain of opposites and thus of life, this last comprehends the entirety of economic doctrine, and the result is that the laws governing the development of goods become at the same time the laws deciding that struggle between personal and natural elements in human society.[22]

The first book of his *Lehrbuch der Volkswirthschaft*, is likewise based upon a doctrine of goods, in which goods are defined as such by reference to human wants and needs.

Indeed, if one were to identify a specifically German trait in economic writing in mid-century, it would not be the provenance of a historical method in economic writing, but rather this universally accepted conception that the point of departure for the consideration of economic life was the human being and its needs. The existence of such human needs and wants generated a realm of economic activity

---

[20] See his *System der Staatswissenschaft*, 2 vols., J. G. Cotta, Stuttgart 1852, 1856; *Lehrbuch der Volkswirthschaft*, Wilhelm Braumüller, Vienna 1858.
[21] Cited in E.-W. Böckenförde, 'Lorenz von Stein als Theoretiker der Bewegung von Staat und Gesellschaft zum Sozialstaat', *Staat, Gesellschaft, Freiheit*, Suhrkamp Verlag, Frankfurt a. M. 1976, p. 149.   [22] Stein, *System der Staatswissenschaft*, Bd. 1, p. 22.

in which these needs were satisfied. The exchanges that occurred in this realm were summarised in the all-embracing *topos* of *Verkehr* – communication, commerce, social intercourse, traffic, exchange. Economic man was here conceived as *der verkehrende Mensch*. *Verkehr* is the axiom that unites studies of telegraphs, railways, stock exchanges, banks, and trade with a conception of the marketplace as a location[23] at which the activities of individuals transmuted into an ordered economic whole. The economic meaning of the term *Verkehr* originates with the development of *Nationalökonomie* at the beginning of the century, growing in importance through the century, and, as we shall see below, it formed an organising principle for a section of Max Weber's 1898 lecture outline. In addition to this it also helps us understand how Karl Knies, as a historical economist, could devote entire books to the subjects of the telegraph and railway communication.

Menger's *Grundsätze der Volkswirthschaftslehre* does not at first sight belong to this tradition; it is usually thought to embrace an abstract account of marginal utility, hence focusing on a problem, and employing a method, at odds with contemporary German economics. True enough, Menger's student Wieser, who did espouse the new marginalism, promoted Menger's claim to be a founder of neo-classical economics; but the basis for such a claim has always been shaky.[24] Assigning Menger to neo-classicism certainly makes explanation of the *Methodenstreit* easier, but there is in fact little of substance in such an assignation. True, Menger's approach was abstract; but it was an abstraction allied to a radical subjectivism continuous with the conventional German concern with goods and human needs. The abstraction that Menger introduced into his treatment involved conceiving the relationship between goods, needs, and satisfaction in terms of utilities (*Nützlichkeiten*); but he only ranked these utilities, and did not presuppose a scale of 'utility', since this would have violated his subjectivist approach. There was therefore no way in which he could conceive of marginal increases in utility after the fashion of his contemporary Jevons.[25]

---

[23] Note that from von Thünen to Alfred Weber, the classical theories of the location of economic activity are German in origin.
[24] See the brief outline of the problem in P. Mirowski, *More Heat than Light*, Cambridge University Press, Cambridge 1990, pp. 259–61.
[25] Wieser published an outline of the Austrian School's treatment of value and utility in 1891 that consistently refers to Jevons, rather than Marshall, in this connection – see 'The Austrian School and the Theory of Value', *Economic Journal*, vol. 1 (1891), pp. 108–21.

For Menger, utilities are objects that can effect the satisfaction of human needs; and those which are accessible for acquisition or exchange are called goods. In an entirely conventional manner this statement appears in the third paragraph of the first chapter of the *Grundsätze*, 'The General Theory of Goods'.[26] A footnote appended to it lists a number of previous authors who had discussed the nature of economic goods, among them Hufeland's *Neue Grundlegung* of 1807 as cited by Roscher, as well as Roscher's *System*.[27] This focus on goods and needs was therefore not only conventional, but this fact was emphasised by Menger himself.

What was not so conventional was the manner in which Menger, in seeking to elaborate an idea of goods and their relation to the satisfaction of needs, pursued an abstract, rather than generalising, method. It was usual in treatises on general economics to begin with an introductory section on 'Basic Concepts', but then move on to a treatment of the diverse areas of economic activity. This does not happen in Menger's *Grundsätze*. Schmoller in a dismissive review of the book suggested that, by focusing on an exposition of utility and value, Menger simply rewrote the classical fiction of an ahistorical economic man. On the contrary, argued Schmoller, the way forward in economics was to direct research into historical and statistical material.[28] This encapsulates the real difference between the two writers: on the one hand Menger, seeking to clarify the theoretical basis of economics by reducing propositions to their most abstract, ideal-typical form; on the other hand Schmoller, arguing that progress could only come through amassing comparative data and searching for general laws of economic development within it. Stated in this way the *Methodenstreit* becomes less a debate over the status of historicism than an argument over deductivist versus inductivist method.

Part of the difficulty must have been that Menger dealt in the same basic concepts as his contemporaries, while developing a framework compatible with marginal analysis, but non-mathematical in form. This can be seen in the passages where he develops his explanation of the relationship of value, need, and utility. The value of a good, argued Menger, was defined not in itself, but rather in relation to our

---

[26] C. Menger, *Grundsätze der Volkswirthschaftslehre*, Gesammelte Werke, Bd. 1, p. 2; originally published in Vienna 1871.

[27] Menger had in fact dedicated the *Grundsätze* to Schmoller.

[28] By 'statistical' here is simply meant descriptive numerical data – Schmoller, review of Menger, *Literarisches Centralblatt für Deutschland*, 1 February 1873, no. 5, pp. 142–3.

needs. These needs could in principle be ranked, from the most vital
for the existence of life (10 on Menger's scale) to the least vital (ranked
1). The goods that satisfied these needs were however not themselves
homogeneous; the fundamental need for one, such as food, gave it a
greater range of potential satisfactions than that for, say, tobacco.
However, even for a comparatively vital good such as food, there
came a point where satisfaction was excessive compared with the
degree of urgency of another need. The subjective approach was
necessary to resolve the problems arising from this, since it was up to
the consumer to arrive at an appropriate balance between the various
goods available.[29] Utility, as a subjective phenomenon, was a continuous variable, but the lack of homogeneity between the goods to
which it was imputed meant that such goods could only be ranked in
order of the subject's preference, and not ordered by reference to
utility as an independent and uniform standard of value. Jevons on
the other hand derived the conception of utility from the binary
alternatives of pleasure and pain, providing a basis for the treatment
of consumers' utilities in terms of a mathematical function.[30]

Many of the leading ideas of neo-classical economic analysis are
embedded in Menger's approach, but the implications are neither
elaborated nor interpreted – in fact the formulations summarised
above occur on three pages of the *Grundsätze*, after which the
discussion passes on to more general considerations of value. Menger
in any case had little command of mathematics, and this would have
been necessary for any elaboration of his treatment of subjective
utility. The major advance that Menger made was in his treatment of
the manner in which choices were made between goods with varying
incremental levels of satisfaction, or their 'marginal utility' as von
Wieser called it in 1884.

Without launching into a comprehensive survey of German economics in the later nineteenth century, it is possible on the basis of the
foregoing to contend that, firstly, the content and style of 'German
economics' in the nineteenth century was continuously distinct to the
English tradition exemplified by Ricardo, Malthus, Senior and John
Stuart Mill; and, secondly, that up until the 1880s the varying

[29] Menger, *Grundsätze*, pp. 92–4.
[30] Jevons argued that utility, as a continuous variable, was essentially mathematical in
character; but that the balance of pleasure against pain involved a choice that was
generalisable and susceptible to aggregation – see *The Theory of Political Economy*, 2nd edn,
Macmillan, London 1879, pp. 14–17, and Chapter 2ff.

'schools' of German economics drew upon a relatively stable set of basic axioms concerning the domain of human need and economic life. Where these schools differed was in their derivation and elaboration of human need and economic life. Despite some similarities, this cannot be reduced to a familiar divergence of analytical versus historical method, or even deductive versus inductive method as such: Menger ended his life after all seeking to rewrite his *Grundsätze* as a comprehensive economic sociology.[31] The differences which existed can however be elucidated on the basis of the varying terminology for 'economics' in the German language. It was on these distinctions that Menger built his critique of the Historical School in his *Untersuchungen über die Methode der Socialwissenschaften, und der Politischen Oekonomie insbesondere*,[32] the text which was the opening shot in the *Methodenstreit*, and for this reason alone we should pay some attention to this terminological question.

A variety of terms is available in the German language to denote economic activity and its representation. Although many of these terms have for the most part been used synonymously since the early nineteenth century, this potential lexical variety has at critical times been employed as a means of establishing important distinctions. Furthermore, obsolete terms associated with the eighteenth-century tradition of the *Cameralwissenschaften* continued in modified use to the end of the nineteenth century. The first variation available in the German language is an option between the classical Graeco-Roman *oeconomia*, borrowed in the sixteenth century, and a root derived from middle High German, *Wirt*.[33] In both cases early usage was closely linked to the idea of household management, such that 'economising' activity was in this sense synonymous with well-ordered activity. The special connotation of thriftiness is not essential to this usage and was a later accretion, as it was in the English language.[34] English is of course restricted to the Graeco-Roman derivation for its usage, although it is likely that the variation in French and English spelling from that of

---

. [31] See K. Yagi, 'Carl Menger after 1871', draft translation of his *Osutoria Keizai Shisoushi Kenkyu*, Chapter 2 (1988).   [32] Duncker und Humblot, Leipzig 1883.

[33] See for 'Ökonomie' Grimm, *Deutsches Wörterbuch*, Bd. 7, cols. 1268–9, and for 'Wirt', Bd. 14/2, cols. 629–30.

[34] In both the OED and Grimm the eighteenth-century examples of the usage economic/ *Ökonomie* involve conceptions of order and organisation, rather than thrift *per se*. See 'economic', 'economical' in the *Oxford English Dictionary*, vol. v, 2nd edn, pp. 58–9. There is an analogous development with respect to the term 'management', for which there is no direct German equivalent with the range of meaning of the English – see for a discussion of this my 'Cameralism and the Science of Government', above, pp. 16–17.

the German is in part a result of the term being reintroduced into medieval Latin from contemporary Greek as *yconomus*.[35] Whereas, by the nineteenth century, the English language uses the terms 'economy' and 'economic' to signify both a neutral, descriptive meaning (a specific region or branch of purposive activity), and as a prescriptive (the sense of thrift in the exercise of this activity), contemporary German usage did not necessarily involve this connotation, thanks in part to the manipulation of Graeco-Latin and Germanic lexical foundations. One outcome of this was the existence, in the last third of the century, of several variant terms for 'economics', each of which could be systematically distinguished along some conceptual axis from the remaining terms. *Staatswirthschaftslehre, Nationalökonomie, Politische Ökonomie, Wirthschaftslehre*, and *Volkswirthschaftslehre* could in this way be treated either synonymously, or as defined parts of the general science of economics.

In making his critique of the Historical School, Menger made the following basic distinction between three distinct domains of economics:

(a) the historical sciences dealing with the *Volkswirthschaft* (history and statistics);
(b) *theoretische Nationalökonomie*;
(c) practical sciences of the economy, laying down foundations of purposive action in individual domains of economic activity (economic policy, financial science).

Politische Oekonomie, according to Menger, united (b) and (c): 'By *politische Oekonomie* we shall mean that totality of theoretico-practical sciences of the economy (*die theoretische Nationalökonomie, die Volkswirthschaftspolitik und die Finanzwissenschaft*), which are today usually characterised in this way.'[36] Menger argued in the Preface to his critique that contemporary Political Economy was characterised by a plurality of methods that derived from a failure to distinguish consistently between the precepts of theoretical economics, and the methods to be followed in the practical investigation of economic forms. As a consequence, there was a lack of clarity and agreement concerning the nature and purpose of political economy, which led to confusion and purposeless argument. His treatise sought to correct this by directing a systematic critique at the conception that the

[35] OED, vol. v, p. 60.
[36] C. Menger, *Untersuchungen über die Methode der Socialwissenschaften, und der Politischen Oekonomie insbesondere*, Gesammelte Werke, Bd. 2, p. 10. This was first published in 1883.

principles of economics could be identified from a practical study of national economies – or as Roscher had argued in 1843, that the laws of economics could be revealed through study of the formation of economic systems. Menger drew attention to the fact that there was a lack of symmetry between the historical method as practised in law, and as practised in economics. Exponents of the former were capable of identifying clear principles that persistently eluded exponents of the latter – such as Schmoller, Roscher, and Knies.

The basic argument that he advanced was that individualising (historical) and generalising (theoretical) apprehension of economic phenomena were appropriate to different levels, and were not substitutes one for the other. The project of developing a historical approach to theoretical economics (*theoretische Nationalökonomie*) therefore amounted to a methodological solecism.[37] The purpose of scientific study was not, argued Menger, the simple accumulation of knowledge, but furtherance of our understanding of phenomena. Just as empirical knowledge could not be gained through reflection, theoretical knowledge was not accessible through empirical study. But this was the very claim made by Historical Economics; a claim that was ultimately unsubstantiated, but a programmatic principle that sustained the cohesion of a substantial body of work nonetheless.

Schmoller in his review rejected the idea that theoretical *Nationalökonomie* could in fact aspire to the revelation of general economic principles:

Since theoretical economics (*theoretische Nationalökonomie*) in no way has the task of teaching us how to apprehend the universal nature of economic (*volkswirtschaftlicher*) phenomena, but only promote an understanding of a specific, although very important, side of economic human life; so it is a laughable and scarcely conceivable insanity to proceed from the general psychological motives of human action, rather than from the impulse of self-interest. ... The phenomena of the economy (*Volkswirtschaft*) are the consequence of individual economic desires and must therefore be considered from this point of view.[38]

This focus on self-interest was necessarily a concrete one, identifiable only within the fabric of social activity. Only on this practical, concrete and historicising basis could one advance to firm principles which would then permit a degree of deductive reasoning on econ-

[37] Menger, *Untersuchungen*, pp. 12–13.
[38] G. Schmoller, 'Zur Methodologie der Staats- und Sozial-Wissenschaften', *Jahrbuch für Gesetzgebung, Verwaltung und Volkswirtschaft*, N. F. Jg. 7 (1883), pp. 976–7.

omic forms. Menger had not of course denied this, simply arguing that the abstract principles of economic action were not deducible from historical research dedicated to the conception of the individuality of economic phenomena. This line of argument was continued by Weber in his critique of Roscher in 1903;[39] and none of the products of the Historical School showed signs of moving from the phase of historical research to the derivation of general principles. Schmoller suggested that Menger borrowed too heavily from John Stuart Mill's *Logic* and an older Political Economy; a charge which simply reveals his blindness to Menger's debt to German economic writing, and his ignorance of Classical Economics.

An American student attending Schmoller's Seminar in the early 1890s noted the lack of analysis and general eclecticism in Schmoller:

> In his treatment of value and price he showed his acquaintance with the work of the Austrians by freely borrowing their results, not, however, as consequences of a long and difficult chain of deductive reasoning, but simply as the obvious inferences from his own description of market phenomena. In this part of his lectures the student meets only confusion, loose definitions, description instead of careful analysis, and conclusions arrived at, no one knows exactly how.[40]

Given the considerable reverberations of the *Methodenstreit*, the insubstantial nature of Schmoller's rebuttal of Menger comes as a surprise to the modern reader. The patronising tone of Schmoller's review became distinctly nastier when Menger repeated his arguments in the following year; Schmoller simply returned the review copy of his pamphlet with a dismissive letter, which he then printed in place of a review in his *Jahrbuch*.[41] The lines of conflict thus established, there was little further elaboration by either side. Part of the reason for this was that, by the 1890s, a more differentiated awareness of the development of economic argument was emerging. Thus, for example, when in 1895 Hasbach published an outline history of the dispute, he began by demonstrating that the Classical triumvirate of

---

[39] M. Weber, 'Roscher und Knies und die logischen Probleme der historischen Nationalökonomie', in his *Gesammelte Aufsätze zur Wissenschaftslehre* 5th edn, J. C. B. Mohr (Paul Siebeck) 1982, pp. 6–9. This part of the essay was originally published in 1903, the remaining sections in 1905 and 1906.

[40] H. R. Seager, 'Economics at Berlin and Vienna', *Journal of Political Economy*, vol. 1 (1893), p. 250.

[41] *Die Irrtümer des Historismus in der deutschen Nationalökonomie*, Gesammelte Werke, Bd. 3, pp. 1–98. The text of the letter is printed in Hayek's 'Introduction' to the Gesammelte Werke, Bd. 1, p. xxii, n. 16.

Smith, Ricardo, and Malthus was in no respect a unity, methodologi-
cally or theoretically. He pointed out that a dispute had existed
between Malthus and Ricardo over the proper method for Political
Economy, while in an attempt to mediate this Senior had in 1826
introduced a distinction between theoretical and practical aspects of
the science.[42] Hasbach also correctly identified the introduction of a
methodological distinction of an abstract–deductive method with the
writings of Mill and Cairnes, and emphasised that some economists
failed to distinguish properly research method from the method of
presentation. He suggested that the most comprehensive discussion of
the issues raised by these problems was the book by John Neville
Keynes, *The Scope and Method of Political Economy*.[43] Hasbach's treatment of the problem indicates that, by the mid-1890s, there was a
growing appreciation of the complexity of economic argument, and a
move away from the broad methodological contrast of the Historical
School with Classical Economics initiated by Roscher and continued
by Schmoller. The penetration of this more differentiated appreciation of the development of economic analysis eclipsed the certainties
of the *Methodenstreit*, and this in turn undermined the predominance of
a Historical School of Economics which had offered a method for the
divination of economic principles and laws, but had never succeeded
in fulfilling its programmatic intentions.

By the time that Schmoller became Rector of Berlin University in
1897, this discrepancy between aspiration and achievement was
evident, notwithstanding the bitter attack launched by Schmoller
against the academic credentials of non-historicist economists.[44] This
process can be seen at work in the teaching and writing of Max
Weber, who as Professor of Economics, first in Freiburg and then in
Heidelberg, was faced in the 1890s with the task of delivering
comprehensive lectures on economic theory and policy as understood
at the time. Max Weber is today thought of chiefly as a founding
father of sociology, but as an academic his appointments were always
in economics. This, and the fact that his formal professional qualification was as a lawyer, calls for some explanation of his early career; and
this career does itself provide us with some insight into the nature of
contemporary German economics.

[42] W. Hasbach, 'Zur Geschichte des Methodenstreites in der politischen Ökonomie', *Jahrbuch
für Gesetzgebung, Verwaltung und Volkswirthschaft*, N. F. Bd. 19 (1895), Part 1, pp. 465–76.
[43] Hasbach, 'Geschichte', Part 2, pp. 768–83.
[44] See for a discussion of the implications of Schmoller's stance A. Oncken, 'New Tendencies in
German Economics', *Economic Journal*, vol. 9 (1899), pp. 463–5.

It should first of all be noted that economics teaching in German universities was at the time part of a legal education – students attended lectures in economics, but graduated with state examinations in law. Only at the level of graduate study was it at this time possible to gain a qualification in economics, by writing a dissertation under the supervision of a full professor. Students registered by the semester on payment of a tuition fee and followed specific lecture courses, sitting their final examination where and when they chose. Weber therefore attended Knies' lectures in Heidelberg during 1882 and 1883,[45] but went on to sit his examinations in Göttingen during the spring of 1886. This final state examination formally qualified Weber for entry into the law profession; but instead he chose to pursue academic study further and registered as a doctoral student in commercial law with Goldschmidt, working in the Seminar for Land Law and Agrarian History in Berlin. In 1889 he completed a dissertation on medieval trading companies in Spain and Italy, and published it the same year. It is however necessary in the German system to complete a second dissertation, the *Habilitationsschrift*, to gain the right to teach and to begin a career as an academic; Weber pursued this option, while at the same time completing his practical legal training and qualifying as a lawyer. In 1891 he completed his *Habilitation* on Roman agrarian history, and while working in the Berlin courts began in the summer semester of 1892 to deliver lectures on commercial law in place of his old teacher Goldschmidt, who had fallen ill. A career as an academic, or as a practising lawyer, was now open to him. Early in 1893, he was offered an extraordinary Professorship in Commercial and German Law at the University of Berlin. 'Extraordinary' professors were aspirants to full 'ordinary' professorships, assisting the full professor in the obligatory teaching associated with a particular chair. These *Ordinarien* constituted an academic core of fully-paid state employees who, once appointed to a post, were expected to teach the full range of material associated with that post. Given the nature of Weber's academic work at this time, it could therefore be anticipated that he would have soon gained a chair in legal history, and built his career upon the interface of law and classical history.[46]

---

[45] For Weber's comments on Knies see W. Hennis, *Max Weber: Essays in Reconstruction*, Allen and Unwin, London 1988, pp. 128–9.

[46] See the description of this point in his career in Marianne Weber, *Max Weber. Ein Lebensbild*, J. C. B. Mohr (Paul Siebeck), Tübingen 1926, pp. 174ff.

However, during 1892 he had completed his study for the Verein für Sozialpolitik on rural labour conditions in eastern Germany,[47] and presented his findings to the annual meeting of the Verein in the summer. His mastery of the detail of the eastern rural economy made a great impression upon those attending the meeting – among whom were of course many of the leading economics professors of the day. Furthermore, Weber disliked the academic politics of the Prussian universities,[48] dominated as they were by the figure of Friedrich Althoff, and so when in the course of 1893 he was offered a post as a full professor of economics in Freiburg, he accepted, turning down at the same time the offer made by Berlin to appoint him Professor of Commercial Law.

The post in Freiburg was for *Nationalökonomie und Finanzwissenschaft*, vacant because of the appointment of von Philippovich to a chair in Vienna. The Philosophy Faculty Appointments Commission, under the leadership of Philippovich, had originally drawn up a list of two candidates, placing first von Wieser, the student of Menger, and in second place Max Sering, at that time professor at the Berlin Agricultural College. Either the Ministry in Karlsruhe or the candidates themselves turned these proposals down, for a new list was then drawn up with Weber in first place, followed by Fuchs and Lotz.[49] In July 1893 Weber accepted, but at this point Althoff intervened and informed the Baden Ministry that Weber had a brilliant legal career in front of him, and would only use the Freiburg appointment as a springboard to a less remote post. This spoiling manoeuvre caused the round of negotiations to falter, until in January 1894 the faculty drew up yet another list, once more placing Weber first, followed by Elster and Oldenberg.[50] Weber once more accepted, and he was subsequently appointed in April 1894. He took up his teaching duties that autumn, throwing himself into intensive preparation for teaching in a

---

[47] See for the background to this my essay 'Prussian Agriculture – German Politics: Max Weber 1892–7', in K. Tribe (ed.), *Reading Weber*, Routledge, London 1989, pp. 98–9.

[48] German universities were and are under the control of state governments, and all professorial appointments have to be approved by the relevant Ministry. The faculty is able only to put forward a ranked list of preferred candidates, and a Minister who is so minded can alter this ranking and impose this on the faculty.

[49] Carl Johannes Fuchs (1864–1934) was at the time extraordinary professor at Greifswald, while Lotz (1865–1941) was a full professor in Munich.

[50] Ludwig Elster was professor at Breslau, while Oldenberg was a Privat Dozent in Berlin. It was with Oldenberg that Weber was to clash in 1897 at the annual congress of the Evangelisch-soziale Verein over Germany's future economic policy – see Weber, 'Germany as an Industrial State', in Tribe, *Reading Weber*, pp. 210–20. The details of the Freiburg appointment can be found in F. Biesenbach, 'Die Entwicklung der Nationalökonomie an der Universität Freiburg i. Br. 1768–1896,' Dissertation, University of Freiburg 1968, pp. 200–2.

subject in which his only formal preparation had been Knies' lectures in Heidelberg, some ten years previously. Such was Weber's dedication to this new discipline that his new wife feared for his health; looking back, she recalled the difficulty she had once had in persuading him to spend an hour with her strolling in the Berlin Tiergarten.[51]

During his period in Freiburg Weber regularly delivered two courses each semester, lecturing twelve hours a week in combination with a two-hour seminar.[52] In this way he covered both economic theory and policy, and a more specialised treatment of finance, as was required by his appointment:[53]

WS 1894/5
(1) *Allgemeine und theoretische Nationalökonomie*
(2) *Finanzwissenschaft*
SS 1895
(1) *Praktische Nationalökonomie (Volkswirthschafts-politik)*
(2) *Die deutsche Arbeiterfrage in Stadt und Land*[54]
WS 1895/6
(1) *Allgemeine und theoretische Nationalökonomie*
(2) *Geld-, Bank- und Börsenwesen*
SS 1896
(1) *Allgemeine und theoretische Nationalökonomie*
(2) *Geschichte der Nationalökonomie*
WS 1896/7
(1) *Finanzwissenschaft*
(2) *Börsenwesen und Börsenrecht*

Weber was assisted by Schulze-Gävernitz, extraordinary Professor of *Volkswirtschaftslehre*, who, appropriate to the title, lectured in the areas of economic policy, economic history, labour questions, and Russo-German trade.[55] Responsibility for the core teaching in theoretical economics was therefore borne almost entirely by Weber, which in the

---

[51] Weber married Marianne Schnitger on 20 September 1893; the reference to Weber's intensive work routine is in Marianne Weber, *Max Weber*, p. 208.

[52] D. Käsler, *Einführung in das Studium Max Webers*, C. H. Beck, Munich 1979, p. 16.

[53] This list can be compared with a general survey of teaching on economics and law at German universities published in the second part of 'Instruction in Public Law and Political Economy in German Universities', *Annals of the American Academy of Political and Social Science*, vol. 1 (1890), pp. 78–102; 272–88.

[54] This course must have drawn heavily upon the work he had done on German rural labour; and in October 1893 he had delivered a series of eight lectures on agrarian policy to a Protestant–Social Congress school in Berlin – see his lecture outline *Landwirtschaft und Agrarpolitik*, Berlin 1893.

[55] Biesenbach, 'Entwicklung der Nationalökonomie', p. 207. Schulze-Gävernitz, a pupil of Brentano, replaced in June 1893 Heinrich Herkner, who was in 1912 eventually to become Schmoller's successor in Berlin.

light of his accepted status as founding father of sociology is striking enough. However, the fact that at this time he also possessed a detailed grasp of the operation .of financial and commodity markets has attracted even less attention in the literature of Weber commentary. Fügen suggests that the impulse for this involvement lay in his impatience with the prevailing, but superficial, view that these markets were nothing more than a conspiracy against the working man and farmer.[56] So in 1894 Weber published the first part of a general introduction to financial markets in Naumann's *Göttinger Arbeiterbibliothek*, the second part appearing in 1896. He also wrote some entries for reference works at the same time, but most conspicuous among these writings is the outline he wrote of the official enquiry into financial and commodity markets, published in four parts in 1895 and 1896. This runs to 325 pages in all – like much of Weber's writing, what appear to be articles turn out on closer examination to be substantial books published in serial form.[57]

As was usual for the time, Weber's appointment as a professor responsible for teaching economics was in the Philosophy Faculty, although most of the students attending the lectures would have been studying law. In June 1895 Weber applied to the Philosophy Faculty for the transfer of the *staatswissenschaftlichen Fächer* to the Law Faculty, creating in this way a new Rechts- und Staatswissenschaftlichen Fakultät. It certainly made sense to combine the teaching of law students within the one faculty; although the justification advanced by the Law Faculty at the time, that this was the practice at Würzburg and Strasburg, was very thin, since these were hardly representative of the university system as a whole. Weber's proposal was accepted by the Ministry in the following year, and over the subsequent two or three decades increasing numbers of institutions followed this pattern.

Meanwhile at the University of Heidelberg, in the same state of Baden and therefore administered by the same Ministry, Weber's old teacher Knies was nearing the age of retirement. Within the *Staats- und Cameralwissenschaften* of the Philosophy Faculty Knies was the sole full

---

[56] H. N. Fügen, *Max Weber*, Rowohlt, Reinbeck bei Hamburg 1985, p. 57.

[57] M. Weber, 'Die Ergebnisse der deutschen Börsenenquete', *Zeitschrift für das Gesaammte Handelsrecht*, 4 parts: Bd. 43 (1895), pp. 83–219, 457–514; Bd. 44 (1896), pp. 29–74; Bd. 45 (1896) pp. 69–156. Bd. I.5 of the *Max Weber Gesamtausgabe* has been reserved for his writings on finance and markets, and has a projected length of 650 pages.

professor, assisted by Emil Leser.[58] From the mid-1870s Knies had regularly lectured on 'Allgemeine Nationalökonomie' in the summer semester, and 'Praktische Nationalökonomie und Finanzwissenschaft' during the Winter Semester. Knies and Leser shared these two courses from semester to semester, while in WS 1896–7 for example Knies also took the Political Economy practical class on Saturdays from 11–1pm.[59]

As the first move in the process of replacing Knies, the Philosophy Faculty proposed in November 1896 the following candidates for the succession: Georg Friedrich Knapp in first place; Karl Bücher in second place; and Max Weber in third.[60] The Memorandum noted that Weber should be offered the chair in case the others did not accept, since it was better paid than his Freiburg post and this would keep him in Baden. It went on: 'Among the younger teachers of political economy he has a very special place ... even today he promises to be one of the leading men in his field.'[61]

In early December both Knapp and Bücher turned the *Ruf* down,[62] whereupon Weber accepted, with the proviso that resources be made available to establish a *Seminar* for *Nationalökonomie and Finanzwissenschaft*. This condition, combined with the clear difference in age between Weber and the other candidates, lends emphasis to Weber's distinction as an academic economist. In Heidelberg, as in Freiburg, he was responsible for the core teaching in economics; his move to unite the *Staatswissenschaften* with the Law Faculty in Freiburg

---

[58] Leser had been given the post of extraordinary Professor in 1881, but no salary. In 1893 he had been awarded the Knight's Cross First Class, but even then received no salary from the Ministry. In 1894 he applied for some payment, supported by Knies, arguing that he had in any case been lecturing in place of the ailing Knies. This gained him an annual award of 1,000 RM, on which modest sum he continued to teach for another twenty years, although still officially unpaid. In Freiburg, for example, Weber had received an annual housing allowance of 760 RM in addition to his salary of 4,760 RM. See V. Hentschel, 'Die Wirtschaftswissenschaften als akademische Disziplin an der Universität Heidelberg (1822–1924)', in N. Waszek (ed.), *Die Institutionalisierung der Nationalökonomie an deutschen Universitäten*, Scripta Mercurae Verlag, St Katharinen 1988, pp. 203–4.

[59] *Anzeige der Vorlesungen, welche im Winter-Halbjahr 1896/97 auf der Grossh. Badischen Ruprechts-Karls-Universität zu Heidelberg gehalten werden sollen*, p. 16.

[60] Knapp (aged 54) was professor at Strasburg and is known chiefly for his work on agrarian history and currency; Bücher (aged 49) was professor at Leipzig and is mainly known for writings in economic history. Weber was at this time 32 years old – Hentschel, 'Wirtschaftswissenschaften', p. 205.

[61] Cited in Hentschel, 'Wirtschaftswissenschaften', p. 205.

[62] There is a convention in Germany that the offer of a chair is a 'call' that can be accepted or rejected; hence when a chair is filled the candidate 'accepts the call' rather than being, more prosaically, appointed.

likewise underscores his concern that the teaching of economics be lent additional rigour. By this time a distinction had emerged between, on the one hand, routine teaching in lecture courses to students who sought only a general competence in a subject; and, on the other, teaching in a *Seminar*, where students presented papers to a professor and worked under his guidance. The *Seminar* was in this sense both the name for a structured discussion between students and teachers (as it is today), but also in addition the name for a library and study facilities used by advanced students, which therefore require adequate funds.[63] If a professor were to develop research and stimulate young students, a *Seminar* was an absolute necessity. Knies had neglected to build such a group; Weber saw this deficiency and appreciated the importance of its remedy.

In Heidelberg Weber began teaching in the summer semester of 1897 with the course on 'Allgemeine (theoretische) Nationalökonomie', read daily at 11am, with Leser delivering *praktische Nationalökonomie* the hour before. In the winter semester of 1897–98 they repeated the switch that Knies and Leser had practised for many years: Weber lectured on *praktische Nationalökonomie* (12–1pm daily) and in addition agrarian policy on Mondays from 6–8pm, while Leser lectured daily on *Nationalökonomie* (11–12 noon). On Thursdays from 6–8pm Weber held the *Seminar* practicals for the new *Volkswirthschaftliches Seminar* alongside the older and virtually moribund *Staatswissenschaftliches Seminar*. In May 1898, shortly after the beginning of the summer semester, Weber was forced by the onset of his long illness to break off teaching, although he did continue until 1903 with some duties; and in any case his courses continued to be announced in the lecture lists under his name.[64]

Some light is thrown upon the degree to which 'Historical Economics' survived as an active force by 1900 if we consider the process by

---

[63] The function of the *Seminar* is explained in S. J. Wickett, 'Political Economy at German Universities', *Economic Journal*, vol. 8 (1898), pp. 149–50. See for a contemporary account of the relative merits of Wagner's seminar in Berlin, and Böhm-Bawerk's in Vienna, H. R. Seager, 'Economics at Berlin and Vienna', *Journal of Political Economy*, vol. 1 (1893), pp. 236–62.

[64] Weber continued to participate in faculty meetings and doctoral examinations. In WS 1899–1900 he held a small course on *Agrarpolitik*; this was the last course that he gave in Heidelberg. For SS 1900 he announced the course on *theoretische Nationalökonomie* and the related seminar, but retracted shortly before the beginning of the semester. In SS 1903 he once more announced a course on *Agrarpolitik*, but was not able to deliver it. Repeated requests to be relieved of his duties were finally approved In June 1903, with effect from 1 October – Hentschel, 'Wirtschaftswissenschaften', p. 206.

which Weber was replaced as a teacher in Heidelberg. Who in fact succeeded Weber when he eventually resigned? There was a long history of the Philosophy Faculty seeking to recruit Sombart for a second chair alongside Weber, and then as Weber's successor, but this was consistently blocked by the Ministry. Weber had sought to provide Leser with a salary for his extraordinary professorship, but without success. However, pressure for a second full chair was eventually successful, and in March 1900 the faculty listed Sombart (Breslau), Rathgen (Marburg), and Hasbach (Kiel) in order of preference for this post. The faculty sought an appointment that would complement Weber, since at this time it was assumed that he would, eventually, return to teaching; although as Hentschel points out, Sombart was more similar in style and interests to Weber than this argument would justify.[65] The Ministry simply ignored the faculty's ranking and appointed Rathgen, arguing that he would be a suitable appointment because of his affinity with Weber, which in turn was not the point. Rathgen began teaching in the winter semester of 1900–1 with a main course of practical economics, following this in the summer semester of 1901 with theoretical economics and finance, the areas usually covered by Weber; and he continued this pattern of teaching until he left for the Hamburg *Kolonial Akademie* in 1907. On the acceptance of Weber's request for 'early retirement' in June 1903, the faculty proposed, in order of preference, the names of Gothein, Sombart, and Helfferich. Gothein, professor at Bonn, accepted and remained at Heidelberg until his death in 1923.

Gothein had earlier been Professor of *Nationalökonomie* at the Technische Hochschule in Karlsruhe, moving in 1890 to Bonn, where he had there played an important part in the establishment of the Cologne Handelshochschule. He was to repeat this experience in Heidelberg, playing a not unimportant part in the organisation of the Mannheim Handelshochschule, following on from an initiative that Max Weber had taken in the late 1890s in conjunction with the Mannheim Chamber of Commerce.[66] In Heidelberg, Gothein covered the three chief lecture courses – *Allgemeine Volkswirtschaftslehre, Finanzwissenschaft* and *praktische Nationalökonomie* – reading them in a

---

[65] Hentschel, 'Wirtschaftswissenschaften', p. 208.
[66] For a discussion of this see my essay, 'Business Education at the Mannheim Handelshochschule, 1907–1933', (forthcoming).

regular cycle, combined with some teaching in economic history, which was his specialism.

The departure of Rathgen in 1907 presented yet another opportunity for the faculty to seek to appoint Sombart, although the general idea now was to complement Gothein's historical and policy-oriented interests by appointing a more theoretically oriented candidate. Sombart was not only included, but placed at the top of the list ahead of Heinrich Herkner (by then at Zürich), and Max's brother, Alfred. As it happened, Herkner had just accepted an appointment at the Technische Hochschule in Berlin, so the Ministry appointed Alfred, given their blank refusal to have anything to do with Sombart. By 1910, Gothein and Alfred Weber were teaching the main economics courses, with Gothein developing his interest in economic history and Weber dropping finance in favour of economic sociology. In addition to this, opportunity was provided by the growing numbers of students for an increase in the number of Privat-Dozenten, prominent among whom were Edgar Salin and Emil Lederer. The latter, after a period at Leipzig, became Gothein's successor upon his death in 1923.

While it could be suggested that Gothein's interest in economic history preserved some vestiges of a historical tradition, by 1910 the intellectual scenery had been shifted, and this commitment no longer commanded the predominating role that it had before. This is also apparent in Max Weber's work after his partial recovery, for this too reflects the changes that were taking place in the social sciences. Weber's resignation did not of course terminate his academic career, although his relationship to the emergent discipline of economics was never again so direct, despite occasional expression of a wish to resume the work of a theoretical economist.[67] When he in 1904 slowly resumed the level of scholarly output that he had sustained during the period 1892–97, his contribution was to be both more academic, and more broadly based. Weber assumed once more the formal role of a university professor shortly before his death in 1920, but at no time after his retirement from the Heidelberg chair was there any question of his standing as a scholar. If nothing else, his contribution to the work of the *Archiv für Sozialwissenschaft und Sozialpolitik* and his promotion of the *Grundriss der Sozialökonomik* project ensured a continuing working involvement with academic life of a kind no different

[67] See W. Hennis, 'The Pitiless "Sobriety of Judgement". Max Weber between Carl Menger and Gustav von Schmoller – The Academic Politics of Value Freedom', *History of the Human Sciences*, vol. 4 (1991), pp. 28–9.

to other university professors. However, one aspect of his work in the 1890s left to one side in the outline above is his heavy involvement in local associations and national societies; as the agrarian writings demonstrate, most of his contributions to the debate on rural labour and economic development during the 1890s, to which he in effect directly owed his initial appointment at Freiburg, were made in such contexts.[68] Although this kind of activity continued in the period after 1904,[69] the greater part of his published writings now took the form of essays in academic publications. This is a reflection of changes in the organisation of scholarship and teaching in Germany, and in German domestic politics. But also at work is a discursive shift that can be loosely termed 'the formation of modern social sciences', a shift to which Weber made a large personal contribution and which also involved the final demise of the Historical School of Economics as a coherent enterprise. This is a complex process and no pretence can be made here of presenting even an overview, given the scarcity of reliable signposts for this crucial period in the development of modern social sciences.[70] However, in conclusion we can turn back to Weber's period as a Heidelberg Professor of Economics to assess the degree to which, by the later 1890s, his avowed allegiance to the 'Younger School of German Historical Economists' had any substance.

A useful source for consideration of this issue is the reading guide and lecture outline constructed for his WS 1897–98 economics lectures.[71] The reading guide is a 23-page structured listing of references lecture by lecture, giving some insight into the distribution of material and the general contents; while the more detailed lecture outline presents a 34-page summary of the first three sections of the lectures, under the title 'The Conceptual Foundations of Economics'.[72]

The reading guide begins with an introductory section, 'Tasks and

---

[68] See my essay 'Prussian Agriculture', *passim*.

[69] Areas of particular importance here would be his interventions in academic politics, and his writings on the political implications of the First World War.

[70] Hennis, 'Pitiless Sobriety', and the writings of Lawrence Scaff and David Frisby provide some indication of the terrain.

[71] The following remarks are based upon a preliminary discussion of this guide in my 'Introduction' to *Reading Weber*, pp. 4–8.

[72] The reading guide, *Grundriss zu den Vorlesungen über Allgemeine ('theoretische') Nationalökonomie*, is divided into six 'books' and twenty sections of unequal length. *Erstes Buch. Die begrifflichen Grundlagen der Volkswirtschaftslehre* has the appearance of detailed lecture notes. Since five lectures were given a week over the semester, the relation between individual lectures and these outlines is not ascertainable.

Methods of Theoretical Economics', headed by the main works of the 'Older Historical School' (Roscher's *Grundriss*, Hildebrand's *Nationalökonomie*, and Knies' *Politische Ökonomie*) and including the main writings of the *Methodenstreit* by Menger and Schmoller. It also includes Cairnes, *Character and Logical Method of Political Economy* and Cliffe Leslie's *Essays on Moral and Political Philosophy*. These are the only English-language texts among a list of sixteen; and although he cites the second edition of Cairnes' *Logical Method*, containing as it does a pointed critique of Jevons' 'mathematical' economics, Jevons does not figure elsewhere in the list. More importantly perhaps for Weber's position in the emergent profession of economics is his neglect, in this first section, of J.N.Keynes' *Scope and Method of Political Economy* (1891). As noted above, Hasbach had in 1895 suggested that this work was the most accessible summary to date of methodological debates within political economy. Keynes' basic distinction between 'abstract, theoretical and deductive political economy' on the one hand and 'ethical, realistic and inductive political economy' on the other gained rapid acceptance in the discussions of the methods proper to economics and formed the methodological counterpart to Marshall's *Principles* (which does find a place among the foreign textbooks and compendia cited by Weber) in the development of economics teaching in Britain. But Weber, for whatever reason, fails to list this text.

The importance of this 'omission' is not that it indicates Weber's lack of awareness of recent developments in economics; as we have seen, in citing Cairnes Weber is citing a book which takes issue with Jevons, a figure who is today regarded as one of the most important later nineteenth-century economists. The fact that Weber does not introduce Jevons or Keynes at an appropriate point into his survey of relevant literature is more likely an indicator that he thought them irrelevant for his purposes. Why should this be so?

If Weber's 'Historical Economics' were simply a systematisation of economic history in the manner of Schmoller then we should not expect his central course to begin with methodological issues. Neither should we expect this to be followed by a section entitled 'The Conceptual Foundations of Economics', in which the list of books is headed by the names Menger, Böhm-Bawerk, and Pierson, proceeding on through Auspitz and Lieben, Patten, and Walras. These names indicate that his appreciation of the conceptual foundations of contemporary economics was, for the time, thoroughly modern and international. In Section §2.2 of the lecture outline, Weber then defines 'abstract theory' as based upon 'modern occidental Man and his activity. It strives initially to disclose the most elementary life-phenomena of the fully mature person.'[73] The focus is thus upon the conditions of modern economic activity, and does not seek to grasp the nature of economic life as the product of a long process of historical development.

For this purpose it presupposes a *constructed* 'economic subject', in respect of which, by *contrast* to empirical men, it

    a. *ignores* all those motives not specifically *economic* in nature; considers, that is, among all those motives that influence empirical men, only those arising from the satisfaction of material needs and treats the remainder as *not present*;

    b. *fabricates* the presence of specific qualities in empirical men, when they are in fact either *absent* or only *partially* present, to wit

      i) complete *insight* into the prevailing *situation* – perfect economic knowledge;

      ii) unfaltering selection of the *most appropriate means* for a given end – absolute 'economic rationality';

      iii) exclusive devotion of one's own powers to the attainment of economic goods – unwearying economic endeavour.

    It therefore argues on the basis of *unrealistic* men, analogous to a mathematical ideal.[74]

This last comment is perhaps the most significant in the entire passage. It has been customary to regard the existence of a 'Marginal Revolution' as a major turning point in the theoretical development of modern economics, although there has always been difficulty in accounting for the lack of uniformity between the work of the three chief protagonists: Jevons, Walras, and Menger. It would be more accurate to think of the changes in economics during the last third of the nineteenth century as deriving from the introduction of mathematical analysis. The idea of the science of economics as the optimisation of the allocation of resources, in which the realisation of optimality is the product of marginal, rather than total, variations in the satisfaction of wants, clearly lends itself to mathematical formulation. The contrast which Weber is seeking to make above is not one that turns on an opposition of historical to analytical method, nor one which turns on the deductive-inductive opposition emphasised by Keynes. What Weber had no time for was a mathematical apprehension of economic phenomena, as practised by Jevons, and as developed by

---

[73] *Erstes Buch. Die begrifflichen Grundlagen der Volkswirtschaftslehre*, p. 1 (1898, unpublished).
[74] *Ibid.*, p. 2.

Marshall. The reason for this was not some innate hostility to mathematical models, but rather his belief that the confinement of economic science to these terms left out a considerable proportion of the subject matter proper to economics. If we are to identify a relevant contrast separating the economics of Weber from that of Marshall or Fisher, then the distinction would perhaps turn on his opposition to the development of a mathematically based science of economic behaviour and his belief in the material variety of economic life.

For Weber, economics was a 'Science of Man', as emphasised by Wilhelm Hennis.[75] In the lecture outline the critique of 'abstract theory' is followed by a discussion of economic needs and the constitution of 'goods' as means for the satisfaction of these needs, a discussion entirely in harmony with the introductory arguments of Menger, Roscher, or even Hufeland. 'Utility' could not be objectively determined, argued Weber; it only gained meaning in terms of the satisfaction of subjectively apprehended human needs. Here 'The standpoint of *man* is decisive. Economics is *not* a science of nature and its properties, but rather of man and his needs.'[76] However, this standpoint does not involve an assimilation to a historical economics and a rejection of recent economic theorising. Weber goes on to describe the formation of value in terms of the allocation of scarce goods and the satisfaction of demand. Satisfaction of need is a question of marginal utility, such that estimation of value arises from the subjective perception of need and the objective availability of goods.[77]

In the lecture outline Weber contrasts these categories of economic action appropriate to an 'isolated economy' with conditions prevailing 'in an entirely different economic formation: the *Verkehrswirtschaft*.'[78] This is elaborated further as the lecture course develops. The second section of his lecture course, entitled 'The Natural Foundations of the Economy' deals with the natural conditions of economic activity in terms of political geography, population, and racial characteristics – the material foundations of economic activity. There then follows 'The Historical Foundations of the Economy', covering primitive peoples, theories of the family, settlement and the development of property, the development of commerce, the nature of ancient economy, the agrarian foundations of medieval economies, and the emergence of the modern enterprise, completing the eight-

---

[75] '"A Science of Man". Max Weber and the Political Economy of the German Historical School', in his *Max Weber*, pp. 107–45.   [76] *Erstes Buch*, p. 4.
[77] *Ibid.*, p. 7.   [78] *Ibid.*, p. 13.

page section with a sub-section entitled 'The Emergence of the Economy'. If we look at the reading listed here we find that, far from a simply historicising account of economic processes, Weber covers under this heading the development of contemporary economic institutions such as the factory, the banks, the stock exchange, and the institutions of trade.[79]

There are three more sections of unequal length in the course. 'Book 4. The Stages of Development of Economic Theory', is divided into pre-Smithian, classical, and socialist economics, in which the last interestingly enough contains twenty-three references including *Capital* and Engels' *Anti-Dühring*. The fifth book is longer, being devoted to a 'Theoretical Analysis of the Modern Economy (*Verkehrswirtschaft*)'. *Verkehr* is here the mode in which the analysis of production and distribution are integrated into an exposition of economics that involves both theoretical and practical levels. The organising concept of *Verkehr* does however make for some strange combinations to those used to the regularities of Classical Political Economy, with its emphasis on value forms. While the reading begins conventionally enough with Cannan's *History of the Theory of Production and Distribution in English Political Economy*, the following sections on industrial and agricultural enterprises emphasise the fact that production and distribution are understood as material processes, and not exclusively as moments in the valorisation process. The sub-section '*Verkehr* and its Theoretical Problems' covers means of transport, the telegraph, shipping, currency, the organisation of credit, banking and foreign exchange, followed by markets, exchanges, and the institutions of trade. Only then does Weber arrive at price formation and income distribution, devoting most attention to the 'Typical Categories of Income in the *Verkehrswirtschaft*' – profit, rent, and wages. Finally, Book 6 covers the development of social and economic ideals in an extremely cursory manner, adding texts by Stammler and Sombart to literature already cited, and concluding the reading guide with Weber's own Inaugural Address.

An adequate evaluation of Weber's teaching in economics would require a detailed survey of the contemporary state of economics and the social sciences in German universities such as we do not yet have. As noted above, research of this kind would contribute significantly to our understanding of the formation of modern social sciences, an understanding which is as yet at a very rudimentary level. Nevertheless, the purpose of this essay has been to demarcate more exactly the

[79] *Grundriss*, pp. 7–14.

provenance of the German Historical School of Economics. This has been approached in three stages.

Firstly, it was argued that no sharp disjunction marks the formation of the School, and that in substance the work of Roscher, Knies, and Hildebrand marks a development of, rather than a departure from, the German economics of the 1820s and 1830s. Historical Economics certainly differed in style and substance from the Classical Economics of France and England; but then so did the *Nationalökonomie* practised in the first three decades of the century.

Second, the *Methodenstreit* provides a useful focus for the evaluation of Schmoller's self-definition of Historical Economics. Notable in his response to Menger is the fact that his critique owes more to academic condescension than theoretical substance. Schmoller's academic achievement lay in his contribution to academic politics, and his various historical writings. Most noteworthy in his contribution to the *Methodenstreit* is his inability to engage in theoretical argument: a failure of knowledge and a failure of intellectual capacity. Both disqualify him from the title 'economist' even in the broad terms acceptable at the time. If the German School of Historical Economics is identified by reference to Schmoller, then this intellectual project was moribund by the early 1890s.

Thirdly, this contention is illustrated by the early academic career of Max Weber. Although Weber described himself as a member of the 'Younger Historical School', he owed little as an economist to the positions defended by Schmoller. It is evident that Weber is quite capable of elaborating a coherent critique of 'abstract economic theory' that owes little to conventional historicist principles. For the 1890s, these arguments are, if not entirely novel, certainly advanced. However, the period of relative academic inactivity that Weber spent between 1898 and 1904 is a period in which agendas shifted and a new generation of scholars appeared. In some respects Weber's teaching in Heidelberg was a swansong, not for Historical Economics, but for a style of economic reasoning that had been developed from the beginning of the century. Weber presented to his students perhaps the most refined version of this economic doctrine. When, in the years following his recovery he expressed the desire to return to the life of a theoretical economist, this could have been no more than a yearning for past certainties. For by then, the emergent discipline was in the hands of younger specialists, and was developing in a fashion not entirely to Weber's methodological liking.

CHAPTER 5

The Handelshochschulen *and the formation of* Betriebswirtschaftslehre, *1898–1925*

> The relationship between theory and practice in commercial
> education is, ... in both America and Germany, the reverse of
> that which is generally anticipated. Germany, the land of
> thinkers and dreamers, conducts commercial training in a
> primarily practical fashion; America, the land of the practical
> man par excellence, has, for general want of practical
> commercial training, to everywhere adopt a purely theoretical
> pedagogy, and falls over itself in the invention and foundation
> of ever newer institutions for commercial education.[1]

It is generally assumed today that business education at university
level is an American invention. This belief finds reinforcement in the
style and substance of management education as it diffused throughout Western Europe in the 1950s and 1960s. Modern management
meant the introduction of American business methods; training in
these methods meant the use of American curricular models and
textbooks. But this propensity to turn to an American model was not
unique to the postwar years; we can find traces of it at the beginning of
this century. When, in 1902, W. J. Ashley presided over the creation
of the first Faculty of Commerce at a British university, he appealed to
the precedents set by recent American developments. Ashley, an
Oxford history graduate, had been hired back from North America to
lead the faculty: first Professor of Political Economy and Constitutional History at Toronto from 1888 to 1892, then the inaugural
Professor of Economic History at Harvard University, his knowledge
of developments in North American business education was considered of critical importance to the success of the Birmingham
faculty. Ashley wrote in the prospectus of the new Faculty of
Commerce that

---

[1] I. Jastrow, 'Kaufmannsbildung und Hochschulbildung in Amerika', *Berliner Jahrbuch für
Handel und Industrie*, Bd. 1 (1904), p. 422, reporting on a trip to the United States preparatory
to the establishment of the Berlin Handelshochschule, of which he became first Director.

Birmingham will be the first English University to realise the importance and the educational value of proper training in this subject, and to appoint a Professor to take it in charge. In giving Accounting a place in a commercial curriculum it will only be following the example recently set by several of the greater American universities, – by Harvard University and the Universities of Michigan and Wisconsin; and it proposes to use the term 'Accounting', which has come into common use in America, rather than 'Accountancy', to indicate that what it aims at is not so much the preparation of professional accountants for their future occupation (though it expects to do something in that direction), as to teach the ordinary business man the proper use and interpretation of accounts.[2]

It was not therefore intended that the new courses of instruction would displace existing arrangements for professional training and qualification; rather, that a general understanding of the function and purpose of accounting and related commercial techniques be conveyed to future managers and administrators. There was an entirely analogous argument with respect to commercial education and the law: businessmen needed to be acquainted with aspects of company and contract law, but they neither required, nor had the time for, a professional legal training. Ashley's invocation of accounting is therefore of importance in representing the purpose, scope, and limits of higher commercial education.

If we turn to modern histories of and commentaries upon accounting and accounting education, we are confronted with a story that re-emphasises these Anglo-American origins. Johnson and Kaplan's critique of the evolution of accounting practice, for example, identifies a shift away from engineers' costing practices (customary in the early years of the century) towards auditors' financial accounting information, a shift which was facilitated by the emergence of university business courses that focused upon financial reporting.[3] In Britain, academic accountants were themselves chiefly interested in the problems of auditing company accounts, as their publications testify.[4] Present-day histories of accounting and accounting education

[2] W. J. Ashley, *The Faculty of Commerce in the University of Birmingham*, n. p., Birmingham 1902, pp. 9–10.

[3] H. T. Johnson and R. S. Kaplan, *Relevance Lost. The Rise and Fall of Management Accounting*, Harvard Business School Press, Boston 1987, p. 132.

[4] Dicksee was the first Professor of Accounting at Birmingham, appointed in 1902; this was in effect a part-time appointment and he also taught at the LSE for several years, eventually being made Professor of Accounting and Business Organisation there in 1914. His first book, published in 1892, was *Auditing*; this ran to twelve editions in his lifetime, was published in the United States in 1905 edited by R. H. Montgomery, whose own *Auditing Theory and Practice* of 1912 inaugurated American financial accounting literature. See J. Kitchen and R. H. Parker,

reiterate this emphasis upon developments in business education in the United States and Britain; and so it seems natural for English readers to conclude that business education was primarily an American invention, dating initially from the later 1890s, diffusing to other, latecomer economies after the Second World War.

It is true that the postwar development of business education has been dominated by an American model, but it is not true that business administration as a university discipline was invented by the Americans, as implied by Ashley's remarks. In fact, as Johnson and Kaplan note in passing, there was virtually no regular tuition in accounting in American colleges and universities before 1900, so it remains a mystery as to what Ashley thought he was referring when he invoked American precedents.[5] We do know that the Department of Economics at Harvard University introduced a course in accounting for second-year students in 1900–1, but no academic credit was given for this; a half-credit was given in 1901–2, and a full credit only in 1905–6.[6] Lockwood has drawn attention to the general dearth of suitable university-level textbooks, and teachers, at the turn of the century – Hatfield at the University of Chicago reportedly even relied upon a German textbook in the absence of a suitable English-language text.[7] True, the Wharton School of Finance and Economy had existed at the University of Pennsylvania since 1881, but even twenty years after its foundation it had failed to develop an imitable business curriculum, despite the propagandising efforts of E. J. James. A distinctive business curriculum suitable for university-level study only began to take shape with the foundation of the Harvard Graduate School of Business Administration in 1908, and, even here, there was difficulty in developing a second-year curriculum that properly followed on from the first.[8] Consolidation set in around 1914,

Accounting Thought and Education: Six English Pioneers, Institute of Chartered Accountants of England and Wales, London 1980, pp. 57–9.

[5] The School of Commerce at the University of Wisconsin, for example, taught very little law or economics, and no accounting in 1900–1, according to its prospectus – see L. C. Marshall (ed.), *The Collegiate School of Business*, University of Chicago Press, Chicago 1928, pp. 71–2.

[6] M. T. Copeland, *And Mark an Era. The Story of the Harvard Business School*, Little, Brown and Company, Boston 1958, p. 22.

[7] The textbook was one by Schär, on double-entry bookkeeping. See J. Lockwood, 'Early University Education in Accountancy', *Accounting Review*, vol. 13 (1938), pp. 133–4. Schär later taught at the Berlin Handelshochschule, and his work is discussed below.

[8] See S. A. Sass, *The Pragmatic Imagination. A History of the Wharton School 1881–1981*, University of Pennsylvania Press, Philadelphia 1982, pp. 154–7; and Copeland, *And Mark an Era*, pp. 37–41. At the Harvard Business School the teaching programme was nominally over two years, but initially designed around the first year's intake. It was assumed, given the elective basis of the

was then interrupted by America's involvement in the First World War, and then properly took off in the 1920s, which were boom years for American universities in general, and business education in particular.

But there was still no model curriculum commanding widespread assent. Large numbers of students might graduate from the some 180 business schools existing by the mid-1920s, but the quality and relevance of the training that they received was very variable. A few major schools offered recognised courses, but there was no generally-accepted curricular form, and little success in the development of textbooks in commercial law and business economics. Two separate surveys of business education at that time concluded that the expansion of numbers had at least temporarily hindered, rather than aided, the development of a business curriculum relevant to the needs of American industry.[9] American business education certainly flourished in the 1920s, but only from a quantitative point of view; the rapid increase in demand far outstripped the supply of competent teachers and textbooks, so that almost everywhere unversed instructors were pressed into service, and existing courses in law, economics, English and history were hastily repackaged as part of a business degree. Business education existed in the United States, but the discipline of Business Administration, with its own courses, textbooks, instructors and degrees, had yet to be invented.

Here the United States was far behind Germany. For business education as a coherent programme of study aimed at training managers, administrators, and commercial teachers already existed in Germany. By the early 1920s, it had its own name – *Betriebswirtschaftslehre* (BWL) – and by the end of the decade some of the Commercial Colleges had gained the right to award doctorates in commerce.[10] The first of these new Commercial Colleges was founded in 1898, where a joint two-year course was established by the University of Leipzig and the local School of Commerce, combining

programme, that the curriculum for the second year would then naturally develop as these students progressed through their first year into the second. However, there was a high dropout rate after the first year, and this phenomenon hindered the elaboration of a coherent two-year course for several years.

[9] F. Ruml, 'The Existing Curriculum and Offerings in Collegiate Education for Business', in L. C. Marshall (ed.), *The Collegiate School of Business*, University of Chicago Press, Chicago 1928, pp. 75–95; and J. H. Bossard, 'The Organisation of the Business Curricula', in J. H. Bossard and F. Dewhurst, *University Education for Business*, University of Pennsylvania Press, Philadelphia 1931, Chapter 11.

[10] Berlin in 1927; Mannheim and Nuremberg 1929; Leipzig and Königsberg 1930. 'Commercial College' is used here as a translation of *Handelshochschule*.

existing teachers and courses. Shortly afterwards courses were also established at the Aachen Technische Hochschule, although this initiative was never a great success, and closed in 1908. The next foundation, in 1901, was the municipal Commercial College in Cologne, the first truly autonomous institution and which later formed the nucleus of the University of Cologne. In the same year an Akademie für Sozial- und Handelswissenschaft was founded in Frankfurt am Main, likewise the institutional basis of the present University of Frankfurt. All of these institutions combined relevant parts of the existing university economics and law syllabi with practical aspects of commerce and administration, admitting students not ordinarily qualified for university entrance, but subjecting them to courses and examinations based upon the university model. The creation of the Städtische Handelshochschule Berlin in 1906 represented the first systematic advance upon its predecessors by removing teaching in economics from its pre-eminent position within the curriculum, and replacing it with 'commercial science'. Cologne and Berlin were thus the models in whose image the remaining foundations were shaped, in Mannheim (1907), Munich (1910), Königsberg (1915) and Nuremberg (1919).[11]

By 1920 there was a cumulative total of 4,197 graduates of the Handelshochschulen with the qualification *Diplom-Kaufmann*;[12] by 1933 this total had risen to 15,906, the original four-semester course had been extended to six, and a *Diplom* introduced for university economics students that was complementary to the existing business diploma. Within thirty years of their first appearance the Handelshochschulen had become accepted as specialist higher education institutions alongside the much older mining, forestry, agricultural, and veterinary academies.

The Handelshochschulen were supported by a combination of municipal, state, and private funding, and were distinct from the

---

[11] Mention should also be made here of the Exportakademie des K. u. k. österreichischen Handelsmuseums, Vienna (1898; after 1919 renamed the Hochschule für Welthandel); and the Höhere Schule für Handel, Verkehr und Verwaltung, St Gallen (1898; from 1911 the Handelshochschule).

[12] Hayashima, 'Die Absolventen der Leipziger Handelshochschule', Table II/2: Graduates of Handelshochschulen 1900–1920 by institution 1920–1933, p. 121. The graduates were distributed as follows, with the number of graduates with the Handelslehrerprüfung in brackets: 1,477 (378) from Leipzig; 1,033 (293) from Cologne; 379 (190) from Frankfurt; 773 (378) from Berlin; 151 (87) from Mannheim; 357 (0) from Munich; and 27 (25) from Königsberg. Nuremberg did not have at this time any graduates, since it had just begun its courses.

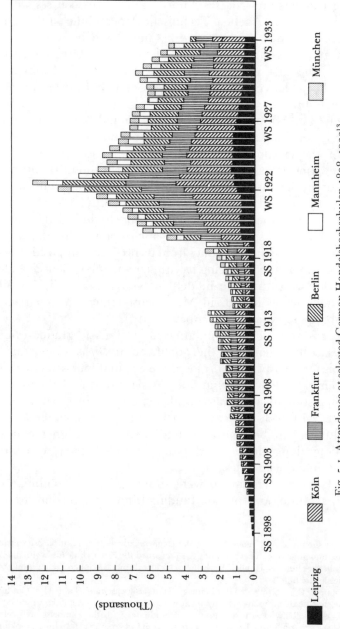

Fig. 5.1. Attendance at selected German Handelshochschulen 1898–1933[13]

Leipzig   Köln   Frankfurt   Berlin   Mannheim   München

(Thousands)

14
13
12
11
10
9
8
7
6
5
4
3
2
1
0

SS 1898   SS 1903   SS 1908   SS 1913   SS 1918   WS 1922   WS 1927   WS 1933

university system in that they were autonomous institutions with control over courses, student recruitment, and staff. The curricular development of the leading institutions did not greatly vary, however, and they tended to follow converging evolutionary paths. By the early 1920s there was common agreement on the main components of higher commercial education, so that the introduction of an intermediate qualification (the *Diplom*) for university economics students in 1923 could be clearly linked to a parallel commercial curriculum. Teaching in the Handelshochschulen was by this time organised around the new discipline of *Betriebswirtschaftslehre*, a neologism that first gained wide acceptance in 1920 but which emerged out of disputes between teachers of economics and commerce shortly before the war. The development of this new 'business economics' was therefore prompted by the practical problems of organising a coherent curriculum for higher commercial education. The process by which it was configured is therefore closely related to curricular development within the institutions themselves; and so to understand the manner in which this new business economics distinguished itself from existing teaching we need to consider in detail the aims, organisation, and educational impact of the new Handelshochschulen.

A comprehensive account of the new Handelshochschulen and their teaching does not yet exist.[14] Two recent English-language accounts of the development of business education in Germany provide a useful introduction to the area, but neither sheds a great deal of light on the singularity of German developments.[15] In the case of Lindenfeld's essay, this limitation derives from his immediate

[13] Based on figures in A. Hayashima, 'Die Absolventen der Leipziger Handelshochschule 1900–1920', *Kwansei Gakuin University Annual Studies*, vol. 36 (1987), Appendix I. Aachen is excluded, as are the later, more marginal, colleges in Nuremberg and Königsberg. A decline in the later 1920s is evident from this graph, a decline which accelerated during the 1930s; this is part of a general decline in student numbers, but which was in fact more marked in law and medicine than in economics and BWL. In addition to this general trend, it is quite probable that the Handelshochschulen overestimated actual labour market demand for its graduates, and that students only began to adjust to this in the later 1920s. For a discussion of this see my essay in Minerva (forthcoming) on the Mannheim Handelshochschule.

[14] Akira Hayashima has made a detailed study of the Handelshochschulen and has published, in German, several extremely valuable essays on the Prussian colleges. His principal focus has been on the Cologne Handelshochschule, on which he has announced a forthcoming monograph.

[15] R. R. Locke, *The End of Practical Man. Entrepreneurship and Higher Education in Germany, France, and Great Britain 1880–1940*, JAI Press, Greenwich, Conn. 1984; and D. F. Lindenfeld, 'The Professionalization of Applied Economics: German Counterparts to Business Administration', in G. Cocks and K. Jarausch (eds.), *German Professions, 1800–1950*, Oxford University Press, Oxford 1990, pp. 213–31.

concern with the role of the Handelshochschulen in the creation of a
business career structure, rather than with the nature and quality of
the teaching carried on in the institutions themselves. As a contribution to a survey of German professions, there is no intention on
Lindenfeld's part of providing a comparative account of business
education that might illuminate its curricular distinctiveness. Locke's
study, by contrast, does set out to provide a comparative account of
engineering and business education in Britain, France, and Germany,
but with distinctly mixed results. His book gives a useful overview of
the development of the Handelshochschulen, due criticism being
levelled at the failings of comparative educational histories in which
the unit of comparison is the national educational apparatus, rather
than individual institutions, their curricula, students, and the relationship of vocational institutions to the labour market. Nonetheless,
the comparative aspirations of Locke's study are compromised by a
number of idiosyncracies. The account of British developments in
business education is defective; it either recycles outdated conventional wisdom, or, where it ventures beyond this, becomes speculative
and erroneous. The attention given to German business education
usefully highlights the importance of the Handelshochschulen, but
misinterprets the nature of their teaching. Locke is correct to focus on
the curricula of the Handelshochschulen, but the analysis that he
provides is faulty. He contends, wrongly, that it was developments in
German accounting theory (in particular, dynamic accounting as
developed by Schmalenbach) that prompted the emergence of
Betriebswirtschaftslehre.[16] Schmalenbach's work was highly innovative,
and it is important to our understanding of the nature of *Betriebswirtschaftslehre*. Locke, however, both overstates the structural role of
dynamic accounting, and fails to relate it to contemporary Anglo-
American accounting theory and practice. Dynamic accounting was
certainly distinctive, and its leading features are outlined below; but
this distinctive nature is not what made *Betriebswirtschaftslehre* different from the *Volkswirtschaftslehre* taught in German universities at the
turn of the century. To understand this difference, and by extension
the difference between German and American business education, we
need to examine the teaching programmes offered by the new

---

[16] Locke, *The End of Practical Man*, pp. 155ff. This point is explored in greater depth in my essay
'Business Education at the Mannheim Handelshochschule, 1907–1933', *Minerva*, vol. 32
(1994), pp. 158–85.

Handelshochschulen, and identify the pedagogic issues which these new programmes sought to resolve.

The Handelshochschulen were an institutional response to widespread demand for higher commercial education. In their early years, however, the new institutions found some difficulty in distinguishing themselves from the teaching of commercial schools on the one hand, and universities on the other. *Betriebswirtschaftslehre* was invented as the solution to this problem: a body of teaching that went beyond the vocational routines taught in commercial schools, and the academic law and economics taught in universities.

The Handelshochschule zu Leipzig, founded in 1898 as a joint enterprise between the university and the Chamber of Commerce, exemplifies this dilemma. It was not an independent institution, being placed under the control of the state government; but it had its own Senate, constituted out of representatives from the state government, the city government, the Chamber of Commerce, the university, and the existing Commercial College.[17] Its teaching programme combined a menu of existing courses from the university and the local Commercial College, such that the Handelshochschule was in effect an academic holding company offering no courses of its own. It did however offer its own Diploma, and from its inception directed its efforts towards two distinct groups of student: young men at the beginning of their careers in business, and teachers from commercial schools. There was a clear recognition that a dual task existed for higher commercial education: the education of a new business class, and the education of the teachers of lower commercial schools.

This feature was taken over by all subsequent Handelshochschulen, as well as the regulations concerning entry and period of study. University entrance in Germany was open only to those with nine years of secondary schooling and an Abitur from a Gymnasium, Realgymnasium, or an Oberrealschule. The Handelshochschule was likewise open to such students, but added three further classes of eligible students:

(1) graduates of higher commercial schools;
(2) teachers who had passed their second teaching examination;
(3) commercial employees who had acquired the right of one-year

---

[17] 'Ordnung für die Handelshochschule zu Leipzig genehmigt durch Verordnung des Königleichen Ministeriums des Innern vom 18 Februar 1898', §3, reprinted in H. Raydt (ed.), *Erster Jahresbericht der Handelshochschule zu Leipzig*, Max Hesse's Verlag, Leipzig 1899, p. 11.

voluntary military service, had finished their apprenticeship, and possessed the 'necessary intellectual maturity'.[18]
A matriculation committee decided on this last attribute, which meant that the Handelshochschule was in a position to admit any candidate thought to be suitable, whether the candidate came from Germany or abroad. Here then a decisive difference existed with respect to university practice, but this genuine difference was moderated by two factors: firstly, university entrance was rapidly increasing during the period 1890–1914 as a growing number of Abiturienten began university studies;[19] and secondly, over the years Abiturienten became an increasingly large proportion of domestic students at all Handelshochschulen. Although the regulations of the Handelshochschulen represented a considerable extension of access to higher education, they were not inferior institutions in terms of the practical qualifications of their entrants; and to an increasing extent they drew upon the same pool of recruits as the universities, offering them a complementary, as well an alternative, course of study. By 1914 there was a marked convergence with the university system in terms of teachers and students, which in turn laid the basis for the reforms of the 1920s.

At Leipzig, the centrality of economics to the commercial curriculum was lent emphasis by the manner in which students were explicitly, and uniquely, directed to attend the lectures on *allgemeine Volkswirtschaftslehre* during their first semester, and before they attended any other economics courses. The 'Plan of Studies' listed first all the university economics lectures, and then a selection of law lectures, which could be attended in any sequence that was thought convenient.[20] The third section of the 'Plan' outlined geography lectures that might be taken[21] – these appear to have been entirely optional, but the fact that they precede the commercial courses accentuates the way in which university-based courses were given

---

[18] §7. Aufnahmebedingungen in 'Ordnung für die Handelshochschule zu Leipzig', p. 12. The first intake in April 1898 for the summer semester numbered 97 students, of whom 77 were from Germany. Of these, 18 were Abiturienten, 18 were teachers, and 37 those with the one-year certificate – Table 1, Raydt, *Erster Jahresbericht*, p. 8.

[19] In 1891 there were 27,398 students at German universities; by 1914 this had grown to 60,741 – Hayashima, 'Die Absolventen der Leipziger Handelshochschule', Table 1: Student numbers by type of institution, p. 118.   [20] Raydt, *Erster Jahresbericht*, p. 18.

[21] Ratzel, who lectured on Central European Geography and Political Ethnography in Leipzig, was on the Handelshochschule Senate together with Bücher, who took the principal lecture courses in Economics and in Finance. In commercial courses of the time it was usual to deal with trade and markets under the rubric of Geography.

precedence within the general organisation of commercial studies. Besides these university lectures, courses in commercial correspondence, commercial arithmetic, bookkeeping, commercial practice, textile technology, and chemical technology were supplied by teachers from the commercial college. Courses in foreign languages, stenography, and typewriting were also recommended.[22]

The Leipzig initiative had been given financial support by the Chamber of Commerce for two years only in the first instance; but the college immediately proved far more attractive to students than initially anticipated, demonstrating the existence of a strong demand for higher commercial education. This demand came principally from the sons of independent traders and manufacturers – just over half of the students during the years 1898–1902 were from such a background, with only 3.6 per cent from the families of managers.[23] Although the initial proportion of entrants with an Abitur was, at 34 per cent, below that of those with a one-year certificate (43.3 per cent), this relationship rapidly altered, so that by 1906 around two-thirds of entrants had an Abitur of some kind. By 1920–21, 40.7 per cent of students entering the Leipzig Handelshochschule were graduates of Gymnasia and Realgymnasia; and the proportion of graduates who had entered with a one-year certificate fell from 61 per cent in 1901–2 to 36.8 per cent in 1914–15.[24] This trend towards conventional school qualifications and away from vocational qualification was followed in some degree by all the Handelshochschulen, lending emphasis to their convergence with university institutions in terms of students, staff, and curricula.

Combining university courses in economics, law, and geography with the existing teaching of a practical commercial college did have definite limitations. A curriculum created from the marriage of academic teaching in law and economics with practical commercial subjects was at best provisional, whatever its initial success in attracting students might be. The strong demand for places at Leipzig prompted the formation of similar institutions, but none of them

[22] Raydt, *Erster Jahresbericht*, p. 19.
[23] Hayashima, 'Die Absolventen der Leipziger Handelshochschule', Table 3: Social background of students at the HH Leipzig 1898–1920, p. 123.
[24] Hayashima, 'Die Absolventen der Leipziger Handelshochschule', Table 4: Educational background of students at the HH Leipzig 1898–1920, p. 124; and Table 5, Graduates with Diplom Kaufmann 1901–1919, p. 127. Hayashima is cautious with the details of this analysis because of the high proportion of foreign students (more Russians than native Saxons before the First World War; 1906–7 almost as many Russians and Germans); this introduces uncertainty into the exact educational and social background.

imitated Leipzig's teaching arrangements. Furthermore, the Leipzig college was handicapped by its institutional association with university and state government; not only was it entirely reliant on existing teaching, this reliance meant that it had no basis upon which to introduce its own courses. Although many of the subsequent foundations drew upon existing teaching resources, only Aachen remained bound to them, and this initiative soon failed. Cologne, for example, drew initially upon the academic resources of the nearby University of Bonn, but unlike Leipzig it was from the very beginning more than a pedagogic holding company, and it rapidly established its academic autonomy by recruiting its own full- and part-time staff.

Part of the reason for this was that a substantial sum of money had long been available in Cologne to found a higher commercial academy; financial constraints were never a problem here, and there was no need for the provisional character and initial caution of the Leipzig initiative. The immediate success of the Leipzig Handelshochschule in exceeding its planned intake proved that a substantial pool of potential entrants existed. Throughout the 1890s, there had been inconclusive discussions in Cologne concerning the foundation of a new commercial college, always on the assumption that their college would be the first such institution in Germany. In 1898 they were suddenly faced, not only with the inauguration of the Leipzig Handelshochschule, but with the formation of a Handelshochschule within the nearby Technische Hochschule at Aachen. The City Assembly noted with some alarm at a meeting in July 1900 that by the following Easter, Handelshochschulen would be formed in Hanover and Frankfurt; while plans were also far advanced in Berlin, Hamburg, and Mannheim.[25]

Proposals had been made several times in the 1850s for some form of higher commercial and technical education in Cologne. The principal supporter of these schemes was Gustav von Mevissen, a local industrialist, who, on the occasion of the golden wedding anniversary of the Kaiser and queen in 1879, set down his arguments in a memorandum and set aside railway shares approaching the value of 200,000 Marks, to be used for a commercial college in Cologne.

[25] Verhandlungen der Stadtverordnetenversammlung zu Köln vom 12 Juli 1900, Anlage 7 in A. Hayashima, 'Zur Geschichte der Kölner Handelshochschule', *Kwansei Gakuin University Annual Studies*, vol. 30 (1981), p. 204. The plans for Hanover and Hamburg were eventually realised in a rather different form, and the inauguration of the Berlin Handelshochschule was delayed until its own building was opened. Nevertheless, the consternation of those in Cologne was evident.

Mevissen argued in his 'Denkschrift' that very few leaders of industry and commerce had benefited from a university education, in part because of a general belief that its emphasis was more upon theoretical than practical knowledge; and from a widespread prejudice that a university education would rob the sons of business families of the capacity to apply themselves to the demands of a commercial life. Without denying the value of a university education, he proposed that the rising business class would be better served by an institution directed specifically to their vocational needs.[26]

Mevissen had stipulated that his gift was for the foundation of a Handelshochschule; but he had also mandated that the fund must first reach a capital of 1 million Marks before being so used, implicitly forcing the municipal authorities to add to the initial benefaction. The gift was formally accepted by the king of Prussia in 1880, but the city authorities took no further action. In 1893 Mevissen came into contact with Eberhard Gothein, then Professor of Economics at the University of Bonn, and Gothein agreed to visit and report on the organisation of commercial colleges in Paris and Vienna on Mevissen's behalf. Then, in the mid-1890s, the support of the local Chamber of Commerce was won for the project, but when put to the City Assembly the proposal failed to gain the necessary majority. Mevissen died in August 1899, leaving a further 300,000 Marks to the fund which, thanks to the accumulated dividend, now stood at 400,000 Marks. Together with property revenue earmarked for the college, the city had at its disposal more than 700,000 Marks for the creation of a Handelshochschule.[27] Gothein revised Mevissen's original plan in May 1900, and in July the city sought the approval of the Prussian government, presenting Gothein's memorandum as the basis of their application.[28]

Gothein's memorandum took up Mevissen's earlier argument that a conventional university education was unattractive to those entering a life in business; not only was the scholarly life one which could

---

[26] Mevissen's 'Denkschrift über der Gründung einer Handelshochschule in Köln, zum 11 Juni 1879' can be found in J. Hansen, *Gustav von Mevissen. Ein rheinisches Lebensbild 1815–1899*, vol. II, Georg Reimer, Berlin 1906, pp. 627–36, and is reprinted in Hayashima, 'Zur Geschichte der Kölner Handelshochschule', pp. 185–91.

[27] K. van Eyll, 'Die Gedanke zur Gründung einer Universität oder einer Handelshochschule in Köln bei Gustav Mevissen', in F.-W. Henning (ed.), *Handelsakademie – Handelshochschule – Wirtschafts- und Sozialwissenschaftliche Fakultät*, Böhlau Verlag, Köln 1990, p. 37.

[28] Letter of Mayor Becker to Prussian Ministers of Culture and Trade, 13 July 1900, reprinted in A. Hayashima, 'Der Kölner Weg zum Promotionsrecht. Zur Geschichte einer deutschen Handelshochschule', *Kwansei Gakuin University Annual Studies*, vol. 31 (1982), pp. 27–9.

distract the student from the demands of commercial life, the substance of its teaching was ill-adapted to commercial instruction. For this reason the approach adopted in Leipzig, where students attended university lectures in law, economics, and geography, was no adequate substitute for a systematic course of commercial studies. At the same time, Gothein emphasised that study in a Handelshochschule must be based upon the same elective principle of *Lernfreiheit* as prevailed in the universities; without this, he argued, a German institution of higher education was inconceivable.[29] He accordingly rejected the rigidity of the fixed courses and regular examinations that he had found at the École des Hautes Études Commerciales in Paris, and argued that what was needed in a higher commercial college was a two-year course combining obligatory and optional lecture courses.

The natural basis for such a commercial course, argued Gothein, was the study of economics. This should begin with general lectures of a broadly similar character to those delivered in the university, following this with a range of applied subjects not normally covered in such depth in the university context, and taught by the College's own specialist staff. By contrast, for the courses on law – procedure, civil law, and administrative law – Gothein considered that the college would be permanently reliant on the teaching of academic and practising lawyers. Instead of augmenting the university curriculum as in the case of economics, he envisaged an abbreviation of the university law curriculum, through the omission of subjects such as historical and criminal law. Alongside the teaching in law and economics, courses in commercial subjects were to extend throughout all four semesters. This teaching would centre upon an *allgemeine Handelslehre* presented over two semesters; beginning with *Comptoir-kunde*, it would proceed to cover domestic and external trade, techniques of trade, means of payment, and other related subjects. Gothein's vision of the commercial curriculum did not therefore diverge sharply from the Leipzig curriculum, combining academic courses in law and economics with systematic preparation in commercial skills based upon the curricula of the commercial schools. It was the project of delivering most of the teaching within an independent institute that marked the real departure in this proposal; while the

---

[29] E. Gothein, 'Denkschrift über Errichtung einer Handelshochschule in Köln, Mai 1900', in Hayashima, 'Zur Geschichte der Kölner Handelshochschule', p. 199. *Lernfreiheit* opened all lectures of a university to the students, who were in principal free to follow whatever lectures they wished. Although studies terminated with state examinations covering a fixed syllabus, it was not prescribed when, or where, these should be sat.

economics teaching in Cologne might simply extend the existing university curriculum with respect to applied economics, the fact that the courses were to be taught by the college's own staff was a significant development. Likewise with 'Allgemeine Handelslehre': although the detail of the teaching in this area might not differ so markedly from that in Leipzig, it was conceived as part of a unitary subject, a *Lehre*, even though this might as yet be inadequately elaborated.

The Prussian Ministers of Culture and Trade gave their approval to the City Administration's proposal in September 1900, with one proviso: that all appointments be subject to the approval of the Ministry of Trade.[30] The following month Becker proposed three names to the Ministry. The office of *Studiendirektor* was to be combined with the principal teacher of Nationalökonomie, and for this Becker put forward Hermann Schumacher, an Extraordinary Professor at the University of Kiel. In addition, a teacher from the Barmen Realgymnasium was proposed for a position in modern languages, and a Privat Dozent at the Aachen Technische Hochschule was put forward as a teacher for bookkeeping, correspondence and commercial arithmetic.[31] A letter in December named three further appointments in a list headed by Carl Grünberg, then at the University of Vienna, as teacher of Nationalökonomie and Finanzwissenschaft;[32] also proposed were a teacher of chemistry and chemical technology (from the University of Bonn), and a teacher of mechanical technology (from the railway section of Siemens and Halske in Berlin). The key academic positions in the teaching programme at Cologne were therefore filled by candidates already developing their careers within the existing higher education system; the fact that a new Handelshochschule could attract such staff testifies to the seriousness with which this initiative was received.

[30] Letter from Prussian Ministers of Culture and Trade to Ober-Bürgermeister Becker, 19 September 1900, in Hayashima, 'Der Kölner Weg zum Promotionsrecht', p. 30. At the same time they pointed out that the title of 'Professor' was one reserved to the universities and conferred only by the King. This was to cause some difficulties, resolved only by a meeting in June 1902 in which it was agreed that a maximum of two-thirds of the full-time teachers at Cologne and Frankfurt might be permitted to use the title 'Professor', provided that it was made clear that their appointment was at the Handelshochschule or Akademie. See Hayashima, p. 37.

[31] Becker to Handelsminister Brefeld, 10 October 1900, in Hayashima, 'Der Kölner Weg zum Promotionsrecht', p. 31.

[32] Grünberg at first accepted the *Ruf*, then declined on domestic grounds. A student of Lorenz von Stein and Anton Menger, he was in 1924 appointed the first director of the Frankfurt Institut für Sozialforschung. See U. Migdal, *Die Frühgeschichte des Frankfurter Instituts für Sozialforschung*, Campus Verlag, Frankfurt a. M. 1981, Chapters 3 and 4.

The college opened in May 1901 in the premises of the existing municipal Handelsrealschule, with five of its own teachers: in economics, languages, mechanics, chemistry and commerce. Their teaching was augmented by eleven professors from Bonn, plus twelve practitioners in law and commerce from Cologne. Sixty-eight students were admitted under terms modelled on those introduced at Leipzig: twenty of this first intake had an Abitur from a Gymnasium, while forty-three entered as employees with several years practical experience. Students were admitted at the beginning of every semester, and not all of the first intake completed the allotted two years of study; but the number of regular students quickly rose to over two hundred by the summer semester of 1903, and reached 304 by the summer of 1906.[33] In addition to these regular students, occasional students were also admitted: these were either *Hospitanten*, persons over the age of seventeen with nine years of schooling, or *Hörer*, adults admitted to public evening lectures. In the winter semester of 1903, for example, forty-four of the former and 1,220 of the latter were registered.[34]

The Cologne curriculum followed Gothein's memorandum in placing economics at its core:

The lectures in this most important principal discipline are aimed at instilling in students an understanding of modern economic life, its organisation and its fundamental problems. ... The student should be placed in a position, after his departure from the college, of being able to himself observe economic phenomena, explain their causes, and comprehend their interrelationship as a whole.[35]

The introductory lecture course was repeated every semester, so that it could be taken by all entrants at the beginning of their studies at the college. Attendance at these lectures was a condition for entry into the remaining economics courses, for which no particular sequence was prescribed, although it was apparently expected that students would attend between four and six economics lectures a week over the four semesters of study.[36] Courses on economic policy and applied economics ranged more widely than would be usual in a university – international trade, money and banking, commercial policy, social policy, and colonial policy were all the object of one or more courses.

[33] Hayashima, 'Zur Geschichte der Kölner Handelshochschule', p. 210.
[34] C. Eckert, *Die städtische Handels-Hochschule in Cöln. Bericht über die zwei Studienjahre 1903 und 1904*, Verlag von Julius Springer, Berlin 1905, p. 30.
[35] C. Eckert, *Bericht über die zwei Studienjahre 1903 und 1904*, pp. 45–6.
[36] See the comments on p. 50 of C. Eckert, *Bericht über die zwei Studienjahre 1903 und 1904*.

Other courses were more condensed than would normally be the case in universities, so that the lectures on finance only covered the major topics, and those on statistics only economic statistics. Many of the lectures were given by officials: for instance, a course on posts and telegraphs was delivered by a *Postrat*, and one on health and safety at work by a privy councillor. Other courses were given by professors from the University of Bonn, and a number of specialised supplementary lectures were also available. An economics *Seminar* had been formed and students were encouraged to present papers on a regular basis for discussion with staff and businessmen. There was naturally a degree of improvisation in all this, but it should be noted that from the very beginning all teaching took place within the college precincts. Whereas in Leipzig the students of the Handelshochschule simply attended existing lecture courses alongside university students, here the teachers came to the Handelshochschule and delivered their courses exclusively to its members.

Next in line was the legal curriculum:

Law has of course to be taught differently in a Handels-Hochschule than in universities. For it cannot be the object in a college of trade and industry to train finished jurists. The young businessman should not for example be placed in a position where he can dispense with experienced legal opinion in difficult cases. He should simply be placed in a position whereby, in such cases, he is able to communicate with the professional lawyer in a manner better than that usually possible today.[37]

The task was therefore a dual one. Firstly, students had to be given a general understanding of the significance of law in economic and business life. Secondly, they had to be instructed in those particular aspects of law that they would encounter in their future employment. Here it was important, for example, to be conversant with contract law, the conditions governing foreign exchange, and the legal provisions relevant to commercial organisations. Instruction should therefore begin with an introductory course on civil law based on Books 1–3 of the *Bürgerliches Gesetzbuch*,[38] with special emphasis on commercial law. In addition to this some acquaintance with legal procedure and solvency law should be included as part of the introductory course. Following on from this were lectures on commercial law, in particular company law, which subjects should be dealt with at far greater length than was customary in the university. Law of the Sea and the

---

[37] C. Eckert, *Bericht über die zwei Studienjahre 1903 und 1904*, p. 57.
[38] Books 4 and 5 covered Family Law and the Law of Inheritance, which were of little relevance.

Law of Domestic Waterways were almost entirely neglected in university teaching, but these were treated as of great importance in the teaching of a commercial college, and were consequently made available. These and other related subjects were taught not by academics from Bonn, but by by practising lawyers and officials from Cologne.

A foundation in the principles of economics and law was required of all students, and there were in addition to this a number of elective subjects available, including topics in insurance, geography, 'knowledge of goods' (*Warenkunde*), natural science and technology. However, these were distinct from the practical basis of the college's curriculum, which was assembled under the heading 'commercial technique' (*Handelstechnik*), and introduced as follows:

Commercial Technique strives to provide a comprehensive picture of business practice. It is intended to serve the individual interests of merchants and industrialists and should be regarded, in contrast to *Volkswirtschaftslehre*, as a part of *Privatwirtschaftslehre*. Commercial Technique begins where the modern office, training virtuosi in detailed work along established lines, goes awry; it seeks to provide an overview of the entire range of business skills, and identify their nature and effects.[39]

This is the area that Gothein had referred to as *Handelslehre*, covering all the areas of practical business affairs. Given the novelty of teaching these subjects within a higher education institution, those charged with their teaching had, in addition to their regular teaching, the task of developing disparate elements into a coherent discipline. The purpose of such teaching was not the provision of routinised training in the various practical aspects of business life, as was the task of commercial schools; it was instead intended to furnish a comprehensive overview of commercial administration, combined with a reliable insight into its detailed aspects.

The first major component of these studies was bookkeeping, in which a survey of the different methods of accounting and balances was covered, enabling the student to create and maintain accounts appropriate to any particular enterprise. Commercial arithmetic was a separate area of study; it was taught by a mathematician from Bonn, who dealt with its theoretical foundations, and a 'Handelstechniker', who concentrated on the economic significance of the material. Eugen Schmalenbach, a graduate of the first intake at Leipzig, held the latter post from April 1904; in 1906 he was made Professor of

[39] C. Eckert, *Bericht über die zwei Studienjahre 1903 und 1904*, p. 75.

Handelstechnik, and then with the conversion to university status, *Professor für Betriebswirtschaftslehre.*[40]

Schmalenbach devoted his efforts to a new area of commercial calculation, that of 'Bilanzkritik', the analysis of balances.

With the growth of mobile capital, especially of share capital, the need arose in business practice of creating a basis for share valuation, and this basis was primarily to be found in balance analysis. Led by the major German financial papers, the methods of calculating the so-called 'inherent value' of shares from given balances have been extensively improved. At the same time it became ever more difficult to read the balance, for beginners without guidance almost impossible, and the methods used were in need of scientific elaboration.[41]

This problem in financial accounting was therefore the area covered by Schmalenbach, and he set about creating a large archive of accounting records as a basis for the systematisation of accounting practices.

The teaching in accounting and commercial calculation was followed by instruction in the organisation of commercial enterprise, covering commercial correspondence, sales, international trade, markets and exchanges, duties, insurance, export and import. A commercial seminar was created by Schmalenbach in the winter semester of 1903–4, in which students were introduced to the financial and commercial press, and were further required to discuss the week's events as reported in the press.

The last component of the curriculum was modern languages, but this part of the course was no afterthought, as testified by the large amount of space devoted to languages in the Cologne annual reports. It was taken for granted in all European higher commercial colleges of the time that facility in two foreign languages was an important element in the training of future managers and administrators, and a substantial amount of the students' time at Cologne was taken up by teaching, conversation, and reading in English, French, Italian, Spanish, Portuguese, Russian, Dutch, Norwegian, and Danish.[42] English and French were the principal foreign languages; but the programme went beyond the familiar territory of commercial

---

[40] Perhaps it is this change of title from *Handelstechnik* to *Betriebswirtschaftslehre* that led Locke to his belief that Schmalenbach's dynamic accounting was the basis of BWL. As will be made clear below, the evolution is rather more complex than this.

[41] C. Eckert, *Bericht über die zwei Studienjahre 1903 und 1904*, p. 79.

[42] All these languages were supported in the Handelshochschule in 1903 and 1904: see C. Eckert, *Bericht über die zwei Studienjahre 1903 und 1904*, p. 81.

correspondence, conversation, and translation. The English *Seminar* organised for teachers covered English philology, the work of Spenser, Shakespeare, Byron, on to Kipling, and 'Jerome', author of *Three Men in a Boat* and of course *Three Men on the Bummel*.[43] In addition to this, the library of the Handelshochschule subscribed not only to German specialist literature, but also a selection of their English and French equivalents. So, for example, we can find the *Economist, Journal of Political Economy*, and the *Revue du Droit Internationale* listed in the library's periodical collection, as well as the *Illustrated London News* and *Punch*.[44]

In part the extent of these study resources in the new college were a reflection of its wealth, founded as it was with Mevissen's donations and the financial support of the Chamber of Commerce and the City Council. The fund of 1 million Marks with which the college had begun in 1901 was further augmented in 1903 with 300,000 Marks from the will of Mevissen's widow. The resulting total provided an annual income of around 60,000 marks per annum during the early years, although by 1907 the contribution to current income from this source was exceeded by direct municipal support: expenses during the first year were 128,050 Marks, rising to 320,506 Marks in 1909, at which time the income from Mevissen's fund covered 20.15 per cent of current expenditure, as against 27.9 per cent provided by the City Council.[45] Mevissen's fund played an important structural role in the financing of the college's activities: while insufficient in itself to finance the annual shortfall in revenue, its existence allowed the City Council to commit itself to meeting the balance of operating costs and thus give the new college a secure financial basis. The college was therefore freed of the requirement to cover its cost out of current income, while at the same time establishing a direct relationship with the city authorities. This was an important element in financing new accommodation for the college.

Mevissen's proposal had never been simply for a commercial

---

[43] C. Eckert, *Bericht über die zwei Studienjahre 1903 und 1904*, pp. 89–90. These two books by Jerome K. Jerome were first published in 1889 and 1900 respectively. A later report noted that English comedies had been read, together with aspects of the work of Bernard Shaw and Oscar Wilde – C. Eckert, *Die städtische Handels-Hochschule in Cöln. Bericht über das Studienjahr 1908*, Paul Neubner, Cologne 1909, p. 52.

[44] C. Eckert, *Bericht über die zwei Studienjahre 1903 und 1904*, pp. 105–10.

[45] C. Eckert, *Die städtische Handels-Hochschule in Cöln. Bericht über die Entwicklung der Handels-Hochschule im ersten Jahrzehnt ihres Bestehens unter besonderer Berücksichtigung der Studienjahre 1909 und 1910*, Paul Neubner, Cologne 1911, pp. 204–5. The balance of income was provided by student fees.

college in the sense of staff and students using rented accomodation (as was for example the practice of the London School of Economics in the early 1900s), but envisaged a purpose-built and adequately equipped college. Preparations for a new building began in 1902; a prize competition during 1903 resulted in the submission of sixty-seven designs,[46] and final approval was given to both plans and costings in November 1904.[47] The foundation stone was laid in July 1905, and a spacious and imposing building completed in time for the beginning of the academic year 1907–8. Sited in the Römerpark on the banks of the Rhine, the new building had eleven lecture rooms with capacities ranging from 252 to 16, seven seminar rooms, a library with two reading rooms, an assembly hall for nearly 500 students, fourteen staff offices, a gymnasium, a fencing hall, a canteen and six flats for librarians and caretakers. Indeed, for some years after its opening the capacity of the building exceeded the demands made upon it; 363 full-time students were registered for the first semester in the new building, rising to a peak of 624 in the summer semester of 1914. The provision of adequate accommodation was nevertheless an important step in lending the movement for higher commercial education a degree of permanence and substance, a process that was replicated in Berlin.

The Berlin college was explicitly modelled upon its forerunner in Cologne, but it had a rather different genesis and its administrative and teaching organisation also varied in important respects. Mevissen's agitation for higher commercial education, coupled with the provision of substantial funds, had been the initial impulse in the foundation of the Cologne college; but here private philanthropy was linked to municipal initiative and funding, so that it was the Cologne City Council that in the event underwrote the new college's running costs, and in addition financed the construction and equipment of a new college building. The administration of the Cologne college was in the hands of a permanent academic director appointed by the city mayor in consultation with a governing body of academics and other representatives. In effect the director was then able to organise the teaching in whatever manner he deemed appropriate, and his ability to recruit staff was subject only to the approval of the Prussian

---

[46] An account of the planning and construction of the new college can be found in C. Eckert, *Bericht über die Entwicklung der Handels-Hochschule ... 1909 und 1910*, pp. 199–203.

[47] The land was bought for 1.36 million Marks, and the building itself cost 2,480,552 Marks – C. Eckert, *Die städtische Handels-Hochschule in Cöln. Bericht über das fünfte Studienjahr*, Paul Neubner, Cologne 1906, p. 10.

Table 5.1. *Full-time students in Cologne and Berlin*

	Cologne	Berlin
SS 1901	86	
WS 1901	136	
SS 1902	159	
WS 1902	205	
SS 1903	230	
WS 1903	238	
SS 1904	239	
WS 1904	254	
SS 1905	266	
WS 1905	303	
SS 1906	335	
WS 1906	331	213
SS 1907	330	228
WS 1907	363	369
SS 1908	388	339
WS 1908	413	402
SS 1909	443	400
WS 1909	463	410
SS 1910	462	288
WS 1910	472	448
SS 1911	463	419
WS 1911	462	478
SS 1912	498	486
WS 1912	533	511
SS 1913	561	484
WS 1913	597	590
SS 1914	624	562

Source: A. Hayashima, 'Die Absolventen der Leipziger Handelshochschule 1900–1920', *Kwansei Gakuin University Annual Studies*, vol. 36 (1987), Appendix 1, p. 134.

Ministry of Trade and Industry. The Berlin college, by contrast, was established by the Elders of the Berlin *Korporation der Kaufmannschaft* on land owned by the *Korporation* adjoining the Stock Exchange, and headed by a *Rektor*, a position filled from the existing staff on a rotating basis, overall control of the college administration being retained by the Elders.[48] The formal link between the college and the

[48] Berlin, Mannheim, Leipzig, Frankfurt, and Nuremberg were all headed by a *Rektor* whose period of office lasted from two to three years – C. Eckert, 'Handelshochschulen', *Handwörter-buch der Kommunalwissenschaften*, Bd. 2, Gustav Fischer Verlag, Jena 1922, p. 471.

business community was therefore more direct than in Cologne, although this also carried with it the danger that friction between academic and business interests in the running of the college could occur.[49]

A lecture by Apt to the *Verein junger Kaufleute* in March 1900 proposed the foundation of a Handelshochschule in Berlin, and this suggestion was formally adopted by the Elders in May 1903.[50] As in Britain at this time, it was generally assumed that the United States had the most advanced system of commercial education, and the Elders commissioned Jastrow (future inaugural *Rektor* of the Berlin foundation) to conduct a survey and report on what he found. The result was an interesting comparative review of the existing state of on-the-job and vocational training in Germany and America, which highlighted the deficiencies of both business education and practical training in the United States. Jastrow found that in the United States on-the-job training was largely informal, or more exactly, non-existent – employees were simply expected to pick up the skills needed to perform their work as they went along. The formal, academic commercial education available was, by contrast, highly general and non-vocational. Jastrow also encountered in the United States a widespread belief that the skills of German employees derived from commercial education, rather than systematic practical training, a belief which fuelled the further development of non-specific academic commercial education, rather than vocational training.[51]

Jastrow's survey disabused the Elders of their assumption that an imitable model for business education existed in the USA. Instead, they followed the example set by the Cologne Handelshochschule; not because it was German, therefore, but because it was the most successful and imitable institution of its kind in 1904. One positive feature of the American commercial education had been identified by Jastrow: noting that the academically educated businessman was an everyday occurrence in the United States, he properly inferred that, for the American businessman, academic qualification was a cultural, rather than a vocational, asset. This raised the question of the purpose

[49] As illustrated by the scandal in 1914 when Jastrow was deemed to have resigned after refusing to renegotiate his contract as Professor of Economics. Georg Simmel highlighted the singular nature of this clash between the worlds of business and academia in his article 'Der Fall Jastrow', *Die Zukunft*, 10 October 1914, pp. 33–6. My thanks to David Frisby for bringing this to my attention.

[50] G. Obst, 'Die deutschen Handelshochschulen', *Zeitschrift für Handelswissenschaft und Handelspolitik*, Bd. 1, H. 6 (1908), p. 194.

[51] Jastrow, 'Kaufmannsbildung und Hochschulbildung in Amerika', pp. 421–4.

of academic education for the commercial class; and he concluded
that this purpose lay not so much in the transmission of practical
knowledge, but in the general education of leading businessmen.

Jastrow was appointed professor of the Staatswissenschaften and
Rektor of the college during the period 1906–9.[52] Although it would
have been possible to find temporary accommodation, no students
were admitted until the new premises were ready, building taking
place during the years 1904–6 on a scale and plan similar to that at
Cologne.[53] The college opened for the winter semester of 1906–7 with
nine full-time teachers and some thirty-three part-timers, the range of
subjects covered by the permanent staff being strictly comparable to
that of Cologne in 1901: economics, law, *Handelswissenschaften*,
chemistry, and physics, together with a chair of Business Education
and Geography. The formal opening took place in October 1907 in
the presence of the Crown Prince, 213 full-time students being
registered for the first semester. Numbers rose quickly, if not so
continuously as at Cologne, which in 1914 still had rather more full-
time students than Berlin. However, occasional students were an
important feature of the Berlin college, simply because of its location
in the centre of the German capital. During the first semester there
were, for example, 263 *Hospitanten* (part-time students admitted to
specific courses) and 917 *Hörer* (attending lectures on an *ad hoc* basis).
There was considerable seasonal fluctuation in the numbers of
occasional students, and while the number of *Hospitanten* did not
significantly increase over the first three years, the number of *Hörer*
during the winter semester rose to 1,350 by WS 1908–9.[54]

Some 20 to 25 per cent of full-time students were foreign, primarily
from Austro-Hungary but with significant representation from Russia, and later Romania. In his three-year report Jastrow made light of
this foreign presence, but by 1913 the proportion had risen to 35 per
cent, the number of Russians, for example, outnumbering those
drawn from the city of Berlin itself.[55] By the summer semester of 1914
the proportion of foreign students reached 38 per cent of full-time

[52] Werner Sombart had a position as the second Professor of the Staatswissenschaften.
[53] The main assembly hall, for example, had seating for 500–600, the largest lecture theatre held
300, and there were a number of other lecture and seminar rooms; I. Jastrow, *Die
Handelshochschule Berlin. Bericht über das erste Studienjahr Oktober 1906/7*, Georg Reimer, Berlin
1908, p. 17.
[54] I. Jastrow, *Die Handelshochschule Berlin. Bericht über die erste Rektoratsperiode Oktober 1906–1909*,
Georg Reimer, Berlin 1909, p. 38.
[55] A. Binz, *Bericht über das siebente Studienjahr der Handels-Hochschule Berlin. Oktober 1912/1913*,
Georg Reimer, Berlin 1913, p. 13.

students, later reports recording with evident relief that the war had had the benign effect of removing these troublesome non-native speakers.[56] Admission requirements were the same as in Leipzig and Cologne, the proportion of those admitted with proof of employment training in the first three years being around 60 per cent, as opposed to 15 to 20 per cent with an *Abitur*. This latter proportion increased only very slightly before the First World War. As in Cologne, the majority of students were sons of independent businessmen, just under half being from business families of all descriptions, with an average age of 23–24.[57] Among the occasional students, the *Hospitanten* had a variety of backgrounds, the largest single group being students of Berlin University, whereas the *Hörer* were overwhelmingly businessmen, clerks, and secretaries.[58]

The course of study at the Handelshochschule was intended to last four semesters, but the dropout rate was considerable during the first few years. Of the 213 full-time students who entered the first semester in 1906, 161 survived into the second semester, 107 into the third and only 65 completed four semesters. However, Jastrow suggested that the figures he compiled on duration of study in Berlin could be affected by students entering after completing one or two semesters at another college (19 per cent had done so in WS 1908–9), while on the other hand students might leave Berlin to complete their studies elsewhere – this was a quite normal feature of the German university system, and it was reasonable to suppose that it would be carried over into the Handelshochschulen.[59]

By modern standards, the teaching programme of the college was intensive, a situation promoted by the payment of a block fee rather than payment by course. Full-time students were permitted to attend up to 24 lecture hours per week, the recommended number being 20; but the overwhelming majority of students recorded attendance rates of 23 and 24 hours per week.[60]

[56] P. Eltzbacher, *Handels-Hochschule Berlin. Bericht über die Rektorats-Periode Oktober 1913/1916*, Georg Reimer, Berlin 1917, p. 17. The non-German speaking students were described here as 'störend empfunden'.

[57] Jastrow, *Die Handelshochschule Berlin. Bericht über die erste Rektoratsperiode*, pp. 46–8.

[58] A. Binz, *Bericht über das vierte und fünfte Studienjahr der Handels-Hochschule Berlin. Oktober 1909/ 1911*, Georg Reimer, Berlin 1911, pp. 23–4.

[59] Later reports did not repeat Jastrow's table of wastage rates. Sixteen students gained the Diplom in SS 1908, fourteen in WS 1908–9, and thirty-two in SS 1909. Jastrow, *Die Handelshochschule Berlin. Bericht über die erste Rektoratsperiode*, pp. 40–1, 201–2.

[60] Jastrow, *Die Handelshochschule Berlin. Bericht über die erste Rektoratsperiode*, pp. 48–9. The mean in the semesters before the war varied around 20 hours per week: A. Binz, *Bericht über das siebente Studienjahr der Handels-Hochschule Berlin. Oktober 1912/1913*, p. 15.

Table 5.2. *Graduates of the Berlin Handelshochschule*[a]

	Diplom-Kfm.	Handelslehrerzeugnis
SS 1907	3	
WS 1907	3	1
SS 1908	16	5
WS 1908	14	2
SS 1909	32	6
WS 1909	29	14
SS 1910	37	11
WS 1910	43	15
SS 1911	47	3
WS1911	34	9
SS 1912	41	5
WS1912	51	9
SS 1913	48	7
WS 1913	37	15
SS 1914	55	12

Note:
[a] Based upon the Annual Reports of the college.

The curriculum in Berlin was distinguished by the priority given to the *Handelswissenschaften*, although this was still in 1907 a fairly loose collection of practical subjects. Nevertheless, whereas Cologne placed an introductory course in economics at the beginning of its study programme – repeated every semester and required for entry into later courses – Jastrow created in Berlin a general introductory course providing an overview of the work of the Handelshochschule. The official recommendation was to supplement this during the first semester with lectures on accounts and commercial arithmetic, and a foreign language. In addition, it was suggested that students take an introductory course either in economics, or law, or physics, or chemistry, or economic geography.[61] A similar pattern, without the introductory course and following on at a higher level from individual subjects selected in the first semester, was recommended for the second semester. The third and fourth semesters involved further specialisation along the path already established, with the addition of practical classes permitting students to develop specific areas of interest in association with individual teachers. Quite evident from this is the clear break with the core role of law and economics lectures

[61] Jastrow, *Die Handelshochschule Berlin. Bericht über das erste Studienjahr Oktober 1906/7*, pp. 164–5.

on the university model. Students were still able to specialise in these areas if they so wished; for in Jastrow and Sombart the college had two experienced economics teachers, and the range of specialised topics available was great. Indeed, apart from languages, economics continued as the subject with the greatest number of lecture hours devoted to it.[62] Whereas in Leipzig business education was in practice ancillary to an academic understanding of the general subject matter of law and economics, in Berlin the curriculum and pattern of teaching facilitated the development of an autonomous business curriculum.

Quite how advanced Berlin's position was for the time is illustrated by discussions that took place at the annual meeting of the Verein für Sozialpolitik in 1907, whose theme was the 'vocational training of economic officials' and which therefore directly addressed the curricular issues at stake in the Handelshochschulen. The topic was prompted not so much by the rapid contemporary development of the Handelshochschulen, as by the problem to which the Handelshochschulen had provided one kind of solution: the absence of any university qualification in economics, apart from the doctorate. This issue was not in fact resolved until after the war, by the introduction of an economics diploma directly related to the qualification of Diplom-Kaufmann. At the 1907 meeting, however, Karl Bücher reviewed the issues before the meeting in an introductory speech which assumed, firstly, that the university was the appropriate institution within which to train officials; secondly, that the Handelshochschulen could provide no more than a preliminary grounding for candidates who then went on to enter a university; and thirdly, that the ideal curriculum should be organised around obligatory courses in economics, law, and statistics. Specialised courses could be taken, but commercial studies played a minor role in the menu proposed.[63] Bücher had of course been closely associated, as Professor of Economics at the University of Leipzig, with the formation of the Leipzig Handelshochschule, and so he is here in effect defending the original curricular structure of the college. In the event most of the contributors to discussion at the Verein meeting disregarded the function of

---

[62] Out of 247 weekly hours in WS 1910–11, economics took up 41 hours, *Handelswissenschaften* 33, and law 22: Binz, *Bericht über das vierte und fünfte Studienjahr der Handels-Hochschule Berlin. Oktober 1909/1911*, p. 25.

[63] K. Bücher, 'Die berufsmäßige Vorbildung der volkswirtschaftlichen Beamten', *Verhandlungen der Generalversammlung in Magdeburg, 30 September 1907, Schriften des Vereins für Socialpolitik*, Bd. 125, pp. 9–39.

the Handelshochschulen in providing a serviceable economic qualification, insisting that a form of economic curriculum and examination should be introduced into the university system equivalent to the existing structures in law.

The difficulty with recasting the established university disciplines was that no generally accepted standards existed for teaching and examining 'commercial sciences'. As can be inferred from the outline of the courses on offer given above, Berlin discarded (with good reason) the pedagogical organisation provided by academic law and economics, but did not immediately replace them with direct alternatives. Instead, students were provided with a general introduction to the study of commercial subjects and then left to construct their own path through the available courses on an entirely elective basis. Nominally, *Handelswissenschaft* provided the core of commercial studies, but the material which it brought together was inherited from the teaching of commercial schools, and was not directly applicable to a higher educational institution. An article published in 1906 had already identified this problem, and outlined an approach which would assist the development of a new and autonomous science. Hellauer, a teacher at the Vienna Export Academy, first distinguished between the internal practices of a commercial enterprise (*kaufmännische Betriebslehre*), and the trading relationships formed between such enterprises (*Handelslehre*). The former, he suggested, could be subdivided into two distinct sections:

(1) Enterprise organisation;
(2) Enterprise administrative technique.[64]

The latter was composed chiefly of accounting, bookkeeping, and commercial calculation, familiar techniques that were well established, albeit at a non-academic level. These familiar techniques were insufficient in themselves to constitute a new commercial science, for which it was necessary to develop a general analysis of enterprise organisation. Furthermore, Hellauer proposed that this should be systematically linked to an understanding of the relationship between enterprises and their markets (*Handelslehre*), so that one would be able to progress in a deliberate manner from the internal organisation of the enterprise to domestic and international trade. Conceived in such a manner, one could then construct a systematic commercial science.

Hellauer recognised that this new commercial pedagogy could only

---

[64] J. Hellauer, 'Versuch einer Gliederung der Handelswissenschaften als Hochschuldisziplin', *Deutsche Wirtschafts-Zeitung*, Jg. 2, Pt. I (1906), cols. 416–7.

be developed over time within the Handelshochschulen; Berlin's placing of *Handelswissenschaft* at the centre of their new curriculum did at least make this a possibility. For the time being, however, examinations in Berlin were simply adapted to the acquired knowledge of the student: in 1909 for example students were no longer set compulsory examination subjects, and merely had to sit four examinations, two of which they could nominate as their principal courses, and two as their subsidiaries.[65] There was widespread discussion of the problems that this presented so long as no clear agreement existed on the nature of commercial science, and in 1912 representatives of the Prussian Handelshochschulen in Berlin, Cologne, and Frankfurt finally agreed on common regulations for the Diplom examination.

The new regulations left untouched the student's right to nominate subjects for examination, but these subjects were more clearly defined and ranked. The material covered by the Diplom was divided into nine sections, from which students were then to select their examination topics:

(1) Privatwirtschaftslehre (Handelswissenschaft);
(2) Volkswirtschaftslehre;
(3) Law;
(4) Chemistry, with special reference to technology;
(5) Physics, with special reference to applied physics;
(6) Geography, with special reference to Economic Geography;
(7) Insurance;
(8) Co-operative organisation;
(9) Foreign languages.

At first glance, it looks as though economics had been placed back in its pre-eminent position, swallowing the nascent *Handelswissenschaft*. Our appreciation of the exact nature of curricular evolution involved is aided by referring to the definition of *Privatwirtschaftslehre* (PWL) that is given in the new regulations:

To the general part [of PWL] belongs a knowledge of the general principles of enterprise and of enterprise organisation, of the relationships between enterprises and the institutions facilitating commercial transactions (*Verkehr*). The examination covers the theory of the enterprise, the foundations of business organisation, bookkeeping, accounting, commercial calculation, purchase and sales, and monetary and capital exchanges.

In the special part the candidate must choose one of the branches taught at the college, at present the economy (*Privatwirtschaftslehre*) of commodity

---

[65] Binz, *Bericht über das siebente Studienjahr der Handels-Hochschule Berlin. Oktober 1912/1913*, p. 50.

markets, industrial enterprises or banking. Thorough knowledge of the organisation and running of the chosen branch is required.

In both parts the candidate has to demonstrate a mastery of the fundamentals of calculation and bookkeeping.[66]

Hence what is 'private' about this branch of economics is that it deals with the organisation of economic activity within discrete units; its genesis can be traced right back to the conception of the household economy as originally elaborated by Aristotle and Xenophon. *Volkswirtschaftslehre* addressed the general principles of economic life without reference to the institutional forms within which economic activity took place – it focused upon price formation, distribution, money and credit, and economic policy. It was precisely this feature of *Volkswirtschaftslehre* that had prompted the objection that the economics taught in universities was of little relevance to commercial education, since it dealt in generalities giving little direct guidance as to the rational conduct of economic institutions – be they factories, banks, or department stores.

Cologne had placed *Volkswirtschaftslehre* at the head of its curriculum, and the rubric cited above providing a rationale for this position continued to appear in the college's reports.[67] In the original curricular sequence the second place was occupied by law, which then together with economics formed a compulsory part of the course. By 1912 this had altered: the second principal section of the curriculum was no longer law, but *Privatwirtschaftslehre*, covering those areas previously dealt with under the heading of *Handelstechnik*, 'techniques of trade'. Furthermore, it was made plain that some dispute surrounded this subject – there was disagreement over its status as a science or as an art, and its relation to *Nationalökonomie* was also a matter for disagreement. Up to WS 1906–7 Cologne had continued with the tripartite division of bookkeeping, correspondence, and commercial arithmetic inherited from the commercial schools and which formed the mainstay of *Handelstechnik*. This material was then rearranged under the rubric of 'Commercial organisation, including bookkeeping and techniques of commerce', under which heading teaching continued for five years.[68] A further reorganisation of the

---

[66] 'Ausführungsbestimmungen zu der Ordnung für die Diplomprüfung an der Handels-Hochschule Berlin', §1 in Binz, *Bericht über das siebente Studienjahr der Handels-Hochschule Berlin. Oktober 1912/1913*, p. 53.

[67] The passage cited in n. 35 above recurs for example in C. Eckert, *Die städtische Handels-Hochschule in Cöln. Bericht über die Studienjahre 1911 und 1912*, Paul Neubner, Cologne 1913, p. 60.

[68] *Ibid.*, p. 82.

subject then took place, creating a greater degree of specialisation and distinguishing four main sections:

(1) General *Privatwirtschaftslehre*;
(2) *Privatwirtschaftslehre* of factories;
(3) *Privatwirtschaftslehre* of retail and wholesale trading enterprises;
(4) *Privatwirtschaftslehre* of banks.[69]

This involved a complete rearrangement of the lectures, techniques of accounting and commercial calculation being distributed throughout, rather than taught as separate subjects. Industrial, commercial, and banking enterprises differed in respect of the detail of their internal organisation and management, but are treated as variants of business organisation. The business enterprise now became the object of economic analysis, and this development was assisted by the publication of textbooks which lent shape to this curricular development.

In 1910 Hellauer (who, as noted above, had in 1906 outlined an intellectual basis for the reorganisation of commercial science) published his *System der Welthandelslehre*, considering international trade from the standpoint of its daily practice: the chapters covered trading organisations, orders and deliveries, commodity markets, and the various practical and legal aspects of commercial contracts.[70] During the following year J. F. Schär, who had been a 'Professor der Handelswissenschaften' in the Berlin Handelshochschule from its foundation, published his *Allgemeine Handelsbetriebslehre*, a comprehensive, if wordy, treatment of commercial science working outward from the management of the individual enterprise to trade, competition, cartels, future markets, and speculation.[71] Schär had taught for many years in commercial schools, and was already in his late fifties when appointed to the Berlin Handelshochschule, and so it is not so surprising that his synthesis of the subject should be somewhat vague and diffuse. This was not however the case with Nicklisch's *Allgemeine Handelsbetriebslehre*,[72] which underwent some radical rewriting after its

[69] *Ibid.*, p. 83.
[70] J. Hellauer, *System der Welthandelslehre. Ein Lehr- und Handbuch des internationalen Handels. Erster Band: Allgemeine Welthandelslehre 1. Teil*, 8th edn, Puttkamer und Mühlbrecht, Berlin 1920. The text of this printing is unchanged from that of the first, apart from a short prefatory note and some corrections. Hellauer had taught at the Vienna Exportakademie, which accounts for his interest in international trade.
[71] J. F. Schär, *Allgemeine Handelsbetriebslehre*, 4th edn, G. A. Gloeckner, Leipzig 1921. The overall structure of the work was unchanged from the first edition.
[72] H. Nicklisch, *Allgemeine Kaufmännische Betriebslehre als Privatwirtschaftslehre des Handels und der Industrie*, Bd. I, Verlag Carl Ernst Poeschel, Leipzig 1912.

initial appearance in 1911 and which presents an altogether sharper image of the new commercial science, as will be outlined below.

During 1912 this linkage between curricular development, new textbooks, and examination reform was reflected in a sharp debate over the relation between *Privatwirtschaftslehre* and *Volkswirtschafts-lehre*, which served chiefly to signal the autonomy of the new commercial curriculum with respect to existing university teaching in law and economics. Prion, a teacher at the Munich Handelshoch-schule, raised the question of the status of the developments in commercial sciences in reviewing yet another new textbook, whose title 'Foundation and System of a Scientific Privatwirtschaftslehre' paraded the academic ambitions of commercial education.[73] The review drew a sharp distinction between the general issues of econ-omic welfare and productivity dealt with by the *Nationalökonomie* taught in universities, and the principles informing the rational management of economic enterprises. The absence of a clear frame-work for the latter task had been one of the principal reasons for the foundation of the Handelshochschulen, argued Prion, but the problem of the appropriate level of instruction in these new institu-tions persisted.[74]

Later in the same year Lujo Brentano published an attack on these developments which, while seriously confused, demonstrated that the development of a new commercial *Privatwirtschaftslehre* was not uncontested. Referring to a review by Schär of Weyermann and Schönitz, in which criticism was raised of the general and abstract nature of *Volkswirtschaftslehre*, Brentano pretended that these comments could only apply to what he called 'state socialist' thinkers, for whom he could not answer. Confusion was deepened by his insistence that *Nationalökonomie* dealt with an economic totality, whereas a commercial *Privatwirtschaftslehre* was in thrall to special interests. It was, argued Brentano, important to retain the perspective of the economy as a whole:

---

[73] The book under review was M. Weyermann and H. Schönitz, *Grundlegung und Systematik einer wissenschaftlichen Privatwirtschaftslehre und ihre Pflege an Universitäten und Fachhochschulen*, Karls-ruhe 1912. I have not been able to trace a copy of this work. Textbooks are a curious form of literature: when new they are commonplace and familiar, when old, extremely rare and esoteric. This is probably because they are one of the few forms of literature which librarians are willing to discard, making space for ever-newer textbooks.

[74] W. Prion, 'Wissenschaftliche Privatwirtschaftslehre', Part 1, *Deutsche Wirtschafts-Zeitung*, Jg. 8 (1912), cols. 211–14.

[Those entrusted with new teaching positions in this new branch of economics] ... should constantly treat their material from the standpoint of the general interest, and never from the private interest of the individual enterprises – otherwise the differences among special interests will necessarily lead to a complete degeneration of the science.[75]

This naturally completely miscontrues the issues at stake, a situation not assisted by a reply from Richard Ehrenberg, an early leader of the movement for commercial education, which argued that the conditions for economic viability were identical for both individual enterprise and national economy, and there was therefore no requirement for a new business economics.[76] Other contributions during the years 1912 and 1913 sought to define the principles of a new *Privatwirtschaftslehre*, adding little clarification to the substantive issues at stake, apart from indicating, by their existence, that there was some dispute concerning the purpose and scope of economics as hitherto taught in universities.[77]

In these exchanges little is registered except the existence of a disagreement over the utility of general economic concepts in the business of enterprise organisation. Academic economics as taught in the universities might provide workable explanations of the general foundations of economic activity, but it did not supply those whose task it was to manage economic enterprises with a framework in whose terms they might judge the economic rationality of their activities. Then, as now, mainstream economic principles did not furnish businessmen and officials with a coherent framework for decision-making. The curricular development of the Handelshochschulen had, on the other hand, been directed to the elaboration of a new commercial science adapted to the functional requirements of

[75] L. Brentano, 'Privatwirtschaftslehre und Volkswirtschaftslehre', *Bank-Archiv*, Jg. 12 (1912), p. 4.
[76] R. Ehrenberg, 'Keine "Privatwirtschaftslehre"!', *Bank-Archiv* Jg. 12 (1912) pp. 55–7.
[77] See for example K. Diehl, 'Nationalökonomie und Handelsbetriebslehre', *Jahrbücher für Nationalökonomie und Statistik*, III Folge, Bd. 43 (1912), pp. 94–112; E. Schmalenbach, 'Die Privatwirtschaftslehre als Kunstlehre', *Zeitschrift für Handelswissenschaftliche Forschung*, Jg. 6 (1911/12), pp. 304–16; J. F. Schär, 'Das Verhältnis der Nationalökonomie zur Privatwirtschaftslehre im allgemeinen und zur Handelsbetriebslehre im besonderen', *Deutsche Wirtschafts-Zeitung*, Jg. 9 (1913), cols. 513–22; K. Diehl, 'Privatwirtschaftslehre, Volkswirtschaftslehre, Weltwirtschaftslehre', *Jahrbücher für Nationalökonomie und Statistik*, III Folge, Bd. 46 (1913), pp. 435–82; A. Calmes, 'Die Entwicklung der Handelswissenschaft zur privatwirtschaftlichen Lehre der Erwerbswirtschaft', *Handels-Hochschul-Nachrichten*, (1913), pp. 13–17, 25–32; G. Obst, 'Verhältnis der Privatwirtschaftlehre zur Volkswirtschaftslehre', *Zeitschrift für Handelswissenschaft und Praxis*, Jg. 5, H. 12 (1913), pp. 357–62.

business organisation. As exposed in the textbooks of Schär and Weyermann and Schönitz, however, this seemed to offer little more than a descriptive account of the economic components of business and trading organisations, and an outline of the practices of business administration. Schär for example spent a considerable amount of time in his textbook recounting the development of economics and the fundamental principles of economic life before he finally reached the principles of business organisation.

Nicklisch's textbook was however quite different; not only did it distinguish itself on its first appearance by its focus on the organisation of the enterprise, but it made the 'commercial balance' the focus of its analysis. Prion in his review of the book suggested that it lacked an adequate definition of the enterprise, and a satisfactory review of enterprise forms. However, he considered the strength of the book to lie in its distinction of the capital of the enterprise from its property. Contemporary accounting practice treated the capital of a firm as its total stocks minus debts, equalling the net property of the enterprise or of the entrepreneur. In this approach, the sum appearing on the capital account could be distorted by the existence of capital held in other accounts, or by the existence of hidden reserves, which formed one of the major concerns of contemporary auditing practice. Nicklisch was not especially concerned with these problems of audit; he sought to identify the net *property* of the enterprise. This was equivalent to its stocks of goods, whether in the form of machinery, goods, or money, minus whatever debts existed at any one time, leaving an abstract accounting sum representing the net worth of the enterprise.[78] Nicklisch argued that a distinction could usefully be introduced between property and capital: the former as a concrete collection of goods, machinery, and money, while the latter was an accounting abstraction indicating only who owed what to whom.[79] The purpose of this distinction was to separate the physical assets of the enterprise off from the question of who, at any one time, might formally have title to portions of their value. Furthermore, the operation of the enterprise alters the relationship between the various forms in which the stocks were held. The composition of property could be broken down as land and machinery, turnover goods (cash,

[78] That is to say, this represented an attempt to arrive at a conception of the value of the enterprise as a going concern, independently of any valuation based upon share prices or upon conventional methods of depreciation and write-offs.

[79] W. Prion, 'Kaufmännische Betriebslehre', *Handels-Hochschul-Nachrichten*, (1913), p. 66.

money of account, commodities, bills of exchange), guarantees, and reserves, and then cast up in terms of profitability, liquidity, and security, presenting an image of the viability and profitability of the enterprise separate from any balance sheet representation. Depending on the particular type of enterprise concerned (whether it be an insurance company or a wholesaler), it was then possible to divide up the enterprise as components of capital with varied earning capacities. This approach to the profitability and viability of the enterprise opened the way to a reconstruction of the commercial sciences around the going concern as the object of analysis.

The outbreak of war in 1914 temporarily halted discussion of these and related issues, but by 1919 a review of the teaching practice in the Handelshochschulen indicated that a degree of standardisation had taken place, centred on the model contained in the regulations agreed in 1912 for Berlin, Cologne and Frankfurt. *Privatwirtschaftslehre*, *Volkswirtschaftslehre*, and law were here the foundation of commercial curriculum, the first of these being described as 'the specialised discipline of the Handelshochschulen'.[80] By 1921 Nicklisch was talking, in a public lecture to students of the Berlin Handelshochschule, of a new name for this discipline – *Betriebswirtschaftslehre*, a name 'which will rapidly find general acceptance'.[81]

The sixth edition of his 1912 textbook appeared in 1922 with an altered title: *Wirtschaftliche Betriebslehre*. Its subject matter was defined in the first few lines of the introduction as follows:

Alongside *Volkswirtschaftslehre* there stands today *Betriebswirtschaftslehre*.

At the centre of this science is placed the undertaking (*die Unternehmung*), the enterprise (*der Betrieb*). This science seeks to investigate and represent the regularities of enterprise activities. It distinguishes those phenomena important to the internal life of the enterprise from those that are of significance when considering transactions (*Verkehr*) between enterprises.

... Business Economics (*wirtschaftliche Betriebslehre*) concerns itself above all with the economy (*Wirtschaftlichkeit*) of mental and manual labour performed in the enterprise, and with the distribution of the product of this labour among all those who have taken part in its production, whether through the provision of capital, or personally with direct activity.[82]

[80] F. Werner, 'Die Handelshochschule als Hochschule für die Verwaltung', in C. Eckert (ed.), *Der Eintritt der erfahrungswissenschaftlichen Intelligenz in die Verwaltung*, Ferdinand Enke, Stuttgart 1919, p. 111.

[81] H. Nicklisch, 'Betriebswirtschaftslehre. Was ist bei ihren Studium vor allem anderen zu beachten?', *Zeitschrift für Handelswissenschaft und Handelspraxis*, Jg. 14 (1921), p. 97. Public lecture to students of the Berlin Handelshochschule, 25 May 1921.

[82] H. Nicklisch, *Wirtschaftliche Betriebslehre*, 6th edn, C. E. Poeschel, Stuttgart 1922, p. 1.

The first section of the text presented the customary definitions of economics: man as the beginning and end of all economising activity, with the concepts of need, goods, value, and price given logical priority over consumption, production, and trade.[83] Nonetheless, due recognition is given to the principle of marginal utility, taking the discussion of value and price formation beyond the simple reiteration of platitudes concerning supply, demand, and markets. Once these basic economic principles have been got out of the way, the logical point of departure can be broached: the enterprise.

Textbooks are of course instruments for teaching, and as such are designed to present to unversed readers a structured introduction to their subject matter. There is usually little of great interest or novelty in them to attract the interest of practitioners or even of historians. The individual formulations that we can find in *Wirtschaftliche Betriebslehre* are certainly commonplace enough, but the overall organisation was, for its time, unusual, and illuminates the definite break that had been made with the more conventional university economics. The chapter headings provide some indication of this structure (see Table 5.3).

As can be seen from the outline of contents in Table 5.3, Nicklisch's textbook develops an economic analysis which progressively exposes the various activities of the enterprise. Beginning with a definition of *Betrieb* that equates it with human economic activity, the argument moves quickly into more substantive distinctions between enterprise forms and the particular issues that they pose – whether, for example, they are created to transform their property into commodities (manufacturing) or maintain it (banking and insurance).[84] A further distinction is then introduced, that of the firm or trading company, a legal entity with relations with other forms of enterprise. This then leads to a discussion of the capital and property of the firm, and the manner in which the activities of the firm alter the composition of its capital over time through the linked processes of production and turnover.

The internal organisation of the enterprise is dealt with first through a consideration of labour, its management and productivity, and then more abstractly by chapters on the various forms of assets possessed by the enterprise, their composition and valuation. The 'movement of value' represents the production activities of the

[83] 'Man is the beginning and end of all economic activity . . . ' *Ibid.*, p. 5.
[84] *Ibid.*, pp. 47–8.

Table 5.3. *Contents of Nicklisch's* Wirtschaftliche Betriebslehre *(1922)*

1. The Foundations of Business Economics
   a) Need, Commodity, Value, Price
   b) Consumption and Generation of Value; Trade
   c) The Organisation of Economic Activity
2. The Undertaking; the Enterprise
   a) Forms and Types of Enterprise; the Firm
   b) Labour in the Enterprise
   c) Capital and Assets
   d) The Movement of Value through the Enterprise; Productivity and Profit
3. The Organisation of Labour
   a) Division of Labour
   b) Scientific Management (*wissenschaftliche Betriebsführung*)
   c) Wage and Performance
4. The Organisation of Assets
   a) The Composition of Assets
   b) The Determination of Asset Value
   c) Enterprise Involvement in Assets
5. The Progress of Value
   a) The General Movement of Value
   b) The Composition of Value Movements
   c) Cost Theory
   d) Important Aspects of Circulation
6. The Yield
   a) Productivity
   b) Security, Risk and Liquidity
7. Bookkeeping and Statistics
   a) Balance and Inventory
   b) Statistics

enterprise, in which the assets are deployed together with labour to create a return, the scale of which is determined by the costs of production. Having presented the economic activity of the enterprise in this fashion, the result of its functioning can then be summarised under the heading of performance, or 'yield' – and not, it has to be emphasised, profitability, which is in this perspective a quite different matter.[85] The distinction between own and alien capital, originally

---

[85] Discussion in Chapter 6 does consider *Rentabilität*, which is often translated as profitability, but in this context such a translation would be misleading. Nicklisch uses the term *Rentabilität* in the sense of 'economic viability', assessing the various elements of enterprise organisation with respect to their contribution to overall performance, or balance, of the enterprise. 'Profitability' should here be reserved for an evaluation of alterations to the book value of the enterprise as a whole; it is an abstract accounting magnitude, rather than an aspect of departmental turnover.

discussed by Prion in his review of the 1912 edition, is used by Nicklisch to discriminate between the financial performance of the enterprise's assets, and the actual economic viability of the enterprise.[86]

The final chapter of the book deals with cost accounting: the proper attribution of costs and revenue to the internal accounts of the enterprise, establishing the viability of the enterprise as an economic, rather than a financial unit. The conception of the dynamic balance sheet, introduced by Schmalenbach, here provides a means of evaluating the enterprise as such, rather than the capital of the entrepreneur. The focus of this approach is on the performance of the enterprise as a complex process of production and turnover, in which the function of accounting is to identify the precise areas in which yields are generated and losses made. The assumption lying behind this approach is that no reliable long-term judgement can be made from a simple setting of costs, stock, and debt against revenue from sales. As Nicklisch forcefully maintains, the concept of balance can only be derived from the 'organic apprehension of all enterprise phenomena.'[87] Nicklisch's textbook terminates in a detailed discussion of accounting theory and enterprise statistics, the purpose of which is to render the balance sheet as a proper reflection of the viability of the enterprise as a physical entity.

Nicklisch's textbook draws together the various elements of the commercial sciences and provides them with a systematic framework. Much of the inspiration for this does however come from the work of Eugen Schmalenbach, who developed a new approach to enterprise accounting methods known as 'Dynamic Accounting', but who never generalised them into a systematic and comprehensive analytical structure.[88] Schmalenbach's point of departure was the argument that accounting theory had hitherto treated the factory as a fixed sum of capital that, over time, produced money. If the enterprise was viewed in this manner as a *Geldfabrik*, its sole purpose was conceived as the production of profit; but viewed as a machine for producing profit, it was not at all clear what the source of this profit might be. The development of industrial techniques had increased the role of production costs in establishing the profitability of an enterprise; and, as a result of this shift in the composition of assets, emphasis had

---

[86] Nicklisch, *Wirtschaftliche Betriebslehre*, p. 225.   [87] *Ibid.*, p. 274.
[88] See for an outline of Schmalenbach's work S. Hundt, *Zur Theoriegeschichte der Betriebswirtschaftslehre*, Bund Verlag, Köln 1977, Chapter 2.

shifted away from the exploitation of the price mechanism and markets to the regulation of the production process as the route to profitability. Schmalenbach's argument was that the entrepreneur could not do very much to influence prevailing market conditions, but he was on the other hand in a stronger position to have a direct influence upon enterprise performance. This could only be achieved, however, if the actual economic performance (*wirtschaftliche Leistung*) of the enterprise could be isolated from external contingencies. The basic principles of Schmalenbach's project can be summarised as firstly, the isolation of enterprise performance from market conditions; and secondly, the establishment of a clear dynamic framework within which enterprise performance could be assessed. The role of the balance sheet here was therefore not the determination of asset value, but rather of profit and the overall level of activity.[89] These were, and remained, essentially problems in accounting theory and practice; but when linked to the progressive detachment of commercial science from *Volkswirtschaftslehre*, it provided the means to knit together the apprehension of the enterprise as the object of economic analysis.

Schmalenbach had published his first article on the problem of costs, distinguishing costs of production according to their variation with scale and time, while studying at the Leipzig Handelshochschule. He returned to this theme in an article published during 1908, arguing that in the determination of production costs the first task must be to identify the manner in which they alter with scale and time – are they proportional to output, fixed, degressive, or progressive?[90] Once the various technical and physical factors generating these differing cost levels had been distinguished it was possible, argued Schmalenbach, to proceed to the pricing of input. The accepted accounting practice here was to employ historic costs, attributing costs of production on the basis of the actual costs of acquisition of the factors of production. Quite plainly, however, where the price of the input was subject to fluctuations, the use of such prices would obscure the viability of the enterprise, and he consequently argued that replacement costs current at the time of consumption should be used, rather than actual costs.

[89] See A. Schranz, 'Modern German Accountancy', *Accounting Review*, vol. 5 (1930), p. 165.
[90] E. Schmalenbach, 'Theorie der Produktionskosten-Ermittelung', *Zeitschrift für Handelswissenschaftliche Forschung*, Jg. 3 (1908), pp. 41–4. 'Degressive' costs increase at a lower rate than output, ie. marginal costs are below average costs. 'Progressive' costs are where costs increase at a higher rate than that of output, since marginal cost is above prevailing average costs.

A paid price is nothing but a reminiscence of an act of sale. It is not a property hewing to the object, and is certainly not its value. Value is a relation of one thing to other things. This relationship does not possess the thing *in concreto*. The value of an object, kept under lock and key, changes in just the same way as the value of the same object in the marketplace. If we use the object, then we use a value – not a historical value, but rather an actual, real value.[91]

An article published the following year elaborated upon this line of argument. Schmalenbach argued that it was necessary to make a clear distinction between the function of the price mechanism in market co-ordination (and as treated by *Volkswirtschaftslehre*) and the quite different problems of internal enterprise co-ordination and administration; here market prices were not necessarily reliable, and a range of imputed prices had to be deployed.[92]

Once more, it was the intervention of overlapping time periods which created this need, such that costs and revenues might fall in differing periods, while the process of production and stockbuilding itself imposed constraints upon the accounting framework. In Schmalenbach's schema, assets are conceived as deferred charges, and liabilities as obligations to perform future services; they are treated as flows and not stocks. The dynamic balance sheet treats costs and revenue likewise as elements of turnover, in which there is a complex interaction between, for example, output for which no revenue has been received, and revenue for which no output has yet been produced. The periodisation of costs and expenditures had to be properly taken into account if, beneath these complementary but unrelated flows of cash and goods, the fundamental viability of the enterprise was to be determined. The balance was not simply a memory aid: rather, 'it shows us, in a manner of speaking, the reserves stored in the undertaking. It shows the relationship of active and passive reserves.'[93]

Schmalenbach never produced a synthesis of his work, nor was it reprinted extensively in an accessible form. But it should be evident from the foregoing that the principles that he advocated in the creation and evaluation of the enterprise balance sheet were complementary to the efforts to create a curriculum for the Handelshochschulen independent of the economics taught in the university.

[91] *Ibid.*, p. 52.
[92] E. Schmalenbach, 'Über Verrechnungspreise', *Zeitschrift für Handelswissenschftliche Forschung*, Jg. 3 (1909), pp. 165–85.
[93] E. Schmalenbach, 'Grundlagen dynamischer Bilanzlehre', *Zeitschrift für Handelswissenschaftliche Forschung*, Jg. 13 (1919), p. 26.

Initially conceived as, at most, a branch of *Volkswirtschaftslehre*, *Privatwirtschaftslehre* developed into a *Betriebswirtschaftslehre* that became the core of the commercial curriculum. The uneasy combination of general economic principles with the practical techniques of the counting house that had marked Leipzig's initial teaching was, within twenty years of the first commercial courses, entirely superseded. By the beginning of the 1920s the Handelshochschulen were rapidly expanding, and teaching a standardised curriculum centred around the new commercial science of BWL, the new business economics. The regulations for the Diplom-Kaufmann introduced in the 1920s had four compulsory areas: General BWL, Special BWL, law, and economics.[94] Having established BWL as the core of the curriculum, economics could be re-introduced as a distinct, but related, examination subject.

The story does not end there, however, for over this same period university economics had not been static. It has already been noted in passing that economics was taught in universities primarily to students of law, who were obliged to take a course of introductory economics as part of their qualification to sit the state examination in law. There was however no state examination in economics, and those who wished to study the subject had to proceed directly to a doctorate. During 1900–1 some twenty-five doctorates in economics were awarded in Prussian universities, the number rising to seventy-eight in the year before the outbreak of war.[95] The creation of the Universities of Cologne and Frankfurt shortly after the end of the war greatly increased the number of students reading economics in universities: by the winter semester of 1919–20 Weber estimated that there were 1,660 such students in Berlin, 1,600 in Frankfurt, and 1,250 in Cologne. Obst extrapolated these figures and concluded that some 6,000 students might be seeking to gain a doctorate in economics during the years 1920–23.[96] The strength of student demand was not the sole problem: given the existence of the Handelshochschulen, it was no longer entirely clear what function was served by the teaching of economics at university level, and the nature of the demand. There

[94] A. W. Fehling, 'Collegiate Education for Business in Germany', *Journal of Political Economy*, vol. 34 (1926), p. 575.

[95] Figures taken from Adolf Weber's contribution to the volume edited by Jastrow, *Die Reform der staatswissenschaftlichen Studien, Schriften des Vereins für Sozialpolitik*, Bd. 160, Duncker und Humblot, Munich 1920, p. 58.

[96] G. Obst, 'Die Reform des wirtschaftswissenschaftlichen Studiums', *Zeitschrift für Handelswissenschaft und Handelspraxis*, Jg. 13, H. 5 (1920), p. 97.

was an evident requirement for some kind of reform in the study and teaching of economics, and at its meeting in 1919 the management committee of the Verein für Sozialpolitik appointed Jastrow to assemble a volume of commentary and opinion on the subject. This would be circulated in advance of the meeting for 1920, at which the issues it highlighted would form the main theme for discussion.

In his contribution to Jastrow's report Eckert identified four chief objectives of teaching economics in universities:

(1) the economic education of future *Staats- und Gemeindebeamten* – judges, lawyers, and administrators. These persons would not be primarily concerned in their future career with economic affairs, but they did require a degree of economic understanding;

(2) the economic education of future business, commercial and agrarian personnel;

(3) the education of assistants and advisers to businessmen and administrators;

(4) the methodical development of a small but significant number of future economic theorists.[97]

The first group was adequately served by the conventional introductory economics teaching at universities, except that at some universities applied economics was too historical, barely passing beyond the early stages of agricultural and handwork production. However, the transfer of economics from the Philosophy Faculty to the Law Faculty, a process that had gained momentum shortly before the war, would eventually correct this. As for the second group, these would be better served by the existing teaching of the Handelshochschulen and other specialised institutions. The third and fourth group required by contrast more specialised tuition, on a broader basis than generally available at that time.

Jastrow in his contribution to the 1920 meeting proposed a wholesale overhaul of the relation of tuition in law and economics at university level, broadening the study of economics and thereby moderating premature specialisation for legal practice. He proposed a two-part teaching structure for economics, the first covering a more descriptive and applied treatment of economic phenomena, and the second dealing with more theoretical and specialised parts of economics. At the head of the first part he placed *Privatwirtschaftslehre*.[98]

[97] C. Eckert, 'Lehrziele und Lehrmittel der Volkswirtschaftslehre an der Universität Köln', in Jastrow, *Die Reform der staatswissenschaftlichen Studien*, pp. 36–7.

[98] I. Jastrow, 'Leitsätze über die Reform der staatswissenschaftlichen Studien', Verhandlungen der außerordentlichen Generalversammlung in Kiel 21 bis 23 September 1920, *Schriften des Vereins für Sozialpolitik*, Bd. 161, Duncker und Humblot, Munich 1921, p. 40.

Some eight years after the exchanges had taken place between Brentano and the proponents of this newly defined area of economic analysis, in which the validity of *Privatwirtschaftslehre* had been questioned, it was now being proposed as a foundation for economic study at university level.

By January 1922 agreement had been reached on the introduction of the new intermediary qualification of Diplom-Volkswirt. Proof of six semesters of study at a German university was required, and eight subjects for examination were listed, the eighth of which was *Privatwirtschaftslehre* – or, where tuition was not available, two other subjects chosen from a list including economic history, labour law, and insurance.[99] Students wishing to proceed to a doctoral examination had to study for a minimum of two further semesters, adding two semesters on to the previous minimum and hence diverting candidates from doctoral to Diplom-level qualification. These proposals were discussed at the inaugural meeting of economics teachers (*Dozenten der Wirtschaftswissenschaften an deutschen Hochschulen*) in September 1922,[100] and they then came into force in April 1923.

By the mid-1920s there were some 3,913 students of economics registered at the twelve Prussian universities, with an additional 2,009 studying BWL at Cologne and Frankfurt.[101] In the other universities facilities for the study of BWL were poorly developed, and it is reasonable to assume that the extension of teaching staff in no respect kept pace with student demand. The conclusion that one could draw from this could be that the inclusion of BWL within the Diplom-Volkswirt examination was an effective option only for students of economics in Cologne and Frankfurt. However, it should also be borne in mind that even before the war large numbers of university students attended lectures of the Berlin Handelshochschule as *Hospitanten*; for economics students in Berlin, Munich, or even Heidelberg for that matter, there was little difficulty in gaining access to lectures in *Betriebswirtschaftslehre*.

The creation of an Economics *Diplom* provided for the first time a means of qualifying in economics at sub-doctoral level. Teaching in

99 The terms agreed at the Meiningen conference are reprinted in A. Weber, 'Das Diplomexamen für Volkswirte', *Jahrbücher für Nationalökonomie und Statistik*, III. Folge, Bd. 65 (1923), pp. 302ff.

100 See L. Pohle, 'Diplomprüfung für Volkswirte und staatswissenschaftliche Promotion', *Jahrbuch für Gesetzgebung, Verwaltung und Volkswirtschaft*, Jg. 46 (1922), pp. 861–74.

101 F. Schmidt, 'Die Zukunft der Betriebswirtschaftslehre', in Fs. Robert Stern, *Zur Entwicklung der Betriebswirtschaftslehre*, Berlin 1925, p. 149. He also noted that there were thirty-eight full Professors of Economics in Prussian universities, as against eight full Professors of Betriebswirtschaftslehre.

economics was just completing its transfer from Philosophy to Law Faculties; but the new *Diplom* opened out the teaching of economics beyond the needs of law students, and so it was only a matter of time before this teaching was relocated in independent social science faculties. The existence of the Handelshochschulen, with their two-year *Diplom*, undoubtedly played a role in this, but a discrepancy between the Handelshochschulen and universities still existed, since students in the former institutions studied for a minimum of four semesters, and not six. This disparity was soon eradicated. In 1924 new regulations extended the minimum number of semesters required for admission to the Diplom-Kaufmann examinations at the Handelshochschulen from four to six. At the same time, the qualifications of Diplom-Kaufmann, Diplom-Volkswirt and Diplomhandelslehrer were granted equal status for entry, after two semesters further study, to a doctoral examination.[102] In addition, the Handelshochschulen had altered their entry requirements so that only those in possession of an Abitur were eligible for entry into the Diplom examination; although by this time the majority of entrants to the Handelshochschulen possessed this school-leaving qualification. By the mid-1920s, barely two decades after their inception, reforms to curricula and examinations had narrowed the distance between the Handelshochschulen and the universities, although in this process both institutions had altered their character.

The evolutionary path followed by the Handelshochschulen did not entail a simple accommodation to existing university models of curricula and disciplines; convergence became possible because the Handelshochschulen created their own distinct discipline, and placed it at the centre of their teaching. This then had a significant impact on the reform of economics teaching in the universities, breaking its linkage with the law curriculum and laying the foundation for the development of the discipline of economics on a new basis. In France, on the other hand, where economics had likewise been taught in Law Faculties since the mid-nineteenth century, the role of economics as an auxiliary to the teaching of law prevailed until the later 1930s, when proposals were made for the creation of independent social science faculties.[103] Commercial colleges in France dated from the 1870s and early 1880s, but they had never developed an academic

---

[102] Fehling, 'Collegiate Education for Business in Germany', pp. 574–9.
[103] G. Pirou, 'Les Facultés de droit', in *L'Enseignement Économique en France et à l'étranger*, Special 50th Anniversary Issue of *Revue d'Économie Politique*, (1937), pp. 1–21.

character. Their teaching and organisation owed more to the spirit of a school than to that of a university: weekly exams were still the norm in the early 1900s, and it was only in the later 1920s that efforts were made to develop their organisation beyond the form originally created in the early 1870s.[104]

None of the Handelshochschulen survived the Second World War, the remaining institutions being incorporated into existing universities, or dissolved. The discipline which they had created nonetheless flourished in the postwar period, being elaborated during the 1950s with the incorporation of neo-classical price theory, operational research, and financial accounting: an amalgam that is still without any equivalent in British management education, where these topics are treated as strictly separate components of management science education. Whether the systematic combination of these and other related topics represents any pedagogical advantage is unclear; just as any direct linkage of educational provision to economic performance is, at this level, of dubious validity. Too many disturbing factors intervene: schooling, cultural selection, career structures, and the organisation of industry all play a role in the creation of managerial competence quite independently of the direct training which managers receive. Nonetheless, although we might conclude that the extent of the contribution made by German business education to the postwar successes of the German economy is, strictly speaking, indeterminate, that it has played a significant role seems well within the bounds of possibility.

[104] M. Meuleau, *Histoire d'une Grande Ecole*, HEC, Jouy-en-Josas 1981, pp. 66, 70. A three-year course in place of the existing two-year programme was first proposed in 1929.

CHAPTER 6

The Logical Structure of the Economic World – the rationalist economics of Otto Neurath

> I agree with your view that the previous form of free
> economy ... will not return, or if it does then heavily modified
> by financial or exchange considerations – not for any other. I
> will not shed a tear for if it should so turn out. But I judge the
> matter in a manner similar to Eulenburg ... and regard plans
> for a 'planned economy' as dilettantish, *objectively* as *absolutely
> irresponsible* recklessness of a kind that can discredit 'socialism'
> for a hundred years, and which will draw everything that
> might be realised now into the depths of crass reaction. That is
> what I unfortunately see coming, and here lies the difference
> between us. I fear that you contribute to the increase of this
> danger, which you massively underestimate.[1]

The World War of 1914–18 brought to a definite end the 'long'
nineteenth century and inaugurated the age of modernity. Many who
recognised this also assumed that nineteenth-century capitalism
would be replaced by a new form of twentieth-century, planned
economy; that the correlate of the modern world was an organised
economy in which rational deliberation would replace profit and the
market as the mechanism for the allocation of resources. The Russian
Revolution was but the most advanced form of this development;
radicals and socialists everywhere looked forward eagerly to the new
world that was opening up, a world of social, political, and economic
change in which the old constellation of forces no longer prevailed.
Industrial capitalism, creation of the nineteenth-century bourgeoisie,
was to be superseded by a more rational and egalitarian economic
order; and Max Weber was far from alone in his relative indifference
to the impending demise of capitalist organisation as it had developed
in the course of the nineteenth century.

[1] Letter of Max Weber to Otto Neurath, Munich 4 October 1919; *Gesammelte Politische Schriften*,
Drei Masken Verlag, Munich 1921, p. 488.

He did, however, view contemporary developments with the deepest foreboding. His lecture 'Politics as a Vocation', delivered to Munich students just a few days after the bloody suppression of the Spartakist rising and the murder of Luxemburg and Liebknecht,[2] hinged on a clear distinction between *Verantwortungs-* and *Gesinnungs-ethik*: between action based upon a sense of responsibility for its consequences, and action judged only in terms of an absolute morality and the cause which it served. This was not in itself an exclusive distinction, nor immediately applicable to contemporary events in Germany and Russia. But this 'carnival that adorns itself with the proud name of a "revolution" '[3] was seen by Weber as precipitate and impetuous, a flight into the future that would be rapidly and brutally overwhelmed by the forces of reaction which it provoked. A *Flucht nach vorn* on the part of radical groupings already threatened to shatter the prospects for democratic politics in the aftermath of war. Dilettantism in the transition from capitalism to socialism was at best likely to postpone, at worst destroy, the socialist project itself.

Otto Neurath, to whom Max Weber expressed this sentiment, is more usually remembered today as a member of the Vienna Circle, the co-author with Hans Hahn and Rudolf Carnap of its manifesto, *Wissenschaftliche Weltauffassung: Der Wiener Kreis*, and the moving spirit behind the *Encyclopedia of Unified Science*. As such, he shared in the Vienna Circle's dedication to scientific rationalism, a thorough-going logical empiricism that sought to rebuild philosophical reasoning on a logical basis adequate to developments in contemporary mathematics and physics. He had, however, also been for a period in 1919 head of the Central Planning Office of the short-lived Bavarian Soviet Republic. In July of the same year Weber had testified at his subsequent trial,[4] having been called by the defence as a character

---

[2] Rosa Luxemburg and Karl Liebknecht were murdered by soldiers on 19 January 1919 in Berlin. On 21 January Kurt Eisner, Prime Minister of the Bavarian 'Free State', had been assassinated by a rightist officer; his funeral took place in Munich on 26 January. Weber's lecture to Bavarian members of the Freistudentischer Bund was delivered in the shadow of these events, on 28 January – see W. Schluchter, 'Wertfreiheit und Verantwortungsethik. Zum Verhältnis von Wissenschaft und Politik bei Max Weber', in his *Rationalismus der Weltbeherrschung*, Suhrkamp Verlag, Frankfurt a. M. 1980, p. 238.

[3] Weber, 'Politik als Beruf', *Gesammelte Politische Schriften*, p. 435.

[4] Weber noted in evidence that Neurath had, in his most recent work, to some degree lost touch with reality. 'In the political arena and perhaps to some extent in economic affairs Neurath lacked a sense of proportion, since he really too easily permitted himself to be carried away by utopianism.' 'Zeugenaussage im Prozeß gegen Otto Neurath', in W. J. Mommsen (ed.), *Zur Neuordnung Deutschlands*, Max Weber Gesamtausgabe I, Bd. 16, p. 495.

witness on the basis of Neurath's contributions to the *Archiv für Sozialwissenschaft und Sozialpolitik*.[5] These contributions are alluded to by Weber in his letter, for it was Eulenburg who had vigorously contested Neurath's proposition that the wartime economy represented a qualitatively different form of economic organisation. Notwithstanding their differences, Weber did, however, take Neurath's arguments seriously; for it is Neurath's conception of natural economy that prompted Weber's critique of socialist calculation that appears in *Economy and Society*.

At almost exactly the same time, but quite independently of Max Weber, Ludwig von Mises drafted his renowned appraisal of socialist economic calculation, first published in the *Archiv* during 1920. Weber's arguments have attracted less attention than those of Mises, in part because of the context in which they were published. *Economy and Society* was conceived as a contribution to a multi-volume reference work and was itself unfinished at Weber's death. The section in which Weber's comments on natural economic calculation appear was first published in late 1921, by which time this type of formal demonstration of the impediments to effective socialist calculation was generally thought to have originated with Mises. The subsequent debate on market and planned economies was thus shaped largely in response to Mises' critique of socialist economy, and disregarded Weber's own contribution. But Weber's approach, while formally similar to that of Mises, has some important distinctive features.

Firstly, Weber's arguments are part of a general evaluation of forms of economic organisation left incomplete in his manuscripts at his death in April 1920. The manner in which *Economy and Society* was then prepared for publication by Max Weber's widow, and then, much later, Johannes Winckelmann, has long been a source of

---

[5] Neurath had completed his *Habilitation* in Heidelberg during the war and had, since 1918, announced courses in the 'Staats- und Kameralwissenschaften' section of the Philosophy Faculty. In the summer semester of 1918 he is recorded as offering lectures on 'Comparative Economics, with special reference to Eastern Europe and the Near East', and on the 'Theory of Administrative Economy', as well as classes on 'The Natural Economy of the Past and the War Economy of the Present'. However, at the back of the *Vorlesungsverzeichniß* there is a section giving the addresses of professors and *Privat-Dozenten*, and here Neurath is simply recorded as being on war service (*Anzeige der Vorlesungen der Grossh. Badischen Ruprechts-Karls-Universität zu Heidelberg für das Sommer-Halbjahr 1918*, pp. 23, 38, 44). In 1919 he entered his Vienna address, not exactly helpful for the Heidelberg student; he was in any case on remand during most of the 1919 summer semester. It can be doubted, therefore, whether Neurath ever did teach in Heidelberg, although he was certainly, as a *Privat-Dozent*, entitled to do so.

controversy.[6] Secondly, however, besides the formal structure of Weber's argument, we need to consider the context within which it was shaped and the function of the object of criticism, namely Neurath's conception of natural economy. Viewed in this way, from the perspective of Weber's critique of Neurath, the debate over market and planned economies of the 1920s and 1930s appears in a fresh light. Not least, Weber's critique of socialism, unlike that of von Mises, does not imply a denial of socialist values. There is in Weber no trace of von Mises' assumption that 'market forces' necessarily produce entirely benificent and rational outcomes. Weber's critique of central planning as a means for the rational allocation of resources is, on the contrary, firmly placed within his vision of modernity as an 'iron cage'. In this view, bureaucratisation is not a monopoly of planned economies, but is an inherent feature of all modern social and economic organisation, whether 'free market' or 'planned'. It makes no sense from this standpoint, therefore, to criticise the rationality of central planning through invocation of the allegedly inherent super- iority of market rationality, since the market mechanism is equally capable of generating its own forms of irrationality. Instead, 'rational planning' should be rejected as a means of preserving and extending those areas of modern life in which the rule of officials, managers, and those 'uninventive specialists' anticipated in the closing pages of the *Protestant Ethic and the 'Spirit' of Capitalism* can be resisted.

Neurath was not a Marxist economist; he did not derive his proposals for socialist economic administration from any specific political doctrine. His arguments for natural economy and the administration of economic life with respect to defined social ends derived from his belief in the essential rationality of 'modern man' and his ability purposefully to order the world in a socially optimal fashion. Weber's critique of socialist rationality therefore directly confronted the function of rationality in the modern world, and the clash of 'modern' and 'antimodern' forces within it.

Today, it is usual to view 'plan' and 'market' as polar forms of rational economic organisation; for Weber, on the other hand, neither could plausibly fulfil the claims to rationality and efficiency that they made. In his view, there was little to choose between 'planned' and 'market' bureaucracies, except that the latter held the prospect of

---

[6] See F. H. Tenbruck, 'Abschied von *Wirtschaft und Gesellschaft*', *Zeitschrift für die gesamte Staatswissenschaft*, Bd. 133 (1977), pp. 702–35.

keeping the 'iron cage' at bay. This is an altogether darker conception of modern economic organisation than that inherited from von Mises, and one which, at the close of the twentieth century, is proving more relevant to our understanding of the dilemmas of the modern world.[7]

It was evident to Max Weber, and many of his contemporaries, that no theoretical or practical blueprint could be found in existing socialist literature for the creation of a socialist economy. Neurath's proposals for economic organisation based on natural economic calculation therefore provided a unique focus for a critique of post-capitalist strategies. Marx's economic analyses had been deliberately focused on the self-dissolution of capitalism through the conditions and forces that it engendered, the 'developmental tendencies' of capitalism; the subsequent (socialist or communist) order was therefore not something to be planned for, it was a condition that would come about, that would happen. Accordingly, the construction of socialism was considered to be a political, and not an economic, task. Discussion of the future organisation of a socialist economy which went beyond the kind of vague nostrums formulated by Marx in his writings on the Paris Commune or in his *Critique of the Gotha Programme* was consequently ruled out. Too great an interest in the shape of the future raised questions of its relation to the present, and encouraged discussion of the manner in which a progression from capitalism to socialism might be deliberately set in train. Discussion of this kind was dismissed by orthodox Marxists as either utopian, or revisionist. Indeed, it was just this refusal to contemplate in any serious manner the nature of the coming socialist order that served to define Marxist orthodoxy, and not an allegiance to any particular doctrine derived from the corpus of Marx's work.

As the debate over Bernstein's 'revisionism' showed, Orthodox Marxism was constituted not by reference to Marx, but by reference to its Other, Revisionism, the hallmark of the latter being that it

---

[7] Don Lavoie's recent account of the planning debate in *Rivalry and Central Planning. The Socialist Calculation Debate Reconsidered* (Cambridge University Press, Cambridge 1985) perpetuates many of the misconceptions inherent in the standard history of the debate on market and plan, despite claims to the contrary. For example, Lavoie's treatment of non-Austrian economists as 'neo-classical' is anachronistic; this label properly belongs to the 1950s and 1960s, and is an inappropriate generalisation for the 1920s and 1930s. Secondly, the attempt to demonstrate a Marxist heritage for the association of socialism with planning is erroneous at several levels: Marx's writings themselves demonstrably fail to make such an association, indeed Marx's theoretical stance involved deep hostility to anything beyond the vaguest statements on a socialist future. As the case of Otto Neurath shows, and indeed of many contemporary admirers of the Soviet Union, it was quite possible to be an enthusiast for central planning without being in any sense a Marxist, or even a socialist in the accepted sense of the term.

sought to identify feasible strategies for a transition to socialism. What counted as Orthodox Marxism therefore shifted from time to time according to the substance of the 'revisionist' arguments to which it was opposed, maintaining the purity of orthodoxy through a constant repudiation of the feasible and pragmatic. Mises scornfully remarked in his essay that orthodox socialists thus placed themselves in the position of suggesting that 'in the land of milk and honey roast pigeon will fly into the mouths of the comrades, but they unfortunately neglect to demonstrate how this wonder will come about.'[8]

The manner in which needs would be assessed, and economic life organised for their satisfaction in a future socialist society, remained a matter for speculation on the part of socialists – and the orthodox Marxism forged under the direction of Kautsky, Plekhanov, and Lenin contained only the barest of outlines of the actual structure of the 'new order'. Furthermore, the economic categories with which they operated were geared only to the analysis of capitalism; while Marxism laid emphasis on the economic foundations of exploitation and class struggle, it remained mute when confronted with the economic structure of a possible future society, despite the fact that the economic organisation of socialist society was expected to deliver the material foundations for the enhanced social welfare and equality that would appear with the supersession of capitalism.

Serious discussion of the nature of socialist economic organisation was therefore left to the unorthodox, and the critics. Systematic analysis of the conditions for socialist economic administration was first conducted at the turn of the century, and these early contributions are usefully gathered together in Hayek's *Collectivist Economic Planning*, published in 1935. First in Hayek's collection is Pierson's essay, originally published in Dutch in 1902, in which attention is drawn to the problems involved in determining individual needs, exchanging goods, and making investment decisions in the absence of a universal equivalent.[9] This form of economic criticism was given further shape in 1909 by Barone in his famous article 'The Ministry of Production in the Collectivist State', which counterposed the free to the collectivist form of economic organisation. In the latter, all decisions associated with general welfare are made by a central

[8] L. von Mises, 'Die Wirtschaftsrechnung im sozialistischen Gemeinwesen', *Archiv für Sozialwissenschaft und Sozialpolitik*, Bd. 47 (1920), p. 86.
[9] N. G. Pierson, 'The Problem of Value in the Socialist Society', in F. A. von Hayek (ed.), *Collectivist Economic Planning*, George Routledge, London 1935, pp. 74ff.

agency, such that the intervention of a ministerial bureaucracy substitutes for the market mechanisms of the free economy. The problem posed by Barone therefore assumes the following form: how is the economy able to find an equilibrium state if all relevant decisions are taken not by economic subjects, but by state officials? The purpose and organisation of a 'collectivist' economy is for Barone subordinate to the principle that economic order demands the existence of equilibrium conditions, and his conclusion is that, since an equilibrium condition cannot result from the economic decisions of state officials, a socialist economy is not a real possibility.[10] Important in this line of argument from Barone is that the market mechanism is associated with the generation of equilibria, and that the function of a central plan is to imitate the process by which such equilibria are achieved. Barone's proof of the non-viability of socialist economic planning is consequently one whose validity depends on very restrictive assumptions concerning the function of market and plan.

These analytical demonstrations of the impracticality of a socialist economic order met with little response from the ranks of the socialist intelligentsia and Marxists, and it was not until 1920 that the issue was raised once more and given a comprehensive treatment in Mises' article. He began by establishing a series of structural conditions for the existence of a socialist economy. First among these was that means of production be the exclusive property of the community, their disposition and use being the responsibility of a specific state apparatus. This carried the implication that the state apparatus, unlike the 'free' owner of producer goods, was exclusively concerned with the needs and requirements of other economic agents; the option of the free agent to either produce, consume, or not produce at all was denied to the state agency. Its imperative was to satisfy the needs of its population, although these needs could not be easily specified, nor was it clear how available resources should be allocated. As Mises observed, 'Who should consume, and what each should consume, this is the socialist distributional problem.'[11] He also noted that a founding principle of socialism was the fact that no conversion could be effected from factor contributions to distributive shares, since it was not evident that the needs and capacities of an individual were matched to each other. In a free market economy this problem could be resolved through an economic calculus, making use of the prevailing

[10] E. Barone, 'The Ministry of Production in the Collectivist State', in Hayek, *Collectivist Economic Planning*, pp. 245–90.   [11] Mises, 'Wirtschaftsrechnung', p. 88.

system of wages and prices; but socialism was meant to do away with the inequalities that this system generated. The socialist distributional problem identified by Mises became therefore a political, rather than an economic issue, and hence a non-issue in the appraisal of socialist economic organisation. So far as the proponents of socialist economic organisation were concerned, the crucial feature from the economic point of view was that all agents received a transfer from the community; the details of the calculation and composition of this transfer was not thought to be of any relevance.

Assuming for the sake of argument that all received equal amounts, corrected for differentials arising from age, sex, and health, Mises pointed out that exchanges could take place between agents with respect to these consumer goods, either directly (in kind), or indirectly (in the form of the certificates allocated to each agent); hence there was space for the existence of money as a means of exchange and allocation. Money would here be a general means of exchange signalling the need for the redistribution of resources, and this process would generate prices in a 'grey' market which the central authority would have to take into consideration when allocating goods. The task of the central authority was thus not only to achieve a 'just' distribution of goods, it also had to take account of the effects of its own activities with respect to the economy. The existence of monetary calculation as a means of administrative calculation was however applicable only to consumer goods, for here needs could be identified and the grey market used to monitor the impact of allocative decisions. Producer goods, however, did not enter into exchange in this way, so there was no means of checking allocative efficiency; decision-making with respect to producer goods was therefore entirely administrative and not susceptible to monetary calculation.[12] Labour time could not be used as an alternative measure or standard, since labour was heterogeneous and irreducible to a single unit of comparison. In any case, as had already been established, factor contributions in the sphere of production were independent of general calculations of allocation in the economy as a whole. In whatever manner this problem was resolved, the central authority was faced with the dilemma that it could not employ a universal valorising standard in its calculations, but had to employ at least two incommensurable standards.

[12] *Ibid.*, p. 90

It is an illusion to believe that monetary calculation could be replaced by calculation in kind (*Naturalrechnung*) in a socialist economy. In a non-commercial economy calculation in kind can only apply to consumer goods, it fails completely at the level of higher-order goods. As soon as free price formation for higher-order goods is abandoned, rational production is made impossible. Every step that leads us away from separate ownership of the means of production and from the use of money also leads us away from rational economy. . . . Without economic calculation no economy. Since the implementation of economic calculation is impossible in the socialist community, an economy cannot exist in our sense at all.[13]

In the subsequent debate economic theorists, such as Oskar Lange and Fred Taylor,[14] argued that monetary calculation with respect to producer goods on the part of the central authority was indeed possible, utilising the price mechanism as a planning instrument – and discussion of the economics of planning has since the 1920s, in fact, turned almost entirely on this calculative interface of market and plan.

But as is evident from the above, Mises not only emphasised the non-universality of monetary calculation, he also specifically denied the applicability of calculation in kind. In doing so, he was not referring to the contemporary attempt in Russia to build a direct path to socialism through a 'Proletarian Natural Economy' under conditions of War Communism;[15] he had in mind the wartime German economy, in which the allocation of key goods and raw materials had become the task of a government bureaucracy. In Britain, the organisation of the economy for war occurred in a piecemeal and gradual fashion;[16] it was assumed that the most pressing economic problem posed by the onset of war and its future conduct was financial, and this assumption was one shared by politicians and economists alike.[17] Neither German politicians nor German economists saw things this way. In August 1914 the German government

[13] *Ibid.*, pp. 99–100.
[14] Fred Taylor's 1928 Presidential Address to the American Economic Association, 'The Guidance of Production in a Socialist State' was republished, together with Oskar Lange's essay in the *Review of Economic Studies*, vol. 4 (1936–37) as *On the Economic Theory of Socialism*, University of Minnesota Press, Minneapolis 1938.
[15] For a discussion of this neglected phase of the Russian Revolution see A. Hussain and K. Tribe, *Marxism and the Agrarian Question*, 2nd edn, Macmillan, London 1983, pp. 259–63.
[16] See T. Wilson, *The Myriad Faces of War*, Polity Press, Cambridge 1988, Chapters 20, 21.
[17] It is evident from the pages of the Royal Economic Society's *Economic Journal* that British economists considered their expertise most appropriately applied to questions of war finance. This formed the centre of discussion on the outbreak of war and continued to play an important part throughout the war, especially of course in the work of the *EJ*'s editor, Maynard Keynes.

sought to gain immediate control of the allocation of strategic commodities, and to this end they established the *Kriegsrohstoffabteilung* (KRA) as an agency with centralised control of raw materials. Although a section of the War Ministry, its activities were modelled upon the management practices of the Allgemeine Elektricitäts-Gesellschaft (AEG), one of Germany's greatest industrial combines, and it was headed by Walther Rathenau, who was himself Director of the AEG. The swift action of the German government in taking control of the allocation of raw materials, and hence of the composition of output, was without parallel in France or in Britain.

German economists did pay attention to the financial and monetary implications of a protracted war, but discussion quickly turned to the structural impact of war on production and employment. As Emil Lederer noted,

However important this organisation of technical means for the process of circulation and maintenance of the credit system is ... one should not forget that currency and credit are only the rails upon which economic life rolls, and that a shock that goes to the core of economic life itself cannot be stabilised through simple adjustments to monetary policy and currency.[18]

Lederer noted that the mobilisation of men into the armed services reduced the manpower available to industry and agriculture, while at the same time dislocating production by alterations in demand. Transport and trade were likewise thrown into disarray, and added to the changed structure of demand unavoidable constraints in the adaptation of supply. This created a situation of crisis, but with the peculiarity that the armed services had an overriding priority in the consumption of food and munitions.[19] In these circumstances Lederer proposed a variety of measures to moderate the rigidities resulting from this novel constellation of forces, involving credit, co-operation between sectors of the economy, price controls, and emergency modifications to commercial law. Another article in the same year directed attention to the problems of food supply, pointing out, for example, that restrictions in the consumption of bread generated increased demand for other foodstuffs.[20]

These and other issues were taken up in a subsequent essay by Franz Eulenburg which focused on the dislocation occasioned by the

[18] E. Lederer, 'Die Organisation der Wirtschaft durch den Staat im Kriege', *Archiv für Sozialwissenschaft und Sozialpolitik*, Bd. 40 (1915), p. 118.   [19] *Ibid.*, p. 127.
[20] E. Lederer, 'Die Regelung der Lebensmittelversorgung während des Krieges in Deutschland', *Archiv für Sozialwissenschaft und Sozialpolitik*, Bd. 40 (1915), p. 779.

war in the spheres of consumption, price formation, production, and finance. This systematised and extended the points raised by Lederer, drawing attention to the manner in which wartime economic organisation could only be provisional in nature. While, for example, the increase of government procurement boosted economic activity, Eulenburg argued that this was at the cost of private consumption and long-term private investment.[21] The normal functioning of market economies was therefore not superseded by wartime economic organisation, merely suspended – a point reiterated in a direct reply to Neurath a year later.[22]

The work of the KRA exemplified this principle, for it presupposed the continuing existence of market mechanisms, albeit in a heavily modified form. Typically, the option between market and plan is assumed to counterpose business rationality with bureaucratic rationality, such that one of the sources of inefficiency in plan-oriented decision-making is considered to be the remoteness of state officials from market forces and managerial practices. This is for instance the guiding assumption of Hayek's famous critique of socialism, *The Road to Serfdom*.[23] A polarity between market and plan set up in this way disregards, however, the increasing degree of planful activity inherent in developed market-based economies. As business historians recognise, the increasing size of private enterprises towards the end of the nineteenth century had the effect of reducing contact with market mechanisms, and hence reduced the flow of information required for effective managerial decision-making. The development of modern corporate structures and accounting procedures was induced by the need to establish internal structures and procedures that would provide the information required for rational decision-making, in the

---

[21] F. Eulenburg, 'Zur Theorie der Kriegswirtschaft. Ein Versuch', *Archiv für Sozialwissenschaft und Sozialpolitik*, Bd. 43 (1916/17), p. 395. Eulenburg noted that this essay outlined arguments that would be developed in his forthcoming contribution on 'War Economy' for the *Grundriß der Sozialökonomik*, edited of course by Max Weber.

[22] F. Eulenburg, 'Die wissenschaftliche Behandlung der Kriegswirtschaft', *Archiv für Sozialwissenschaft und Sozialpolitik*, Bd. 44 (1918), pp. 775–85.

[23] Routledge and Kegan Paul, London 1944. Hayek treats the plan as the outcome of collectivist politics, and ignores the implications for market mechanisms of developments in German and American industry after 1900. His image of the market is the economic corollary of his formalised conception of the rule of law. While in the nineteenth century such constructs represented an ideal-typical representation of legal and economic institutions, this was no longer true of the twentieth, as Max Weber clearly perceived. Hayek's critique is thus essentially utopian in character, since it bases a critique of mid-twentieth-century economic management upon nineteenth-century ideal types.

absence of reliable market signals.[24] Rathenau's AEG was an early, but not unique, exemplar of this trend. The business-orientation of the KRA was lent further emphasis by the way in which Rathenau staffed it with managers seconded from German industry. The German war economy can thus be characterised as one in which central state planning was conducted in combination with large-scale private organisations, adapting modern business procedures to the task of co-ordinating a wartime economy.

During the first two years of its operations the command exercised by the KRA over the disposal of raw materials succeeded in maintaining a balanced output of munitions while slowly increasing productive capacity. However, the British resources mobilised during the Battle of the Somme in July 1916 made a powerful impression on the Germans, leading to criticism of the direction of the war economy. As a result of this Hindenberg was appointed Chief of Staff in August 1916, with Ludendorff his Quartermaster General, who took immediate steps to alter established War Ministry policies. The 'Hindenberg Programme' was formulated, proposing a doubling of the output of munitions, and a tripling of output of machine guns and artillery, by the spring of 1917. The net outcome of this attempt to raise output dramatically by simply doubling and trebling planned production levels met, initially, with modest success. During the course of the winter, however, these measures contributed to a progressive dislocation of transport and supply, slowing the completion of new productive capacity and tying-up resources in large numbers of half-finished factories.[25] Such attempts to raise output by *diktat*, and the inevitable subsequent progressive dislocation of production and consumption, later became a notorious feature of Stalinist economic management; but it turns out that this particular form of planful disorder was invented not by the Russians, but the Germans. It seems in retrospect ironic that these prototypical failures of macroeconomic management should have first been rehearsed by Ludendorff acting in the name of Hindenberg, who later became the figurehead of the German Right.

Many radicals saw the wartime coalition of government and big

[24] The most accessible account of this process is the work of Alfred Chandler, especially his *The Visible Hand*, Harvard University Press, Cambridge, Mass. 1977.
[25] G. D. Feldman, Army, *Industry and Labor in Germany 1914–1918*, Princeton University Press, Princeton, NJ 1966, pp. 149–54.

industry as signalling the demise of competitive capitalism – the capitalism for which Max Weber would 'not shed a tear'.[26] The generally acknowledged early success of the KRA in directing the production and distribution of steels, coal, building materials, and foodstuffs added further weight to arguments that, in the wake of the war, centralised direction of the economy should be carried over into the task of meeting the needs of a peacetime economy. It was in this climate of opinion that Otto Neurath's arguments became pre-eminent, for he had been developing his proposals for 'natural economic calculation' since 1909, when he first formulated his conception of 'war economy'. Neurath treated 'war economy' as an ideal-typical form of economic organisation that emerged in response to the economic conditions of modern warfare; his arguments thus had a more general character than those of his contemporaries reacting to the experiences of the 1914–18 war. The establishment of the KRA exemplified his arguments, rather than prompted their elaboration. The manner in which Neurath's conception of war economy underlies his later arguments on socialist economic calculation, but predates the war, calls for some discussion of the genesis of his ideas, before proceeding to a consideration of the way in which his conclusions were criticised by Max Weber.

Otto Neurath was born in Vienna in 1882, the son of Wilhelm Neurath, a self-taught teacher of economics. From 1901 he studied mathematics at the University of Vienna, where he struck up friendships with Philipp Frank and Hans Hahn. He took his doctorate in Berlin, submitting a dissertation in 1906 on 'Ancient Conceptions of Trade, Commerce and Agriculture'; he then returned to Vienna where he began in 1907 to teach at the Neue Wiener Handelsakade-mie, marrying in the same year Anna Schapire, with whom he co-edited in 1910 a popular reader of economic doctrine. The yearbook of the Akademie for that year also contained an article by Neurath which proposed that the conditions of economic organisation in societies at war could be systematised into a theory of 'war economy' (*Kriegswirtschaftslehre*), and this was to be the first of some forty-five pieces devoted to this theme. In 1912 he gained a Carnegie grant to develop his work on the nature of 'war economy', and part of the year was spent travelling in the Balkans. Soon after his mobilisation in

---

[26] Rathenau himself contributed to the cultural-critical literature which supposed that the free market economy was a relic of the past – see his *Autonome Wirtschaft*, Eugen Diederichs, Jena 1919.

1914 he managed to persuade his commanding general that the prevailing wartime conditions represented a golden opportunity to develop research into war economies – and this led to the formation of a section in the War Ministry dedicated to the study of the war economy run by Neurath. In fact, by this time Neurath already had an established reputation as the originator of the theory of 'war economy', having published an entry on the subject in a popular encyclopedia as well as an article in a major academic journal.[27]

The most important articles on this theme were however collected in a book published in 1919 entitled *Through War Economy to Natural Economy*, where the introduction, dated April 1919, states that 'the present book assembles essays which contribute to the idea that the time of free economy (*Verkehrswirtschaft*) is coming to an end, and that the time of administrative economy is beginning, money economy is dissolving, making way for a thoroughly organised natural economy.'[28] The first of the essays is reprinted from the *Weltwirtschaftliches Archiv* of 1913, and describes the nature of 'war economy' as a separate discipline. Here Neurath notes that economic studies had never paid any attention to war, nor had there been any systematic attempt to study the effect of war on industry, trade, and agriculture. War had always been treated as an accidental phenomenon, even in Sombart's *Krieg und Kapitalismus* of 1913; but an adequate comparative framework for the study of economic systems should include 'war economy' as a specific economic form, since wartime economic organisation went beyond the more customary forms of crisis management.

Neurath had suggested in his original essay of 1910 that in medieval times war had been a means of exploitation; the resources of rulers had to be concentrated to wage war, and the political outcome had definite economic consequences for victor and vanquished. In early modern Europe the relation between states became increasingly expressed in commercial terms, the various tariffs and prohibitions through which trade was conducted gradually being displaced by a system of free trade. Once this had come about, the previous economic function of waging war disappeared; henceforth warfare became a disturbing element in the international world of commerce, while at

[27] 'Kriegswirtschaft' in *Meyers Großes Konversations-Lexicon*, Bd. 24, 6th edn, Jahres Supplement 1911–12, Leipzig 1913, pp. 523–8; 'Probleme der Kriegswirtschaftslehre', *Zeitschrift für die gesamte Staatswissenschaft*, Jg. 69 (1913), pp. 438–501.
[28] O. Neurath, *Durch die Kriegswirtschaft zur Naturalwirtschaft*, Verlag Georg D. W. Callwey, Munich 1919, Geleitwort.

the same time involving a redirection of domestic economic activity. Adam Smith, noted Neurath, wrote only of defence, not of warfare in general.[29] In the modern economy, argued Neurath, waging war meant the rearrangement of economic factors for the prosecution of this particular end, and this rearrangement was essentially a task of economic administration on the part of the government. Since the conduct of war focuses attention on the quantity of goods at hand, rather than monetary values, the possibility is opened up of suspending money calculation and substituting calculation in kind – both for the provisioning of the army and population, and for the production of armaments.[30] The waging of war by a modern industrial state required purposeful economic administration; once this was generally recognised, it would then also become apparent that this planful 'natural' organisation of modern economies could be extended to peacetime.

These arguments were put forward in 1910; in the following years they were repeated and extended into a systematic confrontation of *Verkehrswirtschaft* with *Verwaltungswirtschaft*, of market-based and administratively-based economic orders. Or, in other terms: decentralised versus centralised calculation. *Verwaltungswirtschaft*, or the administered economy, was not however synonymous with socialist economy:

The administered economy is above all characterised by the use of an economic plan as the basis of its measures. If a central office is to promulgate decrees on consumption and production etc. it has to be clear about the effects of these measures and for this purpose have an overview of the entire economic order.[31]

In the free economy such a plan does not exist; each economic subject strives to maximise its own income, and while one can argue that the resulting distribution of resources is rational and optimal, it does not follow that this is the only method of achieving a rational allocation of resources:

this view of the economic nature of *Verkehrswirtschaft* is no necessary precondition for its continued existence. . . . While monetary calculation has been in the foreground of the *Verkehrswirtschaft* of the last decades, the administered economy has to consider things directly, hence ascertaining

---

[29] O. Neurath, 'Die Kriegswirtschaft', reprinted from *Jahresbericht der Neuen Wiener Handelsaka-demie* (1910) in *Durch die Kriegswirtschaft*, p. 11.   [30] *Ibid.*, p. 29.
[31] Neurath, 'Kriegswirtschaft, Verwaltungswirtschaft, Naturalwirtschaft', reprinted from *Europäische Wirtschaftszeitung* (1917) in *Durch die Kriegswirtschaft*, p. 149.

quantitatively production, stockbuilding, consumption, export, import and the entire domestic economy. In ascertaining the various fluctuations in a quantitative manner and hence gaining a general overview of the manner in which this all influences the provisioning of men and women (consumption statistics express this most clearly) administrative economy conducts natural calculation, which plays a far greater role today than earlier.[32]

In wartime, Neurath goes on, the administered economy possesses three advantages: speed of decision and execution; optimal distribution of means (with respect to military objectives); and an enhanced evaluation and utilisation of inventions. Two disadvantages are identified by Neurath: the centralisation of all decision-making can hinder simple exchanges, and productivity can be reduced.

This second problem could, suggested Neurath, be dealt with by the introduction of the Taylor system; and although this line of thought was also later taken up by Lenin, we should note here that Neurath responds to the question of work-organisation simply by introducing a rationalist plan. Neurath's argument for centralisation and planning for need is not one that is rooted in a contemporary socialist politics; the basis for his argument is a pure rationalism, apparent in his attempt to make a *Felicitologie* the basis of a systematic comparative method.[33] This is even more apparent in his postwar writings, in which this approach is extended to develop 'rational arguments for socialism'.

'To *socialise* an economy means to conduct *planful administration in favour of society through society*' stated Neurath on 25 January 1919 before a plenary meeting of the Munich Workers' Council.[34] In the later phases of the war Neurath had been involved in the development of a 'War Economy Museum' in Leipzig, but this project collapsed with the armistice. Instead, he was persuaded to draw up a plan for economic socialisation, and in so doing he noted that socialists and communists had failed to produce any programme for the administration of the future society they sought to create. In Munich he discussed this problem with Edgar Jaffé, editor of the *Archiv* and soon to become Minister of Finance in the Bavarian Republic; and the

[32] *Ibid.*, p. 149.
[33] This comprehensive comparative treatment of economic forms is organised by key terms such as *Lebenstimmung, Lebensboden, Lebenslage*, all of which are to be combined into a *Felicitologie*, a kind of topology of human welfare in which a tabulation of welfare could be built upon household budget data: 'Das Begriffsgebäude der vergleichenden Wirtschaftslehre und ihre Grundlagen', *Zeitschrift für die gesamte Staatswissenschaft*, Bd. 73 (1918), pp. 487, 501–2.
[34] Neurath, 'Wesen und Weg der Sozialisierung', published as a pamphlet and reprinted in *Durch die Kriegswirtschaft*, p. 209.

outcome was his presentation, as a technical adviser to the Workers' Council, of the lecture 'Nature and Means of Socialisation'. At this time plans had already been drawn up for Saxony, proposing the creation of a Central Economic Office whose first task was to survey the productive forces of the land, and ascertain the movement of raw materials, energy, and commodities. In this, it was not values and balances that were of importance, but a material inventory expressed in physical quantities. The 'universal statistical survey' that resulted was to be used by the Natural Calculation Centre of the Central Economic Office, the object being to formulate an economic plan. It was not the purpose of such a plan to identify a unique economic strategy; instead, the purpose was to construct a number of variant *Lebenslagen* on the basis of available resources, choice between them being left to a representative body.[35]

Neurath made quite clear in his approach that socialisation required the creation of a central planning instance – administration of the economy was to be exercised through this central office, not by any other agency. This had to be done immediately, so that commercial exchanges could be replaced by direct exchanges among governmental and other agencies.[36] Perhaps it was to quell any opposition to this emphasis on centralisation, and hence a diminution of the role of workers' councils, that he immediately proceeded to define as a socialist anyone who was in favour of this.[37] A kind of socialist 'monarchy' was quite feasible, suggested Neurath; but social democracy was a possibility if the bureaucracy was ruled by a council system. This would however need to be established independently from enterprise councils, which were by their nature concerned only with the well-being of the economic undertakings with which they were connected. Socialist economic administration could of course lead to the democratisation of enterprises, but this was not a necessary consequence; in individual enterprises it was perfectly possible for a form of absolutism to prevail. In any case, argued Neurath, a complete democratisation of the workplace crippled production.[38]

The role of the central office was to treat the economy 'as a giant enterprise' calculating in material terms. Money would exist in the economy, but the decision-making process with respect to the allo-

---

[35] H. Kranold in the foreword to O. Neurath, *Die Sozialisierung Sachsens*, Verlag des Arbeiter- und Soldatenrats im Industriebezirk Chemnitz, Chemnitz 1919, pp. 3–4.
[36] *Ibid.*, pp. 17–21.   [37] Neurath, 'Wesen und Weg', in *Durch die Kriegswirtschaft*, p. 209.
[38] *Ibid.*, p. 211.

cation of resources would be made neither with respect to circulating currency nor money of account (*Girogeld*). By drawing up plans in this way 'everything becomes transparent and controllable';[39] workers could see directly the effects of their demands and it would be possible to introduce direct exchanges between enterprises, and between industry and agriculture. 'Socialisation' meant the introduction of a rational allocation of resources according to human need, not according to existing wealth or status. Viewed in this way, socialism was a matter of economic rationality, not of politics:

The entire organisation of the economy is a closed totality. The *means* of *political power* through which it is realised is without great significance for the internal functions of the whole structure. Without corresponding power, whether it derive from a parliamentary democracy or a soviet republic, even the best socialisation plan is quite worthless.[40]

This bland indifference to political structure, so long as rational economic order prevailed, demonstrates the fact that natural economic calculation exercised by a central economic instance was for Neurath more the product of logic than politics. Furthermore, it ran counter to the prevailing emphasis on workers' councils as the keystone to socialisation – instead, he argued that the object of socialisation was not to reform the administration of enterprises, but to transform the economy. In this vision, then, workers' councils were at most a means for the training of socialist administrators.

Neurath's conception of the centrally planned economy thus descended directly from his proposition that a war economy administered on the basis of natural calculation provided a model for a modern peacetime economy. Weber not only argued against this position, but suggested, like Mises, that in the absence of a generalised means of calculation economic rationality could not exist: 'one cannot talk of a rational "planned economy" as long as there is no means for the purely rational construction of a "plan" in the all-determining instance'.[41] Rational economic activity was defined by Weber under four headings:

[39] *Ibid.*, p. 213.
[40] O. Neurath, *Betriebsräteorganisation als Wirtschaftsorganisation*, Verlagsgenossenschaft 'Neue Erde', Vienna 1920, p. 6. Neurath includes a diagram here of the relation of economy and polity; the latter is characterised as 'some form of administration'. For Neurath, the polity was an administrative device, not a domain of political struggle and decision-making.
[41] M. Weber, *Wirtschaft und Gesellschaft*, 5th edn, J. C. B. Mohr (Paul Siebeck), Tübingen 1972, p. 56.

(1) the planful distribution of utilities in the present and in the future (in the form of savings);

(2) the planful distribution of utilities between employments according to their marginal products;

(3) the planful acquisition, through production or introduction, of those utilities for which all appropriate means were in the hands of an agent;

(4) the planful acquisition of secure powers of disposal over utilities originating from a number of sources.[42]

However, Weber did not treat rationality as a singular and universal concept, for he made a distinction between formal and material rationality. *Formal* rationality was defined in terms of the degree of technical calculability applicable to any given economic action. *Material* rationality by contrast derived from an evaluation of the degree to which the actual satisfaction of human needs corresponded to the evaluative principles in whose terms allocations were made.

This distinction between formal and material rationality is critical to his evaluation of socialist economic calculation, since it implies that there is no general criterion of rationality that can be applied to economic action. As he went on,

the concept of *material* rationality is entirely ambiguous. .... purposively rational calculation with the technically most appropriate and feasible means is *not* enough, rather a variety of ethical, political, utilitarian, hedonistic, *ständisch*, egalitarian or any other imperatives exist and ... evaluate economic action according to *evaluative rationality* or *material* purposive rationality.[43]

Weber argued that, from the point of view of formal rationality, it was the question of calculability that was paramount, and that consequently 'From a purely technical point of view money is the "most complete" means of economic calculation'.[44] However, it was possible to envisage conditions under which natural economic calculation could be employed, especially where income and expenditure were not monetised, and money-values could not easily be imputed. This could occur in household calculations, but was effective only as long as goods were not heterogeneous, and the objective was not the optimal allocation of resources. Calculations in kind, whether the marginal factor was surplus labour or the satisfaction of need, made the determination of the scale of urgency problematic. Formal rationality in the determination of the marginal utility of goods – and

---

[42] *Ibid.*, pp. 35–6.   [43] *Ibid.*, p. 45.   [44] *Ibid.*, p. 45.

here it is worth emphasising that Weber unambiguously associated optimality with the allocation of resources according to their marginal utilities – could therefore never be fully realised in economies operating with natural economic calculation. Indeed, this was one of the features of such societies which made them 'traditional' in character, constituting an obstacle to change.

According to Weber, then, in the absence of money as a standard of economic calculation, decisions that are made outside the household get into difficulties that can only partially be resolved by imputation. Natural economic calculation is essentially oriented to the satisfaction of specifiable needs; it relates to the sphere of consumption. Once one considered entrepreneurial activity, oriented as it was to profitability rather than marginal utility, money and the price mechanism became indispensable. Calculation in *natura* is unable to express priority or necessity; it can only present a range of possible combinations that cannot be rendered comparable by any agreed standard. Moreover, in such calculations it was not possible to arrive at a satisfactory schedule of comparative costs and benefits. While this might not be critical for a household, it did become of paramount importance once one considered the conditions for the production of consumption and producer goods.

Material calculations were certainly made in enterprises, establishing the annual requirements for raw materials for example; but this form of calculation could not be employed in the evaluation of production processes of different types, with instruments of different kinds and multiple applications. Natural economic calculation within enterprises reached the limit of its rationality with the problem of imputation.

If natural economic calculation were to regulate the rational long-term utilisation of producer goods, it would have to generate 'value indices' for individual objects, which would assume the role played by 'balance prices' in current forms of calculation. It is in any case difficult to foresee quite how they could be developed and *policed*: on the one hand for individual, locationally distinct, enterprises, on the other hand with respect to 'social utility', i.e. that of present *and future consumption requirements*.[45]

These problems, argues Weber, are fundamental to any future 'comprehensive socialisation', and there could be no question of a rational planned economy so long as there was no means for the rational construction of a plan.

[45] *Ibid.*, p. 55.

Weber's excursus on natural economic calculation was prompted by Neurath's articles on the subject, and his endeavour to develop a critique of capitalist economic organisation on the basis of war economies. Weber did not deny that money calculation, while formally rational, was a poor indicator of the manner in which needs were actually met. However, wartime economies were run rather like a bankrupt's enterprise – the allocation of resources was conducted primarily according to technical, not economic, criteria. Insofar as there was a choice of objectives, it was possible to introduce rough and ready forms of economic calculation according to the principle of marginal utility, but these involved the kinds of decision made in a household and were incapable of assuring a durable and rational solution in the distribution of labour and producer goods.[46] This form of economic organisation had only a limited relevance for a critique of the material rationality of capitalist economic order, since its utilisation of resources was geared to immediate and definable military ends, and not the long-term development of the economy. This was not to deny that calculation in money and calculation *in natura* were both rational techniques; only that they were not complete substitutes for each other and did not exhaust all forms of economic organisation. The greater facility with which monetary calculations could be made had perhaps hindered the full development of calculation *in natura*; but even if this were admitted, such forms of calculation were not suitable for the sustained reproduction of an exchange economy.

Weber's critique of socialist economic calculation was therefore embedded within a more general evaluation of the rational bases of economic organisation, drawing equally on contemporary economic theory and his own extensive knowledge of ancient and medieval economies. This line of argument was particularly difficult for Neurath to counter, since he had of course completed a doctoral dissertation on aspects of ancient economic organisation; in this respect Weber confronted him on his own intellectual territory. Neurath did not in any case further pursue his contention that the organisation of economies in time of war provided a model for future socialist economies. Instead, in the course of the 1920s he progressively integrated this idea into a conception of 'modern man' and the prospects for social and economic organisation. The prison sentence passed upon him for his part in the Munich Soviet Republic was never carried out, and in the summer of 1919 he returned to Vienna, where

[46] *Ibid.*, p. 57.

he immediately became involved in the workers' housing movement and other projects.

Within this new context he argued for a socialism that did not emphasise expropriation, or any one particular form of political organisation, but rather focused on the just distribution of social goods. Rathenau's vision of guild socialism was criticised by Neurath for its over-reliance on monetary calculation and the profit, while other proposals, such as those of Popper-Lynkeus, over-emphasised the sphere of distribution. Instead of these structural schemes, Neurath proposed that social welfare should be increased by a direct calculation of needs in respect of housing, food, clothing, education, and entertainment.

> Socialism seeks to remove the preferment of one group, replacing the economy of rulers with a communal economy which will distribute everything which is part of the 'life situation' (*Lebenslage*) and the most important preconditions of living conditions (*Lebenstimmung*) – housing, food, clothing, education, entertainment, labour and leisure time – according to general principles which take account of the level of activity, age, health, gender etc. of the individual. Such a form of distribution will not be according to inherited or acquired privileges of property.[47]

This conception of a direct assessment of material need and the allocation of goods on this basis does not escape Weber's strictures concerning the long-term reproduction of an economy run on this basis, nor the allocative efficiency involved. Viewed in the light of these criticisms, Neurath's proposals are unworkable and utopian. But it is this emphasis upon natural economic calculation that forms the basis for Neurath's developing interest in the representability of economic processes, and which forms the rational foundation for much of his work until his death in 1945.

In 1924 Neurath was appointed director of the Social and Economic Museum in Vienna, a post he was to hold until his exile in 1934. This project aimed at presenting to its public a clear and comprehensive image of social and economic conditions in the modern world – 'life situations' were thereby to become the subject of 'visual education' based on the 'Vienna method' of pictorial statistics. Here the role of a material inventory and a 'universal statistical survey' previously exposed in connection with the work of a Central Economic Office re-emerge as educational devices. 'Social conditions' such as birth and death rates, nutrition and the allocation of housing were represented

---

[47] O. Neurath, *Vollsozialisierung*, Eugen Diederichs, Jena 1920, p. 11.

in symbolic form, employing a consistent system of signs. This was in turn to be the basis of the International System of Typographic Picture Education (ISOTYPE), the development of which became ever more central to Neurath's endeavours through the 1930s. As he stated in an article on the new museum in 1931: 'The method of visual education has an important contribution to make to general education: to give fundamental, strictly scientific information for social understanding, even to the less educated, without depressing him in the way learned books and statistical tables do. Charts condense information without confusing.'[48] The project of developing visual displays of social and economic statistics in the Vienna Museum drew upon the same physicalist appreciation of socio-economic organisation that Neurath had developed in his studies of war economies. Instead of forming the basis for a rational organisation of economic life, this now became the substance for a 'transparent and visible' representation of economic life for pedagogic ends. The universal comprehensibility of standardised images became the foundation of the ISOTYPE system, replacing natural languages with a form of communication independent of language, or, indeed, literacy.[49]

The manner in which this approach was linked to broader conceptions of socialism and economic planning is demonstrated by a book published in 1925. Here, *Capital*, volume 1 is transformed into a treatise on diverse life situations (*Lebenslagen*).[50] Two central arguments are presented. The first proposes that economic subjects derive differential degrees of utility from common goods. While these utilities can be aggregated and goods allocated according to the highest general level of satisfaction, it was more useful to combine these differential increments of satisfaction into a *Lebenstimmungsrelief* – a kind of topology of living conditions. Choices could then be made in a rational and substantive manner among the various combinations revealed – in the case of a socialist society, the choice would be made by a representative body. As already noted, Neurath was not

[48] O. Neurath, 'Bildhafte Pädagogik im Gesellschafts- und Wirtschaftsmuseum in Wien', *Museumkunde* N. F. III, H. 3 (1931); reprinted in Neurath, *Empiricism and Sociology*, D. Reidel, Dordrecht 1973, p. 217.

[49] 'Education by pictures in harmony with the ISOTYPE system, advertisement by ISOTYPE signs, will do much to give the different nations a common outlook. If the schools give teaching through the eye in harmony with this international picture language, they will be servants of a common education all over the earth, and will give a new impulse to all other questions of international education.' O. Neurath, *International Picture Language*, Kegan Paul, Trench, Trubner and Co., London 1936, p. 18.

[50] O. Neurath, *Wirtschaftsplan und Naturalrechnung*, E. Laub, Berlin 1925, pp. 23–4.

especially interested in the form that this body would take. This then leads to the second argument: such calculation is conducted without the mediation of money; it is instead made in a direct manner, on the basis of the kind of statistical information which absolutist rulers of the eighteenth century had begun to collect on their subjects: the *Statistik* developed by Achenwall and Schlözer.[51] This information is irreducible to one particular measure – neither money nor labour is an adequate unit of calculation – there is only a diversity of heterogeneous utilities.

The data with which the central planning office would operate included factors such as living space, calorific intake, accident frequency, morbidity, labour time, all of which were then to be combined into what Neurath later termed a *Lebenslagephysiognomie*.[52] Any attempt to reduce this heterogeneous data into some standardised index automatically resulted in the loss of the very information which was needed if planning were to be rationally executed. Hence, according to Neurath, the introduction of monetary calculation in a planned economy destroyed the possibility of conducting rational economic management, since decision-making was based upon an abstract aggregate unit that did not adequately represent the diversity of material conditions and need. Rational economic calculation for Neurath therefore means: a choice between different *Lebenslagephysiognomien*, or an evaluation of the 'silhouette of the standard of living' as he later called it.[53]

It is evident that the component parts of these various *Lebenslagephysiognomien* are not only material, but 'representable' in the manner that Neurath had developed in his Vienna Museum. Upon his exile to The Hague in 1934, Neurath shifted his concerns more directly to the development of the ISOTYPE system of signs, and the publication of books based upon this system. As Neurath stated in his 'Foreword' to one of the first results of this project, *Modern Man in the Making*,

Nations, classes, states, well-to-do and poor people are described by means of simple charts and simple statements in this report, without the use of personal names. An attempt has been made to evolve for this purpose a special

---

[51] See A. F. Lueder, *Kritische Geschichte der Statistik*, Johann Friedrich Römer, Göttingen 1817; and V. John, *Geschichte der Statistik*, Verlag von Ferdinand Emke, Stuttgart 1884.

[52] O. Neurath, *Was bedeutet rationale Wirtschaftsbetrachtung?*, Einheitswissenschaft Heft 4, Verlag Gerold und Co., Vienna 1935, p. 17.

[53] O. Neurath 'Inventory of the Standard of Living', *Zeitschrift für Sozialforschung*, Jg. 6 (1937), p. 143. Neurath's attempt to delineate degrees of satisfaction has of course a direct filiation to Menger's scale of incremental satisfactions discussed above pp. 73–5.

picture-text style which should enable anybody to walk through the modern world that is beginning to appear about us and see it as he may see a landscape with its hills and plains, woods and meadows.[54]

This combination of text and image is well illustrated by the presentation of the distribution of personal income in Britain (see Figure 6.1).[55] As Neurath suggests, this arrangement of economic data 'shows connexions between facts instead of discussing them.'[56]

Modern Man in the Making presented an image of modernity through the combination of signs drawn from the ISOTYPE system. This system of uniform signs was built up in a purely additive manner and was independent of spoken languages; the emphasis was on visual comparison of standard measures, or simple visual indication of function. It is in the latter sense that we are perhaps today most familiar with this rationalised form of representation. Presented in books, the ISOTYPE system was a logical development of graphical representations of economic phenomena which go back to William Playfair's *Commercial and Political Atlas* of 1785;[57] and thus, while novel, they are not unique. Such is, however, not the case for the use of ISOTYPE images as public signs, for here a picture language is substituted for a national language. This, too, is quite familiar from the everyday world, but the originality of Neurath's work in this area is evident from the way in which his images are so immediately familiar. Consider this typical ISOTYPE guide to the use of a public telephone, which would only require slight technical modification to be immediately comprehensible to any modern user (see Figure 6.2).[58] What then is the nature of the connection between images such as these, and Neurath's wider rationalist project?

The natural economic arguments arising from Neurath's conception of war economy, arguments so brusquely rejected by Weber and von Mises, did in fact develop into an unanticipated payoff – the development of systems of visual representation, together with a strict set of norms for their employment. The ISOTYPE system was a form of communication that did not require the mastery of any particular national language for it to function. The world was, through the medium of ISOTYPE, rendered transparent and comprehensible.

[54] O. Neurath, *Modern Man in the Making*, Secker and Warburg, London 1939, p. 7.
[55] *Ibid.*, p. 93.   [56] *Ibid.*, p. 8.
[57] See for a general discussion of many of the issues raised by Neurath in the use of visual and textual information, E. R. Tufte, *The Visual Display of Quantitative Information*, Graphics Press, Cheshire, Conn. 1983.   [58] Neurath, *International Picture Language*, p. 19.

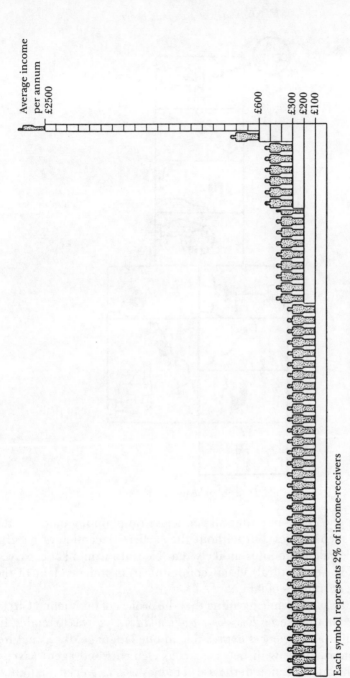

Average income
per annum

£2500

£600

£300
£200
£100

Each symbol represents 2% of income-receivers

Fig. 6.1. Profile of personal incomes in Great Britain in 1934

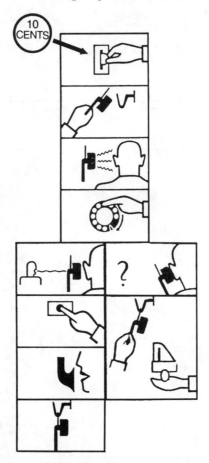

Fig. 6.2. How to make use of the telephone

Perhaps one could not after all run a central planning office on the basis of such images; but without the earlier conception of natural economic calculation it is unlikely that Neurath would have arrived at this idea of 'natural' visual communication independent of the national currencies of language.

Here it is worthwhile recalling that the project of the Vienna Circle, expressed in their series *Encyclopedia of Unified Science*, was to render the statements of all sciences expressible in one language. By its nature, the economy deals with heterogeneous elements and agents; Neurath's constant objection to the use of money as a universal medium of calculation was precisely that it was not able to represent adequately this real heterogeneity. Defining rational economic calculation in terms of monetary calculation, contended Neurath, left important factors unconsidered; rational choices could no longer be made since the objects of choice were occluded by a monetary sign. The proposal that natural statistical information should form the medium of calculation, the resulting profiles being visually representable, was of course never a serious candidate for socialist and capitalist planning in the 1930s. But this was more than an economic eccentricity, since it resulted in the systematisation of a form of communication which had been until that time seriously underestimated, and which has become of increasing importance in rendering economic conditions intelligible to the non-specialist and student.

Neurath spent his last years working on ISOTYPE; expelled from Vienna, first he established a new Institute in Holland, then fled to England in 1940 and established an Institute in Oxford, where he died in December 1945. ISOTYPE promised a means of rendering social and economic conditions directly comparable and 'readable'; the sciences and society were to be rendered 'appraisable' through the medium of a universal language, built up from images rather than words. Here again, poised at the threshold of a logical positivist science of society, we might be forgiven for wondering whether rationalism can be taken too far. But it should at least be apparent that it can lead us in unanticipated directions. Max Weber saw modernity as a world of isolation and specialisation, a world of 'specialists without spirit, sensualists without heart'. The universally intelligible systems of signs which Neurath spent the last few years of his life developing have become part of our own world; and they seem tailor made for 'modern men', inhabitants of the anonymous public spaces which public institutions have become: our colleges, hospitals, offices, airports, and road systems. The equanimity with which Neurath transforms the world into a system of universal signs for the guidance of these 'modern men' is directly linked to his view that the world should be organised in a rational and transparent manner.[59] But there is of course another aspect to this transparency. When arguing in the 1920s for a new form of physicalist statistics he had referred in passing to the role of *Statistik* in the absolutist state. Schröder, writing in the later seventeenth century, had suggested that

---

[59] The notion that the accessibility of personal computers is enhanced by the use of icons, and the very dubious conceptions of 'simplicity' associated with this, is clearly of a piece with Neurath's thinking here.

an inventory of manufactures would supply the ruler with a pair of *Staatsbrille*, 'state spectacles' with whose assistance proper judgements could be made on .the best means of increasing population and commerce.[60] The 'clearsighted' absolutist ruler would thus be placed in a position analogous with that of the central planning office furnished with the kind of statistical information that Neurath envisaged.

Neurath's ability to shuttle between the conceptual world of absolutism and that of the 1930s in this manner is not just the product of a free-ranging eclecticism; for the rationalism which he espouses is universalistic in its claims, expressive of a belief in the progressive force of rationality. 'Modern men' were, for Neurath, beings emancipated from superstition and tyranny, autonomous spirits liberated from tutelage, realisations of Kant's dictum *sapere aude*.[61] His work, for all its superficial eccentricity, therefore expresses the manner in which modern rationalism is a product of the Enlightenment. This is its characteristic and its limit. It appears eccentric to us not because it is anachronistic, but because of the relentless manner in which it pushes a form of rationalism to this limit. That modern men could find themselves caught up in a new form of absolutist rule was not something which Neurath could easily comprehend. The fact that Max Weber did understand this is evident from the comments that he made in his letter to Neurath with which this essay begins.

---

[60] W. von Schröder, *Fürstliche Schatz- und Rentkammer*, Leipzig 1686, p. 65 in the 1752 edition.

[61] '*Tutelage* is the inability to make use of one's own understanding without the direction of others. ... Sapere aude! Have the courage to make use of your *own* knowledge! This is the slogan of the Enlightenment.' I. Kant, 'Was ist Aufklärung?', *Werke*, vol. VIII, Walter de Gruyter, Berlin 1968, p. 35.

CHAPTER 7

Capitalism, totalitarianism and the legal order of National Socialism

Fifty years after its first appearance, Franz Neumann's *Behemoth* remains unsurpassed as the classic study of National Socialism.[1] This is not for want of scholarly attention to the subject. The *NS-Zeit*, brief as it was, retains its power to generate debate and controversy, assuring in turn a continuing and high level of academic scrutiny devoted to the period. Historians and social scientists have played a prominent and public role in recent controversies, as evidenced by the Kujau affair and the *Historikerstreit*.[2] Despite this ready association of scholarly investigation and popular interest in the phenomenon of National Socialism, *Behemoth*, written in New York during 1941, endures as the most successful attempt to outline its structure and dynamics.

As sometimes happens, however, *Behemoth*'s analysis was so readily, and widely, accepted that little attention was paid to its possible limitations or deficiencies. It was quickly assumed that the text was heavily indebted to Marxist categories and concepts, and when a German translation was eventually published during the 1970s it seemed natural to add an afterword placing *Behemoth* in the context of recent Marxist discussions of Fascism.[3] Certainly Neumann describes

---

[1] See for recent comments J. Caplan, *Government without Administration*, Oxford University Press, Oxford 1988, pp. 331–2; and P. Hayes, *Industry and Ideology. IG Farben in the Nazi Era*, Cambridge University Press, Cambridge 1987, p. 319, n. 2.

[2] The Kujau affair involved the purchase by *Stern* magazine of Hitler's diaries; the fact that they were obvious forgeries is of lesser importance than the motivations of *Stern*'s editors and publishers – see R. Harris, *Selling Hitler*, Faber and Faber, London 1986. The *Historikerstreit* can be dated from an essay by Habermas in *Die Zeit* (11 July 1986) in which he commented upon views expressed by several German historians concerning the army on the Eastern Front, and the singularity of the Holocaust – 'Eine Art Schadensabwicklung', reprinted in R. Augstein *et al.*, >*Historikerstreit*<, R. Piper, Munich 1987, pp. 62–76. See Geoff Eley's account of the events and arguments in 'Nazism, Politics and the Image of the Past: Thoughts on the West German *Historikerstreit* 1986–1987', *Past and Present*, 121 (1988), pp. 171–208.

[3] G. Schäfer, 'Franz Neumanns *Behemoth* und die heutige Faschismusdiskussion', Afterword to *Behemoth*, Europäische Verlagsanstalt, Cologne 1977.

National Socialism as 'Totalitarian Monopoly Capitalism'; but it should be noted that when he investigates the structure of National Socialism he chooses to do so in terms of the institution of property, invoking Karl Renner.[4] Throughout, Neumann has constant recourse to legal categories and arguments – whether in characterising the ideology of National Socialism by reference to Carl Schmitt, considering the public status of the NSDAP, or analysing the social structure of contemporary Germany. It is this feature that lends the work its rigour and longevity, but we should note at once that it is a very curious form of Marxist analysis that devotes so much attention to law, and so little to class formation, exploitation, and capital.

Moreover, this constant recourse to legal categories underscores the lasting thematic core of the book, which concerns the problem of order and the power of coercion in modern society. By generally accepted democratic values, the National Socialist seizure of power suspended legal order and civil security in 1933, and these were only restored by the victory of the Allied armies in May 1945. This victory was seen by Neumann and his colleagues in the Office of Strategic Services (OSS) as the only certain way of ending Nazi tyranny. One could envisage a certain brand of Marxist theorising that would confidently predict the eventual collapse of National Socialism under the burden of its all-too-evident contradictions, but there is not a trace of this in *Behemoth*.[5] National Socialist Germany was conceived by Neumann as a disorderly monster (hence the title) that had to be destroyed. By late 1941, with both the United States and the Soviet Union at war with Germany, this looked for the first time to be simply a question of time, production, and human resources. But this only lends emphasis to an implicit assumption in *Behemoth* that the National Socialist system of rule violates conceptions of order, rationality, and the maintenance of social and political equilibrium that were systematised in the European Enlightenment, and which had since become the foundations of modern economic and political theory. It was, from this modern social scientific perspective, inconceivable that a régime as brutal and volatile as National Socialism could survive, and then go on to impose its will on a European

[4] Franz Neumann, *Behemoth. The Structure and Practice of National Socialism*, 2nd edn, Oxford University Press, New York 1944, p. 255. The second edition differs from the first solely through the addition of an appendix, which updates the substantive sections of the 1942 edition. The conclusion remains unrevised.
[5] The need for a military defeat of National Socialism is emphasised in the preface to *Behemoth*, p. xiii.

Imperium the like of which had not been seen since Roman times. Such a violation of all prevailing preconceptions concerning political order and legitimacy would surely founder, or adapt in the face of internal and external pressures. This was in essence the stance adopted by governments during the 1930s, a stance that was abandoned only with reluctance in September 1939. Conceptions of social equilibrium were pushed to one side in favour of the apparent certainties provided by military action.

Nevertheless, if one is to seek understanding of the phenomenon of National Socialism, one can only deploy concepts and categories that are available. Neumann faces up to this dilemma, but at a certain cost. For the very rigour of his analysis depends on a theoretical apparatus embedded in the modern European tradition of politics and law, which apparatus presupposes that rationalism and the rule of law generally prevail. *Behemoth* is a study of the failure of democratic order; but it is at the same time a demonstration of the inadequacy of modern political theory faced with intransigent and disorderly realities. Viewed in this light, the text is far more than a classic analysis of National Socialism, but a substantial contribution to our understanding of the dilemmas of the modern world. It is for this reason that we need to know more about Franz Neumann and the construction of his *Behemoth*.

Of course, we might say that Franz Neumann was a lawyer, and that this is sufficient explanation for the analytical construction of *Behemoth*. Except that until 1933 Neumann was a labour lawyer, and it was only after his emigration that he turned his attention to more general theoretical and constitutional issues. Or again, the fact that *Behemoth* was researched and written while Neumann was a member of the Institute of Social Research suggests that we might order the text to the work of the Frankfurt School, and evaluate it in these terms. However, since it is evident that Neumann was a peripheral figure in the work of the Institute – he was recruited because of his legal and administrative skills, not for his research potential[6] – this interpretive strategy results in a marginalisation of the text. Indeed, Martin Jay in his account of the School is led to argue that it was only after 1942 that Neumann developed a sensitivity to the importance of

---

[6] Horkheimer was unfamiliar with Neumann's work and turned to Leo Löwenthal for advice; see R. Erd (ed.), *Reform und Resignation. Gespräche über Franz L. Neumann*, Suhrkamp Verlag, Frankfurt a. M. 1985, pp. 86–7. See for a detailed discussion of this and related matters P. Intelmann, 'Zur Biographie von Franz L. Neumann', *1999*, Heft 1 (1990), pp. 39–41.

the political sphere, diminishing in this way the significance of anything that predated Neumann's association with the Institute.[7]

Neumann's publications of the 1920s and early 1930s, although for the most part devoted to legal technicalities, are nevertheless of the greatest importance in understanding the analytical framework developed in *Behemoth*. They represent an engagement with the legal and political structure of the Weimar Republic, which engagement then provides the foundation for Neumann's later work on legal and political theory. During his time at the Institute Neumann certainly developed his understanding of National Socialism through discussion and research, but the analytical framework that he deploys in *Behemoth* is continuous with arguments that he had been developing since the later 1920s. An investigation of the strengths and weaknesses of *Behemoth* as a classical analysis of National Socialism must therefore begin with these writings, and with Franz Neumann's activities as a trade union lawyer during the Weimar years.

Neumann was born in Kattowitz in 1900. In 1918 he entered the University of Breslau to study economics, philosophy, and law, switching to Leipzig in the winter semester, and to Rostock for the summer semester of 1919. It was about this time that he joined the Social Democratic Party (SPD). In the autumn of 1919 he took up his study of law at the new university of Frankfurt am Main, sitting his qualifying law examination in December 1921.[8] His early studies concentrated on legal theory, while after his examination he completed a doctoral dissertation under the supervision of the neo-Kantian Max Ernst Mayer.[9] However, he was also heavily influenced by Hugo Sinzheimer, who was not only Germany's leading labour lawyer, but substantially responsible for the economic sections of the Weimar Constitution. After three years as Sinzheimer's *Assistent*

---

[7] M. Jay, *The Dialectical Imagination*, Heinemann, London 1973, p. 118. The posthumous collection of Neumann's essays, edited by Herbert Marcuse under the title *The Democratic and the Authoritarian State*, (Free Press, New York 1957), underscores this approach to Neumann; only two of the eleven essays were published before 1942, and these two date from 1937 and 1940, thereby obscuring an extensive bibliography reaching back to 1924. See W. Luthardt, 'Ausgewählte Bibliographie der Arbeiten von Franz L. Neumann' in J. Perels (ed.), *Recht, Demokratie und Kapitalismus*, Nomos Verlag, Baden-Baden 1984, pp. 217–27.

[8] The most comprehensive and reliable biography of Neumann is that of Peter Intelmann, 'Zur Biographie'. He lists a number of sources for Neumann's biography (n. 1, pp. 14–15), many of which however simply duplicate each other, often in so doing repeating surmise and error in the guise of biographical detail. Rather than cite and criticise these contributions individually, the following account refers exclusively to Intelmann and avoids other sources.

[9] 'Rechtsphilosophische Einleitung zu einer Abhandlung über das Verhältnis von Staat und Strafe', Frankfurt 1923, summarised in Intelmann, 'Zur Biographie', pp. 16–19.

Neumann completed his legal training in 1927, and at once opened a practice in Berlin with his Frankfurt colleague, Ernst Fraenkel. He was soon appointed lawyer to the Building Workers' Union, and Fraenkel to the Metal Workers' Union. Both rapidly built up heavy case-loads – Intelmann records that Neumann appeared in more than 500 cases in Leipzig during this period, representing a range of trade unions for the Allgemeine Deutsche Gewerkschaftsbund. In addition to this he gave lectures on industrial and business law at the Hochschule für Politik, where, among others, Carl Schmitt and Hermann Heller also taught.

His writings at this time directed themselves to aspects of labour law, and usually appeared in trade union publications.[10] Two essays from this period stand out by the manner in which they address more general, constitutional issues, and in so doing reveal the character of Neumann's theoretical instrumentarium at this time. The first of these dates from 1930, and deals with the manner in which the Weimar Constitution dealt with issues of freedom and equality.[11] The second, which appeared the following year, outlines a critique of the Weimar political order, couched in terms of a discussion of the conditions of a new economic constitution.[12] Modern capitalism, it is suggested, should be characterised as *monopoly* capitalism; the leading characteristic of this new form of capitalist order is that the central function of the free entrepreneur is no longer effectively exercised. The question is then posed: is this leading characteristic of the era of monopoly capitalism compatible with the general legal conditions for the functioning of the capitalist economy?

It can now be asked whether the *legal conditions* for the functioning of capitalist economic order exist. Capitalist economy is based upon the legal institutions of *private property* in the means of production, with its associated institutions – *freedom of contract, freedom of trade* and the *right of inheritance*, securing the bourgeois order of succession.[13]

---

[10] Intelmann notes some 40 publications up to 1933; see for example 'Der Kampf um den Zwangstarif', *Die Arbeit*, Jg. 2 (November 1925), pp. 694–703; 'Gesellschaftliche und staatliche Verwaltung der monopolistischen Unternehmungen', *Die Arbeit*, Jg. 5 (July 1928), pp. 393–404; 'Betriebsrisiko', *Arbeitsrechts-Praxis*, Jg. 1 (October 1928), pp. 219–23; and *Die politische und soziale Bedeutung der arbeitsgerichtlichen Rechtsprechung*, E. Laubsche Verlagsbuchhandlung, Berlin 1929.

[11] 'The Social Significance of the Basic Laws of the Weimar Constitution', in F. Neumann and O. Kirchheimer, *Social Democracy and the Rule of Law*, Allen and Unwin, London 1987, pp. 27–43. Originally published in *Die Arbeit*, Jg. 7 (1930).

[12] 'On the Preconditions and the Legal Concept of an Economic Constitution' in Neumann and Kirchheimer, *Social Democracy*, pp. 44–65. Originally published in *Die Arbeit*, Jg. 8 (1931).

[13] Neumann, 'Preconditions', p. 46.

Neumann argues that, while the legal institutions of capitalist economy are still secured, they have ceased to perform their function in
fostering the development of market relations. Instead, the market is
subordinated to the interventionist activity of the state on the one side
and to the power of monopolists on the other, so that in many areas
the self-regulating property of the market is suppressed. The legal
guarantee of freedom of contract has thus become a formality,
because the economic subject is no longer the individual free entrepreneur, but rather a monopolist or the government bureaucracy.

Neumann develops this argument about the nature of monopoly
capitalism in terms of the contemporary discrepancy between constitutional norm and constitutional reality. He lists five central points:
(1) in the modern pluralist democracy parties, trade unions, and
     associations of diverse kinds have appropriated control of state
     decision-making processes;
(2) the judiciary has assumed the right of review of parliamentary
     legislation and constituted itself as a high court with the ability to
     interpret the constitution;
(3) the public economic sector is increasingly autonomous, or 'poly-
     cratic', to use the term introduced by Popitz;
(4) pluralism and polycracy combine within the parliamentary
     apparatus to produce the problem of federalism – state decision-
     making is dominated by federal bodies which are themselves
     autonomous;
(5) parliament has lost control of the administrative apparatus,
     which has become a ministerial bureaucracy.[14]
There is a great deal to be said for this assessment of the constitutional
problems of late Weimar, but we should note that it is not original.
Neumann's formulation of the problem coincides almost exactly with
that of Carl Schmitt, soon to become the 'Crown Jurist' of the Third
Reich.[15] Furthermore, Schmitt was to be mobilised in *Behemoth* as
National Socialism's leading ideologist.[16] This aspect of Neumann's

---

[14] *Ibid.*, pp. 49–51.
[15] See on this J. W. Bendersky, *Carl Schmitt. Theorist for the Reich*, Princeton University Press,
Princeton, NJ 1983, pp. 204ff; and E. Kennedy's review of Bendersky, *History of Political
Thought*, vol. 4 (1983), pp. 579–89. The ambivalence provoked by Schmitt among German
intellectuals is thoughtfully outlined in V. Neumann, 'Carl Schmitt und die Linke', *Die Zeit*,
28 (8 July 1983), p. 32. Schmitt's own view of his situation in 1933–36 is presented by E.
Straub in 'Der Jurist im Zwielicht des Politischen', *Frankfurter Allgemeine Zeitung*, 163 (18 July
1981).
[16] Other candidates for this post are variously Alfred Rosenberg, Hans Frank, Christoph
Steding, and of course Hitler himself. Neumann's election of Schmitt is symptomatic of a
general difficulty in identifying with any degree of certainty 'National Socialism' other than

analytical strategy is thus somewhat paradoxical, and requires some consideration.

Neumann had attended Schmitt's seminar in Berlin and taught alongside him at the Hochschule für Politik. Up to the date of his entry into the NSDAP on 1 May 1933 Schmitt had been an implacable conservative opponent of the enemies of the Weimar state. The concepts and arguments mobilised by Schmitt were directed against many of the phenomena opposed by Social Democrats and liberals, and such was their incisiveness that they were readily taken over by those who, like Schmitt, supported the Weimar Republic, but who also happened to be his political opponents. Schmitt's critique of parliamentary democracy and party politics, his definitions of the political, of the nature of sovereignty and of legitimacy are fundamental to constitutional argument during the 1920s and early 1930s. Neumann's analytical apparatus was to a great extent borrowed from Schmitt, but, unlike Schmitt, he employed it as a means of assessing the conditions and possibilities of capitalist order. The result was not without ambivalence; and it is in part because of this that the leading principles of Schmitt's critique of Weimar democracy (and indirectly, of parliamentary democracy in general) have to be outlined before considering the manner in which they were absorbed into Neumann's theoretical instrumentarium.

The principal target of Schmitt's criticisms was formed by those legal doctrines which, in embracing the concept of the rule of law, treated this as a régime in which political neutrality prevailed. The rule of law was conceived in this way as a rational order in which legal negotiation replaced political struggle. Borrowing a phrase from Donoso Cortès, he dubbed this ideal of the Enlightenment and nineteenth-century Liberalism as a 'discussing society' – an interminable forum in which discussion replaced decision, in which the vote of a majority substituted for political action, and in which the consent of outvoted minorities was consigned to the region of 'legitimacy'. As Ellen Kennedy puts it,

The necessity for discussion is no less epistemological than it is political; in liberalism, the search for truth goes on as a conversation from which force is absent and where reason and persuasion prevail. Liberal political theory thus depends on an assumption that political conflict can be transformed into a matter of opinion ...[17]

as a social and political phenomenon to be known only by its effects, rather than by its objectives.

[17] E. Kennedy, 'Introduction: Carl Schmitt's *Parlamentarismus* in its Historical Context', in C. Schmitt, *The Crisis of Parliamentary Democracy*, MIT Press, Cambridge, Mass. 1985, p. xix.

Schmitt had personally witnessed the demise of the Munich Soviet Republic, which left him with a passionate attachment to the virtues of political order. But this attachment did not lead him to ignore the realities of political life; for him, politics was struggle, and ultimately beyond rationalistic attempts to convert this fact of struggle into the considered application of a rule of law.

The political arena was for Schmitt a domain in which decisions were made and acted upon. Such decisions were not simply the pre-programmed product of political machinery; they were arrived at by a sovereign body, and not by a set of procedures. Characteristically, Schmitt formulated his conception of sovereignty in a bald statement which opens his *Political Theology*: 'Sovereign is he who decides upon the exception'.[18] This was, he immediately adds, a limiting concept, but one which had a number of virtues. Firstly, the 'state of exception' cannot be defined in advance; and so the existence of a state of exception is registered by the exercise of sovereignty on the part of an agent with the power both to decide whether such a state exists, and to take measures to deal with it. This is quite distinct from the idea of dictatorship; for that form of rule denotes a permanent state of domination, while Schmitt's emphasis on the state of exception presupposes the general existence of order as a state of normality. Secondly, this way of defining the notion of sovereignty lays emphasis on decision as the characteristic of political life, not discussion, nor domination. Such decision cannot reside in the Constitution; this can only indicate who in a specified case is permitted to act. As Schmitt states:

There is no norm which could be applied to a situation of chaos. Order must be produced, so that the legal order has meaning. A normal situation must be created, and sovereign is he who definitively decides whether this normal condition actually prevails. ... In this there lies the essence of state sovereignty, which can be legally defined not as a monopoly of compulsion or of domination, but rather as a monopoly of decision.[19]

Associated with this approach is the infamous definition of the political, whose architecture is similar to that of the definition of sovereignty: 'The specifically political differentiation to which political actions and motives can be reduced is the distinction between friend and foe. This provides a conceptual definition in the form of a

---

[18]   C. Schmitt, *Political Theology*, MIT Press, Cambridge, Mass. 1985, p. 5.
[19]   *Ibid.*, p. 13, my translation from the second (1934) edition of *Politische Theologie*, p. 20.

criterion, not an exhaustive definition nor a particular substance.'[20] This does not mean that the foe is an outlaw, to be eliminated; it rather emphasises that the domain of the political is defined by the presence of conflict and opposed interests. As Schmitt suggests, the political foe need not be morally evil or aesthetically monstrous; he need not be an economic competitor and it may be possible to do business with him. He is rather the 'other', the agent with which in extreme cases conflict is possible, conflict which then cannot be settled through a general application of norms laid down in advance, nor through the influence of a 'disinterested' third party.[21]

By combining these concepts of the political and of sovereignty Schmitt is able to produce a powerful critique of contemporary political theories. He explicitly rejects the pluralist theory of the state advanced by Cole and Laski, which in his view simply reduces the state to one association among many competing with them on an equal basis. In Schmitt's view, the specifically political character of the state and its exercise of sovereignty is overlooked by Cole and Laski, and submerged into a state of heterogeneity.[22]

Schmitt certainly did recognise heterogeneity in the development of political forces and agencies, but viewed the elevation of such a condition into a theory of modern democracies as an intellectual evasion. Modern parliamentarism was in a state of crisis, he argued, because the conditions of modern mass democracy had rendered argument and public discussion a formality.

The parties (which according to the text of the written constitution officially do not exist) do not face each other today discussing opinions, but as social or economic power-groups calculating their mutual interests and opportunities for power, and they actually agree compromises and coalitions on this basis ... One may therefore assume as well known today that it is no longer a question of persuading one's opponent of the truth or justice of an opinion but rather of winning a majority in order to govern with it.[23]

Parliament, government by discussion, had been overtaken by the development of mass parties whose electoral support derived from their identification of, and appeal to, specific constituencies of

[20] C. Schmitt, *Der Begriff des Politischen*, Duncker und Humblot 1963 (reprint of 1932 edn), p. 26. See G. Schwab's introduction to his translation of this text under the title *The Concept of the Political*, and Schwab's *The Challenge of the Exception* (Duncker und Humblot, Berlin 1970) which, unlike Bendersky's treatment, focuses on Schmitt's central texts and concepts.
[21] Schmitt, *Begriff*, p. 27. 'The foe is hostis, not inimicus in its widest sense ... ', p. 29.
[22] *Ibid.*, pp. 41, 44. See also on this P. Q. Hirst, 'Carl Schmitt's Decisionism', *Telos*, 72 (1987) pp. 15–26.　　[23] Schmitt, *Crisis*, pp. 6–7.

interest. This did not however mean that democracy was itself directly endangered, for parliament was an idea belonging to liberalism, and it was necessary to clearly distinguish between democracy and liberalism. The latter belonged to the previous century. Democracy, on the other hand, was a system which rested on the principle that 'equals [are] equal [and] unequals will not be treated equally'. 'Democracy requires, therefore, first homogeneity and second – if the need arises – elimination or eradication of heterogeneity ... A democracy demonstrates its political power by knowing how to refuse or keep at bay something foreign and unequal that threatens its homogeneity.'[24]

It is at this point that the difference between the political perspectives of the conservative Schmitt and the Social Democrat Neumann becomes most apparent. The former's critique of the *Koalitionsparteienstaat* is taken up by Neumann; but while Schmitt sees the only hope in a legally bound sovereign executive, Neumann argues that, given the exclusion of party-political interests, some kind of compromise should be possible between the state and economic agencies.[25]

Neumann's approach also owed much to Heller's 'integrationist' perspective. Whereas Schmitt counterposed heterogeneity to homogeneity, Heller laid emphasis on integration. While both homogeneity and integration are concepts of order, they involve divergent conditions for the existence of order. For Schmitt, order required homogeneity, a state which was achieved through the exclusion, by compulsion if necessary, of that which was disorderly. Here we can detect the conceptual foundations of his adaptation to National Socialism. For Heller and Neumann, on the other hand, order required a condition of integration, which is processual, based upon compromise, non-exclusive and open to renegotiation. As Neumann stated in his book on the freedom of association, the political was not only present where the friend–foe opposition arose, but also there 'where disputing forces which wish to contribute to the creation of a state body are present'.[26]

The structure of Neumann's analysis of Weimar, as set out in his 1931 essay, nevertheless displays an astonishing similarity to that of

---

[24] *Ibid.*, p. 9.   [25] V. Neumann, 'Kompromiß', p. 72.
[26] Cited in *ibid.*, p. 68. At the time of writing, the only pieces by Heller available in the English language are his two contributions to the *Encyclopedia of the Social Sciences*, vol. 13 (Macmillan, New York 1933): 'Political Science', pp. 207–24; and 'Power, Political', pp. 300–5. See E. Kennedy, 'The Politics of Toleration in Late Weimar; Hermann Heller's Analysis of Fascism and Political Culture', *History of Political Thought*, vol. 5 (1985), pp. 109–27.

Schmitt in his *Hüter der Verfassung*, which was republished in the same year.[27] Schmitt here characterised the condition of constitutional order in terms of the same three concepts deployed by Neumann – pluralism, polycraty, and federalism.[28] The nineteenth-century distinction of state and society, in which the substantive content of 'society' was everything not already appropriated by the monarcho-military state, had been undermined. By the 1920s, Schmitt argued, the self-organising capacity of the institutions of society had been displaced by the state as the organising instance of society, blurring the distinction between the state as the realm of the political and society as the realm of the non-political. Social and economic problems thus became state problems; the antitheses of politics and economy, of state and culture, of state and law, ceased to exist.

This argument followed the contours of one articulated in the mid-1920s by Alfred Weber, who suggested that the state was threatened by a process of economisation.[29] The consequent assumption by the state of powers hitherto reserved to independent agencies did not, however, render this state all powerful. On the contrary, it became instead hostage to successive attempts, on the part of interest groups and associations, at a colonisation of its machinery and powers, the better to serve the ends of distinct social groupings. It was this condition, in which the neutral state of the nineteenth century was subjected to progressive transformation, that the term 'total state' was minted to define.[30] The 'total' nature of this state rested therefore not in its capacity of ubiquitous command and obedience; the total state was rather a weak state, its powers subsumed in the social and political struggles of the groups whose interests it served. Its ubiquity was instead labile and insecure, penetrating and directing society for want of any other governing force. This precise usage on the part of Schmitt

[27] Volker Neumann has drawn attention to this in his article 'Kompromiß oder Entscheidung? Zur Rezeption der Theorie Carl Schmitts in den Weimarer Arbeiten Franz L. Neumanns', in J. Perels (ed.), *Recht, Demokratie und Kapitalismus*, p. 71. 'Der Hüter der Verfassung' first appeared as an article in the *Archiv des öffentlichen Rechts*, N. F. Bd. 16 (1929), and then in a revised version as an essay in 1931.

[28] Schmitt, *Der Hüter der Verfassung*, J. C. B. Mohr (Paul Siebeck), Tübingen 1931, p. 71.

[29] L.-A. Bentin, *Johannes Popitz und Carl Schmitt. Zur wirtschaftlichen Theorie des totalen Staates in Deutschland*, C. H. Beck, Munich 1972, pp. 2–3.

[30] Schmitt, *Hüter der Verfassung*, p. 79. The concept of 'total war' to describe the socio-economic effects of modern warfare was first used in France in 1918 – L. Herbst, *Der totale Krieg und die Ordnung der Wirtschaft*, Deutsche Verlags-Anstalt, Stuttgart 1982, p. 36. Ernst Jünger took the term up in his conception of 'totale Mobilmachung'; see his *Krieg und Kreiger*, Berlin 1930, pp. 14–16.

and many others in the early 1930s did not survive. Instead, the concept followed two quite distinct lines of development.

First of all, the 'total state' became for a while during the 1930s a category of National Socialist self-understanding. It was in this sense employed to bind together notions of *Bewegung* and *Volk*, gaining a positive sense which was then deployed as a critical tool against the so-called 'liberal state':

The Total State is the antithesis of the Liberal State, it is the state of comprehensive substantiality as contrasted with the Liberal State – a state empty of content, nihilised, minimalised, autonomised by the manner in which supposedly inherent laws are in fact legally underwritten. The Total State is a formula that marks and distinguishes the dawning of a new state, by presenting a pure and contrasting image to a political world still in thrall to liberalistic concepts.[31]

Soon, however, even the generic term 'state' was rejected by National Socialist ideologues as itself a liberal residue, being replaced by an indeterminate combination of *Führer*, *Volk*, and *Bewegung* in what by the later 1930s passed for official political theory. Schmitt did not readily adapt to this; it was no longer possible to pretend that National Socialism could be construed in terms of any coherent set of political or legal categories. Consequently, by 1936 Schmitt found himself out of favour with the leadership, suspected of 'liberal inclinations'.[32]

The second path of conceptual development was one which saw the conception of the 'total state' taken up by critics of the National Socialist régime, and it is in an extension of this sense that we are familiar with the concept today. Starting out from Schmitt's theses, the term was coloured by conceptions of dictatorship and domination quite at odds with its original meaning. In this use of the term the abolition of private and public liberties, combined with the role of command in the management of political and economic spheres, came to the fore. This usage rapidly gained acceptance among critics of anti-democratic régimes, for it proved capable of employment against both Germany and the Soviet Union. A later example of this can be found in Borkenau's *The Totalitarian Enemy*, in which National Socialism is described as 'Brown Bolshevism'.[33]

This was of course the forerunner of more familiar Cold War usage,

[31] E. Forsthoff, *Der totale Staat*, Hanseatische Verlagsanstalt, Hamburg 1933.
[32] See Bendersky, *Carl Schmitt*, pp. 222ff.
[33] F. Borkenau, *The Totalitarian Enemy*, Faber and Faber, London 1940, Chapter 2.

provided in the mid-1950s with its classical formulation by Friedrich and Brzezinski – indeed it would not be unfair to say that it was upon this conceptual foundation that Brzezinski built his subsequent academic and political career.[34] But Neumann, even though he uses the term 'totalitarian' in his analysis of National Socialism, is not employing it in the indiscriminate manner later customary in Cold War political science. Like Carl Schmitt, he kept in view the connection between the conception of a total state and the decline of the rule of law in Weimar; and in so doing he defended the liberal order only insofar as it had the potential to deliver specific rights and a form of justice. This did not imply an unconditional defence of the rule of law. His difficulty was, however, that while his critique overlapped at many points with that of Schmitt, the conclusions drawn are divergent. Moreover, it has to be emphasised that his use of the term 'totalitarian' is developed from debates of the early 1930s in Germany, and is unrelated to any particular position on the nature of the Soviet Union. Borkenau approached the issue the other way around – his application of the term 'totalitarian' to National Socialist Germany was derived from his critique of the Soviet Union. It was only after the war that this position was reversed, so that Soviet Communism was directly associated with National Socialism through the generalised use of the concept of totalitarian rule.

Under a law of 7 April 1933 non-Aryan or communistically active lawyers were barred from practice.[35] This brought to an end Neumann's career as a German lawyer. In early May, having already been arrested and released once, he fled with his family to England. Very soon he had decided that the National Socialist seizure of power was no transitory event, and concluded that his exile was to be a lasting one. Although he remained politically active in the opposition to National Socialism, he was not able to continue in practice while in exile, not least because of the very different legal system in which he found himself. He instead shifted to academic work. Having already made contact with the London School of Economics, in July 1933 Neumann applied to the Royal Society for financial support so that he

[34] C. J. Friedrich and Z. K. Brzezinksi, *Totalitarian Dictatorship and Autocracy*, Harvard University Press, Cambridge, Mass. 1956.
[35] Intelmann, 'Biographie', p. 24. 'Communistically-active' includes for these purposes Social Democrats; later the term was extended to all liberal opponents of the National Socialist régime. Neumann was deprived of German nationality in June 1936 on account of his continued engagement on behalf of the German opposition in exile. Intelmann summarises the relevant government reports and documents in his essay, pp. 30–5.

could finish a book entitled *State and Monopolies*. Work on this, he stated, had begun the previous year, and a contract existed for German publication, but this of course could no longer be realised. Instead, he expressed his intention of writing the book in English, drawing upon English, German, and American law.

Neumann's proposed book was to be divided into seven major sections, beginning with an exposition of the legal basis of free competition, its modification through the emergence of monopolies, the objects and effects of state intervention, and the international aspects of monopolies.[36] The central role of legal categories for the analysis of capitalist economy is evident in this draft, which continues the line of argument already established some years before. Neumann never completed a book on this subject. He did, however, incorporate an account of the *Rechtsstaat*, and its erosion through the economic conditions of the 1920s, into the third part of his second doctoral dissertation, which he wrote in 1936 at the LSE under the supervision of Harold Laski.

Neumann's first publications in exile appear at first glance to recapitulate a conventional Marxist critique of the collapse of the Weimar Republic at odds with the legal analysis outlined above. Thus in 1933 he wrote that 'the National-Socialist Revolution is a counter-revolution of a monopolised industry and the big landowners against democracy and social progress; ... this revolution was only successful because the structure and the practice of the Weimar Constitution facilitated it.'[37] Later in the same article, however, the reader encounters a description of the 'total' nature of modern parties borrowed virtually word-for-word from Carl Schmitt, once more emphasising the manner in which Neumann continued to draw upon distinctly non-Marxist traditions for central theoretical propositions.

This was not simply a form of eclecticism, but betrays the deficiencies of the conventional Marxist analysis of capitalism. Put simply, traditional Marxist political theory is an oxymoron. The analysis of political forces practised by orthodox Marxists had always dealt with the political realm as if it were structured and dynamised by economic forces, requiring itself no special theoretical attention. This was not

---

[36] Letter of Neumann to the Academic Assistant Council, Royal Society, 22 July 1933, pp. 3–5.
[37] F. Neumann, 'The Decay of German Democracy', *Political Quarterly*, vol. 4 (1933), p. 526. Elsewhere Neumann referred to fascism as the ' ... political rule of the petty-bourgeoisie, which veils the economic dictatorship of Monopoly Capitalism' – F. Neumann, *Trade Unionism–Democracy–Dictatorship*, Workers' Educational Trade Union Committee, London 1934, p. 54.

simply a bad habit, but was chartered by the work of Marx himself.[38] The law received similar treatment, whether it involved legal process, or the analysis of statutes and norms; despite, or perhaps because of, Marx's early training in law. Neumann himself drew attention to this problem in a review of 1935, noting the paucity of socialist theorising with respect to the state. In this account, the social democratic theorising of Hermann Heller's recent work is given short shrift: 'one can read on every page the German idealistic philosophy which constitutes its origins.'[39] In particular, Neumann criticised the manner in which Heller argued against the conception of the state as a form of class domination.

In the same essay Neumann suggests that Harold Laski's book, *The State in Theory and Practice*, offers an analysis of class rule and the state that accorded with the Marxist model. Particular emphasis was laid by Laski upon the identity of state and government, and the manner in which relation between state and community was one that rested upon coercion. Neumann himself proceeded in the same essay to propose that the crucial difference between Marxist and bourgeois theories of the state was that the latter treated the state and law as rational constructs, while the former treated them as socio-historical products.[40] The implications of this form of definition are far-reaching, and serve to distance Neumann considerably from the generalisations of Laski.

This point requires some elaboration. From a superficial examination of Neumann's writings of the mid-1930s it would be possible to conclude that it was at this time, in England and under the influence of Laski, that he developed a serious Marxist critique of the capitalist state. Such a break would mark a watershed, dividing off his writings prior to this time (almost exclusively concerned with labour law and directly related constitutional issues), from subsequent publications addressing general theoretical issues, and which are far more critical in tone. The implication of this line of argument would be that the

[38] While the theoretical substance of Marx's *Capital* lays out a systematic treatment of the capitalist mode of production, the same cannot be said for Marx's writings on France, the 1848 revolutions, the First International, or India. In none of these cases can it be said that there is an analytical framework operating that differs significantly from contemporary radical journalism. In these terms, Lenin is not an orthodox Marxist; his political writings develop an understanding of the political realm which owes little to Marx's own writings.

[39] Franz Neumann, 'On the Marxist Theory of the State' in O. Kirchheimer and F. Neumann, *Social Democracy and the Rule of Law*, Allen and Unwin, London 1987, p. 76. The essay originally appeared under the pseudonym 'Leopold Franz' in *Zeitschrift für Sozialismus*, Jg. 2 (1935).   [40] Neumann, 'On the Marxist Theory of the State', p. 82.

analytical structure of *Behemoth* was built upon conceptual foundations laid in the 1930s in Britain, rather than during the 1920s in
Germany.

If we turn to Laski's writings we certainly do find a critique of the
Rule of Law that bears superficial comparison with that of Neumann,
but there is an important distinction in the treatment given to the
concept of sovereignty. For example, Laski observes that, while
parliament is in Britain the legal sovereign, there are in fact many
things that it cannot do; but then he goes on to conclude from this
observation that the concept of parliamentary sovereignty is quite
useless for political theory. As Herbert Deane notes, this conclusion
rests upon a blurring of the distinction between sovereignty as a legal
and as a political concept.[41] Laski operates with an absolutist
conception of sovereignty, which of necessity treats the existence of
alternative political interests and centres of decision-making in the
modern state as corrosive of all sovereignty and, hence, of the state
itself. Consequently, Laski contends that the concept of sovereignty
should be discarded, and replaced with the more relevant concept of
power.[42] These and related ideas were summarised in a new introductory chapter to the 1937 edition of *Grammar of Politics* under the title,
'The Crisis in the Theory of the State'.

Whereas Laski proposed to discard the conception of sovereignty in
favour of power, the former concept is central to Neumann's thesis – as
he states in the first paragraph, 'The modern state shows two basic
characteristics: the existence of a sphere of sovereignty of the state,
and the existence of a sphere of freedom from it. Only if sovereignty
exists can we speak of the state as such.'[43]

The sphere of freedom from the state represents a limitation upon
state power, and is constituted by sets of human rights defined by
general norms. This division, between the sphere of sovereignty and

---

[41] H. A. Deane, *The Political Ideas of Harold J. Laski*, Columbia University Press, New York 1955,
p. 15. Deane acknowledges in his Preface his debt to Neumann as his teacher in preparing this
book.

[42] H. Laski, *A Grammar of Politics*, 4th edn, George Allen and Unwin, London 1937, pp. 44–5: 'It
will be here argued that it would be of lasting benefit to political science if the whole concept
of sovereignty were surrendered. That, in fact, with which we are dealing is power; and what
is important in the nature of power is the end it seeks to serve and the way in which it serves
that end.'

[43] F. Neumann, *The Rule of Law*, Berg, Leamington Spa 1986, p. 3. This is a reprint of the
dissertation, whose full title is: 'The Governance of the Rule of Law. An Investigation into the
Relationship between the Political Theories, the Legal System and the Social Background in
the Capitalist Society', LSE 1936.

the sphere of freedom, gives rise to a contraposition of rights on the one hand, and power on the other.

This counterpoint introduced disintegrative forces into the socio-political order; nonetheless, the existence of such forces does not automatically mean that the Rule of Law is rendered mere appearance, or even that it is fatally undermined. Modern society is, according to Neumann, riven with conflicts, and manifests disintegrative tendencies; but a certain amount of order prevails, and hence a degree of integration is secured. The object of Neumann's study in his dissertation is to consider the important question: how much order, and what degree of integration, is necessary to sustain social order?

Neumann argues that the principle of the Rule of Law was not merely directed to the security of individual freedoms, and the limitation of state power to legal action; in addition the legal nature of state administration was addressed. No particular form of democratic representation need be assumed; only that freedom consisted in freedom from interference by the state, and the application of formal-rational law by an independent judge acting as guarantee to the individual. The legal system associated with this rested on three leading conditions, suggested Neumann: the existence of a system of free competition; the absence of the working-class as an independent movement, and the consequent ability to disregard the existence of class conflict; and the existence of a division of powers integrated at the level of the nation.[44] The development of monopoly capitalism swept away these conditions. The state emerges as a broker between mass political parties, and parliament as a theatre in which conflicts emerge and compromises are made; the nature and status of the laws promulgated by parliament becomes a debated issue, while the judiciary appropriates to itself the right of legislative review.

This argument is developed through three principal sections, although as Neumann readily admits, the second part, presenting a historical review of the analysis of sovereignty, is not sufficiently integrated and simply provides evidential support for the other two parts. Neumann begins his analysis with a discussion of basic concepts such as freedom, state, law, and power. Here themes initially broached in his first doctoral dissertation of 1923 are taken up once more, with the addition of a critique of the idea of a pure theory of law. Neumann also argues that the concept of freedom presupposes the existence of at least two possible options in any given situation, and is

[44] *Ibid.*, pp. 185–6.

therefore closely related to choice and competition. This involves a sociological underpinning of legal theory, in which the realisation of freedom and its associated rights presupposes an appropriate economic basis. It is precisely this economic foundation of the legal structure of competitive capitalism that has, in the course of the twentieth century, been displaced by monopolistic capitalism.

Characteristic of this period is the development of legal argument over issues such as, for example, the meaning of the paragraphs of the Weimar Constitution as 'general laws'. This is the line of attack that was taken by Carl Schmitt, with a consequent emphasis on the role of juridical decision and powers of review. The final part of Neumann's dissertation is devoted to a discussion of these issues, charting the decline of the Rule of Law and its associated principles during the Weimar period. The integrity of the existing legal order, so the argument runs, is being progressively undermined by the extension of polycracy and monopolistic bargaining; but these new phenomena show little sign of creating the basis for an alternative, more robust, legal system. The National Socialist seizure of power is thereby represented as a logical continuation of the problems of the Weimar period; it rests upon the existing (albeit degraded) legal order. But if it be so continuous with the Weimar Republic, could it therefore be claimed that the National Socialist state is based upon the Rule of Law? Three leading features of the new order controvert this idea: the personal nature of rule, the existence of retroactive legislation, and the manner in which *völkisch* conceptions are meant to guide juridical decisions.[45]

Neumann has no clear answer to his question concerning the nature of the legal foundations of National Socialism. His closing paragraph clearly expresses his dilemma: 'We therefore sum up: That law does not exist in Germany, because law is now exclusively a technique of transforming the political will of the Leader into constitutional reality. Law is nothing but an *arcanum dominationis*.'[46] This is certainly a conclusion consistent with the preceding argument, and yet it leaves much unanswered. If, according to Neumann's general argument, law and the legal process function as significant

---

[45] *Ibid.*, pp. 293–6. Neumann points out that the retroactive legislation of the National Socialists not only made punishable previous actions not at the time deemed criminal, but it also decriminalised prior criminal actions, such as the murders associated with the Night of the Long Knives in 1934.   [46] *Ibid.*, p. 298.

integrative forces; and if, furthermore, it is assumed that some measure of integration is required to sustain any form of social and political order; then for a system to maintain itself in being there has to be some process at work which generates this necessary minimum of integration.

That this conundrum struck Neumann with some force is clear from a further book proposal drafted in 1936 following completion of his thesis – it was entitled *Law as an Integrating and Disintegrating Element in Modern Society. A Sociological Analysis in the Forces which Strengthen or Weaken Rational Elements in Law*. Here rational law is defined as 'a general rule of law as opposed to arbitrary individual commands.'[47] He continued: 'It will be found that the primary means of integrating society is the general rule of law which, however, is not only considered to be a basis of calculation but is also related to a distinct notion of justice.'[48] This general rule loses its relationship to the idea of justice in the course of the nineteenth century, becoming merely a basis for calculation. In the course of the twentieth century normative legal thought then disappears: 'The general rule disappears also in theory as well as in practise. Irrational tendencies arise. Law is conceived as a command ... Legal standards of conduct replace rational law. What are the reasons for this change? What seems to me a possible solution is that irrational law prevails where the state is confronted with monopolistic power.'[49] The prospectus concludes with the question of the role of rational law in the 'totalitarian state': does it have an integrative or a disintegrative function?

It was this point that *Behemoth* was to take up and develop; but only after Neumann had secured further financial support, and had moved to the Institute of Social Research in New York. While at the LSE he had already been active on behalf of the Institute and its journal, the *Zeitschrift für Sozialforschung*. His main task concerned the Institute's library, held under embargo by the German authorities. The Institute had formally transferred ownership to the LSE in an attempt to gain its release, and it was Neumann who conducted the lengthy correspondence with the German authorities on behalf of the LSE, without in the end meeting with any success. Unable to practise in Britain because of his lack of relevant qualifications, and faced with the stagnation of the academic labour market, he looked to the

---

[47] Book Proposal, London 1936 (§1).   [48] *Ibid.*, (§2).   [49] *Ibid.* (§4).

Institute in New York for financial support.[50] With Laski's support he gained a temporary appointment; by April 1936 he had arrived in New York, and begun work at the Institute on Morningside Heights. The arrangement was at first only a temporary one; and for the first two years of his association with the Institute he continued with the kind of practical legal work that he had undertaken while still at the LSE. It was only in 1938 that he was he given a more permanent position and permitted to engage in serious research.[51] Work on *Behemoth* began in the summer of 1939.

Many of his former colleagues of that time have emphasised the distance between Neumann's intellectual and political formation and that of the Institute as a whole.[52] Indeed, not only was the book eventually published outside the Institute's programme, but after the war Horkheimer steadfastly refused to reprint it as part of the Frankfurt School's work; he is reputed to have argued, in support of this stance, that its theses opposed those of the Institute.[53] By this he was in all likelihood referring to the controversy over state capitalism that developed in the Institute around 1940, and which brought Horkheimer, Pollock, and Löwenthal together on one side of the debate, with Marcuse, Neumann, Kirchheimer, and Gurland on the other. Pollock, who had earlier published a detailed study of the Russian planned economy,[54] argued that National Socialism represented in certain respects a post-capitalist order, in which the basic principles of capitalist economic order were neither suspended nor transformed, but displaced. This thesis was disputed by Neumann, Marcuse, Gurland, and Kirchheimer, all of whom laid emphasis on the continuity between competitive capitalism, monopoly capitalism, and National Socialism. Dubiel and Söllner suggest that the dispute is one essentially between theoretical and empirical argumentation, but this explanation is unsatisfactory. For one thing, Neumann's analysis

[50] Neumann later argued that the cultural climate of Britain in the later 1930s was inimical to the development of an effective opposition to National Socialism, and that a move to the United States represented a necessary clean break with the past – 'The Social Sciences', in F. Neumann et al., *The Cultural Migration*, University of Pennsylvania Press, Philadelphia 1953, pp. 17–18.

[51] See the account in Erd, *Reform*, pp. 86–8; and in Intelmann, 'Biographie', pp. 36–40.

[52] The distance was expressed not least in the fact that Neumann, the experienced lawyer, was able to dictate whole sections of the book without hesitation; Horkheimer on occasion searched for two hours for the right word, during which time the secretary was allowed to read. Erd, *Reform*, pp. 99–100.

[53] Martin Jay cited in Erd, *Reform*, pp. 125–6.

[54] Pollock, *Die planwirtschaftlichen Versuche in der Sowjetunion 1917–1927*, Schriften des Instituts für Sozialforschung an der Universität Frankfurt a. M. Bd. 2, C. L. Hirschfeld, Leipzig 1929.

is founded upon legal theory as well as a detailed grasp of empirical evidence; and for another, Marcuse's work was never of an empirical nature. Furthermore, it is striking that Neumann and those most closely identified with his interpretation of National Socialism all soon left the Institute to work for the American Government in the OSS; and three of the four chose to remain in the USA after the war and established new academic reputations (Gurland returned to Berlin in 1950). Horkheimer, Pollock, and Löwenthal, by contrast, remained in the Institute throughout the war, and afterwards returned with it to Frankfurt.

During November and December of 1941 members of the Institute contributed to a special lecture series on National Socialism under the auspices of Columbia University, with contributions from Pollock, Neumann, Marcuse, Gurland, and Kirchheimer. Here the arguments that had taken place in Institute seminars during the previous year were made public, and then published in the journal *Studies in Philosophy and Social Science*.[55] Like many others, Pollock saw the First World War as a turning point marking the irrevocable replacement of private capitalism by state capitalism. Three features marked this shift:

(1) the role of the market in balancing production and distribution is lost and replaced with direct control – the autonomy of the market is destroyed;

(2) the state assumes the functions previously performed by the market;

(3) in its totalitarian form, state capitalism is dominated by a new ruling group formed from the fusion of the state bureaucracy with big capital.[56]

Instead of production, consumption, savings, and investment being co-ordinated by the market, state directives deriving from an economic plan are substituted for autonomous market mechanisms. The chief difficulty in forming this plan is not economic in nature, but rather political, involving issues such as the hierarchy of needs and their satisfaction, and levels of social consumption. A division arises

---

[55] H. Dubiel and A. Söllner, 'Die Nationalsozialismusforschung des Instituts für Sozialforschung – ihre wissenschaftsgeschichtliche Stellung und ihre gegenwärtige Bedeutung', in their edited collection, *Wirtschaft, Recht und Nationalsozialismus*, Suhrkamp Verlag, Frankfurt a. M. 1981, pp. 7–8. Reference will be made in the following to this convenient reprint of the relevant essays.

[56] F. Pollock, 'Staatskapitalismus' in Dubiel and Söllner, *Wirtschaft, Recht und Nationalsozialismus*, pp. 82–3.

between the management of enterprises and the investment of capital; the former function is subject to intervention from the state, while the investing capitalist becomes a rentier.[57] Another problem concerns innovation; under the private capitalist system, technological innovation and the development of new commodities is a product of market mechanisms. Under a state-directed system, this stimulus no longer exists. Pollock argues that political competition among the fractions of the ruling groups replaces economic competition as the spur to innovation. This is but one aspect of the emergence of political forces as decisive in the determination of social and economic development; and a consequence is that economic science ceases to play a central part in an understanding of such development, since it has been robbed of its object of study.[58]

These principles were explicitly applied to the case of National Socialist Germany in the final lecture of the 1941 cycle, in which Pollock posed the question: is National Socialism a new order? Employing the model of state capitalism, Pollock concludes that 'a new order is in process of emergence, a new political, legal, economic and social order. ... National Socialism employs in its economic policy a new system of rules – rules which render economic policy more efficient than ever before.'[59]

No specific limits to the new order are envisaged by Pollock; no economic forces are in evidence that can stand in the way of its full development. The command economy has it in its power to terminate the economic causes of depression and unemployment. The conscious and planful co-ordination of the economy, if exploited to its full potentiality, effects an improvement on the economy's 'natural laws'.[60] The National Socialist new order was no exception to this rule. Furthermore, no forces could be identified that might prompt its demise; only military intervention on the part of other state capitalist economies, utilising the potentiality of command and planning to democratic ends, would bring the National Socialist order to an end. This conclusion obviously shares some common ground with Neu-

---

[57] *Ibid.*, p. 91.

[58] *Ibid.*, p. 98. Pollock had also contributed an article to a symposium on the Economics of War in which he recapitulated this exposition under the rubric of a 'preparedness economy', proposing in his conclusion that 'whereas in Germany and Italy, Fascism creates a preparedness economy, in England and France the inherent tendencies in a preparedness economy lay the basis for some kind of Fascism.' 'Influences of Preparedness on Western European Economic Life', *American Economic Review, Papers and Proceedings*, Supplement, vol. 30 (1940), p. 324.   [59] Pollock, 'Staatskapitalismus', pp. 121–2, 123.

[60] *Ibid.*, p. 125.

mann, although Pollock is led, by his use of the state capitalist model, into a different appreciation of the dynamics and structure of National Socialism. In particular, one can note the manner in which Pollock conceives the state as a rational agency, endowed not only with the power of command, but with an innate capacity to form rational plans. This rationalistic conception of the state is quite at odds with that of Neumann. As we have seen, Neumann's analysis of the displacement of competitive by monopoly capitalism does not presuppose a state form capable of systematically displacing market mechanisms. Indeed, it is the real weakness and incapacity of the state that assures the persistence of market forces, albeit under new conditions.

It has been suggested that Neumann chose the title of *Behemoth* as a conscious response to Schmitt's own book *Leviathan*, published in 1937. Hobbes had of course used the mythical pairing in his classical analysis of the state, his *Behemoth* being otherwise known as *The Dialogue of the Civil Wars of England*.[61] Neumann inserted an explanatory note before his Preface, drawing attention to the wider mythical origin of the usage. In Jewish eschatology, he wrote, Behemoth and Leviathan were two monsters, in which the first ruled the land, and the second the sea. They were both monsters of chaos, and the apocalyptic writings prophesied that they would reappear shortly before the end of the world. A rule of terror would be re-established before they were destroyed by God, or, in other versions, before they destroyed each other.

It was Hobbes who made both the Leviathan and the Behemoth popular. His *Leviathan* is the analysis of a state, that is a political system of coercion in which the vestiges of the rule of law and of individual rights are still preserved. His *Behemoth*, or the *Long Parliament*, however, discussing the English civil war of the seventeenth century, depicts a non-state, a chaos, a situation of lawlessness, disorder and anarchy.

Since we believe National Socialism is – or tending to become – a non-state, a chaos, a rule of lawlessness and anarchy, which has 'swallowed' the rights and dignity of man, and is out to transform the world into a chaos by the supremacy of gigantic land masses, we find it apt to call the National Socialist system *The Behemoth*.[62]

The agenda is thereby set for the book, and in the final phrases of this statement the central dilemma is clearly restated – for can one

---

[61] F. Tönnies, 'Preface' to Hobbes, *Behemoth or the Long Parliament*, Simpkin, Marshall and Co., London 1889, p. vii.   [62] Neumann, *Behemoth*, p. xii.

refer to a condition of non-integration, of disorder, as a 'system'? We might here recall Schmitt's words cited above: 'There is no norm which could be applied to a situation of chaos. Order must be produced, so that the legal order has meaning.'[63] Was there some inherent order in National Socialism? If so, how should one go about the task of identifying it?

The book begins with a brief introductory analysis of the collapse of Weimar, which Neumann had had to cut from an original 300 manuscript pages to 60.[64] Part One then outlines the political nature of National Socialism, and in seeking to chart the ultimate aims of the movement suggests that the best clue to this lies in an exposition of its ideology. The identification of a specific National Socialist agenda has always confounded scholars, and *Behemoth* is no exception.[65] Neumann approaches the task by suggesting that the National Socialist critique of the Liberal State turned on the idea that it was a state without substance, where democracy was equated with the rule of the unorganised mass. Unsurprisingly, Schmitt is introduced as the ideologist of this agenda, which agenda can then be elaborated in terms of Schmitt's own arguments. The distinction of parliamentarism from democracy, decisionism, and polycracy are subsequently all ordered to the National Socialist ideological arsenal.[66]

There are two problems with this narrative strategy. Firstly, Schmitt's various writings, even post-1933, do not amount to a consistent adaptation of legal theory to National Socialism, as has already been suggested. An approach to the nature of National Socialism through these writings is thus of dubious merit. Secondly, and more seriously, this direct association of Carl Schmitt's analysis with the corpus of National Socialist ideology obscures the fact that the analytical framework of the entire book is deeply indebted to Schmitt. As is apparent from Neumann's 1931 essay outlined above, he had himself made use of the very concepts and categories that he is now attributing to National Socialism. This contradiction is left unresolved, but does in fact do little damage to the argument of the

[63] See n. 19 above.
[64] Intelmann, 'Biographie', citing a letter of Neumann to Horkheimer of 28 August 1941.
[65] Herbst in his study of National Socialist economic and social organisation falls back on Hitler's *Mein Kampf*, suggesting that, insofar as National Socialist ideology exists, this is the only plausible source – Herbst, *Der totale Krieg*, pp. 42ff. Barkai notes that in *Mein Kampf* the economy is barely mentioned, and turns instead to a number of programmatic statements from Feder, Klagges, and Strasser – A. Barkai, *Das Wirtschaftssystem des Nationalsozialismus*, Fischer Taschenbuch Verlag, Frankfurt a. M. 1988, pp. 27ff.
[66] Neumann, *Behemoth*, pp. 43–9.

book as a whole, since no attempt is made to represent National Socialist ideology as the principal source of integration and social order. This initial presentation of National Socialist ideology can therefore be safely left to one side.

The first substantive section of *Behemoth* is addressed to a discussion of the nature of the National Socialist Party, and its relation to the state. It is not evident that a clear distinction exists: 'Unanimous opinion holds that the party is not subject to any control whatever. The party's property may not be attached for a public or private debt. Moreover, the inner administration of the party, its legislative structure, and its judiciary, are not comparable to those of any other public corporation.'[67] The Party was not liable for the torts of its officials; it generally claimed all the privileges of the civil service, but disclaimed the responsibilities. In sum, the Party occupied a position usually assumed by a sovereign state with respect to another – as Neumann concludes, 'As a result, the state and the party stand side by side. Legally neither controls the other, each is sovereign in its own field – a constitutional situation which is self-contradictory.'[68] The contradiction here is that if sovereignty is the defining characteristic and sole prerogative of a state, then the existence of a parallel institution undermines the integrating force of law, the articulation of state power.

Socrates had put it this way: 'Do you believe that a state in which the decisions of the courts can have no validity, but can be reversed and nullified by particular persons, would subsist rather than perish?' This epigraph appears at the beginning of Ernst Fraenkel's account of the legal system of National Socialism.[69] Fraenkel, who had shared Neumann's Berlin practice, had remained behind in 1933, since his war service gave him a conditional immunity to the legislation that had disbarred Neumann. He continued to practise until 1938, and completed during the late 1930s a manuscript which was then translated and published in New York as *The Dual State*. The image that it provides of the role of the Party and the function of law in National Socialist Germany is one that shares much in common with that of *Behemoth*. However, having registered the freedom of Party matters from due legal process, Fraenkel responds by creating a theoretical construct built precisely upon this conundrum. His 'dual

---

[67] *Ibid.*, p. 73   [68] *Ibid.*, p. 82.
[69] E. Fraenkel, *The Dual State. A Contribution to the Theory of Dictatorship*, Oxford University Press, New York 1941, p. 1.

state' is a system where the 'Prerogative State', constituted out of the merging of state and party bureaucracies, rules not according to established statutes and precedents, but by discretion, expedience, and prerogative. This public sphere is outwith the jurisdiction of the 'Normative State', which is composed of administrative bodies charged with safeguarding the established legal order and securing the ordered and legal functioning of social and economic processes. This is of course much like the Rule of Law; with the difference that anything deemed relevant to the 'political' sphere is outside its jurisdiction. Given that the power of the Prerogative State is discretionary, discretion consists here in deciding what is political and what is not. In principle, anything remotely associated with state and party life can be deemed 'political', and hence outwith the competence of the Normative State and its institutions. The first part of Fraenkel's book is filled with examples of this process.[70] The stability of the system as a whole depends on interventions of discretionary power being extra-ordinary, rather than ordinary, occurrences. So for example contract law, labour law, intellectual property rights, and land law all continued to be upheld by the institutions of the Normative State. Fraenkel lists a number of cases in this area where the various courts were able to reject claims of discretionary powers in cases involving property and contracts, on the grounds that the cases concerned were not sufficiently exceptional.[71]

Fraenkel suggests that, despite this local accommodation between the two state forms, the continued existence of a dual state is problematic. Like Neumann, Fraenkel lays emphasis upon Max Weber's thesis that a rational legal system is indispensable for the operation of a capitalist economic order. Capitalism rests upon rational calculation; the legal framework provides an enduring basis for probabilistic, if not exact, calculation. Under the National Socialist régime the framework existed, but its vulnerability to localised suspension jeopardised the expectational certainties of rational calculation. Fraenkel does not further pursue the implications of this problem, but in any case Neumann rejected the entire approach to the legal order of National Socialism. Fraenkel was a one-time

---

[70] For instance, Fraenkel cites a case where an applicant for a driver's licence was refused on the grounds that he had spent six months in a concentration camp, and that since there were no aspects of life that were non-political, this naturally extended to traffic regulations. Similarly, all journeys made by members of the SA were political acts by virtue of their membership of the SA, and so they were exempt from traffic regulations. Fraenkel, *Dual State*, pp. 43–4.

[71] *Ibid.*, pp. 76ff.

colleague, and Neumann had read the manuscript of *The Dual State* while he was working on *Behemoth*.[72] Neumann brusquely rejected its arguments, stating that no realm of law existed in Germany. Instead, the basis for rational calculation rested upon the manipulation of large numbers of technical rules.[73] This curt rejection of a serious attempt to grapple with the legal order of National Socialism serves to focus our attention even more closely on the problem of order and integration in *Behemoth*. Fraenkel offered an explanation for the problem identified by Neumann, who did not, however, want anything to do with it. How, then, does Neumann go about resolving the contradictions of the legal order of National Socialism without recourse to this dualist conception?

The economy provides a secondary source of order for Neumann in his book. In Part Two, entitled 'Totalitarian Monopolistic Economy', the proposition that National Socialism represents a new form of state capitalist economic organisation is directly addressed. The first chapter is entitled, in a direct questioning of Pollock's theses, 'An Economy without Economics?'[74] Neumann perceives in the 'state capitalist' analysis of National Socialism an affinity with other 'post capitalist', 'post industrial' theories. 'State capitalism', argues Neumann, is nonetheless a contradiction in terms, an attempt to delineate an economic system articulated entirely in political categories. Following the lines of his analysis first broached in the 1920s and early 1930s, Neumann argues that the German economy still functions according to capitalist principles, but under the conditions of cartelisation and monopoly, combined with the regimentation of a totalitarian state.[75]

National Socialism pursues glory and the stabilisation of its rule, and industry, the full utilisation of its capacity and the conquest of foreign markets. German industry was willing to co-operate to the fullest. It had never liked democracy, civil rights, trade unions and public discussion. National Socialism utilised the daring, the knowledge, the aggressiveness of the industrial leadership, while the industrial leadership utilised the anti-democracy, anti-liberalism and anti-unionism of the National Socialist party . . .[76]

Investment, profitability, and sales were certainly altered by the policies of the post-1933 German government, but this was not a

---

[72] Neumann's comments on the manuscript are acknowledged on p. vi of Fraenkel's *Dual State*.
[73] Neumann, *Behemoth*, pp. 467–8, and p. 516, n. 63.   [74] *Ibid.*, p. 221.
[75] *Ibid.*, p. 261.   [76] *Ibid.*, p. 361.

difference of kind compared with developments during the 1920s, when monopoly displaced competitive capitalism. Neumann demonstrates this thesis by an extensive comparison of economic organisation and performance from the 1920s to the later 1930s. As Fraenkel had recognised, the legal institutions underpinning economic activity were not seriously modified; Neumann's differentiation of business by scale furthermore lends emphasis to the fact that, over broad areas of economic activity, significant continuity with the structural conditions of the 1920s persisted. While the political leadership might look with disfavour on the business leaders of Germany, the organisational structures that they had created were mostly left in place. Lacking a clear and distinct conception of National Socialist economics, the leadership had no framework with the aid of which they might impose a consistent alternative schema. The National Socialist remodelling of Germany was considered to be purely a political task; it did not require any specific restructuring of economic relations, so long as enterprises delivered the requisite goods to the armed services. The National Socialist leadership had little regard for economic rationality, treating this as a form of rationality inferior to political calculation. The corollary of this disdainful attitude was that economic ambition was regarded as a purely personal matter; and it was upon this principle that the economic empires of Himmler and Göring were built.

Neumann's account accurately reflects this state of affairs. Although the economy might perform some integrative function in National Socialism, the relatively subordinate role that it played in the system meant that it provided no key to a general understanding of the structure and dynamics of National Socialism as a whole. In his concluding chapter, Neumann returns to the counterpoint of Hobbes's *Leviathan* and his *Behemoth*. The former described a state whose sovereignty is founded upon rational legitimacy and which is not all-devouring. There was by contrast no state in National Socialist Germany. What is the form of order that prevails?

I venture to suggest that we are confronted with a form of society in which the ruling groups control the rest of the population directly, without the mediation of that rational though coercive apparatus hitherto known as the state. This new social form is not yet fully realized, but the trend exists which defines the very essence of the regime.[77]

[77] *Ibid.*, p. 470.

There is no more specific statement than this. Order and integration are generated contingently – by the application of technical rules. Instead of the Dual State, Neumann clearly suggests here that the state is in the process of being superseded. No clear indication is given of the resulting structure of social organisation, but it has clear affiliations with what in the 1950s and 1960s became known as a Police State, where legitimacy had given way to pure coercion.

Such a conclusion is not entirely satisfactory. The concepts mobilised by Neumann direct attention to the legal and political foundations of integration and order, which foundations are to be located in the state. It is precisely in this area that National Socialism violates established forms of political and legal rationality, but this does not amount to a progressive dismantling of the state apparatus. Neumann rejected Pollock's conception of state capitalism in part because it presumed a rationalist intention on the part of the state quite inappropriate, in his view, to the chaotic phenomenon of National Socialism. Neumann concluded that National Socialism had brought to an end the constellation of institutions and powers associated with the state and its sovereignty – instead there reigned a form of chaos, subsisted by a private capitalist economy that retained its own internal ordering principles, but which was subservient to the power of the Party and the ministerial bureaucracy.

It can however be argued that the condition of chaos charted by Neumann is a product of the categories that he employs, rather than an actual condition – it represents an epistemological, and not an ontological, problem. The Third Reich was certainly disorganised and chaotic; but this is not an adequate criterion with which to measure modern societies, all of which are to some degree disordered. Recent studies of legal and economic institutions under National Socialism have demonstrated the manner in which, in diverse spheres, established procedures and forms of rationality persisted. Indeed, far from displacing existing institutions, National Socialism successfully adapted them to its ends, making use of the routines and procedures inherent in institutional functioning.[78]

---

[78] A recent monograph on the practice of civil law has pointed to the way in which established procedures continued after 1933 – R. Schröder, > ... *aber im Zivilrecht sind die Richter standhaft geblieben!* <, Nomos Verlagsgesellschaft, Baden-Baden 1988. See also O. Rammstedt, *Deutsche Soziologie 1933–1945*, Suhrkamp Verlag, Frankfurt a. M. 1986 for a study of the complex adaptation of an academic discipline to National Socialism.

The Third Reich is however marked out by its deliberate programme to exterminate the Jews, a project itself founded in barbarity and criminal irrationality, yet executed with such attention to detail that historians today can in many cases ascertain the exact numbers and destination of each transport and the dates and numbers of gassings. Much recent discussion of the Holocaust and the conception of a European New Order turns on the degree to which these programmes, despite their barbarous intent, embodied the kind of intentional rationality that Neumann had rejected along with Pollock's conception of state capitalism. The historiography of the Third Reich has now moved a long way from debates over the degree to which Hitler 'intended' the annihilation of European Jewry. Likewise the notion that the Third Reich was the culmination of a German *Sonderweg* is now largely discredited. Leaving to one side the revival of totalitarian arguments in the mid-1980s,[79] there are at present two leading lines of argument in analysis of the Third Reich:

(1) the conception that its development was typified by a polycratic competition between social and political groupings, the pluralistic nature of this competitive process making redundant any imputation of intention to the system;[80]

(2) the conception that its development was marked by a deliberate programme of social and economic modernisation.

While not incompatible, proponents of the two approaches do tend to see themselves as occupying differing standpoints, the distinction turning upon the degree of intentional rationality inherent in the system. Along this continuum, the former tend to emphasise the contingent manner in which events unfolded, while proponents of the latter approach place emphasis on the planful and deliberate manner in which the policies of the Third Reich were implemented. In both cases, however, due recognition is given to Neumann's fundamental conviction that a degree of integration has to exist for a social system to remain in being. If the geography of power and coercion is regionalised, such that zones persist in which existing procedures and rules are routinely exercised, while in others different rules are created, then this provides a framework for the construction of some

---

[79] The theses advanced by Nolte and others regarding the 'totalitarian' nature of the Third Reich represent a relativisation, and not a contribution to serious analytical understanding, of the phenomenon of National Socialism.

[80] This approach revives the original meaning of the 'total state' and approaches the perspectives of Neumann and of Fraenkel: see M. Burleigh and W. Wipperman, *The Racial State. Germany 1933–1945*, Cambridge University Press, Cambridge 1991, p. 18.

form of order.[81] If on the other hand we seek to characterise the system as a whole with inappropriate models and concepts, we will simply register the absence of those integrative institutions anticipated in these models, and the presence of chaos. Chaos must by definition be a transitory state; if it persists then there is something which maintains that which is otherwise perceived as 'chaos' in existence. Other models are therefore needed to identify exactly what these forces are.

The concepts and categories deployed by Neumann are universalistic in their claim – descended from the European Enlightenment, they presuppose standards of rationality, equity, human need, and motivation that are universal. It is out of this problematic that modern liberalism and socialism developed, together with an apprehension of society and social order that was systematised in the social sciences. In the course of the twentieth century, however, the presuppositions of homogeneity and universalism have become increasingly embattled. It could be said that the social and political order of the nineteenth century was stratified, such that differing orders of rationality prevailed, but were regionalised in discrete social, temporal, and geographical zones. Modern social and political theory – of class society and democracy – is a product of this environment. In the course of the twentieth century stratification has given way to fragmentation, in which the effective scope of theories that presuppose rationality and intentionality is increasingly limited. This is the process that Neumann registers in his account of the displacement of private capitalism by monopoly capitalism. Pollock's attempt to define this feature of modern industrial economies by means of the term 'state capitalism' represents an attempt to reimpose Enlightenment conceptions of rationality on a process that escapes such definition. The problem that Neumann encounters is, in short, the problem of modernity. Not the 'modernity' of social science modernisation theory of the 1960s, in which social and economic indicators could score the degree of national 'progress' on the path to industrial society. What is modern about National Socialism is the deliberate reconstruction of a social and political order by the application of the modern instrumentaria of power and domination. This fractures the Enlightenment linkage of 'modernity' to 'progress'.

[81] 'Regionalised' is meant here quite literally: at the highest level, the differing administrative regimes of Greater Germany, the occupied European countries, the Generalgouvernment and the Reichskommissariat territories involved quite distinct zones of legal and political order.

The brutality and violence of the National Socialist régime was all the more shocking for its having arisen in an advanced European nation. Over the past fifty years academic effort has been primarily dedicated to charting on the one hand the origins and rise of National Socialism, and on the other its demise. Only comparatively recently has attention turned to the manner in which the system was maintained in being for twelve years, despite the fact that Neumann's study focuses precisely on these issues. His analytical approach presupposed that the inner structure of the National Socialist régime was as pathological as its more evident excesses. Today, however, it is possible to begin understanding the fragmentation of the National Socialist régime not as a mark of its pathological nature, but rather as a normal condition of modern social and political order.

Social 'modernism' has a dual sense here. First of all, it refers to the manner in which social and political life is segmented and fragmented, producing the negative phenomena that become the object of critical appraisal. Secondly, it also refers more specifically to the manner in which, echoing the argument concerning polycracy, that 'modern society' is to a great extent modernised by state intervention. The minimal state of the nineteenth century gave way in the first decades of the twentieth century to a state which increasingly sought positive intervention into the lives of its citizens. This intervention was in turn funded by the steady increase of taxation, so that the state became a major economic agent in its own right, the activity of raising money having just as much impact as the spending or transfer of public funds. Germany had of course been in the forefront of this process, especially in the areas of education and social insurance. Recent research has thrown emphasis upon the way in which social and economic legislation introduced or planned during the National Socialist régime continued this process.

Hitherto, insofar as such manifestations have been recognised, they have usually been considered to be the unintentional products of an essentially backward-looking political leadership, or alternatively as utopian projections.[82] For example, the invasion of Russia and the development of a settlement policy for the East has routinely been treated as the manifestation of an anti-industrial project to re-agrarianise Germany.[83] On the contrary, it is now recognised that

---

[82] Ian Kershaw provides a useful summary of the debate on the nature of the National Socialist 'Social Revolution' in his *The Nazi Dictatorship*, Edward Arnold, London 1985, Chapter 7.

[83] R. Zitelmann, 'Die totalitäre Seite der Moderne', in M. Prinz and R. Zitelmann (eds.), *Nationalsozialismus und Modernisierung*, Wissenschaftliche Buchgesellschaft, Darmstadt 1991,

schemes for the resettlement of the East were closely connected with the creation of a future autarkic New European Order, in which peasant settlements as well as access to raw materials played a role. For the members of the German *Volksgemeinschaft*, and for them alone, the future was to be one of social equality and mobility.[84]

This is evident in the broad area of social policy, where labour market demand, training, and recruitment were to be integrated into a structure that would reconcile the desire on the part of an individual to make a free choice, and the requirement on the part of the economy for specific skills.[85] The provision of suitable vocational training had been a problem addressed during the 1930s, when a functioning and comprehensive system of training and qualification had been established. Provision for social insurance, health care, and leisure was also part of this broader attempt to guarantee to the German people unrivalled conditions of life and work. Indeed, it is now becoming apparent that some part of the successful reconstruction of the German economy in the postwar years can be attributed to these modernising tendencies. The rapid recovery of Germany from the devastation of the war is today most plausibly related to the uneven impact of aerial bombardment on productive facilities, such that much more of Germany's capital stock survived than has usually been anticipated, and what there was was newer than that available in Britain and France.[86] This is no doubt correct; but Germany in 1945 was also, in many important social and political aspects, a more modern society than contemporary France or Britain. This also had implications for the process of European integration that began during the years of postwar reconstruction, as is shown in the concluding chapter below.

Neumann completed the manuscript for his book in August 1941,[87] that is to say: after the invasion of the Soviet Union, but before the world was aware of the systematic murder by *Einsatzgruppen* of Jews as

pp. 14–15. See for another review of the issues J. Alber, 'Nationalsozialismus und Modernisierung', *Kölner Zeitschrift für Soziologie und Sozialpsychologie*, Jg. 41 (1989), pp. 346–65.

[84] See R.-D. Müller, *Hitlers Ostkrieg und die deutsche Siedlungspolitik*, Fischer Taschenbuch Verlag, Frankfurt a. M. 1991. The fate of the non-Germans was, of course, to be very different, but no less 'modern'; Aly and Heim have depicted a convincing picture of the Holocaust and the New Order as social engineering on a grand scale – G. Aly and S. Heim, *Vordenker der Vernichtung. Auschwitz und die deutschen Pläne für eine neue europäische Ordnung*, Hoffman und Campe, Hamburg 1991.

[85] M.-L. Recker, *Nationalsozialistische Sozialpolitik im zweiten Weltkrieg*, R. Oldenbourg Verlag, Munich 1985, pp. 88–95.

[86] See A. Kramer, *The West German Economy 1945–1955*, Berg, Oxford 1991, Chapter 4.

[87] Intelmann, p. 41.

part of the campaign on the Eastern Front. Not until one year later was sufficient information assembled on these massacres and on the early functioning of the extermination camps to permit the conclusion to be drawn that, far from a random brutality, a systematic programme of annihilation was in process.[88] Neumann's book itself appeared in early 1942. Thus our modern understanding of National Socialism primarily in terms of this programme of annihilation is different to that of Neumann, the writer of *Behemoth*: he did not have in view, when conducting his analysis, that feature of the system most obvious to us today. The inherent strength of his analysis is however demonstrated by the manner in which this discrepancy in perspective is not at all obvious to the modern reader.

[88] See Chapter 10 of M. Gilbert, *Auschwitz and the Allies* (1991 edn.) which dates such an awareness from around November 1942, by which time the extermination camps were fully operational.

CHAPTER 8

The genealogy of the Social Market Economy: 1937–48

> If we are to judge the potentialities aright it is necessary to
> realize that the system under which we live choked up with
> attempts at partial planning and restrictionism is almost as far
> from any system of capitalism which could be rationally
> advocated as it is different from any consistent system of
> planning. It is important to realize in any investigation of the
> possibilities of planning that it is a fallacy to suppose
> capitalism as it exists today is the alternative. We are certainly
> as far from capitalism in its pure form as we are from any
> system of central planning. The world of to-day is just
> interventionist chaos.[1]

Today, the phrase 'Social Market Economy' is widely understood as a codeword for a prudent economic centrism. Its terminological predecessor, the 'mixed economy', now conveys the sense of an uneasy relationship between state and economy, in which corporatism and big government determine the balance between private and state enterprise. The Social Market Economy is more overtly capitalistic than this – a capitalism with an acceptable, human face in which greater emphasis is placed upon legal regulation as the means of identifying and achieving social objectives. Stated in this way, we have already lent the term a somewhat clearer profile than it usually assumes in the everyday discourse of journalists and politicians. It is no great exaggeration to say that beyond some general provision for social objectives, its most important connotation is the German *Wirtschaftswunder*; and so anyone seeking to emulate the achievements of the German economy during the 1950s and 1960s could do a lot worse than adopt the terminology of an evidently successful policy. Nonetheless, quite what the Social Market Economy might be,

---

[1] F. A. von Hayek, 'The Nature and History of the Problem', in his *Collectivist Economic Planning*, George Routledge, London 1935, pp. 23–24.

beyond a few slogans and the actual economic and social measures introduced by German governments in the 1950s, remains more or less an enigma. What is the programmatic substance of this 'Social Market Economy', what kind of intellectual heritage does it build upon? The more sceptical among us might argue with justification that we are dealing here with nothing more than a convenient political slogan whose analytical content lacks any specific directives for the formation of policy, but which has the advantage that it promises to modify, in some indeterminate way, those more unsocial aspects of the market economy.

A sceptical attitude to the real substance of a Social Market Economy as a specific economic régime is quite justifiable, on at least three counts.

First of all, the term Social Market Economy did indeed first enter general circulation as a political slogan:[2] as a component of the Christian Democratic Union's *Düsseldorfer Leitsätze über Wirtschaftspolitik, Sozialpolitik und Wohnungsbau* of 15 July 1949, the programme drafted for the first Bundestag election campaign. In distancing itself from the so-called 'free economy' the Party called for state protection for the socially and economically weak, for a 'system of regulatory measures' that would displace the power of public authorities and private monopolies.[3] The original founding manifesto of the CDU, the *Ahlener Programm* of 1947, had pronounced the era of unrestricted free capitalism to be over; the reconstructed German economy was to be an economy planned and guided in the interests of the German people, rather than in the interests of private capital. The reformulation of this position in 1949 relegated such planning functions to a transitional phase of economic reconstruction, and proposed that the future peacetime economy would combine social objectives with the remote and anonymous guidance of the price mechanism.[4] One would not normally expect to find in a party programme precise details of the mechanisms through which this accommodation was to be realised. None were subsequently forthcoming either, however;

---

[2] Although invention of the term itself is usually credited to Alfred Müller-Armack, who first used it in 1947 in the course of a report to the Chambers of Industry and Commerce of Nordrhein-Westfalen – reprinted in his *Genealogie der sozialen Marktwirtschaft*, Verlag Paul Haupt, Bern 1974, pp. 59–65.

[3] R. Walther, 'Exkurs: Wirtschaftlicher Liberalismus' in O. Brunner, W. Conze, and R. Koselleck (eds.), *Geschichtliche Grundbegriffe*, Bd. 3, Klett-Cotta, Stuttgart 1982, p. 814.

[4] See A. R. L. Gurland, *CDU/CSU. Ursprünge und Entwicklung bis 1953*, Europäische Verlagsanstalt, Frankfurt a. M. 1980, pp. 138–40, 145–9.

and so the term quickly became a slogan expressing political aspirations and affirmations, lacking substantive content beyond an association with government policies of the day.

A second reason to doubt the substantiality of the Social Market Economy as a usable economic concept is that the writings of its latter-day exponents are for the most part bereft of analytical rigour or insight. There is of course an extensive literature discussing the accomplishments of the Social Market Economy, but such writing conveys little sense to the modern economist or historian of a close engagement with genuine theoretical or practical issues.[5] Insofar as a blueprint for the Social Market Economy can be identified, then this is universally attributed to the Freiburg School, in particular the writings of Walter Eucken, Professor of Economics in Freiburg from 1927 until his death in 1950. There is certainly a strong filiation here, which will be examined below; but it was only in the postwar period that Eucken, Röpke, Müller-Armack, and Rüstow became identified with the idea of a Social Market. Once this occurred, their writings dating back to the early 1930s were conscripted as the basis for a theoretical heritage, although these writings are by no means directly addressed to this idea. Furthermore, if these writings are examined in detail they reveal a rather different orientation from that usually attributed to them. There is some difficulty here, however, since even by contemporary standards much of this writing is not strictly 'academic': it adopts a popular and general approach which makes little systematic use of theoretical concepts, or consistent reasoning. Wilhelm Röpke, for example, who was during the 1930s one of the first to formulate the conception that economic policy could be classified as either 'market conform' or 'market nonconform', published throughout the 1940s and 1950s a number of works, now largely forgotten, concerning the need for a new humane world order.[6] His most academic publication was probably *Crises and Cycles*, a synthetic account of the Trade Cycle which James Meade described

---

[5] English readers can by way of confirmation refer to the collection of papers edited by A. Peacock and H. Willgerodt, *Germany's Social Market Economy: Origins and Evolution*, Macmillan, London 1989. Contrast this collection with Samuel Brittan's acceptance speech on receiving the Ludwig Erhard Prize for economic writing, in which he puts an intellectual argument for the Social Market Economy with commendable brevity and clarity – see his 'Putting the social in social market', *Financial Times*, 22 February 1988, p. 21. See also his *Restatement of Economic Liberalism*, Macmillan, London 1988.

[6] See for example *Civitas humana*, William Hodge, Edinburgh 1949; *The Social Crisis of our Time*, William Hodge, Edinburgh 1950; *International Order and Economic Integration*, Reidel, Dordrecht 1959.

as 'a first survey for the student of the history of cycles' which however had the familiar failing that 'Many important terms are never defined precisely, and often bare assertion takes the place of analysis.'[7] Moreover, given the fact that the intellectual origins of the Social Market Economy lie in the 1940s, much recent writing on the subject takes the form of reminiscences, *Festschrift* contributions and obituaries, all of which forms of writing are notoriously unreliable historical sources. Judged by such writings, it is difficult to see in the Social Market Economy much more than a well-meaning, but insubstantial, gloss on the workings of the market economy.

Thirdly, for much of its life the Social Market Economy served as a politico-theoretical counterbalance to the socialist economies of the Soviet Union and Eastern Europe. The Social Market Economy was here, both geographically and intellectually, in the frontline of the struggle against socialism:

Faced with the intrinsic dynamics of development in our industrial society, conceptions of a democratic socialism founder everywhere on the deficiencies displayed by a socially guided economy. The Social Market Economy is the sole alternative with which the free world can counter Marxist socialism and secure its own future.[8]

The unfolding of the *Wirtschaftswunder* of the 1950s was accompanied by the parallel development of the German Democratic Republic. The ideological priority given by the Sozialistische Einheitspartei Deutschlands (SED) to the rights and welfare of workers was complemented in the West by social and labour legislation which secured the welfare of employees within a market system. However, with the collapse of the socialist economies of Eastern Europe, and in particular in the process of Unification, the tenets of the Social Marketeers have lost the counter-concept which for so long served to lend the Social Market Economy its political and intellectual focus. This only adds to our sense of the insubstantiality of the term in its modern-day usage.

There is however a further, related, difficulty with this perception of the Social Market Economy as the antithesis of the planned economy. The Social Market Economy of the 1950s confronted the economic claims of the Eastern European economies with a market-based system which produced both wealth and welfare; its success

[7] J. E. Meade, review of Röpke, *Crises and Cycles* (1936), *Economic Journal*, vol. 46 (1936), pp. 694–5.
[8] 'Zur Einführung: Zeitgeschichtliche Notizen', in Müller-Armack, *Genealogie der sozialen Marktwirtschaft*, p. 7.

made it known as a political response to socialist command economies. It would however be a mistake to read the writings of its early
advocates in the light of this Cold War function. The model of the
Centrally Administered Economy that Eucken and Müller-Armack
had in mind during the 1940s was not that of the Soviet Union, since
most of the institutional features now associated with socialist economies were not fully established until the 1950s. When Eucken, Röpke,
Müller-Armack, or Böhm write in the later 1930s and 1940s of the
deficiencies of centralised economic management the primary refer-
ent is not the Soviet Union, but National Socialist Germany. For
them, the planned economy is above all the contemporary German
economy. This strengthens the force of their arguments, since it
implies that their critique of planning does not take the familiar route
of defending capitalism simply by criticising socialism. Ordoliberals[9]
certainly criticised the welfare deficiencies of planning systems, but
sought beyond this to elaborate a conception of the functioning of
market mechanisms. This is not only important for a proper appreciation of the precepts of the Social Marketeers, but places in focus their
strictures on economic reconstruction after the defeat of National
Socialism. If we insist on reading the writings of the 1940s primarily as
a critique of socialist planning we are in danger of going seriously
astray.

Here the link with the writings of Friedrich von Hayek is especially
misleading. Hayek certainly was a close associate of Eucken and
Böhm, taking his place alongside Karl Brandt, Constantin von
Dietze, Friedrich Lutz, Wilhelm Röpke, and Alexander Rüstow on
the Editorial Board of their new yearbook, *Ordo*, in 1948. During the
later 1940s, the London School of Economics became a leading
platform for the dissemination of Social Market economics in the
English-speaking world; and in fact it was while delivering a lecture
series there in 1950 that Eucken died of a heart attack.[10] Moreover,

---

[9] Choice of an appropriate collective term for Eucken and his associates is not easy; later, after
the founding of the *Ordo* yearbook in 1948 it is possible to identify them as its associates, or we
can broadly refer to the Freiburg School. It would be incorrect to refer to these writers as neo-
liberals, since the characteristic feature of the writings discussed here is that they envisage a
wide-ranging programme of social policy reform, whereas the attention of neo-liberals is
focused on competition policy.

[10] This last lecture series was published, with an introduction by John Jewkes, as *This
Unsuccessful Age*, William Hodge, London 1951. Terence Hutchison translated Eucken's
major work as *The Foundations of Economics*, William Hodge, London 1950, as well as other
writings; Alan Peacock translated H. von Stackelberg's *Grundlagen der theoretischen Volkswirtschaftslehre* as *The Theory of the Market Economy*, William Hodge, London 1952; and Peacock
outlined the work of Stackelberg and Erich Schneider in his 'Recent German Contributions
to Economics', *Economica*, NS vol. 17 (1950), pp. 175–87.

perhaps the most widely known critique of socialist planning, Hayek's *The Road to Serfdom*, was first published in 1944, at the same time that Eucken and his colleagues in Freiburg were drawing up their programme for the restoration of market forces in the German postwar economy. It is naturally tempting to read the work of the *Ordo* theorists from the perspective offered by Hayek's more accessible writings. But this would be mistaken. The critique of 'planning' that we find in Hayek has an almost ontological force, in which intervention on the part of the state is rejected not primarily because of the resultant diminution of welfare, but because of the surrender of decision-making to a select few.[11] Hayek developed his critique of socialism and economic planning on the basis of a conception of a 'pure capitalism' that was an ideal type, an economic corollary to the Rule of Law; his conception of 'planning' became the logical counterpart to this, and was equally abstract. There is nothing inherently wrong with this, except that in the hands of Hayek ideal-typical constructions are treated as if they can be directly read into real economies. An ideal-type is supposed to identify the leading characteristics of a given order, and provide some insight into their dynamics. As the epigraph to this essay well illustrates, Hayek's abstractions provide no such insight: writing in the mid-1930s, he sees himself surrounded by disorder, rather than complexity, a sure sign of analytical error. Hayek argued that the rationality and orderliness claimed for a centrally planned economy by its proponents was unrealisable, and that only a capitalist system could deliver welfare and rationality. But the capitalist system which he supposed capable of providing welfare and rationality was every bit as abstract as those rational systems imagined by utopian socialists. For all its evident political appeal to conservatives and libertarians, Hayek's defence of capitalism, as well as his critique of socialism, is as purely theoretical as the arguments of communist ideologues. It is *Kulturkritik* masquerading as economic analysis.

However degenerated discussion of the Social Market Economy might be today, however indistinct as a serious contribution to the

---

[11] 'The choice open to us is not between a system in which everybody will get what he deserves according to some absolute or universal standard of right, and one where the individual shares are determined partly by accident or good or ill chance, but between a system where it is the will of a few persons that decides who is to get what, and one where it depends at least partly on the ability and enterprise of the people concerned and partly on unforeseeable circumstances.' F. A. Hayek, *The Road to Serfdom*, Routledge and Kegan Paul, London 1979, p. 76. For a sober evaluation of the force of Hayek's criticisms of socialist planning see J. Tomlinson, *Hayek and the Market*, Pluto Press, London 1990, pp. 106ff.

understanding of modern economies it might have become, it is nevertheless possible to discover in the writings of Eucken and some of his Freiburg colleagues a conception of economic organisation that represents a genuine effort to move beyond the sterile contraposition of market to plan and vice versa. Despite the limitations of many of their conclusions, there is something to be learned from these efforts to seek ways of managing market forces without subordinating them to a directive apparatus. The initial positions were marked out during the 1930s. During the war they were elaborated as many economists looked towards the future peacetime economy and the manner in which a market economy could be deliberately re-introduced. The defeat of Germany then brought with it occupation forces who, having ended the National Socialist régime, simply replaced it in both East and West with a different form of military economic control, since their natural response to the problems of devastation and shortage was to make plans and issue commands. In this context, arguments advanced by German economists for the ending of controls and regulations and the restoration of market relations became associated with a movement for political emancipation from occupied status. The rapidity with which Germans did regain control of political and economic life through the creation of new institutions and a new republic promoted the *Ordo* theorists to the status of prophets for the new Germany, but, as tends to happen, in the process much of the original sense of their message became forgotten or garbled. The language of the Social Market became an arcane code which lost much in the translation; and over the years this code seems to have worn out with constant repetition, rather than have undergone a process of elaboration and extension. The purpose of this essay is to restore some of this original sense; the better to judge the nature of the work of the Freiburg School, and any connection that we might, on this basis, be able to establish with economic policy in a reconstructed Germany. '

It is customary to date the inception of Ordoliberalism from 1937, when Franz Böhm, Walter Eucken, and Hans Grossmann-Doerth began a series entitled 'Ordnung der Wirtschaft' and prefaced the first volume with an editorial statement.[12] Dieter Haselbach has recently drawn attention to the fact that one of the chief functions of this

---

[12] The first volume in the series was Böhm's *Die Ordnung der Wirtschaft als geschichtliche Aufgabe und rechtschöpferische Leistung*, W. Kohlhammer Verlag, Stuttgart 1937. The statement is translated in Peacock and Willgerodt, *Germany's Social Market Economy*, pp. 15–26 under the somewhat baffling (and unexplained) title 'The Ordo Manifesto of 1936'.

statement was to seek a rehabilitation of economics and law as independent sources of government advice, a position that had, according to the 'Manifesto', been eroded since the later nineteenth century thanks to the impact of the Historical School.[13] As the authors of the Manifesto assert,

Men of science, by virtue of their profession and position being independent of economic interests, are the only objective, independent advisers capable of providing true insight into the intricate interrelationships of economic activity and therefore also providing the basis upon which economic judgments can be made. They are also the only ones who, on the strength of their intimate knowledge of these interrelationships – a knowledge which is constantly being expanded and refined by the continuing penetration of new ideas – are capable of forming an objective judgement, independent of their own immediate economic interests, about economic measures appropriate in particular circumstances.[14]

The authors clearly believed that they had something important to say, and this intellectual posture is one that was steadfastly maintained during the following years. It is important that this guiding feature of their work is kept in mind. First, we should see the involvement of Eucken and others in the work of the Akademie für Deutsches Recht in this light, and the consequent access they thereby gained to officials in the Reichswirtschaftsministerium during the early 1940s. Second, it helps us to understand their sense of frustration after Germany's capitulation; inexplicably (to Eucken and his associates) the American Military Government was not especially disposed to heed advice on the restoration of the price mechanism from resident German economists – initial efforts to make contact were rebuffed. Third, the Currency Reform of 1948 can be viewed as a vindication of

---

[13] D. Haselbach, *Autoritärer Liberalismus und Soziale Marktwirtschaft*, Nomos Verlagsgesellschaft, Baden-Baden 1991, p. 84. The Historical School can be blamed for a great deal, but not for this particular deficiency. Firstly, Eucken and his associates are here adopting a position *identical* with that assumed by German academics within the *Verein für Sozialpolitik* in the 1880s, when the organisation redirected its activity towards the socio-political education of public officials and government: see D. Lindenlaub, *Richtungskämpfe im Verein für Sozialpolitik*, Beiheft 52/53 *Vierteljahrschrift für Sozial- und Wirtschaftsgeschichte*, F. Steiner, Wiesbaden 1967, pp. 27–9. Secondly, Max Weber's criticisms of Schmoller in the early 1900s identified the manner in which his patronage extended only so far as the government permitted; Schmoller was himself a victim of the relation that he had done so much to establish between academics and politicians. See W. Hennis, 'The Pitiless "Sobriety of Judgement": Max Weber between Carl Menger and Gustav von Schmoller – the Academic Politics of Value Freedom', *History of the Human Sciences*, vol. 4 (1991), pp. 40–1.
[14] Böhm, Eucken and Grossmann-Doerth, 'The Ordo Manifesto of 1936' in Peacock and Willgerodt, *Germany's Social Market Economy*, p. 15.

this posture, since it coincided with policies that had been advocated by the Freiburg School since the later war years. Quite how much specific impact their arguments did eventually have on the Allied Government is not clear, but there is no doubt that the need for such a reform as the principal condition for a restoration of the market mechanism had been clearly articulated in discussion papers of the Beckerath Kreis as early as February 1943.

These issues will be taken up below, but first we should return to the passage above. There is more to this than overweening professorial pomposity. The notion of men of science being 'independent of economic interests' is no mere assertion of scientific value freedom;[15] for the counsel of independent scientists had been made necessary by the capture of the state by particular interests. The contours of this argument become clearer if we consider an article on the state and the crisis of capitalism published by Eucken in 1932. After making some remarks on the role of the entrepreneur as the dynamic element in capitalism, Eucken presents an account of the evolution of state and economy from the 'mercantilist-absolutist' period to the present. Essentially, there are three phases. In the first, absolutist, stage, princes sought to control the economy for their own ends, but lacked the power to realise their ambitions; the economy therefore ran its course largely undisturbed by interference from the state. During the nineteenth century liberals sought to extend the autonomy of society from the state, and although the state was more powerful than its eighteenth-century forerunner, economic activity was left to run its course and, conversely, no economic groups sought to win control of the state apparatus for their own ends. By the end of the nineteenth century, however, the German state was increasingly intervening in economic activity on behalf of special-interest groups, leading by the 1920s to the creation of a *Wirtschaftsstaat* in which state and economy have become intermingled; the economy has become politicised. These developments do not imply a strengthening of the state, however, but rather its weakening. The close connection between state and economy means that every deep economic depression strikes at the foundations of the state, as it becomes increasingly the instrument of interest groups. This modern *Wirtschaftsstaat* not only

---

[15] That Eucken entirely misunderstood Weber's critique of the idea of value freedom and his analysis of scientific work is evident from comments in his essay 'Die Überwindung des Historismus', *Schmollers Jahrbuch*, Jg. 62 (1938), p. 197. See also his 'Wissenschaft im Stile Schmollers', *Weltwirtschaftliches Archiv*, Bd. 52 (1940), pp. 468–503.

hampers the entrepreneur, but obstructs the functioning of the price mechanism, controlling the movement of prices in labour, capital, housing, and food markets.[16]

Although this historical appreciation of the development of state and economy might in parts be somewhat eccentric, it is the analysis of the *Wirtschaftsstaat* that is of real importance here. Another name current for this was of course the Total State, and in a footnote Eucken refers to his authority: Carl Schmitt's *Hüter der Verfassung*, published the year before and deployed in Franz Neumann's own critique of Weimar, as demonstrated in the previous essay.[17] Eucken's affinity with Schmitt goes rather deeper than does Neumann's, who freely made use of the conceptual apparatus, while discarding the political standpoint. Both Schmitt and Eucken were supporters of the Papen government, both advocated the strong, conservative rule which, they hoped, would restore political stability in Germany.[18] Liberty would result from a consistently firm *Ordnungspolitik*; which reverses the classical conception of liberalism, where order is supposed to be the consequence of liberty, not its presupposition.[19] Eucken's stance is therefore anything but that of a disengaged and disinterested academic. His problem was the question of how the programme of Ordoliberalism might be realised under National Socialist rule. This puts rather a different perspective upon the work of Eucken and his associates. To understand the implications of this new perspective we need first to outline the main economic tenets of the programme.

Eucken's *Grundlagen der Nationalökonomie* was an immediate success on publication in 1940,[20] being widely discussed at the time, and subsequently reprinted several times during the war. Röpke's earlier *Lehre von der Wirtschaft*, published in 1937 and exposing several themes more usually attributed to Eucken, is nonetheless a more accessible starting-point. Like Eucken, Röpke had gained a full professorship early in his career, at Marburg. However, he had never concealed his hostility to National Socialism and in 1933 was first suspended, and

[16] W. Eucken, 'Staatliche Strukturwandlungen und die Krisis des Kapitalismus', *Weltwirtschaftliches Archiv* Bd. 36 (1932), pp. 301ff.

[17] Eucken's reference to Schmitt is on p. 307 of 'Staatliche Strukturwandlungen'.

[18] One of the most concise statements of Schmitt's position in the closing phases of the von Papen government can be found in his 'Weiterentwicklung des totalen Staats in Deutschland (Januar 1933)' in his *Positionen und Begriffe*, Hanseatische Verlagsanstalt, Hamburg 1940, pp. 185–90.   [19] Haselbach, *Autoritärer Liberalismus*, p. 78.

[20] W. Eucken, *Die Grundlagen der Nationalökonomie*, Gustav Fischer, Jena 1940, translated by T. W. Hutchison as *The Foundations of Economics*, William Hodge, Edinburgh 1950.

then forcibly retired, on the grounds of his 'liberal disposition'.[21] He was appointed Professor of International Economics at the Graduate School of International Studies, Geneva in 1937, from where he could keep in relatively close touch with developments in Germany, and of course with his colleagues in Freiburg. His location in Geneva also gave him ready access to intellectual developments outside Germany; and this is reflected in his writing, highlighting by comparison the more parochial preoccupations of Eucken and Müller-Armack.

Röpke argues that the market economy, co-ordinated by the price system, is intrinsically anarchic; but this does not necessarily mean that it is also chaotic and disorderly. The creation of order by an anarchic system is, he proposes, the central question requiring explanation.[22] The *Lehre von der Wirtschaft* is an introduction to the co-ordination of production and distribution by the price-system, the concluding chapter then being devoted to a general survey of economic systems and the nature of economic crises. Here he sets up a contrast between capitalist and communist economic systems.[23] He suggests that it is an error to contrast a capitalist system driven by profit with a communist system oriented to the production of goods satisfying the needs of the people. The market mechanism of the capitalist economy is no less driven by needs than the planful activity of the communist economy; the difference should instead be seen in motivation and organisation, rather than in the presence or absence of profit. The real question thus becomes one concerning the manner in which each system identifies the needs of its consumers, and seeks to satisfy revealed needs.

There was a popular misconception, he goes on, that a communist system is planful, while a capitalist system is anarchic, lacking any specific plan. On the contrary: at a certain level all state economic

---

[21] Haselbach, *Autoritärer Liberalismus*, pp. 166–7. Röpke taught first in Istanbul, and then in Geneva. He was never to return to a German post; after the war Hartshorne offered him his old job at Marburg back, but Röpke demurred, wishing rather to be called back by his faculty. They never did.

[22] W. Röpke, *Die Lehre von der Wirtschaft*, Verlag von Julius Springer, Vienna 1937, Chapter 1. In this distinction of anarchy from chaos we have already made a considerable advance on Hayek's position in 1935; and also posed the question that Neumann failed to resolve in *Behemoth*.

[23] In the light of the comments made above concerning the need to read these writings against the background of the National Socialist economy, it should perhaps be noted that it was not until 1936 that the German economy began to be seriously modified by the Four-Year Plan; some of the effects of this development are discussed below.

policy must be conducted according to a plan, whether one is considering the setting of tariffs or the management of railways and roads; the initiation of public works programmes in Germany and the United States should not therefore be viewed as the *introduction* of planned activity, for such measures simply extended existing arrangements. The monetary policy of many countries was regulated by the state, without anyone talking about planned economies; so 'if that is all meant to be planned economy, then the concept loses any substance.'

In an unalloyed competitive system the production plan originates with an agent, namely the consumer, whose right cannot be lightly dismissed; whereas the communist system is faced with the dilemma of either imitating the competitive system, basing its plan of production upon the demands of its consumers, however determined, or setting up a plan according to some other perspective, forcing it upon consumers.[24]

On this basis Röpke concludes that a communist system ultimately requires an economic dictatorship, and this in turn necessitates political dictatorship, a conclusion not dissimilar to that of Hayek in 1944.

But not, on the other hand, very similar to that of Hayek in 1935. He concedes that the disturbances to the world economic order since 1929 are more than a cyclical phenomenon, and that their cause lies in the inadequacies of the monetary and credit systems. The kind of capitalist restoration hinted at by Hayek, re-introducing the purity of an order governed by *laissez-faire* principles, would be no solution; instead, an alternative to both *laissez-faire* and planning is required. No specific policies are proposed, but Röpke does suggest that suitable measures

are above all characterised by the fact that they seek to achieve the goal of the market economy in concert with its laws, rather than regulating, commanding and forcing; they seek to restore meaning to the competitive system and at the same time take account of frictions, rigidities, difficulties and overexpansion. In all measures a rigorous distinction will be made between those which are fitting to our economic system, and those which are contrary to its structure ... [25]

This is what became known as the 'Third Way', seeking to make economic policy in a 'market-conform' manner. After the war this 'Third Way' was to be renamed the 'Social Market Economy' by Müller-Armack. As yet however, it was simply a reserved space

[24] Röpke, *Die Lehre von der Wirtschaft*, p. 185. [25] *Ibid.*, p. 191.

between capitalism and socialism, without any specific characteristics of its own.[26] Nevertheless, no matter how indistinct the waymarks are, there is here at the very least a rejection of the terms upon which the arguments over market and plan had been conducted since the early 1920s, and a recognition that a modern economy is a complex order in which, at many levels, planning and regulation are required for it to function.[27]

Eucken's primary contribution was to develop this idea as a classification of economic systems in terms of varying degrees of competition and monopoly on both the demand and the supply side. Rather like Menger's *Grundsätze*, where the passages for which the book is best known occupy at most two pages, the core of Eucken's *Grundlagen* lies in a five-by-five table on page 131, about half-way through the book. The first few chapters direct themselves, somewhat laboriously, to establishing the proper tasks and methods of economic science. This exposition is not without insights – the first chapter makes some pertinent comments about the neglect of time and the spatial location of economic processes on the part of modern economic theory – but there seems to be an undue reticence with respect to the overall purpose of the book. Only in the fourth chapter do we encounter households and enterprises, whose co-ordination is stated to be the task of economic science. From the property of the household economy as an autarkic, patriarchally led organisation he derives the idea of the centrally managed economy,[28] a large-scale economy co-ordinated by deliberate action on the part of a central agency. This is contrasted to the *Verkehrswirtschaft*, in which the price mechanism performs the function of economic co-ordination.

The purpose of making this distinction is not to contrast the substantive economic rationalities prevailing in these two opposed systems. Instead, attention first shifts to a differentiation of managed economies according to the level and degree of directive activity. The

[26] See also the introductory chapter in his *Social Crisis of our Time* (originally published in 1942) which is entitled 'The Great Interregnum – Spiritual Collectivization – The Third Way'.
[27] Röpke's wife was responsible for the German translation of Hayek's *Road to Serfdom*, and Wilhelm Röpke supplied an introduction. His notably laudatory remarks are concluded by a cautionary note, to the effect that support of the market economy not merely permitted, but indeed demanded, a far-reaching programme of economic and social policy – see W. Röpke, 'Einführung' to F. A. Hayek, *Der Weg zur Knechtschaft*, Eugen Rentsch Verlag, Erlenbach-Zürich 1945, p. 13.
[28] As noted elsewhere, there is no native German equivalent to the English 'management'. Eucken uses both *Zentralgeleitete Wirtschaft* (which I translate here as 'centrally managed economy') and elsewhere *Zentralverwaltungswirtschaft*, which was translated as 'centrally administered economy'.

most extreme form is one in which no exchange is permitted and everything is done by direction. Three further forms are distinguished:

(1)   A managed economy with free exchange of consumer goods. A central instance directs the allocation of productive resources, the distribution of products, the technique and site of production; but corrections can be made to these decisions by direct exchanges among consumers.

(2)   A managed economy with free consumer choice – production and allocation are determined, but consumers receive wages and salaries with which they are able to select the goods that they want.

(3)   A managed economy with free consumer choice, where members are in addition able to select their occupation.[29]

Common to all four forms is the fact that decisions concerning production and distribution are made by a central instance, but the varying degrees of choice admitted to the consumer provide some economic data that can be used by the planners. In the light of the contemporary Soviet economy, it would seem pedantic to make these distinctions; but set against the contemporary German economy, these distinctions begin to have a greater significance, since they open up the prospect of centrally managed economies co-existing with private property, free movement of labour, and consumer choice. This is of course far removed from the usual assumption that a planned economy would be based upon state ownership of productive resources; but this was the kind of conundrum facing German economists in the later 1930s, and the *Grundlagen* contributed a framework in which the implications of this co-existence of central management and private property could be analysed.

Whereas the problem of co-ordination is an obvious and characteristic problem for a centrally managed economy, it is not so evident how this is resolved by a *Verkehrswirtschaft*. Some calculable standard is required, and Eucken notes that it should furthermore be borne in mind that every economic unit both supplies goods, and demands them from others. Supply and demand are treated as relatively open or closed, according to the extent of the network to which there is access. This gives rise to a classification by degree of competitiveness on the part both of supply and of demand, from the free competitive system at one extreme to the monopolistic at the other. Twenty-five

[29] Eucken, *Grundlagen*, pp. 96–102.

forms of market organisation are generated in this way, illuminating the manner in which Eucken's basic theoretical approach facilitates a systematic differentiation of forms of economic order.

When account is next taken of the relative openness or closure of the networks to which they have access, whether they overlap or are relatively autonomous, these twenty-five forms are multiplied by a factor of four. The classificatory approach is then reinforced by the introduction of five basic factors with which a market-mechanism has to deal, and which it has to bring into equilibrium: the guidance of production, a distribution of income appropriate to available goods, the fact that production takes place in time and therefore involves investment choices under uncertainty, choice of technique, and location of production and consumption. These variables are then applied to all one hundred open and closed market forms, which then form the basis for the following discussion, the merits of each form being addressed in turn.

In this way Eucken developed a powerful classificatory basis for the analysis of economic organisation, in which inner heterogeneity and the conditions for the establishment of equilibrium were brought to the fore. His principal concern, therefore, was to understand the organisation of the market economy, rather than demonstrate the deficiencies of a socialist economy. A clearer sense of the impact of these arguments is gained from the reception of the book in Germany; this was immediate, positive, and non-partisan, demonstrating that Eucken had succeeded in composing a treatise that could further discussion of economic policy, without at the same time falling foul of the National Socialist authorities.[30] Two separate issues could be addressed in such discussion: first, the nature of the prewar National Socialist economy, and the degree to which the elements of economic planning introduced in the later 1930s would persist into peacetime as a lasting basis for economic organisation; and second, the impact that the financial cost of the war would have upon a postwar economic order. These distinct issues became merged later in the war, but at the time Eucken published the *Grundlagen* they were still treated as separate matters.

The stability of the National Socialist economy had been a matter

[30] See for example the elaboration of the merits of Eucken's book in von Stackelberg's review article, 'Die Grundlagen der Nationalökonomie (Bemerkungen zu dem gleichnamigen Buch von Walter Eucken)', *Weltwirtschaftliches Archiv*, Bd. 51 (1940), pp. 245–81. A meeting of Klasse IV of the Akademie für Deutsches Recht was also devoted to discussion of the book during 1940.

Table 8.1. *Forms of market*

Form of demand	Form of supply				
	Competition	Partial oligopoly	Oligopoly	Partial monopoly	Monopoly (individual or collective)
Competition	Perfect (complete) competition	Partial oligopoly of supply	Supply oligopoly	Partial monopoly of supply	Supply monopoly
Partial oligopoly (Oligopsony)	Partial oligopoly of demand	Bilateral partial oligopoly	Supply oligopoly limited by partial oligopoly of demand	Partial monopoly of supply limited by partial oligopoly of demand	Supply monopoly limited by partial oligopoly of demand
Oligopoly (Oligopsony)	Demand oligopoly	Demand oligopoly limited by partial oligopoly of supply	Bilateral oligopoly	Partial monopoly of supply limited by oligopoly of demand	Supply monopoly limited by oligopoly of demand
Partial monopoly (Monopsony)	Partial monopoly of demand	Partial monopoly of demand limited by partial oligopoly of supply	Partial monopoly of demand limited by oligopoly of supply	Bilateral partial monopoly	Supply monopoly limited by partial monopoly of demand
Monopoly (Monopsony) (individual or collective)	Demand monopoly	Demand monopoly limited by partial oligopoly of supply	Demand monopoly limited by oligopoly of supply	Demand monopoly limited by partial monopoly of supply	Bilateral monopoly

Source: W. Eucken, *The Foundations of Economics*, William Hodge, London 1950, p. 158.

for discussion among economists before the outbreak of war in 1939. Probably the most acute assessment of the German economy in the later 1930s was published by Thomas Balogh in the *Economic Journal* in 1938.[31] Starting out from the problem of whether totalitarian systems were economically stable,[32] Balogh addresses this problem using the instrumentaria of a macroeconomic analysis then only a few years old. The more obvious features of the German economy in the 1930s were a decline in investment and rise of unemployment in early 1930s, followed by a recovery which was popularly associated with National Socialist economic policies on unemployment and re-armament. The recovery fell into two periods: first of all, up to the end of 1934, the increase in employment was more rapid in investment goods industries than in those producing consumption goods; this was accompanied by a rapid deterioration of the balance of trade. Then, beginning in 1935, the acceleration of output from the investment goods industries continued virtually unchanged, while at the same time a deceleration took place in the output of consumer goods. The balance of trade then improved as imports fell and exports began to increase. A slow upward trend in consumption then took place, until by the Spring of 1937 the reserve of unemployed labour was exhausted.

This general appraisal of economic performance is based upon familiar enough categories, but Balogh does not stop at this superficial description of recovery in the German economy. Instead, he turns to consider the manner in which investment was guided and financed. During the first phase of recovery, in which investment flowed primarily into investment goods industries, the increase in public expenditure was achieved mainly by the creation of cash, using bills of exchange rediscountable at the Reichsbank. Once recovery was under way, public expenditure (chiefly re-armament) was not reduced; instead, consumption was aligned with a pre-given level of public spending. Balogh examines in detail the organisation of fiscal and monetary policy, and notes how the control of the money supply was supplemented by prohibitions on the establishment of new

---

[31] Balogh later wrote a devastating critique of the Currency Reform of 1948 (discussed below). Some years later Terence Hutchison used this critique as an example of the general lack of intellectual sympathy among economists for the Social Market, and of a lack of understanding of the German economy: see T. Hutchison, 'Notes on the Effects of Economic Ideas on Policy: The Example of the German Social Market Economy', *Zeitschrift für die gesamte Staatswissenschaft*, Bd. 135 (1979), pp. 437f.

[32] This would at the time have included not only Germany and the Soviet Union, but also Spain and Italy.

companies, the extension of existing plant, and building in virtually all branches of industry.

Some economists had suggested that this economic régime could not last, that it would break down or enter into a period of rapid inflation. Balogh however argued that as long as loan expenditure was kept within the limits of enforced and voluntary individual saving, it could not lead to cumulative inflation, however this might be financed. Capital export was impossible; indeed all external trade was controlled by the state. A range of controls prevented competition for funding between private and public investment projects. Indeed, Balogh wrote that 'The only danger to the present Nazi system lies in the undue increase in consumption demand.'[33] The capital goods industries were fully occupied by state orders. There was no risk involved here in production, and hence in investment. The output of consumer goods industries was restricted, but on the other hand there was a guaranteed sale to the domestic market, given the restrictions on imports effected by state control of foreign exchange dealing. If consumer demand re-emerged as a determinant of output, then there would be difficulties; risk would then once more dominate business activity. Altogether, the specific advantages of the organisation of the German economy in the later 1930s diminished if the objective of economic management shifted from preparation for war to consumer welfare. Balogh concluded that

These considerations seem to demonstrate: a) that the Nazi government has succeeded in evolving an – initially empirical – system which – provided the available powers of control are ruthlessly and skilfully used – is not subject to fluctuations in employment (though subject to fluctuations in real income on account of inevitable changes in the terms of its foreign trade); b) that this system is based on three main controls, of costs, of investment and of international trade; c) that this system is economically stable on its own terms in so far as it does not involve cumulative processes undermining the standard of life; d) that the real sacrifice imposed on the German population by militarisation (rearmament and self-sufficiency) is very much less than commonly supposed. Most of the difficulties and frictions are not necessarily consequences of this system itself, but of the aims which it has been made to serve and which are by no means identical with the system.[34]

Contrary to popular perceptions, therefore, Balogh argued that the system of economic management practised by the National Socialist authorities did not in itself require that it be organised for military

[33] T. Balogh, 'The National Economy of Germany', *Economic Journal*, vol. 48 (1938), p. 497.
[34] *Ibid.*, p. 496.

ends; it was quite possible to envisage the stability of such a system without re-armament as the goal. The implication is evidently that such a system could be run with social, rather than military, objectives.

There is still dispute today among economic historians on this issue – whether, for example, the *Blitzkrieg* strategy was a deliberate choice designed to permit war to be waged with a minimal impact on domestic consumption, or whether it represented the improvisations of an administration caught out by the pace of development of events.[35] Balogh's analysis has been outlined at length here because it enables us to establish two important points. The first of these is the fact that, already in 1938, National Socialist·economic policy was being evaluated in terms of the relationship between investment, consumption, and the risk of inflation, issues that would be addressed by German economists in the early 1940s. The second point is that this analysis simply assumes that the state is in a position to manipulate economic activity, without serious constraints and further consequences, through a battery of monetary, fiscal, exchange, and investment controls. Balogh sets out to evaluate the general stability of a totalitarian, planned economy, and he in effect gives it a clean bill of health. The very modernity of the analytical framework of Balogh's discussion distracts our attention from the more usual framework within which the problems of economic planning had hitherto been posed, and which considered its viability not from the standpoint of stability, but from that of welfare.

Balogh's periodisation and his overall approach takes little account of institutional changes within the German economy. Although he notes that the control of external trade and capital movements had implications for domestic investment and consumption, he pays little attention to the strategic framework within which this was elaborated. This was no great secret: it could be read out of the pattern of external trade and the level of investment in the synthetic production of fuels, textiles, and rubber. National Socialist policy envisaged a future German *Grossraum* which would be autarkic, in which Germany was the manufacturing heartland, together with the bordering

[35] See for example R. J. Overy, 'Hitler's War and the German Economy: A Reinterpretation', *Economic History Review*, 2nd series, vol. 35 (1982), pp. 272–91, which argues that the German economy was geared to long-term and large-scale mobilisation, but which were pre-empted by foreign policy considerations. Herbst likewise argues that the *Blitzkrieg* should be viewed as a temporary expedient on the road to the full mobilisation of resources for total war: see L. Herbst, *Der totale Krieg und die Ordnung der Wirtschaft*, DVA, Stuttgart 1982.

industrial areas of North-east France, Belgium, and Bohemia. The peripheral areas would supply raw materials and foodstuffs to this developed industrial core, and this vision was lent substance by a series of bilateral trade agreements signed with states in South-eastern Europe after 1933.[36] In April 1936 Hitler gave Göring authority over the allocation of raw materials and foreign exchange, and the first step in effecting this was the formation of a small office co-ordinating the work of existing agencies. A secret memorandum drawn up by Hitler in August 1936 then gave primacy to the military objectives of economic policy, with the production of substitutes for imported raw materials wherever possible. The general lines of this policy were not however secret: Hitler announced the 'second' Four-Year Plan at the Party rally in Nuremberg that September, with Göring, supported by a staff drawn from the Air Ministry, placed in overall control of the apparatus.[37]

It is for this reason that Eucken and his associates date the central administration of the German economy from 1936. Caution should however be exercised here in overhasty comparison with the contemporary Soviet planning apparatus.[38] First of all, despite the existence of Five-Year Plans throughout the 1930s in the Soviet Union, these were primarily indicative, since no centralised directive co-ordination of the economy existed. The central Soviet planning instance, Gosplan, itself evolved from a forecasting agency to a central supervisory agency during the period 1925–35. Planning was effected by other agencies on a sector-by-sector basis, with a consequent lack of co-ordination. Only in 1934 were uniform planning indicators adopted, making possible the collection of data on a consistent basis, itself a necessary condition for comprehensive planning. However, even in 1935 data on net investment was not requested; and in fact all that happened was that a rough system of priorities was pursued. Material

[36] A. S. Milward, *War, Economy and Society 1939–1945*, Penguin Books, Harmondsworth 1987, p. 9. During 1935 Göring made several trips to South-eastern Europe proposing the barter of arms for raw materials – A. Kube, 'Außenpolitik und "Großraumwirtschaft". Die deutsche Politik zur wirtschaftlichen Integration Südosteuropas 1933 bis 1939', in H. Berding (ed.), *Wirtschaftliche Integration im 19. und 20. Jahrhundert*, Sonderheft 10, *Geschichte und Gesellschaft* (1984), p. 196.
[37] D. Petzina, *Autarkiepolitik im Dritten Reich. Der nationalsozialistische Vierjahresplan*, Deutsche Verlags-Anstalt, Stuttgart 1968, pp. 48–53.
[38] In a recent article Peter Temin argues for the essential similarity of Soviet and German economic planning in the 1930s, but this argument fails to discriminate sufficiently between planning and regulation, and the diverse nature (and hence, effects) of the instruments employed – see his 'Soviet and Nazi Economic Planning in the 1930s', *Economic History Review*, vol. 44 (1991), pp. 573–93.

balances were calculated for only 105 commodities in 1935, and enterprises reallocated materials between themselves through a network of personal contacts.[39] The trials and purges of the later 1930s had a devastating impact on the operation of both central and local planning agencies precisely because of their reliance upon these personal contacts as channel of communication.[40] As Zaliski emphasises, the common conception of a single, central plan is a myth:

What actually exists, as in any centrally-administered economy, is an endless number of plans, constantly evolving, that are co-ordinated *ex-post* after they have been put into operation. The unification of these innumerable plans into a single national plan, supposedly coherent, takes place rarely ... furthermore, the attempt at unification is only a projection of observed tendencies resulting from extrapolating trends based upon natural forces.[41]

The centralised guidance of any economy, let alone one the sheer size of the Soviet Union, presupposes that the planners possess both reliable information on consumer demands and productive capacity, as well as the appropriate instruments and institutions with which to translate their plans into executive action.[42] Critics of planned economies such as Hayek have invariably laid emphasis on the first of these, while ignoring the implications of the second. This is perhaps because of a belief that a market economy functions the better, the fewer such instruments exist; a bare minimum of interventions, rather than the nature of such intervention, permits an optimal allocation of resources guided by a price mechanism. To say the least, this is not a very practical approach to an understanding of market mechanisms, for it wilfully ignores the manner in which market mechanisms are formed as the outcome of a number of cross-cutting forces. This was well appreciated by Eucken; as has been argued above, his *Grundlagen* can be read as an attempt to open out this appreciation of markets as entities based upon heterogeneous forces overlapping in both space

---

[39] P. R. Gregory and R. C. Stuart, *Soviet Economic Structure and Performance* 3rd edn, Harper and Row, New York 1986, pp. 102–4.

[40] See E. Zaliski, *Stalinist Planning for Economic Growth 1933–1952*, Macmillan Press, London 1980, pp. 168f. For a discussion of the evolution of planning within the Soviet system during the 1930s, see M. Harrison, *Soviet Planning in Peace and War 1938–1945*, Cambridge University Press, Cambridge 1985, Chapter 1.   [41] Zaliski, *Stalinist Planning*, p. 484.

[42] It is seldom noted that early French postwar plans, for lack of national income data, were denominated in physical output quantities and the consequent required levels of investment, just like Soviet plans. Only with the Fifth Plan of 1965 were outputs given monetary values, and targets set both for the aggregate growth of incomes, and for the distribution of growth between consumption, investment, public expenditure and trade – S. Estrin and P. Holmes, *French Planning in Theory and Practice*, George Allen and Unwin, London 1983, pp. 67–8.

and time. The involvement of Eucken and his colleagues in the meetings of Klasse IV of the Akademie für Deutsches Recht[43] – specifically in the sections devoted to economic theory and to price policy – represented a desire to contribute this understanding of market mechanisms to the formation of wartime and postwar economic policy.

The outbreak of a European war in September 1939 moved Germany from a phase in which the economy was directed towards military objectives – covering both the production of war *materiel*, and the development of substitutes for imported raw materials – into a phase in which a war of conquest was fought. Direct control of the principal industrial regions of France, and of Belgium, the Netherlands, and Norway, was achieved by June 1940, and it was subsequently possible to restructure the occupied territories around German economic objectives. Given the existence of a formal state of war, economists could openly discuss the allocation of resources between consumer demand and the requirements of the wartime economy. An entire issue of *Weltwirtschaftliches Archiv* was dedicated to these themes in 1940, reprinting papers from a conference held during February of that year. A number of articles in *Bank-Archiv* were likewise devoted to the question of war finance, contrasting Germany's financial position with that prevailing during the First World War, discussing the relative merits of direct and indirect taxation, and affirming the general superiority of a 'managed economy' (*geleitete Wirtschaft*) over 'state economy' on the one hand, and 'liberal economy' on the other. Up to 1941, these public discussions emphasised the general advantages enjoyed by current economic management compared with the past.[44]

Coupled with this discussion of the appropriate means of financing the war was naturally the question of the impact of various measures on postwar public indebtedness. Although this raised the issue of

---

[43] The Akademie für Deutsches Recht was founded by the National Socialists for the purpose of 'Germanising' the law. Klasse IV was the Economics Section, which was to apply itself to the same task in the domain of economics. However, its organiser, Jens Jessen, had during the 1930s moved from a strongly ideological attachment to National Socialism to being a fervent opponent, and Klasse IV was in part at least constructed as a covertly oppositional forum. Jessen was executed in November 1944 for his part in the July Plot. See G. Schmölders, 'In memoriam Jens Jessen (1895–1944)', *Schmollers Jahrbuch*, Bd. 69 (1949), pp. 9–10.

[44] See for example the essays by F. Terhalle in *Bank-Archiv*: 'Die deutsche Kriegsfinanzierung 1914–1918', Jg. 1939, pp. 549–52; 'Die Aufbringung der Kriegskosten als volkswirtschaftlichen Aufgabe', Jg. 1940, pp. 193–6; 'Staatsschulden – volkswirtschaftlich gesehen', Jg. 1941, pp. 283–6; also R. Stucken, 'Kriegsfinanzierung und Kreditausweitung', *Bank -Archiv*, Jg. 1940, pp. 323–5.

postwar inflation, economists found it difficult to make this a public issue, because of the manner in which, during the early phases of the war, the domestic economy was deliberately insulated from its immediate financial effects. During the early 1940s there had consequently been little public discussion of the potential for future currency depreciation and inflation. In the course of 1942 this altered. An article of that year by Otto Donner discussing the limits on state indebtedness – and there were no technical limits, he declared – examined once more the various ways in which the war could be financed, setting against this the consequences for purchasing power and money supply.[45] The danger existed, argued Donner, that the existence of a wartime 'purchasing-power surplus' could with a return to a peacetime economy be converted into a 'purchasing power overhang' (*Kaufkraftüberhang*).[46] Eucken had himself presented a paper to a meeting of the Klasse IV section for price policy in November 1941 which argued that, given the present constitution of price and credit policy, competitive conditions had been undermined, since all goods could be sold and there was surplus demand.[47] The postwar economy, argued Eucken, would require a far greater supply of consumer goods – goods which were, unlike armaments, heterogeneous by nature and therefore not predictable by a central agency. The market mechanism could not be restored by *fiat*: 'Only when a new monetary order is created which diverges considerably from prevailing conditions will the restraints fall away.'[48] In the course of 1943 the tone sharpened: Jessen's article on the 'Law of the Increasing Extension of the Need for Finance' can be read as a coded critique of wartime finance, deploying British statistics on state revenue and expenditure over the period 1692–1933 and linking the rise of state indebtedness directly to military spending.[49]

[45] O. Donner, 'Die Grenzen der Staatsverschuldung', *Weltwirtschaftliches Archiv*, Jg. 56 (1942), pp. 183–224. Donner was from 1940 to 1943 chief of the Research Section for the Four-Year Plan administration. From 1952 to 1954 he represented Germany at the International Monetary Fund, from 1954 to 1968 at the World Bank: see G. Aly and S. Heim, *Vordenker der Vernichtung. Auschwitz und die Pläne für eine neue europäische Ordnung*, Hoffmann und Campe Verlag, Hamburg 1991, p. 55.   [46] Donner, 'Die Grenzen der Staatsverschuldung', p. 209.
[47] W. Eucken, 'Der Wettbewerb als Grundprinzip der Wirtschaftsverfassung', in G. Schmölders (ed.), *Der Wettbewerb als Mittel volkswirtschaftlicher Leistungssteigerung und Leistungsauslese*, Schriften der Akademie für Deutsches Recht, Gruppe Wirtschaftswissenschaft Heft 6, Duncker und Humblot, Berlin 1942, pp. 29–49.
[48] Eucken, 'Der Wettbewerb als Grundprinzip der Wirtschaftsverfassung', p. 35.
[49] J. Jessen, 'Das "Gesetz der wachsenden Ausdehnung des Finanzbedarfs"', *Schmollers Jahrbuch*, Jg. 67 (1943), pp. 548, 550. See also in this connection O. Veit, 'Geldüberschuß und Wirtschaftslenkung', *Weltwirtschaftliches Archiv*, Bd. 57 (1943), pp. 278–309; and R. Meimberg, 'Kaufkraftüberhang und Kriegsfinanzpolitik', *Weltwirtschaftliches Archiv*, Bd. 58 (1943), pp. 98–130.

By 1943 the public mood had altered, which perhaps accounts for the ability of economists to raise the problem of war finance and suppressed inflation, despite the fact that the declaration of Total War in 1942 had formally prohibited all discussion of postwar conditions. Public suspicion grew that a postwar government, seeking to suppress the inflationary tendencies of an excess of purchasing power, might simply confiscate savings and raise taxation. This suspicion was made manifest in a hoarding of cash, which of course simply had the effect of making such policies more likely. By March 1944 anxiety had become so general that the President of the Reichsbank made a public appeal for calm, criticising the practice of hoarding cash, promising postwar monetary stability and the management of German war debt without resort to 'the deception of inflation'.[50] In fact, a year earlier Funk had recommended a rise in direct taxation to deal with emergent excess purchasing power, but this and related measures were vetoed by Hitler. The existence of a price freeze since 1936 also made it politically impossible to raise indirect taxes as an alternative. In such circumstances cash hoarding and a black market developed, to which the authorities responded with police raids and the *Volksgerichte*. But nothing was done to moderate the development of excess purchasing power, and a considerable *Kaufkraftüberhang* developed, which was indeed eventually to lead to the demise of the Reichsmark as a currency in 1948.

Eucken and his colleagues in Freiburg discussed these and related issues as part of a group of economists later known as the 'Beckerath Circle', after its chairman, Erwin von Beckerath, Professor of Transport and Finance at Bonn. The Circle had begun life as the economic theory section within Klasse IV of the Akademie für Deutsches Recht. In November 1940 the section decided to discuss fundamental problems of economic organisation with a view to the drafting of an economic programme. Three sub-committees were established, in Berlin, Cologne, and Freiburg; but besides some activity between Cologne and Bonn, discussion centred on the Freiburg group. Klasse IV was effectively wound up in March 1943 shortly before the first meeting of the study group was due to be held in Freiburg; but they went ahead and met as the Arbeitsgemeinschaft Erwin von Becker-

---

[50] Funk cited in L. Herbst, 'Krisenüberwindung und Wirtschaftsneuordnung. Ludwig Erhards Beteiligung an den Nachkriegsplanungen am Ende des Zweiten Weltkrieges', *Vierteljahreshefte für Zeitgeschichte*, Jg. 25 (1977), p. 308.

ath.[51] Records of these meetings have survived as summaries of discussion and papers circulated for comment, many of them written by Adolf Lampe, Eucken's colleague in Freiburg. The fact that these are working papers, not intended for publication or for wider dissemination, lends them a clarity and directness lacking in many of the published writings of the Ordoliberals.

An essay by Adolf Lampe dated February 1943 and entitled 'Reconstruction of the Peacetime Economy = Reconstruction of the Market Economy' opens this collection. The initial problem for a postwar economy, he argues, is state indebtedness, the creditors being for the most part their own debtors, that is, taxpayers. However, insofar as the war had been financed through bonds and forced savings, the problem arose of how this debt was to be distributed, for only those who had made investments would be repaid. Furthermore, despite shortages of goods, low incomes and high unemployment would in the immediate aftermath of war generate a low savings ratio, so that if recovery were to be financed out of private savings, this would dictate a very slow pace indeed. The private saver, concluded Lampe, must be forced to accumulate capital; and the only practicable manner of doing so is through taxation and a budget surplus.[52] This position stood in stark contrast with the prevailing view, which was that in a postwar transitional period public expenditure would have to be financed through credit creation. Instead, suggested Lampe, the immediate postwar task should be the eradication of excess purchasing power. If prices were freed straight away[53] it would be impossible to resist wage rises, and hence a resulting increase in the money supply and an inflationary spiral. The general balance of supply and demand could not be the goal of a transitional economy, but was instead its necessary presupposition; only once such an equilibrium had been achieved could the price mechanism function properly.[54]

This question of the phasing of the transition to a peacetime

---

[51] This account is based upon N. Kloten, 'Vorwort' to C. Blumenberg-Lampe (ed.), *Der Weg in die Soziale Marktwirtschaft. Referate, Protokolle, Gutachten der Arbeitsgemeinschaft Erwin von Beckerath 1943–1947*, Klett-Cotta, Stuttgart 1986, pp. 9–10.

[52] The expectation of a low savings-ratio can be squared with the argument for raised taxation in a situation of high unemployment if a large part of the money supply is held in cash, as was in fact the case.

[53] It might be recalled that prices were fixed at 1936 levels.

[54] A. Lampe, 'Wiederaufbau der Friedenswirtschaft = Wiederaufbau der Marktwirtschaft', in Blumenberg-Lampe (ed.), *Der Weg in die Soziale Marktwirtschaft*, pp. 41–4.

economy was addressed in a paper by Eucken later in the same year.[55]
Assuming that at the end of the war the central administration would
continue in being, the prime objective should be to move as quickly as
possible from an emergency situation into an economic order dominated by elements of the market economy, since only the installation
of price signalling would enable production to be guided by real,
rather than artificial, shortages. In the economics of the transition
period, it was important to distinguish two stages: an initial, preparatory stage, and a subsequent stage of actual transition.

In the first of these all the measures of the war economy would
persist, including the control of investment and of external trade.
However, the production of important consumer goods should be
initiated, the budget balanced, and the excess of purchasing power
eliminated. A currency revaluation (*Heraufsetzung der Wechselkurse*)
should then follow, in step with the rise in price levels of leading
trading countries. The exchange rate should be fixed, and here
Eucken suggests that a discussion of the 'Keynes plan' would be
useful.[56] The second stage involved the full transition to a market
economy, which could only begin when the budget was balanced and
excess purchasing power eliminated. Prices would be freed, the system
of rationing discontinued, investment controls dismantled, and direct
orders for the production of consumer goods would cease. So, how is
the excess of purchasing power to be eliminated? The first requisite
was the establishment of a balanced budget; this, it was thought,
would terminate the source of increase in the money supply. Simply
balancing the budget was not enough, however. Further measures
that should be considered were: a reduction in the quantity of money,
an increase of confidence in money (reducing its velocity of circulation), and a limited rise in prices. As with Lampe, the restoration of a
functioning market economy was predicated upon the removal of
excess purchasing power accumulated by households since the later
1930s.[57]

The theoretical underpinnings for these arguments can be found

[55] W. Eucken: 'Beseitigung des Kaufkraftüberhangs in der Übergangswirtschaft' (July 1943),
in Blumenberg-Lampe (ed.), *Der Weg in die Soziale Marktwirtschaft*, pp. 182–6.

[56] Eucken presented a paper on Keynes' proposal for an International Clearing Union to a
meeting in November 1943; this is discussed below.

[57] Full employment was achieved before the war, not with its onset, as in Britain and America.
Furthermore, single-shift working typified 90 per cent of German industry for much of the
war – N. Kaldor, 'The German War Economy', *Review of Economic Studies*, vol. 13 (1945), p.
35. The existence of excess purchasing power was not therefore a result of wartime economic
overheating in the labour market, but a long-term phenomenon.

expressed in a contribution from von Stackelberg of March 1943, in which he outlines the guiding principles of economic management.[58] He argued here that the prime difficulty in satisfying present and future needs derived not so much from the sheer variety of needs and the properties of the existing means for their satisfaction, as from the material and temporal opacity of the path leading from productive capacity, through all the stages of production, to the satisfaction of need. Hence it was not the problem of the assessment of need and the allocation of resources that confronted an economic directorate,[59] but rather the material difficulty of producing and delivering resources according to a rational plan. The evaluation of a given distribution of income was only possible if comparisons were made between households on the basis of a commensurable scale of importance; here Paretian indifference curves could be of use, he suggested. Following Gossen, he continued, utility is then maximised when the marginal utility of all the means of production is equalised. Although this cannot be directly calculated, Stackelberg proposed that the producer seeking the most profitable method of production operated in a fashion as if he had actually calculated the marginal utilities of the various alternatives: 'The competitive economy thus appears as an automatic calculating machine for the determination of magnitudes which could not be ascertained by humans by means of direct calculation.'[60]

Allocation according to marginal utility was fundamental to economic rationality, argued von Stackelberg; but is it not possible, he asked, that a central authority could come to similar conclusions on the basis of sufficient statistical data? Was not the performance of the Soviet war economy sufficient proof of the effectiveness of the planned economy?

The real achievements of the Soviet war economy were certainly great; but they were won at the cost of great waste, which was in turn financed by the foregone consumption of its citizens. Further, even if it were accepted that the centralised administration had been able to

[58] The most concise exposition of Eucken's own views is his article, 'On the Theory of the Centrally Administered Economy: An Analysis of the German Experiment', 2 parts, *Economica*, NS, vol. 15 (1948), pp. 79–100; 173–93.

[59] As was commonly argued by critics of planned socialist economies.

[60] H. Freiherr von Stackelberg, 'Theorie und Systematik der Wirtschaftslenkung', in Blumenberg-Lampe (ed.), *Der Weg in die Soziale Marktwirtschaft*, p. 118. The essay was republished after Stackelberg's death in *Ordo*, Bd. 2 (1949), pp. 193–205. The concept of the price system as a calculating machine was taken up by Eucken in his article, 'Das ordnungspolitische Problem', *Ordo*, Bd. 1 (1948), p. 63.

produce a greater amount more rapidly than would be possible in a
market system, if a longer perspective were taken, then over thirty or
forty years a market economy would eventually produce substantially
more than the most well-managed planned economy.[61]

The leading characteristic of a market economy was, according to
von Stackelberg, that it operated as if it were an automatic calculating
machine. Accordingly, all policy measures had to be considered from
the standpoint of whether they disturbed the operation of this
calculating engine, or were neutral with respect to its dynamics. This
difference could not however be simply reduced to one between direct
and indirect measures, in which the former were *systemwidrig* and the
latter *systemgerecht*. Instead, he proposed the following definition: a
direct measure is one which intervenes at the same point in the
economy at which its intended effect is supposed to occur – in this
sense a direct measure is one which has no side effects. An indirect
measure is therefore one which is applied to one area in the economy,
with the intention of prompting a result somewhere else. For a
Verkehrswirtschaft, all those measures are *systemgerecht* which do not
disturb the calculative structure of normalised prices.

It is however in Eucken's responses to Keynes' plan for an
International Currency Union that the specific character of the
Freiburg School's approach to economic management finds its most
clear expression. The White Paper, 'Proposals for an International
Clearing Union' had been published in April 1943, and Eucken had
obtained a copy of it through contacts in Switzerland.[62] Eucken
began his comments by agreeing that the stabilisation of exchange
rates was the prerequisite for the revival of postwar international
trade. As far as the technical aspects of the proposals went, and the
allocations of *Bancor* which were suggested, he had no substantial
technical objections, regarding the basic principle of the system as
correct. He was however highly critical of the apparatus which was to
oversee the postwar international economy. The UN Food Conference in Hot Springs, which took place in mid-1943, demonstrated

---

[61] It might be noted at this point that this distinctly modern-sounding analysis comes from a
member of the NSDAP since 1931, and also a serving member of the SS.

[62] Keynes' proposals were discussed together with American plans at Bretton Woods in 1944;
the German intellectual origins of the White Paper are discussed in the following essay. There
was in fact no need for Eucken to obtain a copy from Switzerland: both the British and the
American plans were published in Berlin – see A. Predöhl, 'Die angelsächsische Währungspläne und die europäische Währungsordnung', *Weltwirtschaftliches Archiv* Jg. 58 (1943), p. 2,
n. 1.

that the British Government intended to reorganise the postwar international economy, and also to introduce a constant regulation of economic processes via a centralised *Konjunkturpolitik*, stated Eucken. Control of commodity markets was to be effected by the creation of pools for individual goods, managed by representatives of producers, consumers, and governments. The managers of these commodity pools were charged with the pursuit of an expansionary policy, together with the creation of reservoirs, purchasing in times of surplus, and releasing reserves at times of shortage.

The attempt to create such an order and to effect such comprehensive guidance of *Konjunkturpolitik* is highly questionable. All objections against the accumulation of power in the economy, the consequent development of monopolies, and its close association with a centrally administered economy, are relevant here. While in the area of the balance of payments and international currency policy Keynes' Plan represents a serious effort to liberate equilibriating tendencies, the entire organisation of world commodity markets is lacking in equilibrium ... Insofar as the currency plan is part of a comprehensive monopolistic, centrally administered plan, it should be decisively rejected.[63]

The leadership of an International Currency Union should, in Eucken's view, limit their activities to securing payments' balances in respect of stable exchange rates, and nothing further. A deliberate *Konjunkturpolitik* required an agency that would soon assume centralising and monopolistic powers, and so should be rejected. This acceptance of a currency union as a solution to the deficiencies of previous forms of international payment, on the one hand, but the rejection of active intervention in markets to promote growth and stabilisation of commodity prices, on the other, is a clear illustration of the approach taken by Eucken and his associates to the problems of the postwar economy.

At issue here is an evident reluctance to accept the institutional foundations for the policy instruments being proposed. This problem is also evident in a paper written by Lampe on the labour market, in which he recognised the potential for exploitation of employees by employers, but is averse to the 'market solution', that is, trade unions on the one hand and employers' associations on the other. Instead, the need for employers' associations was to be ruled out by the creation of strictly circumscribed workers' associations, establishing a degree of

[63] W. Eucken: 'Bemerkungen zum Währungsplan von Keynes' (November 1943), in Blumenberg-Lampe (ed.), *Der Weg in die Soziale Marktwirtschaft*, pp. 273.

equality with employers and hence securing a more equitable share of the social product. Two specific measures were also envisaged: the introduction of a state unemployment insurance scheme, and the use of labour exchanges to promote control of the labour market and the mobility of labour. A peacetime unemployment rate of between 0.5 per cent and 4 per cent was considered to represent the normal lower and upper limits of the cycle for budgetary purposes.[64]

In another area of policy critical to the future Social Market project, Lampe drafted a paper which considered the relationship between the economic system and fiscal policy. We have already seen that taxation was to be an instrument of forced 'saving', a means of creaming off excess purchasing power. The question is, of course, how could such taxes be introduced without disturbing the 'calculating machine' of the price system? Lampe confined his attention to consumption and income taxes, arguing that other forms, such as transport or property taxes, were structurally faulty, involving no element of ability to pay. Consumption taxes, argued Lampe, reduced productivity, since they reduced confidence and were, in this respect, contributory to inflationary tendencies. Instead of consumption taxes, therefore, Lampe opted for an emphasis upon direct taxation as the appropriate, market-conform, fiscal instrument, representing the most direct and predictable tax with respect to the objectives of fiscal policy. Low levels of taxation could be set for those on low incomes, and, in addition to this, the costs of assessment and collection were fixed, so that the productivity of the tax grew with the concentration of the tax on the better-off.[65] In this discussion, no attention was paid to the manner in which direct taxation itself distorted relative income levels and household incomes; indeed today economic liberals would strongly argue that it is indirect taxes which are more market-conform than direct taxes. Nonetheless, the importance of the criterion of market conformity is evident in the manner in which Lampe constructs his argument, even if his conclusion is somewhat surprising.

Lampe's views on taxation and wage levels were part of the overriding concern with the impact of wartime finance on the postwar economy, and this concern was one widely shared among German

[64] A. Lampe, 'Thesen zur Lohnpolitik' (March 1944), in Blumenberg-Lampe (ed.), *Der Weg in die Soziale Marktwirtschaft*, pp. 301f.
[65] A. Lampe, 'Finanzpolitik der Wiederaufbauwirtschaft' (May 1944), in Blumenberg-Lampe (ed.), *Der Weg in die Soziale Marktwirtschaft*, pp. 345f.

economists of the time. This is also indeed the theme of Ludwig
Erhard's wartime contribution to discussions on postwar stabilisation, a memorandum written for industrialists in 1944 entitled 'War
Finance and the Consolidation of Debts'.[66] At the close of the war,
German economists were concerned not so much with the management of the immediate problems of the German economy, but looked
forward to the restoration of what von Stackelberg had dubbed the
'calculating machine', the price mechanism as the linkage between
producer and consumer. Widespread concern existed among German
economists over the manner in which postwar shortages, the consequent danger of inflation, and the economic administrations of
occupying powers could impede the restoration of a market mechanism; and this helps us understand the symbolic (and mythological)
status assumed by the Currency Reform of June 1948. Very soon after
the German capitulation a clear divergence was evident between
German economists and the occupying authorities. Eucken and his
colleagues often seem to have overlooked the fact that Germany had
lost the war, that the removal of the Nazi régime had necessitated the
occupation of Germany, and that the future welfare of the German
economy was not the first priority of the occupying forces. The
occupying authorities had their own economic advisers; many of
them, of course, of German or Central European origin.[67] There
seemed little need to heed the advice of German economists whose
political background was, at best, obscure.

One of the first positive economic measures taken by the Allies was
to re-affirm the control of prices prevailing before occupation, that is,
the freezing of prices at 1936 levels.[68] Early in 1946 this was confirmed
as the basis for policy for the coming two years. By 1947, it was
estimated that around ten times the 1936 quantity of currency was in
circulation in the four occupied zones, the total of currency plus
deposits being at about five times the 1936 level; the real national
income was by contrast at half the 1936 level. To all intents and
purposes, then, the effect of the Allied administration was to extend

---

[66] Discussed in Herbst, 'Krisenüberwindung und Wirtschaftsneuordnung', pp. 317–21. Herbst
also notes that discussion on the looming postwar discrepancy between purchasing power
and output of consumer goods continued throughout 1943.

[67] See for example Kaldor's 'The German War Economy' for a perspicacious expression of the
view, only later to become an orthodoxy, that German industrial capacity was in relatively
good condition in 1945; for example, in 1943 the German stock of machine tools had been
some 30 per cent higher than that of the United States.

[68] H. Mendershausen, 'Prices, Money and the Distribution of Goods in Postwar Germany',
American Economic Review, vol. 39 (1949), pp. 647–8.

many of the organisational features of the National Socialist economy
into the recovery period, that is, the control of prices was coupled with
a large incipient excess of purchasing power. This was further
compounded by the problems of shortage, the destruction of housing
and communications, and the presence of a large number of refugees.
The defeat had left industrial production severely dislocated,
although as it transpired the capital stock was not so severely
damaged as had been thought. The end of the European and
Japanese wars brought with it severe problems of demobilisation and
the restructuring of international trade, in which the United States
possessed large stocks of goods on the one hand, while on the other
there was a persisting shortage of dollars with which to purchase these
goods. The uneasy relationship between the Big Four, leading to the
de facto partition of Germany into Bizonia and the East Zone in 1947,
dislocated agricultural production; the western region became
dependent on imported foodstuffs where before agricultural products
had been supplied from the eastern regions. The Military Administrations were faced with the immediate problems of housing, feeding,
and clothing millions of people, and it is not difficult to appreciate
why they adopted the control measures that they did – these
immediate tasks were too urgent, one could not just wait patiently for
a readjustment of the economic system through the price mechanism
to take place.

The need for a currency reform has often been set in the context of
economic dislocation and black marketeering; Lutz's essay on the
reform and the subsequent economic revival, for example, begins by
painting a bleak picture of the rise of a barter economy before 1948,
with a consequent dislocation of trade, production, and consumption.[69] This image is at best partial, at worst wildly exaggerated.
There were certainly shortages of food and energy, but this cannot be
directly blamed on the absence of a proper market mechanism; it was
instead linked to general problems of resource allocation in Europe
and the politics of occupation and reconstruction. Throughout the
period, exchanges of goods predominantly took place in money and at
the prices fixed. Price controls mainly affected producers of raw
materials and agricultural goods; manufacturers by contrast often
diversified or reclassified their production and so were able to apply
for new prices which better reflected their costs of production.

[69] F. A. Lutz, 'The German Currency Reform and the Revival of the German Economy',
Economica, NS, vol. 16 (1949), pp. 122–3.

Mendershausen estimates that the black market involved some 5 per cent of imported grains, and 10 per cent of industrial or agricultural production. By contrast, around 90 per cent of turnover in existing luxury goods, such as cameras, jewellery, china, rugs, and furniture, was at unofficial prices. A United States Survey during May 1947 indicated that butter, flour, and stockings changed hands on the black market at one hundred times the legal price; margarine and eggs at seventy-five times; potatoes and beef at fifty times, down to twenty-five times the legal price for coal, suits, and dresses.[70] At these prices, even a small turnover would absorb a large amount of purchasing power; only 8 per cent of transactions would need to be conducted on these levels, with the remaining 92 per cent at legal prices, to absorb five times the volume of money that would be required if all transactions were conducted at legal prices.

For British and American policymakers, the German problem was a complex one that was linked to the regeneration of the European economy, the relation of the European economy to the international economy, and the consequences of the demise of the British Empire as a major world power. The preoccupations of German economists were conspicuously parochial, paying little serious attention to the larger picture within which German recovery would occur.[71] A curious aspect of this domestic preoccupation was that the regeneration of the German economy depended upon the restoration of trade among the European economies, since German industry had been, and would once more become, an export-oriented sector of the economy supplying capital goods to its neighbours. The problems of world economic disequilibrium were therefore a prime constraint on German domestic policy, but the force of this international dimension to the German problem was seldom recognised in the writings of Eucken and his associates during the later 1940s.

So far we have seen that the Ordoliberals placed emphasis upon the evaluation of economic instruments in regard to their impact on the functioning of the price mechanism. That they accepted the necessity for such instruments marks them out from other liberal economists, as does their belief in the necessity of discovering a 'Third Way' between planned and market economies. It was not until 1947 that this Third

[70] Mendershausen, 'Prices, Money and the Distribution of Goods in Postwar Germany', pp. 653–4.
[71] See, for example, the entirely domestic concerns of Müller-Armack's 'Zur Frage der vordringlichen wirtschaftspolitischen Massnahmen', Archiv der Industrie und Handelskammer zu Köln, 1945, reprinted in his *Genealogie der sozialen Marktwirtschaft*, pp. 15–24.

Way became associated with a distinctive menu of social measures; compared with the actual development of social policy under the National Socialist régime, and the existence of future plans for a German National Socialist welfare state, the proposals hitherto raised in discussion among the members of the Beckerath circle were extremely rudimentary.[72] It was Müller-Armack who recast the formula of the Third Way as a 'consciously guided, indeed a socially guided market economy'.[73] The market mechanism was to be constrained by policies which had social objectives; and among other factors this would require emancipation from the tutelage of the occupation administrations, and the creation of an autonomous state. Ordoliberalism was therefore programmed as the intellectual progenitor of German recovery and development.

Müller-Armack outlined the conditions for the creation of a Social Market Economy in May 1948, the need for a currency reform and reduction of the money supply to 10 per cent of its current level being prominent among the initial conditions. He also listed eleven social measures that were to be associated with the Social Market, beginning with the creation of a new participatory enterprise organisation, proceeding through a publicly regulated competition order and the pursuit of anti-monopoly policy in order to forestall possible misuse of power in the economy, provision for the extension of social insurance, and concluding with the need for minimum wages and the securing of individual wages through free wage agreements. The comprehensiveness of this programme of reform is no less striking than the complete absence of its discussion and elaboration by Müller-Armack himself, or by any of his colleagues;[74] discussion which might be thought necessary given the potential conflict between many of the proposals (for example, that concerning a 'market-based equalisation of incomes to remove harmful differences in income and wealth') and the usual strictures on the impairment of the price mechanism. Instead, attention was focused on the need for a reform of the

---

[72] A postwar programme of social policy was drawn up in the early 1940s, including the provision of pensions out of current, rather than past, contributions; health and invalidity benefits; free choice of employment and training; graduated wages according to productivity and difficulty of work; and a right to work. See M.-L. Recker, *Nationalsozialistische Sozialpolitik im zweiten Weltkrieg*, R. Oldenbourg Verlag, Munich 1985, pp. 87ff.

[73] A. Müller-Armack, *Wirtschaftslenkung und Marktwirtschaft*, Verlag für Wirtschaft und Sozialpolitik, Hamburg 1947, p. 88.

[74] Müller-Armack's 'Die Wirtschaftsordnungen sozial gesehen', *Ordo*, Bd. 1 (1948), pp. 124–54, for example, reverts to the woolly generalities concerning the relation of social and economic objectives that plague the literature on the Social Market Economy.

currency, which duly followed in June 1948 and which heralded the introduction of a series of liberalising measures.

As has been shown, as a consequence first of the 1936 price freeze, and then of the looming problems of state indebtedness and inflation after the war, Eucken and his associates had focused on the need for the price mechanism to operate as an effective channel of communication linking consumers and producers in a complex economy. The postwar excess of purchasing power, the effects of rationing and of the black market hindered the transition to a peacetime economy, and the Currency Reform of June 1948 marked a return to an ordered relationship between purchasing power, demand, prices, and the supply of goods. It did this, broadly speaking, through a radical reduction of the money supply, primarily at the expense of those whose assets were in cash, government bonds, or savings deposits. By contrast, those whose assets were in land, commercial and private property, and shares in going concerns were spared the rigours of financial readjustment.[75] The immediate impact of the reform was all the more striking because of a sudden release of consumer goods from stocks that had been built up over the previous months. The large-scale removal of excess purchasing power from the economy, together with the sudden appearance of consumer goods in the shops, represented for the Ordoliberals the turning point: the restoration of the price mechanism for which they had long argued. For them, this marked the first real step in the recovery of the German economy: Germans were once more assuming control of their economy. Since this recovery was then succeeded by a sustained period of unprecedented economic growth, the Currency Reform quickly assumed the status of a founding myth for the new Germany.

The evidence presented above concerning the evolution of ordoliberal thought during the 1940s helps us understand quite why the Currency Reform acquired this mythic quality, and why Ordoliberals should be so closely identified with the successes of German economic recovery. They had, after all, argued for a currency reform since late 1942. In itself, however, the reform was a distinctly inegalitarian measure, not the kind of policy measure one would naturally associate with the proponents of a Social Market. It is

---

[75] In this context, it should be noted that those living in the West with property in the East Zone were later compensated for their loss, without prejudice to later resumption of ownership rights. This has turned out to be one of the biggest obstacles to German Unification, since until property rights are clarified investment and reconstruction is suspended.

largely thanks to the papers of the Beckerath Circle that it can be
established that this discrepancy cannot be shrugged off, for they
demonstrate the extremely limited attention given by Ordoliberals to
the linkage between economic and social policy. Furthermore, discussion of economic policy was programmatic, rather than comparative
and analytic. The chief issue addressed in the Beckerath Circle turned
upon the conditions for the revival of the price mechanism, and this
necessarily required the liquidation of public debt and excess private
purchasing power. The Bank for International Settlements estimated
that, prior to the reform in June 1948, RM 65 billion in banknotes was
in circulation (including occupation notes), plus bank and savings
deposits that brought the total money supply to RM 140–175 billion
By July 1948 the German money supply had been reduced to just
below DM 10 billion, of which DM 5.5 billion represented new cash
allotments, and DM 3 billion, (increasing to DM 5.8 billion) represented the conversion of old currency. In addition DM 1.4 billion of
new credit had been created. Accumulated excess purchasing power
was therefore wiped out along with the German National Debt,
largely at the expense of small savers.[76] The deflationary impact of this
was boosted by the fact that wages were still subject to controls, while
prices were freed and rationing ended in the summer of 1948. There
was a rapid rise in the rate of credit creation in the banking system,
presumably driven by those with real assets using them to acquire
Deutschmarks and take advantage of conditions in consumer and
capital markets. The Bank deutscher Länder responded with further
deflationary measures in November 1948. In addition to this, a
devaluation of the Deutschmark took place in the following year,[77]
prompting further structural adjustment, born exclusively by prop-
ertyless wage-earners – whose savings would have been wiped out by
the Currency Reform, who owned no shares, housing or property,

[76] The terms of the reform involved a limited exchange of RM notes or deposits against DM,
and a conversion of remaining deposits at a nominal rate of 10:1. However, only 50 per cent of
the remaining deposits were made available, and in October 1948 70 per cent of the blocked
deposits were written off. See T. Balogh, *Germany: An Experiment in 'Planning' by the 'Free' Price
Mechanism*, Basil Blackwell, Oxford 1950, pp. 22–4 for a summary of the terms. It was
Balogh's emphasis on the severely inegalitarian features of the reform, and the rise in
unemployment that it brought about, that prompted Hutchison's bitter criticism. Further
details can be found in 'Extracts from British Military Government Law No. 61: First Law for
Monetary Reform (Currency Law), 20 June 1948', in B. R. von Oppen (ed.), *Documents on
Germany under Occupation*, Oxford University Press, Oxford 1955, pp. 292–4.

[77] The devaluation took place in September 1949 from DM 3.33 per $ to DM 4.20; G. Hardach,
'The Marshall Plan in Germany, 1948–1952', *Journal of European Economic History*, vol. 16
(1987), pp. 468.

and who consequently had no collateral with which they might soften the impact of adjustment. But this is of course what structural adjustment is for.

There is dispute today concerning the specific contribution of the Currency Reform to the recovery of the German economy, and any reasoned discussion of the issues involved must necessarily couple an analysis of German monetary policy with an assessment of production and consumption trends in the late 1940s and early 1950s.[78] Furthermore, the various agencies and programmes associated with the Marshall Plan need to be taken into account, as well as domestic and external policy in Britain and the United States. Only within such a broad framework would it be possible to create a clearer picture of the actual 'success' of the reform. But that is not here the issue. It was noted above that the Currency Reform came to have a symbolic status for German economists because of the manner in which the search for a 'Third Way' between plan and market came to place such great emphasis on the functioning of the price mechanism as a 'calculating machine', to use von Stackelberg's phrase. Only in 1947 did this 'Third Way' become directly associated with a menu of social policies, and hence built into the conception of a Social Market Economy. The Currency Reform therefore marked the inception of this new economic programme, a programme which then continued in the 1950s with legislation on cartels and monopolies, a form of participatory democracy in enterprises, and the construction of a modern system of public healthcare and social welfare.

This then is the public face of the Social Market Economy: a market economy combined with social institutions, 'capitalism with a human face'. But is this not very similar to the system of welfare introduced in postwar Britain, its difference today being only in the far higher levels of welfare delivered to the German citizen as compared with the benefits enjoyed by the British descendants of the welfare state of the 1940s? The Ordoliberals did not, apparently, engage in a sustained discussion of British plans – Müller-Armack's proposals in 1947, for instance, involved no reflection on the economic implications of the social policy measures that he there outlined. From the viewpoint of

---

[78] The conventional 'bullish' view can be found expressed in H. Giersch, K.-H.Paqué, and H. Schmieding, 'Openness, Wage Restraint, and Macroeconomic Stability: Germany's Road to Prosperity 1948–1959', in R. Dornbusch, W. Nölling, and R. Layard (eds.), *Postwar Economic Reconstruction and Lessons for the East Today*, MIT Press, Cambridge, Mass. 1993, pp. 4–5. For a contrasting view more in line with the above argument see H. C. Wolf's contribution to the same collection, 'The Lucky Miracle: Germany 1945–1951', pp. 32–9.

the late twentieth century, this is rather a serious oversight. From the foregoing, it would appear that the Ordoliberals were mute on this point: where the constraints of the market economy intersect with the social conditions required for its functioning.

But not entirely so. Röpke's *Civitas Humana*, first published in 1944, contains some comments on the Beveridge Plan, and the ferocity of criticisms there expressed makes quite plain the distance separating social marketeers from market socialists:

> This 'Beveridge Plan' is nothing but the conscientious and extremely logical execution of the old principle of social insurance and social services. . . . It is a gigantic machine for pumping the national income about, described in the Beveridge report on three hundred closely printed pages and with its highly complicated system of pipes, screws and valves and supplied with the most confusing 'directions for use'.
> . . . It is the extreme logical result of a proletarianised society.[79]

This point was touched on by Foucault in his 1979 Collège de France lecture course, recalling Röpke's response to the Beveridge Plan that it 'was quite simply Nazism'.[80] There is some artistic licence at work here: for Röpke does not seem to have committed himself in so many words. But, on the other hand, there is much truth in Foucault's offhand comment. Strange associates these, as progenitors of the social market: Röpke, the ardent republican; Eucken, the austere conservative; von Stackelberg, the autocratic Nazi. In the later 1920s and early 1930s these three could have represented the entire political spectrum: from supporters of Weimar, through its critics and covert restorationists, to the National Socialists who were to be its eventual liquidators. But in the 1940s these three opposing tendencies combine, to become proponents of a new economic order of a rather wider significance than the social and economic policy of a reconstructed Germany. It would be extravagant to label this postwar period as the construction of 'Nazism with a human face'. But there are indeed real continuities that link the social and economic policies of the later 1930s and the 1940s with those of the 1950s, continuities that will be raised by way of concluding these studies of German economics, from Cameralism to Ordoliberalism.

---

[79] W. Röpke, *Civitas Humana*, pp. 142–3.
[80] Transcript of lecture at Collège de France, 7 February 1979.

CHAPTER 9

The New Economic Order and European economic integration

During a radio broadcast in July 1940 Walter Funk, the German economics minister, put forward a plan for the reorganisation of the European economy. His New Economic Order proposed that productive activity in occupied and satellite states be co-ordinated under German direction, concentrating agricultural activity in the East and locating the greater part of European industrial production in Germany itself. The idea of creating a pan-European customs' union was expressly rejected; instead, trade between the different states was to be facilitated by a clearing system, run from Germany and denominated in Marks. Stability of exchange rates was one of the objectives of this system; this would therefore have the consequence that price movements throughout Europe would be controlled from Berlin. Germany's existing system of contract prices for agricultural products would also be extended, farmers and peasants being assured of markets for produce and guaranteed prices.

This scheme was outlined in September that same year by Charles Guillebaud, author of a recently published analysis of the German economic recovery,[1] in a lecture at the Royal Institute of International Affairs, London. Funk's plan was placed by Guillebaud in the context of previous schemes for co-ordination of the European economy, such as List's proposal for an Anglo-German alliance, and Friedrich Naumann's later concept of *Mitteleuropa*, in which the Central European economy was to be directed by the staff of a Central European Economic Commission.[2] Having laid emphasis upon the manner in which the proposed regulation of agricultural prices would insulate European production from fluctuations in world prices, Guillebaud argued that Funk's New Order as a whole had to be

[1] C. W. Guillebaud, *The Economic Recovery of Germany*, Macmillan, London 1939; the book was reviewed by Dennis Robertson in the *Economic Journal*, vol. 49 (1939), pp. 305–8.
[2] See F. Naumann, *Central Europe*, P. S. King and Son, London 1916, Chapters 7 and 8.

rejected, not because it was unsound – 'parts of it may well come to be adopted later in a modified form'[3] – but because it was based upon German hegemony. The postwar European economic order, argued Guillebaud, would nevertheless require political and economic leadership, and Germany was the natural candidate for this role:

Our hopes for the economic future of this area must be based on the emergence after the war of a Germany which will repudiate the false aims of Nazi ideology in so far as they imply the domination of Europe by Germany. The great task of statesmanship after the war will be to secure the willing co-operation of Germany in the economic reconstruction of Europe on a basis of the recognition of the rights and interests of all the peoples involved.[4]

There were, he concluded, two alternatives to this vision for the postwar order. The first involved the extension of Bolshevik rule through Eastern and Central Europe; the second the creation of a vast free trade area throughout Europe, which would leave weaker economies to struggle as best they could. Such a policy was not an immediate prospect:

in the longer run the wide divergences in the different stages of development of the countries of Continental Europe would seem to make the free-trade ideal (which would have to be combined with the unrestricted movement of people) at best a Utopia which might conceivably be reached in some far distant future.[5]

Guillebaud's outline of the developmental paths open to the postwar European economy has proved remarkably prescient; since 1945 all three have played their part in the evolution of European political institutions and economic structures.

Funk's proposals prompted another response. In November 1940 Harold Nicolson, Parliamentary Secretary to the Ministry of Information, wrote to Maynard Keynes asking him to participate in a campaign against the proposed New Order, enclosing notes outlining the main lines of argument to be followed in countering Funk's plan. Keynes demurred:

In my opinion about three-quarters of the passages quoted from the German broadcasts would be quite excellent if the name of Great Britain were substituted for Germany or the Axis, as the case may be. If Funk's plan is taken at its face value, it is excellent and just what we ourselves ought to be

[3] Guillebaud, 'Hitler's New Economic Order for Europe', *Economic Journal*, vol. 50 (1940), p. 458.   [4] *Ibid.*, p. 459.
[5] *Ibid.*, p. 460. See also P. Einzig, 'Hitler's "New Order" in Theory and Practice', *Economic Journal*, vol. 51 (1941), pp. 1–18.

thinking of doing. If it is to be attacked, the way to do it would be to cast doubt and suspicion on its *bona fides*.[6]

Later that same month Keynes was asked to prepare a statement on the German proposals for the Foreign Office. His paper 'Proposals to Counter the German "New Order"' was circulated on 1 December 1940, focusing attention on the prospects of a stable currency system contained in the German proposals:

The virtue of free trade depends on international trade being carried on by means of what is, in effect, *barter*. After the last war *laissez-faire* in foreign exchange led to chaos. Tariffs offer no escape from this. But in Germany Schacht and Funk were led by force of necessity to evolve something better. In practice they have used their new system to the detriment of their neighbours. But the underlying idea is sound and good.[7]

During the following two years Keynes continued redrafting and refining these first reactions, generalising his initial interest in the clearing mechanism established by the Germans and elaborating a scheme for an international currency union. By the time that *Proposals for an International Clearing Union* was published in April 1943[8] reference to the German scheme had long since given way to discussion of the relationship between central banks and to the wider system of trade and finance; and the American counter-proposal for a Stabilisation Fund shifted the emphasis further away from a clearing mechanism facilitating trade towards a general instrument for the co-ordination of the postwar international economy.[9]

Nonetheless, the wartime European clearing mechanism did, despite its more obvious political deficiencies, provide the first

[6] Keynes to H. Nicolson, 20 November 1940, *Collected Writings*, vol. xxv, Macmillan, London 1980, p. 2.
[7] Keynes, Covering note dated 1 December 1940 to 'Proposals to Counter the German "New Order"', *Collected Writings*, vol. xxv, pp. 8–9. The draft statement itself echoed Guillebaud's expectation that German economic leadership would be important for the recovery of the postwar European economy: 'It is not our purpose to reverse the roles proposed by Germany for herself and for her neighbours. It would be senseless to suppose that her neighbours can develop an ordered, a prosperous, or a secure life with a crushed and ruined Germany in their midst. Germany must be expected and allowed to assume the measure of economic leadership which flows naturally from her own qualifications and her geographical position.' *Collected Writings*, vol. xxv, p. 15.
[8] The Preface is printed in *Collected Writings*, vol. xxv, pp. 233–5.
[9] See 'A Comparative Analysis of the British Project for a Clearing Union (C. U.) and the American Project for a Stabilisation Fund (S. F.)', *Collected Writings*, vol. xxv, pp. 215–26. After discussions in Washington these drafts were consolidated into a proposal for an International Monetary Fund, discussed at Bretton Woods in 1944. For a lucid analysis of the Keynes plan see R. Triffin, *Europe and the Money Muddle. From Bilateralism to Near-Convertibility, 1947–56*, Yale University Press, New Haven 1957, pp. 93–109.

working model of a post-gold standard system for multilateral clearing. The International Monetary Fund that resulted from the Bretton Woods Conference of 1944 represented a more ambitious blueprint for the reconstruction of trade and finance in the international economy, for its operation was conditional upon the full convertibility of currencies. States wishing to avail themselves of its facilities for the rectification of temporary disturbances in their overseas trading accounts were required to maintain full convertibility of their currencies. These conditions – applications for assistance to be made only for the correction of temporary imbalances experienced by a member-state maintaining full convertibility – combined to render the IMF ineffective, for they presupposed a world economic order in which no structural financial problems existed; and thus the IMF, under its own rules, was not able to make any serious contribution to the restoration of a functioning world economy. The IMF was in any case not scheduled to begin operation until March 1947; when it did so, the utopian nature of its design quickly became evident, for the United Kingdom Convertibility Crisis that quickly followed ended any prospect of a general return to convertibility among European currencies until the later 1950s.[10] The subsequent recovery of European trade and the reconstruction of national economies therefore occurred without any specific support from the leading international financial institution created at Bretton Woods. Instead, the revival of trade among European economies was facilitated by the European Payments Union, a temporary clearing agency created in September 1950 along lines not dissimilar to the German model that had formed the basis of Keynes' first reflections.[11] This system lasted until convertibility of the major European currencies was established in 1958, fulfilling one of the central functional criteria for the IMF; although the international monetary system collapsed once more in the 1970s, together with the first attempts at the creation of a European Monetary System. By the later 1980s it was evident that accelerated integration of the economies within the European Union required, if the northern economies were not to become *de facto* members of a *Deutschmark* area, at least a functioning exchange-rate mechanism, and at best a single currency.

[10] See on this problem A. S. Milward, *The Reconstruction of Western Europe 1945–51*, Methuen, London 1987, pp. 44–55.

[11] For an account of the creation of the EPU see A. O. Hirschman, 'The European Payments Union. Negotiations and the Issues', *Review of Economics and Statistics*, vol. 33 (1951), pp. 49–55.

Much of this was already evident to Funk and his colleagues in the early 1940s. Introducing a series of lectures delivered during the autumn of 1942 in Berlin, Funk emphasised how the further development of the European economy depended upon a better distribution of raw materials and productive capacity, combined with arrangements for 'multilateral-Clearings'.[12] As Benning, director of the Reichs-Kredit-Gesellschaft concluded in his own lecture,

European co-operation on a continental basis, and the organic development of the economic forces of European countries, is facilitated by the modern instruments of clearing agreements, European economic agreements and the reorganisation of the Continental currency bloc.

The *ultimate aim of the reform of currency policies for our Continent* is ... the creation, with the least possible degree of bureaucratic regulation, of a free system for the clearing of payments between individual European countries, and a comprehensive consolidation of their credit markets; subject to the overriding aim of full employment and an economically secure extended economic space (*Großraumwirtschaft*).[13]

But these lectures on the 'European Economic Community' went further than consideration of trade, currency, and finance in a postwar world; other lectures in the series covered agriculture, industry, labour supply, trade, and transport. These are of course standard headings that one would expect to find in an overview of the European Union (EU) economies; although today they would be dealt with in terms of a neo-classical agenda headed by considerations of market efficiency, growth, and the optimisation of welfare. These were not the terms in which German economists thought about the benefits of integration in 1942. Here, instead of the 'single market', the watchword was *Großraumwirtschaft*, the economy of an extended economic space.

Raumordnung was of course no new idea; it was a central component of the discourse of geopolitics developed during the 1930s, but it was not until the later 1930s that this conceptualisation of space was systematically linked to more general ideas of economic development and integration. Here free use could be made of the work of List, with his conception of the international economy divided into tropical and

---

12 English in the original: W. Funk, 'Das wirtschaftliche Gesicht des neuen Europas', in W. Funk *et al.*, *Europäische Wirtschaftsgemeinschaft*, 2nd edn, Haude und Spenerrsche Verlagsbuchhandlung Max Paschke, Berlin 1943, pp. 32–3. The lectures were organised by the Verein Berliner Kaufleute und Industrieller, the Wirtschafts-Hochschule Berlin, and the *Gau* economic adviser Professor Dr Heinrich Hunke.
13 B. Benning, 'Europäische Währungsfragen', in Funk *et al.*, *Europäische Wirtschaftsgemeinschaft*, pp. 182–3.

temperate spheres; and the manner in which German economic thinking turned upon conceptions of order, rather than of value or of distribution, supported this view of economies as ordered economic spaces. At the theoretical level, one could invoke a tradition reaching from von Thünen, through Alfred Weber and up to Eucken, the last of whom emphasised the temporal and spatial aspects of economic activity in several of his essays during the early 1940s.[14] It was generally supposed by German economists of the time that an economic theory appropriate to the integration of the European economy would supersede liberal theory, tied as it was to a nineteenth-century international economy hegemonised by a single power, Great Britain. As a Spanish economist wrote,

The failure of Liberalism was in part due to the intention of directly creating a world economy; but this can only happen once a number of greater economies have been formed. It was believed that the influence of the international market and far-reaching financial instruments would bring about unitary regulation of the world economy, quite independent of the numerous political tendencies which corresponded to the great number of states whose political sovereignty was merely formal.[15]

A world economy fragmented into a number of blocs created by a few competing great powers created a penumbra of smaller client economies, in which the tenets of free trade had become impractical. Instead, argued Eguilaz, co-ordination of the international economy could only be effected through some form of clearing system, and the development of an international credit system based on mutual deliveries of products.[16]

Another economist, writing in the same year, considered the development of customs' unions as a device for economic integration, emphasising its political aspects. On the one hand, the world economy was in the course of forming itself into large spheres of economic influence; European states could no longer permit themselves the luxury of economic independence, for this would eventually threaten the independence of the entire continent. On the other hand, the classical path of a customs' union could not provide the political

[14] See for example Eucken's essay 'Die zeitliche Lenkung des Wirtschaftsprozesses und der Aufbau der Wirtschaftsordnungen', *Jahrbücher für Nationalökonomie und Statistik*, Bd. 159 (1944), pp. 161–221.
[15] H. P. Eguilaz, 'Probleme einer internationaler wirtschaftlichen Zusammenarbeit', *Weltwirtschaftliches Archiv*, Bd. 54 (1941), p. 163. Eguilaz was General Secretary of the Consejo de Economia Nacional, Madrid, and a member of the National Falangist Council.
[16] *Ibid.*, p. 175.

direction for the successful integration of the European economies: 'a *European Economic Community* (*europäische Wirtschaftsgemeinschaft*) cannot emerge in the liberal-egalitarian manner of the "classical" customs' union in the absence of a prior national will for integration.'[17] Co-operation would be necessary; here, argued Heinrich, Germany could perhaps take the lead. A similar sentiment had already been expressed by Guillebaud and Keynes the previous year, but they had in mind a postwar world and a defeated Germany. At the time Heinrich's essay appeared German forces were about to embark on the invasion of Russia, and in a further war of conquest seek to extend the European *Großraum* from the Atlantic to the Urals.

What is the nature of the economic analysis at work here? Historians of National Socialism have sought, with little success, to isolate a body of economic theory informing National Socialism, or to identify a consistent economic policy pursued by the Nazi régime. For the Soviet Union in the 1930s and 1940s, such difficulties do not exist: successive reorganisations of the Soviet economy throughout the 1920s and the 1930s, as well as opposition to them, were articulated in economic terms, the objectives and instruments being primarily economic in nature. By contrast, there appears to be no such thing as National Socialist Economics, nor by extension any specific National Socialist economic policy. National Socialist rhetoric constantly proclaimed the subordination of economics to politics: the economic sphere was but the instrument of a higher, political domain. Studies of German economic organisation in the 1930s and the early 1940s bear out this view of economic management: that the German economy was not run with a view to efficiency or productivity, but was instead hostage to arbitrary political decision-making.[18]

Nevertheless, the assumption remains that if some kind of consistent framework for economic management could be identified, some additional insight might be gained into the dynamics of the German economy during the later 1930s and the early 1940s. There is however an evident difficulty with the sources. Herbst, for example, in his study of the German war economy, seeks guidelines for economic policy of the 1930s from Hitler's pronouncements in *Mein Kampf*, a

---

[17] K. Heinrich, 'Zollunion und Großwirtschaftsräume', *Schmollers Jahrbuch für Gesetzgebung, Verwaltung und Volkswirtschaft*, Jg. 65, Hb. 1 (1941), p. 299.

[18] See B. H. Klein, *Germany's Economic Preparations for War*, Harvard University Press, Cambridge, Mass. 1959; D. Petzina, *Autarkiepolitik im Dritten Reich. Der nationalsozialistische Vierjahresplan*, Deutsche Verlags-Anstalt, Stuttgart 1968; P. Hayes, *Industry and Ideology. IG Farben in the Nazi Era*, Cambridge University Press, Cambridge 1987.

work which is of course not noted for its economic originality.[19] He also considers the development of the concept of a *Wehrwirtschaft* in the later 1930s, a form of permanently mobilised and militarised economy, which might have provided a framework for an alternative National Socialist economics.[20] He puts forward the suggestion that the adoption of the *Blitzkrieg* in 1939 was an expedient dictated by foreign policy, prematurely launching the *Wehrwirtschaft* onto a wartime footing. But this approach tends to confirm, rather than invalidate, the idea of a primacy of politics. There were nevertheless other writers in the 1920s and 1930s who were National Socialists and who did make some attempt at developing a *Volkswirtschaftslehre* fit for the *Herrenvolk*. Barkai in his study of Nazi economic policy points out that ten of the twenty-five theses in the original Party programme of 1920 dealt with economic issues, and the early anticapitalist tendency in the Party had much to do with a critique of finance capital developed by Feder.[21] By the early 1930s, however, Feder had lost influence over economic policy to Wagener, Darré, and Klagges, the last being entrusted with the task of elaborating a 'National Socialist economic philosophy'.[22] Little came of this; with the seizure of power in 1933 economic policy was improvised by existing specialists, rather than Party ideologues – Barkai's account increasingly drifts into the realms of economic administration and establishes no clear relationship between policy in the 1930s and a specifically National Socialist economic ideology.[23]

   Part of the difficulty in these assessments seems to derive from a rather limited conception of what counts as economic analysis and argument, one divorced from a proper appreciation of the character of German economic argument since the eighteenth century. An

[19] L. Herbst, *Der totale Krieg und die Ordnung der Wirtschaft*, DVA, Stuttgart 1982, Part 1, Chapter 2.

[20] See for example K. Hesse, 'Wehrwirtschaft als Wissenschaft', in K. Hesse (ed.), *Kriegswirtschaftliche Jahresberichte 1936*, Hanseatische Verlagsanstalt, Hamburg 1936, pp. 11–15; he admits, however, that at the time of writing there existed only a number of disparate studies on particular areas of interest. See also H. Hunke, *Grundzüge der deutschen Volks- und Wehrwirtschaft*, Haude und Spenersche Buchhandlung, Berlin 1938; and H. W. Spiegel, 'Wehrwirtschaft: Economics of the Military State', *American Economic Review*, vol. 30 (1940), pp. 713–23.

[21] A. Barkai, *Das Wirtschaftssystem des Nationalsozialismus. Ideologie, Theorie, Politik 1933–45*, Fischer Taschenbuch Verlag, Frankfurt a. M. 1988, pp. 29–30.   [22] *Ibid.*, p. 37.

[23] Mention should also be made here of C. Kruse, *Die Volkswirtschaftslehre im Nationalsozialismus*, Rudolf Haufe Verlag, Freiburg i. Br. 1988. This is a general survey of economics in the period 1933–45 which does not systematically confront the wider political function of economic analysis for National Socialism.

aspect of German economic management that was increasingly evident from the mid-1930s was the emphasis upon autarky, which in turn rested upon the evaluation of economies in terms of their raw materials and patterns of consumption and production.[24] Economic activity was explicitly linked to economic space. The idea of international trade as the instrument of domestic expansion gave way to a policy of stockpiling and import substitution that, from the standpoint of classical economic theory, involved serious inefficiencies and inhibitions to growth. Throughout the 1930s, however, such nostrums were both metaphorically and practically academic, since world trade was declining and free trade was giving way to barter and bilateral agreements. Domestic economic expansion could not therefore depend upon a revival of the international economy; some other route was necessary.

The systematic attempt to create a national economy which, as far as military goods, energy, and food supply was concerned, was independent of world markets, implied a conception of economic autarky and bloc formation closely associated with the doctrine of economic space. This perspective revealed for example that coal was the only major raw material for which Germany had adequate supplies; it had no direct access to natural rubber, like Britain; no oil supply, like the United States; and the armaments industry depended upon imports of high-grade ore from Sweden. There was virtually no domestic supply of non-ferrous metals, some of which were vital for the production of armour. Hitler placed Göring in charge of raw materials and foreign exchange in April 1936, reviving the control of production and consumption that the *Kriegsrohstoffabteilung* had enjoyed during the First World War.[25] Schacht, Economics Minister until his resignation in 1937, had supported the production of synthetic fuels and oil, but saw this as a temporary expedient to be pursued until world markets were in a better position to supply German needs. Göring on the other hand, who succeeded him in 1937, regarded everything from the point of view of a war economy and sought to establish independence from world markets in raw materials. By 1939 German oil requirements for mobilisation could be

---

[24] See W. Andreae, 'Bildung eines Großwirtschaftsraumes im Hinblick auf die Selbstversorgungsmöglichkeiten Großdeutschlands', *Schmollers Jahrbuch für Gesetzgebung, Verwaltung und Volkswirtschaft*, N. F. Jg. 65, Hb. 1 (1941), pp. 71–92.

[25] See the discussion of the work of *Kriegsrohstoffabteilung* during the First World War above, pp. 150–1.

supplied entirely from domestic resources, while between 55 per cent
and 60 per cent of general economic requirements could be met.[26]

The situation with respect to rubber was rather a different story. In
1938 only 5 per cent of the domestic consumption of rubber derived
from synthetic production, and it was only by intensive recycling that
serious inroads could be made into rubber imports. Not until 1942
were significant amounts of synthetic rubber (*Buna*) produced, by
which time it was becoming evident that, for synthetic rubber, the end
of the war would see a situation similar to that which had prevailed in
dyestuffs at the end of the First World War – the emergence of more
efficient and cheaper overseas competitors. By mid-1942 Standard of
New Jersey had licensed buna patents to all-comers without fee, and
the United States government was eventually to spend $700 million
on synthetic rubber production in the course of the war. In 1944
American production of synthetic rubber was four and a half times the
maximum German output. The delays to IG Farben's new plant at
Auschwitz (it never entered full production) can be primarily attributed to the determination to construct a technically advanced plant
that would be economically viable in an open postwar international
economy.[27]

Funk's New Order was not simply an idea; it had a clear relationship to existing German economic management, and it became the
organising principle through which the occupied economies of
Western Europe were exploited. It also has a clear relationship to the
population policy of relocation, resettlement, and extermination
embodied in the *Generalplan Ost*, the plan for the relocation of the
populations of the eastern economies developed in the wake of the
invasion of Russia.[28] Here again, conventional economic categories
are mute: what economic rationale can there be for the systematic
pursuit of wars of conquest, for the deliberate relocation of entire
populations, and for the annihilation of Jews and Slavs? Before
investigating this problem, some further comments are needed con-

---

[26] Petzina, *Autarkiepolitik im Dritten Reich*, pp. 43ff.
[27] Hayes, *Industry and Ideology*, p. 354. The senior directors of IG Farben did not believe that a
German autarkic economy could long survive the war. When asked in 1940 to indicate their
view of the chemical industry in a postwar New Order they simply revamped their earlier
cartel arrangements and gave them a more Germanocentric form; their proposals were built
around an estimation of the future position in foreign markets, and it was stated that autarky
was not a viable long term option for the Greater German Economic Sphere. Hayes, *Industry
and Ideology*, p. 268.
[28] G. Aly and S. Heim, *Vordenker der Vernichtung. Auschwitz und die Pläne für eine neue europäische
Ordnung*, Hoffmann und Campe Verlag, Hamburg 1991, pp. 395ff.

cerning the implementation of the New Order in the occupied countries of Western Europe.

The European New Order was, as both Guillebaud and Keynes indicated, a large-scale German scheme for the exploitation of European capital and labour. It envisaged a two-tier Europe in which the welfare of German citizens was paramount, and in which other citizenries were disadvantaged by virtue of their not being German. German control of European resources operated in part automatically through the clearing scheme, and also through the imposition of occupation costs, whereby individual countries were required to pay the costs of German occupation. French 'occupation costs' had originally been fixed at 20 million RM per day; for these purposes the Franc was valued at 20 Francs to 1 RM, substantially over-valuing the RM;[29] and these direct occupation costs accounted for about 40 per cent of total French taxation revenue from 1940–44. They were remitted to Germany through the clearing mechanism, which systematically, but not uniformly, overvalued the RM, and was linked to a policy whereby import prices were fixed at a low level.

Linked to the mechanism whereby credit and goods were extracted from occupied territories was the direction of labour. A German survey indicated that French workers were more productive in Germany than in France, which was hardly surprising given the abundance of new capital equipment in Germany, and the prospects for greater coercion involved.[30] By the autumn of 1942 there were 5,093,000 male foreign workers employed in Germany, of whom 1,341,000 were French.[31] This extensive mobilisation of European labour was not without its problems: in the French case, ever larger proportions of drafts simply disappeared en route, making off into the countryside and joining the Resistance as the only alternative to working in Germany. As Milward wryly observes, 'The reality in France was that the resistance fighters were composed of bands of unemployed to whom the English distributed weapons by plane.'[32]

Along with the import of labour into Germany, German concerns either directly acquired, or established trusteeship of, European industrial plants. In Bohemia and Moravia, for example, the

---

[29] A. S. Milward, *War, Economy and Society 1939–1945*, Penguin Books, Harmondsworth 1987, p. 137; it is difficult to estimate the ratio exactly since no genuine equilibrium exchange rates had existed with the RM in 1939. By comparison with the US Dollar, the over-valuation of the RM was probably around 50 per cent.   [30] *Ibid.*, p. 142.

[31] A. S. Milward, *The New Order and the French Economy*, Oxford University Press, Oxford 1970, p. 112.   [32] *Ibid.*, p. 173.

Hermann Göring works took control of the Vitkovice steelworks, the Skoda armaments works and vehicle factories, and six other major companies. The Dresdner Bank assumed control of the Tatra car factories, Mannesmann interests took over the Prague Railway Company and a steelworks in Ostrava. About half of the industrial share capital of the Protectorate of Bohemia and Moravia passed into German hands, plus almost all the share capital in coal mining, cement, and paper.[33] This was linked to the command over raw materials that occupation of the Western European economies provided. Some 75 per cent of extracted French iron-ore was taken by Germany during the war; although French steelmaking capacity was absorbed by German firms, production was here again concentrated in the Ruhr, where supplies of coking coal were available.[34] The story was similar with the production of aluminium and of power. Plans were made to develop Norwegian hydro-electric power generation specifically to smelt bauxite brought from France and Hungary. Norway's dependence upon imported food was also addressed: agricultural investment, such as moorland reclamation projects, was planned, together with readjustments in the livestock economy to make it less dependent upon imported feed.[35]

The central feature of all these arrangements, the characteristic that distinguishes German wartime economic management from that developed at the same time in Britain and the United States, was that systematic co-ordination of the European economy was not primarily a consequence of the war. The New Order was a plan for the general integration of the European economy which happened to be developed in the course of a European war; it was not conceived as a wartime expedient, maximising the output of munitions and deliberately suppressing consumer demand, requiring a high level of overall direction of economic activity.[36] If anything, the pressures imposed by war production were, for much of the war, significantly less in Germany than in Britain. If Germany had won the war the New Order would have played a major role in the reorganisation of the

---

[33] Milward, *War, Economy and Society*, p. 158.
[34] This complementarity, whereby the French possessed reserves of iron ore, but became heavily reliant upon Ruhr coal for the production of steel in Northern France, created the political conflict out of which the European Coal and Steel Community was eventually formed in 1951 – see J. Gillingham, *Coal, Steel, and the Rebirth of Europe, 1945–1955*, Cambridge University Press, Cambridge 1991, Chapter 5.
[35] Milward, *War, Economy and Society*, pp. 155–6.
[36] In 1944 some two-thirds of British manufacturing employment was dedicated to war production – *ibid.*, p. 59.

European economy; although it could of course be contended that this was eventually, in any case, what happened.[37]

The New Order was primarily organised in the interests of the German *Volksgemeinschaft*, which was defined to exclude the populations of occupied countries and asocial elements who could not be considered full members. Members of the *Volksgemeinschaft* were to participate, according to Hitler in a speech during November 1940, in the construction of a 'German social state as an example to the rest of the world'.[38] This was to cover health, education, housing, and pension provision, together with an employment and wages policy which would, among other things, provide a premium for those working in the East as part of regional structural policy.[39] As with much of the economic organisation of the New Order, the rapidity with which plans for a postwar order became overtaken by defeats and reverses in the East pushed this original perspective upon the future of Germany and of the European economy to one side. As early as June 1941 the weekly German meat ration, a useful index of general welfare, was reduced from 500g. to 400g. There was every intention of restoring the level as soon as practicable; but what is here of interest is the form of the calculation made in assessing the extent of the resources required to do so. Increasing the meat ration by 100g. per week per person would require an annual production of 300,000 tons of meat; this in turn would require the production of 1.8 million tons of grain. So far this form of reckoning is unremarkable; it is the next stage which is of significance. German economists calculated that the 1.8 million tons of grain that they required for the restoration of the meat ration to 500g. per week was the annual minimum subsistence of more than four million people. This was based upon estimates which put the annual consumption of the Yugoslavian peasant at 300kg.; that of the Russian peasant at 250kg.; while the meat consumption of a German was calculated to require 400–500kg. of grain annually.[40]

This estimate was linked to the general planning of food supplies for the armed forces, in which it was hoped that, during the third year of

[37] In this context Robert Harris' *Fatherland* (Hutchinson, London 1992) provides an imaginative insight into a postwar Europe dominated by a National Socialist Germany.

[38] M.-L. Recker, *Nationalsozialistische Sozialpolitik im zweiten Weltkrieg*, R. Oldenbourg Verlag, Munich 1985, p. 83.

[39] *Ibid.*, pp. 86ff. Recker is here summarising the draft postwar programme drawn up by the Arbeitswissenschaftliche Institut of the Deutsche Arbeitsfront in 1940.

[40] Aly and Heim, *Vordenker der Vernichtung*, p. 371. The official responsible for these calculations was Herbert Backe, a Göttingen-trained agronomist who was Darré's deputy for many years, and then his successor as Minister of Food and Agriculture in 1944.

the war, they could be supplied exclusively from Russia. In a paper drafted by *Wehrwirtschaftsstab Ost*, entitled 'Economic Policy Guidelines for the Economic Organisation of the East, Agricultural Section' and dated 23 May 1941, it was calculated that this redirection of Russian agricultural produce to German use would render superfluous tens of millions of persons in the forested and northern industrial areas of the Soviet Union. Their fate would be either death through starvation, or mass emigration to Siberia. The memorandum continued:

> Attempts to save the population from starvation by the import of surpluses from the Ukraine could only be to the detriment of the supply of food to Europe. These surpluses strengthen the fortitude of Germany in war, they support the ability of Germany and of Europe to withstand blockade. This must be recognised in the clearest terms.[41]

Despite the association made here between food supply and the prosecution of the war, the form of the economic calculation employed is directly related to the ideas of *Großraumwirtschaft* outlined above.

The populations of the European *Großraumwirtschaft*, the 'European Economic Space' were hierarchised in a scale descending from the Germans, through similar Northern European peoples, to the populations of Central Europe, and finally to the Slavic populations of the East. Within this scheme it was the fate of European Jewry to be assigned some indefinite location in the East, where in fact they were then destroyed. The National Socialist ideology of *Lebensraum* was transformed by economists, agronomists, demographers, ethnologists, and sociologists, employed in ministries, research institutes,[42] and universities, into a systematic policy of population resettlement, expropriation, and extermination. They developed the conception of an optimal population for a given region, in which available subsistence was linked to the number of persons that they could support. Size of population and the standard of living were thereby locked into an inverse relationship; for where population density was high, and economic activity concentrated in non-agricultural sectors, the supply of food had to come from an agricultural surplus somewhere else,

---

[41] Reprinted in the proceedings of the Nuremberg trials and cited in Aly and Heim, *Vordenker der Vernichtung*, p. 373. The 'Economic Policy Guidelines' had a print run of several thousand and were distributed widely among the military and economic administrators.

[42] Backe was for example also First Vice-President of the Kaiser-Wilhelm Gesellschaft, forerunner of the present Max Planck Gesellschaft; Aly and Heim, *Vordenker der Vernichtung*, p. 367.

that is, from an underpopulated (in these terms) region.[43] This idea was adopted by academics working at the Institut für Deutsche Ostarbeit in Cracow,[44] and used to express the idea that, since Polish agriculture was overpopulated by a factor of two, half the Polish population was therefore deadweight. If the food supply was insufficient to feed a resident (inferior) population, the thinking went, then the logical course was to remove, in one way or another, the population 'surplus'. Although there were numerous contradictory aspects to the execution of this policy, a constant feature was the deliberate use of specialised academic personnel in planning the reorganisation of the eastern economies.

One of the more striking conflicts concerned the settlement of Germans on the borders of the *Reich*. The official policy was to use ethnic Germans outside the *Reich* as colonial bearers of German culture, extending a policy already promoted in the later nineteenth century for the Germanisation of the Polish borderlands.[45] Heinrich Himmler, sometime agronomy student, appointed in October 1939 *Reichskommissar für die Festigung deutschen Volkstums*, saw things differently.[46] He supported plans drawn up by his officials to resettle thirty million ethnic Germans living outside the *Reich* within its borders. By late October 1939 a short-term plan had been drawn up to move Poles and Jews out of the Warthegau into the General Gouvernement, replacing them with ethnic Germans.[47] A census was due in December, and a long-term plan provided for resettlement according to the results of the census, with ethnic Germans settled at a

---

[43] This idea was originally elaborated by Paul Mombert, Professor of Economics at the University of Gießen from 1922 to 1933, when he was dismissed as part of the purge of non-Aryans from public office – Aly and Heim, *Vordenker der Vernichtung*, p. 107.

[44] See M. Burleigh, *Germany turns Eastwards*, Cambridge University Press, Cambridge 1988, pp. 282–3.

[45] See R. W. Tims, *Germanising Prussian Poland. The H-K-T Society and the Struggle for the Eastern Marches in the German Empire, 1894–1919*, Faculty of Political Science, Columbia University, New York 1941.

[46] R. Breitman, *The Architect of Genocide. Himmler and the Final Solution*, Bodley Head, London 1991, pp. 76ff.

[47] The initial study upon which much of the later work built was T. Schieder, 'Aufzeichnung über Siedlung und Volkstumsfragen in den wiedergewonnenen Ostprovinzen' dated 4–7 October 1939, reprinted in *1999*, Heft 1 (1992), pp. 85–91; with an introduction and commentary from A. Ebbinghaus and K. H. Roth, pp. 62–77 in the same issue. The General Gouvernement was the rump of Poland remaining after the territorial annexations of Germany and the Soviet Union. It was ruled by Hans Frank, whose plans for the territory clashed with those of Himmler, giving rise to some of the contradictions in policy leading up to the Final Solution: see C. R. Browning, *The Path to Genocide. Essays on Launching the Final Solution*, Cambridge University Press, Cambridge 1992, pp. 14ff.

lower level of population density than had hitherto prevailed. Linked to this was the formation of the Deutsche Umsiedlungs Treuhand GmbH (DUT)[48] in October 1939 to regulate the property transfers arising from the resettlement. The abandoned property of ethnic Germans settling in Western Poland was valued by the DUT, and the states from which the ethnic Germans originated were charged accordingly, payment generally being rendered in the form of raw materials and foodstuffs. The settlers should then have been credited in turn, but the DUT instead retained the compensation payments and simply turned over to the incomers the expropriated property of the evacuated Polish and Jewish population.[49]

This systematic uprooting of a settled population and its replacement by incomers was informed by the idea of a 'Central Location', in which space was structured in a hierarchy according to degree of centralisation. This categorisation was then used to site enterprises, communications, administration, services, schools, and hospitals, following ideas first employed in the rural areas of Southern Germany during the early 1930s. Incomers were sorted by occupation and allocated accordingly. The consequent destruction of established social and cultural structures, and their replacement with socially engineered constructs, was one component of a policy aimed at creating a new society, within which the individual person was to be highly mobile and adaptable, bound only to the National Socialist state, and fitted to the demands of a rapidly changing industrial society.[50]

Settlement policy in the East was largely designed by social scientists, many of whom saw themselves engaged in the wider intellectual field of *Raumforschung*, 'space research'.[51] It was comple-

---

[48] The German Resettlement Trustee Company Limited.

[49] See for an account of the activities of the Haupttreuhandestelle Ost R.-D. Müller, *Hitlers Ostkrieg und die deutsche Siedlungspolitik*, Fischer Taschenbuch Verlag, Frankfurt a. M. 1991, Chapter 2: 'Die Wirtschaft: Folgt der Handel der Flagge?'.

[50] Aly and Heim, *Vordenker der Vernichtung*, pp. 161–6.

[51] Diner criticises Aly and Heim for taking the publications and studies of social scientists as preparatory work for the prosecution of mass extermination, and hence intentionally linked to the 'Endlösung' (D. Diner, 'Rationalisierung und Methode. Zu einem neuen Erklärungsversuch der "Endlösung"', *Vierteljahreshefte für Zeitgeschichte*, Jg. 40 (1992), pp. 361–2). But this line of argument is similar to that relating to the 'Hitler Order', the absence of which is read as 'proof' that Hitler either did not authorise, or was not aware of, the Final Solution. Without such academic research the programme of extermination would never have moved beyond the brutal disorder of Babi Yar to the rational extermination of European Jewry from the Mediterranean to Scandinavia. Breitman makes a similar point in a different context, that of *Reichskristallnacht*, a public shambles orchestrated by Goebbels that enraged Himmler, who vowed that a public display of this kind should never recur – see Breitman, *The Architect of*

mented by the activities of officials working in Western Europe, beginning with the reintegration of the Saarland into the German economy in 1935. This had been overseen by Josef Bürckel, advised by Dr Rudolf Gater, who had recently gained his doctorate at the University of Zürich with a dissertation on economic forecasting. In the wake of the *Anschluß*, Bürckel was made *Reichskommissar für Wiedervereinigung Österreichs* in April 1938. Gater was brought in to assist Bürckel once more, and his links with the Hamburg Gauleiter Karl Kaufmann brought further links with Hamburg economists, including Dr Walter Emmerich. A policy of radical concentration was pursued in Vienna, headed by Göring's Four-Year Plan administration, with the aim of readying Germany's economy for war. The specialists who executed this policy openly made use of the opportunity to convert economic rationalisation into a programme of systematic expropriation of Jewish property.[52] The policy of concentration therefore brought the Four-Year Plan administration into direct contact with members of the SS involved in the execution of its plans: such as Adolf Eichmann, his superior Reinhard Heydrich, and Odilo Globocnik, Gauleiter of Vienna. Later, when the Dutch economy was to be reorganised, it was carried out by many of the same personnel who had gained their first experience in Vienna.

It was the same with Poland. In May 1940 Emmerich, originally adviser to the Hamburg City Council and then assistant to Bürckel in Vienna, was made Director of Economic Administration in occupied Poland; Gater followed a few months later as leader of the General-gouvernment section of the Reichskuratorium für Wirtschaftlichkeit, today known as the Rationalisation Board for the German Economy. Both Gater and Emmerich quickly became involved in disputes over the proper management of the Polish ghetto economies, which from the German point of view were costly to maintain. The key issue was whether efforts should be made to reduce the dependence of the ghettos on external supply, or whether such dependence should be the vehicle for the natural dissolution of the ghettos through starvation and disease – a policy which would, however, still be at the cost of

---

Genocide, p. 53. Diner overlooks the function of the German university system in the reproduction of administrative personnel and structures. See also, for a contrasting interpretation to that of Aly and Heim, U. Herbert, 'Labour and Extermination: Economic Interest and the Primacy of *Weltanschauung* in National Socialism', *Past and Present*, 138 (1993), pp. 144–95.

[52] Aly and Heim, *Vordenker der Vernichtung*, pp. 38f.

German resources. The Lodz ghetto,[53] for example, whose creation in
May 1940 had led to the rationalisation of the local textile industry by
the removal of large numbers of small enterprises, quickly showed
signs of running out of the resources to pay for imported food.
Attempts by the Warthegau administration to transport the inmates
en masse into the General Gouvernement were rebuffed. A study of the
Lodz ghetto in January 1941 then concluded that an increase of
expenditure on foodstuffs would improve the condition of the workers
and enable them to be more productive, easing the burden on
German resources.[54] This policy was pursued for some months, but in
December 1941 'unproductive' workers were selected out, trans-
ported to Chelmno and gassed in trucks in one of the earlier phases of
the Final Solution.[55]

Hitler is recorded as remarking that 'the Jewish question really was
a space question which was difficult to solve, particularly for him,
since he had no space at his disposal.'[56] When Hitler talked in this way
he was employing the language of *Lebensraum*, usually regarded as an
ideologically suffused excuse for conquest and territorial expansion.
But it was not Hitler who arranged the Final Solution: he left that to
his subordinates, who worked secure in the knowledge that their
activities had the highest approval. At first sight there seems to be
little to connect the systematic terrorisation and extermination of the
Polish, Jewish, and Slavic populations of Eastern Europe with the
administration of the occupied economies in the West. Aly and Heim
in their detailed analysis of the 'planning intelligentsia' organising the
fate of millions in the East draw no such explicit connection, apart
from a reference to the 1942 lecture series on the European Economic
Community referred to above.[57] Milward, who in his study of the

[53] Lodz was included in that part of Poland annexed by Germany in 1939 and thus was outside
the General Gouvernement.
[54] It was calculated that in early 1941 there were 50,221 skilled and unskilled workers in Lodz
ghetto, but that only 12,000 were working, mainly on military clothing: Aly and Heim,
Vordenker der Vernichtung, p. 306.
[55] See on this C. R. Browning, 'Vernichtung und Arbeit. Zur Fraktionierung der planenden
deutschen Intelligenz im besetzten Polen', in W. Schneider (ed.), >*Vernichtungspolitik*<,
Junius Verlag, Hamburg 1991, pp. 37–51. Browning has shown in his essay 'Nazi
Ghettoization Policy in Poland, 1939–1941' (included in his collection *The Path to Genocide*,
pp. 28–56) that the creation of ghettos in occupied Poland was a local reaction to uncertainty
in Berlin; they were a form of human warehouse until such time as it was decided where they
should go. Local administration was, however, in the meantime confronted with the problem
of their maintenance. In Lodz and Warsaw this developed into a dispute between
productionists and attritionists.
[56] In discussion on 12 March 1940, cited in Browning, *The Path to Genocide*, p. 15.
[57] Aly and Heim, *Vordenker der Vernichtung*, p. 331.

occupied economies of Europe draws attention to the conception of a *Großraumwirtschaft*,[58] makes no reference to its relevance to resettlement policy in the East. And yet these two features of the National Socialist Order are but two aspects of a compact involving social scientists, officials, and Party members in a particular conception of an ordered economic process.

This ordered process was not that spontaneous condition and consequent welfare created and enjoyed by the activities of a free citizenry, as envisaged by Classical Liberalism. It was more akin to the Ordoliberal conception, in which order had first to be created by a strong state resistant to the efforts of interest groups seeking to capture it for their own special purposes. Order must be purposively created before liberty could prevail. This is a bleak enough blueprint for political order in the twentieth century, exceeded in desolation only by the National Socialist version of the same idea, in which however loyalty to the Party was paramount both in the creation of order and in the definition of liberty. Here the German *Volksgemeinschaft* would enjoy the benefits of a European *Großraumwirtschaft* whose citizenry possessed varying social, economic, and political rights. Once this assumption of basic inequalities has been made, then conventional economic concepts of welfare and its optimisation are simply switched off: for the allocation of resources cannot be efficiently determined by market-based competitive criteria when the agents are unfree. Nevertheless, the absence of this special form of economic reasoning does not mean that the system as a whole is therefore based upon irrational principles, in the sense that there is no logic informing its behaviour.

It should be evident from the foregoing that, however warped, there was a clear planful logic governing the administration of the European economy under National Socialist hegemony. There was conflict, of course; the deliberate creation of cross-cutting administrative competences was a key element of National Socialist rule. But all this did was to divert competitive effort, not suppress it, as any industrial economist would recognise. Across competing offices, institutions, and ministries, there was shared understanding of the conditions for the creation and maintenance of economic order. The difficulty which we have today in discerning the nature of this order derives in large part from our inclination to associate orderliness with rationalism and optimality: that an orderly world is one which

[58] Milward, *War, Economy and Society*, pp. 8ff.

corresponds to the categories of our reason. If we cannot discern the rationality of any given state of affairs, or it appears in some respect 'inefficient', we are therefore bound to conclude that it is disorderly.

I have pursued two main lines of argument in the above. The first, substantive, argument seeks to demonstrate that the movement for European integration, articulated as a deliberate policy by a government in a position to carry it forward into actual fact, can be backdated to the New Order of 1940. I have also shown that many of the policy issues raised at that time in connection with European integration are continuous with those of the 1950s and on to the 1990s. The purpose of creating this new, undoubtedly somewhat scurrilous, heritage for the European Union is to alter our perspective upon it. So long as the genesis of the European Union is conceived primarily as the outcome of postwar European politics and diplomacy – of an American desire for a strong bulwark against the Soviet Union; of the mutual positions of France and Germany in a reconstructed Europe; of a tension between the dissolving British Empire and the ambiguities of Britain's 'special relationship' with the United States – then the developmental path of European integration remains contingent upon the fluctuations of political life. The deliberate promotion of economic integration becomes a political matter and is opposed as such. Worse, it is opposed with the argument that free trade requires no special political apparatus, no power base other than that of the sovereign nation state for it to flourish.

The reactions of both Guillebaud and of Keynes to Funk's proclamation of the New European Order in July 1940 demonstrate that a more balanced perspective upon the process of European integration is possible. Instead of seeing the creation of the European Union as part of the political settlement of postwar Europe, it can be seen as a response to forces in the international economy, and thus from the general perspective of the world economic order. The pressures shaping the evolutionary path of the European Union are not short-term contingencies; they are part of the ongoing restructuring of the international order that accelerated in the nineteenth century, with the rise of the new industrial economies.

The German economic tradition, with its focus upon space, time, human need, and the institutional basis of economic order, was peculiarly adapted to the creation of an integrative strategy for the European economy. The circumstances in which this was first essayed, as a New European Order underwriting National Socialist domination of an occupied Europe, itself did a great deal of lasting damage to the intellectual basis from which it had sprung. The remoteness of this tradition of economic argument today is measured by the obscurity of many of the writers and themes discussed in the essays collected together here. Nevertheless, it is arguable that they provide a promising alternative to the general arguments for economic integration underpinning, for example, the arguments advanced by the European Commission in 1988 for the creation of single market.[59]

This last point carries us forward to the second line of argument pursued in this essay. Here there is a different objective, first raised explicitly when discussing Franz Neumann's analysis of National Socialism. It concerns the manner in which order and reason are thought to be linked in a reversible relation: that which is orderly is rational, and that which is rational is orderly (which is of course a variation upon Hegel's famous aphorism concerning the real and the rational). The constant element here is the conception of order as the product of a reasoning mind which recognises in the external world an arrangement homologous with its categories of reason. What has become in the twentieth century mainstream economic theory is an ever-more perfected exemplification of this principle; but one whose claim to identify and prescribe the conditions for rational economic conduct is properly viewed with some scepticism. For the greater the degree of technical purity of an economic principle, the greater the danger that it diverges from a world which does not seem to follow the rules which it prescribes. This implies no criticism of the consistency and rigour of modern analysis; rather, it points to the following paradox: the greater the consistency with which it is applied, the greater the evident inconsistencies which emerge between prescriptive and perceived reality.[60]

---

[59] See M. Emerson (ed.), *The Economics of 1992*, Oxford University Press, Oxford 1989; and the popular version of the arguments in P. Cecchini, *The European Challenge–1992*, Wildwood House, Aldershot 1988. Here economic arguments involving economies of scale and efficiency were pressed into service by a political imperative in an *ad hoc* manner.

[60] The economic argument for the EC Single Market programme laid emphasis upon scale economies and the benefits of rationalisation deriving from integration; these did provide an apparently rational underpinning for political argument, so long as one ignored the fact that economists had largely abandoned such analytic constructs. By the mid-1980s industrial economists were placing more emphasis upon the forces which produced what we might call 'workable competition', rather than identifying the optimal configuration of an industry and then seeking out the barriers to its realisation. Two main points can be made here. Firstly, the dispersion by firms of plants around Europe and the consequent 'sub-optimal', 'fragmented' structure of industries is not accidental. Firms can be expected to hedge in this way as part of a

The proposition that a substantive uniformity links the economic framework governing the management of occupied Western Europe and that deployed in the reorganisation of the conquered East is not intended as a denigration of German economics and social scientists. Nor should it, by implication from the points made in the preceding paragraphs, be taken up as evidence of the dubious origins of European integration. Such a conclusion is possible; but it is not one drawn here. The purpose is instead to highlight the manner in which the rational reorganisation of societies can be diverted into schemes towards which many contribute their technical skills and talents, yet none subsequently acknowledge their complicity in the sometimes calamitous consequences. This is of course one of the properties of the anonymity of market economies; but it is also evident in the workings of command economies. Here, study of National Socialism helps point this up. For the National Socialist régime was not a throwback to an earlier age of terror and cruelty; it is part of the modern age of terror and cruelty, and has to be understood as such.

market-based strategy; the process of 'rationalisation' which the Single Market is supposed to facilitate will therefore either not occur, or at least will not be such as to produce measurable and attributable effects. Secondly, if 'rationalisation' did occur as envisaged, benefits would only accrue from this process if a whole series of related social and economic measures were adopted to cope with the consequent restructuring of industries and regions. In either case, the appeal of the economic argument rests on its textbook simplicity and political function. As serious economic argument it is at best very limited.

Bibliography

Alber, J., 'Nationalsozialismus und Modernisierung', *Kölner Zeitschrift für Soziologie und Sozialpsychologie*, Jg. 41 (1989), pp. 346–65.

Aly, G. and Heim, S., *Vordenker der Vernichtung. Auschwitz und die deutschen Pläne für eine neue europäische Ordnung*, Hoffman und Campe, Hamburg 1991.

Andreae, W., 'Bildung eines Großwirtschaftsraumes im Hinblick auf die Selbstversorgungsmöglichkeiten Großdeutschlands', *Schmollers Jahrbuch für Gesetzgebung, Verwaltung und Volkswirtschaft*, N. F. Jg. 65, Hb. 1 (1941), pp. 71–92.

Anon. [J. G. H. Feder], Review of Adam Smith, *An Inquiry into the Nature and Causes of the Wealth of Nations*, *Göttingische Anzeigen von gelehrten Sachen*, I. Bd., 30. St. (10 March 1777), pp. 234–40.

Anon., Review of Smith, *Untersuchungen der Natur und Ursachen von National-reichthum*, Bd. II, *Allgemeine deutsche Bibliothek*, Bd. 38, l. Th. (1779), pp. 297–303.

Ashley, W. J., *The Faculty of Commerce in the University of Birmingham*, n. p., Birmingham 1902.

Balogh, T., 'The National Economy of Germany', *Economic Journal*, vol. 48 (1938), p. 461–97.
Germany: An Experiment in 'Planning' by the 'Free' Price Mechanism, Basil Blackwell, Oxford 1950.

Barkai, A., *Das Wirtschaftssystem des Nationalsozialismus*, Fischer Taschenbuch Verlag, Frankfurt a. M. 1988.

Barone, E., 'The Ministry of Production in the Collectivist State', in F. A. von Hayek, *Collectivist Economic Planning*, George Routledge, London 1935, pp. 245–90.

Baxa, J., 'Der Ursprung von Friedrich Lists Theorie der produktiven Kräfte', *Zeitschrift für Volkswirtschaft und Sozialpolitik*, N. F. Bd. 3 (1923), pp. 153ff.

Bendersky, J. W., *Carl Schmitt. Theorist for the Reich*, Princeton University Press, Princeton, NJ 1983.

Benning, B., 'Europäische Währungsfragen', in Funk *et al.*, *Europäische Wirtschaftsgemeinschaft*, pp. 162–83.

Bentin, L.-A., *Johannes Popitz und Carl Schmitt. Zur wirtschaftlichen Theorie des totalen Staates in Deutschland*, C. H. Beck, Munich 1972.

Biesenbach, F., 'Die Entwicklung der Nationalökonomie an der Universität Freiburg i. Br. 1768–1896', Dissertation, University of Freiburg 1968.

Binz, A., *Bericht über das vierte und fünfte Studienjahr der Handels-Hochschule Berlin. Oktober 1909/1911*, Georg Reimer, Berlin 1911.

Bericht über das siebente Studienjahr der Handels-Hochschule Berlin. Oktober 1912/ 1913, Georg Reimer, Berlin 1913.

Blumenberg-Lampe, C. (ed.), *Der Weg in die Soziale Marktwirtschaft. Referate, Protokolle, Gutachten der Arbeitsgemeinschaft Erwin von Beckerath 1943–1947*, Klett-Cotta, Stuttgart 1986.

Böckenförde, E.-W., 'Die Historische Rechtsschule und das Problem der Geschichtlichkeit des Rechts', in his *Staat, Gesellschaft, Freiheit*, Suhrkamp Verlag, Frankfurt 1976, pp. 9–41.

'Lorenz von Stein als Theoretiker der Bewegung von Staat und Gesellschaft zum Sozialstaat', in his *Staat, Gesellschaft, Freiheit*, Suhrkamp Verlag, Frankfurt a. M. 1976, pp. 146–84.

Böhm, F., *Die Ordnung der Wirtschaft als geschichtliche Aufgabe und rechtschöpferische Leistung*, W. Kohlhammer Verlag, Stuttgart 1937.

Borkenau, F., *The Totalitarian Enemy*, Faber and Faber, London 1940.

Bossard, J. H., 'The Organisation of the Business Curricula', in J. H. Bossard and F. Dewhurst, *University Education for Business*, University of Pennsylvania Press, Philadelphia 1931, Chapter 11.

Bourne, E. G., 'Alexander Hamilton and Adam Smith', *Quarterly Journal of Economics*, vol. 8 (1894), pp. 328–44.

Braun, H. J., 'Economic Theory and Policy in Germany 1750–1800,' *Journal of European Economic History*, vol. 4 (1975), pp. 301–22.

Breitman, R., *The Architect of Genocide. Himmler and the Final Solution*, Bodley Head, London 1991.

Brentano, L., 'Privatwirtschaftslehre und Volkswirtschaftslehre', *Bank-Archiv*, Jg. 12 (1912), pp. 1–6.

Brittan, S., *Restatement of Economic Liberalism*, Macmillan, London 1988.

Browning, C. R., 'Vernichtung und Arbeit. Zur Fraktionierung der planenden deutschen Intelligenz im besetzten Polen', in W. Schneider (ed.), >*Vernichtungspolitik*<, Junius Verlag, Hamburg 1991, pp. 37–51.

The Path to Genocide. Essays on Launching the Final Solution, Cambridge University Press, Cambridge 1992.

Brückner, J., *Staatswissenschaften, Kameralismus und Naturrecht*, C. H. Beck, Munich 1977.

Brüggemann, K. H., *Dr. Lists nationales System der politischen Ökonomie*, W. Cornelius, Berlin 1842.

Brunner, O., *Land und Herrschaft*, Wissenschaftliche Buchgesellschaft, Darmstadt 1973 (originally published 1939).

Adeliges Landleben und Europäischer Geist, Otto Müller, Salzburg 1949.

Bücher, K., 'Die berufsmäßige Vorbildung der volkswirtschaftlichen Beamten', Verhandlungen der Generalversammlung in Magdeburg, 30 September 1907, *Schriften des Vereins für Socialpolitik*, Bd. 125, pp. 9–39.

Burleigh, M., *Germany turns Eastwards*, Cambridge University Press, Cambridge 1988.

Burleigh, M. and Wipperman, W., *The Racial State. Germany 1933–1945*, Cambridge University Press, Cambridge 1991.

Calmes, A., 'Die Entwicklung der Handelswissenschaft zur privatwirtschaftlichen Lehre der Erwerbswirtschaft', *Handels-Hochschul-Nachrichten*, (1913), pp. 13–17, 25–32.

Caplan, J., *Government without Administration*, Oxford University Press, Oxford 1988.

Carey, M., *Essays on Political Economy*, H. C. Carey and I. Lea, Philadelphia 1822.

Cecchini, P., *The European Challenge–1992*, Wildwood House, Aldershot 1988.

Chandler, A., *The Visible Hand*, Harvard University Press, Cambridge, Mass. 1977.

Chaptal, J. A. C., *De l'industrie Françoise*, 2 vols., A.-A. Renouard, Paris 1819.

Cohn, G., 'Wilhelm Roscher', *Economic Journal*, vol. 4 (1894), pp. 558–60.

Cooper, T., *Lectures on the Elements of Political Economy*, Columbia 1826.

Copeland, M. T., *And Mark an Era. The Story of the Harvard Business School*, Little, Brown and Company, Boston 1958.

Deane, H. A., *The Political Ideas of Harold J. Laski*, Columbia University Press, New York 1955.

Diehl, K., 'Nationalökonomie und Handelsbetriebslehre', *Jahrbücher für Nationalökonomie und Statistik*, III. Folge, Bd. 43 (1912) pp. 94–112.

'Privatwirtschaftslehre, Volkswirtschaftslehre, Weltwirtschaftslehre', *Jahrbücher für Nationalökonomie und Statistik*, III. Folge, Bd. 46 (1913) pp. 435–82.

Diner, D., 'Rationalisierung und Methode. Zu einem neuen Erklärungsversuch der "Endlösung"', *Vierteljahreshefte für Zeitgeschichte*, Jg. 40 (1992), pp. 359–82.

Dithmar, J. C., *Einleitung in die Oeconomische Policey und Cameralwissenschaften*, New edn, Frankfurt a. O. 1745.

Donner, O., 'Die Grenzen der Staatsverschuldung', *Weltwirtschaftliches Archiv*, Jg. 56 (1942), pp. 183–224.

Dreitzel, H., 'Ideen, Ideologien, Wissenschaften: Zum politischen Denken in Deutschland in der Frühen Neuzeit', *Neue Politische Literatur*, Jg. 25 (1980), pp. 1–25.

Dubiel, H. and Söllner, A., 'Die Nationalsozialismusforschung des Instituts für Sozialforschung – ihre wissenschaftsgeschichtliche Stellung und ihre gegenwärtige Bedeutung', in H. Dubiel, and A. Söllner (eds.), *Wirtschaft, Recht und Nationalsozialismus*, Suhrkamp Verlag, Frankfurt a. M. 1981, pp. 7–31.

Dupin, C., *Forces productives et commerciales de la France*, 2 vols., Bachelier, Paris 1827.

Eckert, C., *Die städtische Handels-Hochschule in Cöln. Bericht über die zwei Studienjahre 1903 und 1904*, Verlag von Julius Springer, Berlin 1905.

Die städtische Handels-Hochschule in Cöln. Bericht über das fünfte Studienjahr, Paul Neubner, Cologne 1906.

Die städtische Handels-Hochschule in Cöln. Bericht über das Studienjahr 1908, Paul Neubner, Cologne 1909.

Die städtische Handels-Hochschule in Cöln. Bericht über die Entwicklung der Handels-Hochschule im ersten Jahrzehnt ihres Bestehens unter besonderer Berücksichtigung der Studienjahre 1909 und 1910, Paul Neubner, Cologne 1911.

Die städtische Handels-Hochschule in Cöln. Bericht über die Studienjahre 1911 und 1912, Paul Neubner, Cologne 1913.

'Lehrziele und Lehrmittel der Volkswirtschaftslehre an der Universität Köln', in Jastrow, *Die Reform der staatswissenschaftlichen Studien,* (1920), pp. 36–58.

'Handelshochschulen', *Handwörterbuch der Kommunalwissenschaften* Bd. II, Gustav Fischer Verlag, Jena 1922, pp. 469–77.

Eguilaz, H. P., 'Probleme einer internationaler wirtschaftlichen Zusammenarbeit', *Weltwirtschaftliches Archiv,* Bd. 54 (1941) pp. 159–77.

Ehrenberg, R., 'Keine "Privatwirtschaftslehre"!', *Bank-Archiv,* Jg. 12 (1912), pp. 55–7.

Einzig, P., 'Hitler's "New Order" in Theory and Practice', *Economic Journal,* vol. 51 (1941), pp. 1–18.

Eley, G., 'Nazism, Politics and the Image of the Past: Thoughts on the West German *Historikerstreit* 1986–1987', *Past and Present,* 121 (1988), pp. 171–208.

Eltzbacher, P., *Handels-Hochschule Berlin. Bericht über die Rektorats-Periode Oktober 1913/1916,* Georg Reimer, Berlin 1917.

Emerson, M. (ed.), *The Economics of 1992,* Oxford University Press, Oxford 1989.

Erd, R. (ed.), *Reform und Resignation. Gespräche über Franz L. Neumann,* Suhrkamp Verlag, Frankfurt a. M. 1985.

Estrin, S. and Holmes, P., *French Planning in Theory and Practice,* George Allen and Unwin, London 1983.

Eucken, W., 'Staatliche Strukturwandlungen und die Krisis des Kapitalismus', *Weltwirtschaftliches Archiv,* Bd. 36 (1932), pp. 297–321.

'Die Überwindung des Historismus', *Schmollers Jahrbuch für Gesetzgebung, Verwaltung und Volkswirtschaft,* Jg. 62 (1938), pp. 191–214.

Die Grundlagen der Nationalökonomie, Gustav Fischer, Jena 1940.

'Wissenschaft im Stile Schmollers', *Weltwirtschaftliches Archiv,* Bd. 52 (1940), pp. 468–503.

'Der Wettbewerb als Grundprinzip der Wirtschaftsverfassung', in G. Schmölders (ed.), *Der Wettbewerb als Mittel volkswirtschaftlicher Leistungssteigerung und Leistungsauslese,* Schriften der Akademie für Deutsches Recht, Gruppe Wirtschaftswissenschaft Heft 6, Duncker und Humblot, Berlin 1942, pp. 29–49.

'Die zeitliche Lenkung des Wirtschaftsprozesses und der Aufbau der Wirtschaftsordnungen', *Jahrbücher für Nationalökonomie und Statistik,* Bd. 159 (1944), pp. 161–221.

'On the Theory of the Centrally Administered Economy: An Analysis of the German Experiment', 2 parts, *Economica*, NS, vol. 15 (1948), pp. 79–100; 173–93.

'Das ordnungspolitische Problem', *Ordo*, Bd. 1 (1948), pp. 56–90.

The Foundations of Economics, William Hodge, London 1950.

This Unsuccessful Age, William Hodge, London 1951.

Eulenburg, F., 'Zur Theorie der Kriegswirtschaft. Ein Versuch', *Archiv für Sozialwissenchaft und Sozialpolitik*, Bd. 43 (1916/17), pp. 349–96.

'Die wissenschaftliche Behandlung der Kriegswirtschaft', *Archiv für Sozialwissenchaft und Sozialpolitik*, Bd. 44 (1918), pp. 775–85.

Fabian, D., 'Staat, Gesellschaft, Wirtschaft in ihren Beziehung zueinander', Dissertation, Gießen 1928.

Fehling, A. W., 'Collegiate Education for Business in Germany', *Journal of Political Economy*, vol. 34 (1926), pp. 545–96.

Feldman, G. D., *Army, Industry and Labor in Germany 1914–1918*, Princeton University Press, Princeton, N J 1966.

Feldman, W., 'Modewörter des 18. Jahrhunderts. 2. Teil', *Zeitschrift für deutsche Wortforschung*, Bd. 6 (1942), pp. 346–7.

Ferrier, F.-L.-A., *Du Gouvernement considéré dans ses rapports avec le commerce*, 3rd edn, Pelicier, Paris 1822.

Florinus, *Oeconomus prudens et legalis*, Nuremberg 1702.

Forsthoff, E., *Der totale Staat*, Hanseatische Verlagsanstalt, Hamburg 1933.

Fraenkel, E., *The Dual State. A Contribution to the Theory of Dictatorship*, Oxford University Press, New York 1941.

Friedrich, C. J. and Brzezinksi, Z. K., *Totalitarian Dictatorship and Autocracy*, Harvard University Press, Cambridge, Mass. 1956.

Fügen, H. N., *Max Weber*, Rowohlt, Reinbeck bei Hamburg 1985.

Fulda, F. C., *Grundsätze der ökonomisch-politischen Kameralwissenschaften*, Tübingen 1816.

Funk, W., *et al.*, *Europäische Wirtschaftsgemeinschaft*, 2nd edn, Haude und Spenerrsche Verlagsbuchhandlung Max Paschke, Berlin 1943.

Garve, C., 'Vorrede des Uebersetzers' to A. Smith, *Untersuchung über die Natur und die Ursachen des Nationalreichtums*, Bd. 1, Breslau 1794.

Gehring, P., *Friedrich List*, J. C. B. Mohr (Paul Siebeck), Tübingen 1964.

Giersch, H., Paqué, K.-H., and Schmieding, H., 'Openness, Wage Restraint, and Macroeconomic Stability: Germany's Road to Prosperity 1948–1959' in R. Dornbusch, W. Nölling, and R. Layard (eds.), *Postwar Economic Reconstruction and Lessons for the East Today*, MIT Press, Cambridge, Mass. 1993, pp. 1–27.

Gilbert, M., *Auschwitz and the Allies*, Mandarin, London 1991.

Gillingham, J., *Coal, Steel, and the Rebirth of Europe, 1945–1955*, Cambridge University Press, Cambridge 1991.

Gregory, P. R. and Stuart, S. C., *Soviet Economic Structure and Performance* 3rd edn, Harper and Row, New York 1986.

Guillebaud, C. W., *The Economic Recovery of Germany*, Macmillan, London 1939.

'Hitler's New Economic Order for Germany', *Economic Journal*, vol. 50 (1940), pp. 449–60.

Gurland, A. R. L., *CDU/CSU. Ursprünge und Entwicklung bis 1953*, Europäische Verlagsanstalt, Frankfurt a. M. 1980.

Habermas, J., 'Eine Art Schadensabwicklung', reprinted in R. Augstein *et al.*, *>Historikerstreit<*, R.Piper, Munich 1987, pp. 62–76.

Hamilton, A., *The Report on the Subject of Manufactures, Papers of Alexander Hamilton*, vol. 10, Columbia University Press, New York 1966, pp. 230–340.

Hansen, J., *Gustav von Mevissen. Ein rheinisches Lebensbild 1815–1899*, vol. II, Georg Reimer, Berlin 1906.

Hardach, G., 'The Marshall Plan in Germany, 1948–1952', *Journal of European Economic History*, vol. 16 (1987), pp. 433–85.

Harris, R., *Selling Hitler*, Faber and Faber, London 1986.

Fatherland, Hutchinson, London 1992.

Harrison, M., *Soviet Planning in Peace and War 1938–1945*, Cambridge University Press, Cambridge 1985.

Hasbach, W., 'Zur Geschichte des Methodenstreites in der politischen Ökonomie', *Jahrbuch für Gesetzgebung, Verwaltung und Volkswirthschaft*, N. F. Bd. 19 (1895), Pt. 1, pp. 465–76.

Hasek, C. W., *The Introduction of Adam Smith's Doctrines into Germany*, Faculty of Political Science, Columbia University, New York 1925.

Haselbach, D., *Autoritärer Liberalismus und Soziale Marktwirtschaft*, Nomos Verlagsgesellschaft, Baden-Baden 1991.

Haushofer, H., 'Das Problem des Florinus,' *Zeitschrift für Agrargeschichte and Agrarsoziologie*, Jg. 30 (1982), pp. 168–75.

Hayashima, A., 'Zur Geschichte der Kölner Handelshochschule', *Kwansei Gakuin University Annual Studies*, vol. 30 (1981), pp. 181–218.

'Der Kölner Weg zum Promotionsrecht. Zur Geschichte einer deutschen Handelshochschule', *Kwansei Gakuin University Annual Studies*, vol. 31 (1982), pp. 21–88.

'Die Absolventen der Leipziger Handelshochschule 1900–1920', *Kwansei Gakuin University Annual Studies*, vol. 36 (1987), pp. 113–94.

Hayes, P., *Industry and Ideology. IG Farben in the Nazi Era*, Cambridge University Press, Cambridge 1987.

Heckscher, E., *Mercantilism*, 2nd edn, George Allen and Unwin, London 1955.

Heinrich, K., 'Zollunion und Großwirtschaftsräume', *Schmollers Jahrbuch für Gesetzgebung, Verwaltung und Volkswirtschaft*, Jg. 65, Hb. 1 (1941), pp. 281–301.

Hellauer, J., 'Versuch einer Gliederung der Handelswissenschaften als Hochschuldisziplin', *Deutsche Wirtschafts-Zeitung*, Jg. 2 (1906), Pt. 1, cols. 416–17.

System der Welthandelslehre. Ein Lehr- und Handbuch des internationalen Handels. Erster Band: Allgemeine Welthandelslehre 1. Teil, 8th edn, Puttkamer und Mühlbrecht, Berlin 1920.

Heller, H., 'Political Science', *Encyclopedia of the Social Sciences*, vol. 13, Macmillan, New York 1933, pp. 207–24.

'Power, Political', *Encyclopedia of the Social Sciences*, vol. 13, Macmillan, New York 1933, pp. 300–305.

Henderson, W. O., *Friedrich List. Economist and Visionary 1789–1846*, Frank Cass, London 1983.

Hennis, H., 'The Pitiless "Sobriety of Judgement". Max Weber between Carl Menger and Gustav von Schmoller – The Academic Politics of Value Freedom', *History of the Human Sciences*, vol. 4 (1991), pp. 27–59.

Hennis, W., *Max Weber: Essays in Reconstruction*, Allen and Unwin, London 1988.

Hentschel, V., 'Die Wirtschaftswissenschaften als akademische Disziplin an der Universität Heidelberg (1822–1924)', in N. Waszek (ed.), *Die Institutionalisierung der Nationalökonomie an deutschen Universitäten*, Scripta Mercurae Verlag, St Katharinen 1988, pp. 192–232.

Herbert, U., 'Labour and Extermination: Economic Interest and the Primacy of *Weltanschauung* in National Socialism', *Past and Present*, 138 (1993), pp. 144–95.

Herbst, L., 'Krisenüberwindung und Wirtschaftsneuordnung. Ludwig Erhards Beteiligung an den Nachkriegsplanungen am Ende des Zweiten Weltkrieges', *Vierteljahreshefte für Zeitgeschichte*, Jg. 25 (1977), pp. 305–40.

Der totale Krieg und die Ordnung der Wirtschaft, Deutsche Verlags-Anstalt, Stuttgart 1982.

Hesse, K., 'Wehrwirtschaft als Wissenschaft', in K. Hesse (ed.), *Kriegswirtschaftliche Jahresberichte 1936*, Hanseatische Verlagsanstalt, Hamburg 1936, pp. 11–15.

Hildebrand, B., *Die Nationalökonomie der Gegenwart und Zukunft*, Literarische Anstalt (J. Rütten), Frankfurt a. M., 1848.

Hirschman, A. O., 'The European Payments Union. Negotiations and the Issues', *Review of Economics and Statistics*, vol. 33 (1951), pp. 49–55.

Hirst, M. E., *Life of Friedrich List and Selections from his Writings*, Smith, Elder, and Co., London 1902.

Hirst, P. Q., 'Carl Schmitt's Decisionism', *Telos*, 72 (1987), pp. 15–26.

Hoffmann, J., *Die Hausväterliteratur und die Predigten über den christlichen Hausstand*, Julius Beltz, Weinheim 1959.

Hufeland, G., *Neue Grundlegung der Staatswirthschaftskunst*, Bd. 1, Gießen 1807.

Hundt, S., *Zur Theoriegeschichte der Betriebswirtschaftslehre*, Bund Verlag, Cologne 1977.

Hunke, H., *Grundzüge der deutschen Volks- und Wehrwirtschaft*, Haude und Spenersche Buchhandlung, Berlin 1938.

Hussain A. and Tribe, K., *Marxism and the Agrarian Question*, 2nd edn, Macmillan, London 1983.

Hutchison, T., 'Notes on the Effects of Economic Ideas on Policy: The Example of the German Social Market Economy', *Zeitschrift für die gesamte Staatswissenschaft*, Bd. 135 (1979), pp. 426–41.

Ingram, J. K., *History of Political Economy*, 2nd edn, A. and C. Black, London 1907.

Intelmann, P., 'Zur Biographie von Franz L. Neumann', *1999*, Heft 1 (1990), pp. 14–52.

James, E. J., Giddings, F. H., and Falkner, R. P., 'Instruction in Public Law and Political Economy in German Universities', *Annals of the American Academy of Political and Social Science*, vol. 1 (1890), pp. 78–102, 272–88.

Jastrow, I., 'Kaufmannsbildung und Hochschulbildung in Amerika', *Berliner Jahrbuch für Handel und Industrie*, Bd. 1 (1904), pp. 418–44.

Die Handelshochschule Berlin. Bericht über das erste Studienjahr Oktober 1906/7, Georg Reimer, Berlin 1908.

Die Handelshochschule Berlin. Bericht über die erste Rektoratsperiode Oktober 1906–1909, Georg Reimer, Berlin 1909.

'Leitsätze über die Reform der staatswissenschaftlichen Studien', Verhandlungen der außerordentlichen Generalversammlung in Kiel 21. bis 23.September 1920; *Schriften des Vereins für Sozialpolitik*, Bd. 161, Duncker und Humblot, Munich 1921, pp. 38–46.

Jastrow, I., (ed.) *Die Reform der staatswissenschaftlichen Studien, Schriften des Vereins für Sozialpolitik*, Bd. 160, Duncker und Humblot, Munich 1920.

Jay, M., *The Dialectical Imagination*, Heinemann, London 1973.

Jessen, J., 'Das "Gesetz der wachsenden Ausdehnung des Finanzbedarfs"', *Schmollers Jahrbuch*, Jg. 67 (1943), pp. 539–58.

Jevons, W. S., *The Theory of Political Economy*, 2nd edn, Macmillan, London 1879.

John, V., *Geschichte der Statistik*, Verlag von Ferdinand Emke, Stuttgart 1884.

Johnson, H. T, and Kaplan, R. S., *Relevance Lost. The Rise and Fall of Management Accounting*, Harvard Business School Press, Boston 1987.

Jünger, E., *Krieg und Kreiger*, n. p., Berlin 1930.

Kähler, W. 'Die Einleitung des staatswissenschaftlichen Unterrichts an der Universität Halle', in H. Paasche (ed.) *Festgabe für Johannes Conrad*, Sammlung nationalökonomischer und statistischer Abhandlungen, Bd. 20, Gustav Fischer, Jena 1898, pp. 113–82.

Kaldor, N., 'The German War Economy', *Review of Economic Studies*, vol. 13 (1945), pp. 33–52.

Kant, I., 'Über den Gemeinspruch: Das Mag in der Theorie richtig sein, taugt aber nicht für die Praxis', *Werke*, Bd. VIII, Walter de Gruyter, Berlin 1968, pp. 273–314.

'Was ist Aufklärung?', *Werke*, Bd. VIII, Walter de Gruyter, Berlin 1968, pp. 33–42.

Käsler, D., *Einführung in das Studium Max Webers*, C. H. Beck, Munich 1979.

Kennedy, E., Review of Bendersky, *History of Political Thought*, vol. 4 (1983), pp. 579–89.

'Introduction: Carl Schmitt's *Parlamentarismus* in its Historical Context', in C. Schmitt, *The Crisis of Parliamentary Democracy*, MIT Press, Cambridge, Mass. 1985, pp. xiii-l.

'The Politics of Toleration in Late Weimar; Hermann Heller's Analysis of Fascism and Political Culture', *History of Political Thought*, vol. 5 (1985), pp. 109–27.

Kershaw, I., *The Nazi Dictatorship*, Edward Arnold, London 1985.

Keynes, J. M., *Collected Writings*, vol. xxv, Macmillan, London 1980.

Kitchen, J. and Parker, R. H., *Accounting Thought and Education: Six English Pioneers*, Institute of Chartered Accountants of England and Wales, London 1980.

Klein, B. H., *Germany's Economic Preparations for War*, Harvard University Press, Cambridge, Mass. 1959.

Kramer, A., *The West German Economy 1945–1955*, Berg, Oxford 1991.

Krüger, D., *Nationalökonomen im wilhelminischen Deutschland*, Vandenhoeck und Ruprecht, Göttingen 1983.

Kruse, C., *Die Volkswirtschaftslehre im Nationalsozialismus*, Rudolf Haufe Verlag, Freiburg i. Br. 1988.

Kube, A., 'Außenpolitik und "Großraumwirtschaft". Die deutsche Politik zur wirtschaftlichen Integration Südosteuropas 1933 bis 1939', in H. Berding (ed.), *Wirtschaftliche Integration im 19. und 20. Jahrhundert*, Sonderheft 10, *Geschichte und Gesellschaft* (1984), pp. 185–211.

Ladenthin, E., *Zur Entwickelung der nationalökonomischen Ansichten Fr. Lists von 1820–1825*, Verlagsbuchhandlung Carl Konegen, Vienna 1912.

Laski, H., *A Grammar of Politics*, 4th edn, George Allen and Unwin, London 1937.

Lavoie D., *Rivalry and Central Planning. The Socialist Calculation Debate Reconsidered*, Cambridge University Press, Cambridge 1985.

Lederer, E., 'Die Organisation der Wirtschaft durch den Staat im Kriege', *Archiv für Sozialwissenschaft und Sozialpolitik*, Bd. 40 (1915), pp. 118–46.

'Die Regelung der Lebensmittelversorgung während des Krieges in Deutschland', *Archiv für Sozialwissenchaft und Sozialpolitik*, Bd. 40 (1915), pp. 757–83.

Lindenfeld, D. F., 'The Professionalization of Applied Economics: German Counterparts to Business Administration', in G. Cocks and K. Jarausch (eds.), *German Professions, 1800–1950*, Oxford University Press, Oxford 1990, pp. 213–31.

Lindenlaub, D., *Richtungskämpfe im Verein für Sozialpolitik*, Beiheft 52/53, *Vierteljahreschrift für Sozial- und Wirtschaftsgeschichte*, F. Steiner, Wiesbaden 1967, pp. 27–9.

List, F., *The National System of Political Economy*, J. B. Lippincot and Co., Philadelphia 1856.

Schriften/ Reden/ Briefe, 10 Bde., Verlag von Reimar Hobbing, Berlin 1927–35.

The Natural System of Political Economy, Frank Cass, London 1983.

Locke, R. R., *The End of Practical Man. Entrepreneurship and Higher Education in Germany, France, and Great Britain 1880–1940*, JAI Press, Greenwich, Conn. 1984.

Lockwood, J., 'Early University Education in Accountancy', *Accounting Review*, vol. 13 (1938), pp. 131–44.

Lueder, A. F., *Ueber Nationalindustrie und Staatswirthschaft. Nach Adam Smith bearbeitet*, Berlin 1800.

Kritische Geschichte der Statistik, Johann Friedrich Römer, Göttingen 1817.

Luthardt, W., 'Ausgewählte Bibliographie der Arbeiten von Franz L. Neumann' in J. Perels (ed.), *Recht, Demokratie und Kapitalismus*, Nomos Verlag, Baden-Baden 1984, pp. 217–27.

Lutz, F. A., 'The German Currency Reform and the Revival of the German Economy', *Economica*, NS, vol. 16 (1949), pp. 122–42.

Maier, H., *Die ältere deutsche Staats- und Verwaltungslehre*, 2nd edn, C. H. Beck, Munich 1980.

Marchet, G., *Studien über die Entwicklung der Verwaltungslehre in Deutschland*, R. Oldenbourg, Munich 1885.

Marshall, L. C. (ed.), *The Collegiate School of Business*, University of Chicago Press, Chicago 1928.

Marx, K., 'Draft of an Article on Friedrich List's Book *Das Nationale System der politischen Ökonomie*', in Marx and Engels, *Collected Works*, vol. 4, Lawrence and Wishart, London 1975, pp. 265–93.

McCoy, D. R., *The Elusive Republic*, University of North Carolina Press, Chapel Hill 1980.

Meade, J. E., Review of Röpke, *Crises and Cycles* (1936), *Economic Journal*, vol. 46 (1936), pp. 694–5.

Meimberg, R., 'Kaufkraftüberhang und Kriegsfinanzpolitik', *Weltwirtschaftliches Archiv*, Bd. 58 (1943), pp. 98–130.

Mendershausen, H., 'Prices, Money and the Distribution of Goods in Postwar Germany', *American Economic Review*, vol. 39 (1949), pp. 646–72.

Menger, C., *Grundsätze der Volkswirthschaftslehre*, Gesammelte Werke Bd. I, 2nd edn, J. C. B. Mohr (Paul Siebeck), Tübingen 1968.

Untersuchungen über die Methode der Socialwissenschaften, und der Politischen Oekonomie insbesondere, Gesammelte Werke Bd. II, 2nd edn, J. C. B. Mohr (Paul Siebeck), Tübingen 1968.

Die Irrtümer des Historismus in der deutschen Nationalökonomie, Gesammelte Werke Bd. III, 2nd edn, J. C. B. Mohr (Paul Siebeck), Tübingen 1970.

'Friedrich List', *Gesammelte Werke* Bd. III, pp. 247–57.

Meuleau, M., *Histoire d'une Grande Ecole*, HEC, Jouy-en-Josas 1981.

Meuser, E., 'List oder Raymond?', *Zeitschrift für die gesamte Staatswissenschaft*, Bd. 69 (1913), pp. 104–15.

Migdal, U., *Die Frühgeschichte des Frankfurter Instituts für Sozialforschung*, Campus Verlag, Frankfurt a. M. 1981.

Milward, A. S., *The New Order and the French Economy*, Oxford University Press, Oxford 1970.

The Reconstruction of Western Europe 1945–51, Methuen, London 1987.

War, Economy and Society 1939–1945, Penguin Books, Harmondsworth 1987.

Mirowski, P., *More Heat than Light*, Cambridge University Press, Cambridge 1990.

Müller, A., *Die Elemente der Staatskunst*, 3 Bde., Berlin 1809.

Müller, R.-D., *Hitlers Ostkrieg und die deutsche Siedlungspolitik*, Fischer Taschenbuch Verlag, Frankfurt a. M. 1991.

Müller-Armack, A., *Wirtschaftslenkung und Marktwirtschaft*, Verlag für Wirtschaft und Sozialpolitik, Hamburg 1947.

'Die Wirtschaftsordnungen sozial gesehen', *Ordo*, Bd. 1 (1948), pp. 124–54.

Genealogie der sozialen Marktwirtschaft, Verlag Paul Haupt, Bern 1974.

Naumann, F., *Central Europe*, P. S. King and Son, London 1916.

Neill, C. P., *Daniel Raymond. An Early Chapter in the History of Economic Theory in the United States*, Johns Hopkins University Studies in Historical and Political Sciences, 15th series, vol. 16, Johns Hopkins University Press, Baltimore 1897.

Neumann, F., 'Der Kampf um den Zwangstarif', *Die Arbeit*, Jg. 2 (November 1925), pp. 694–703.

'Betriebsrisiko', *Arbeitsrechts-Praxis*, Jg. 1 (October 1928), pp. 219–23.

'Gesellschaftliche und staatliche Verwaltung der monopolistischen Unternehmungen', *Die Arbeit*, Jg. 5 (July 1928), pp. 393–404.

Die politische und soziale Bedeutung der arbeitsgerichtlichen Rechtsprechung, E. Laubsche Verlagsbuchhandlung, Berlin 1929.

'The Social Significance of the Basic Laws of the Weimar Constitution', in F. Neumann and O. Kirchheimer, *Social Democracy and the Rule of Law*, Allen and Unwin, London 1987, pp. 27–43.

'On the Preconditions and the Legal Concept of an Economic Constitution' in F. Neumann and O. Kirchheimer, *Social Democracy and the Rule of Law*, pp. 44–65.

'On the Marxist Theory of the State' in F. Neumann and O. Kirchheimer, *Social Democracy and the Rule of Law*, pp. 75–84.

'The Decay of German Democracy', *Political Quarterly*, vol. 4 (1933), pp. 523–43.

Trade Unionism–Democracy–Dictatorship, Workers' Educational Trade Union Committee, London 1934.

Behemoth. The Structure and Practice of National Socialism, 2nd edn, Oxford University Press, New York 1944.

'The Social Sciences', in F. Neumann *et al.*, *The Cultural Migration*, University of Pennsylvania Press, Philadelphia 1953, pp. 4–26.

The Democratic and the Authoritarian State, Free Press, New York 1957.

The Rule of Law, Berg, Leamington Spa 1986.

Neumann, V., 'Carl Schmitt und die Linke', *Die Zeit*, no 28 (8 July 1983), p. 32.

'Kompromiß oder Entscheidung? Zur Rezeption der Theorie Carl Schmitts in den Weimarer Arbeiten Franz L. Neumanns', in J. Perels (ed.), *Recht, Demokratie und Kapitalismus*, Nomos Verlag, Baden-Baden

1984, pp. 65–78.

Neurath, O., 'Kriegswirtschaft' in *Meyers Großes Konversations-Lexicon*, 6th edn, Bd. XXIV, Jahres Supplement 1911–1912, Leipzig 1913, pp. 523–8.

'Probleme der Kriegswirtschaftslehre', *Zeitschrift für die gesamte Staatswissenschaft*, Jg. 69 (1913), pp. 438–501.

'Das Begriffsgebäude der vergleichenden Wirtschaftslehre und ihre Grundlagen', *Zeitschrift für die gesamte Staatswissenschaft*, Bd. 73 (1918), pp. 484–520.

Durch die Kriegswirtschaft zur Naturalwirtschaft, Verlag Georg D. W. Callwey, Munich 1919.

Die Sozialisierung Sachsens, Verlag des Arbeiter- und Soldatenrats im Industriebezirk Chemnitz, Chemnitz 1919.

Betriebsräteorganisation als Wirtschaftsorganisation, Verlagsgenossenschaft 'Neue Erde', Vienna 1920.

Vollsozialisierung, Eugen Diederichs, Jena 1920.

Wirtschaftsplan und Naturalrechnung, E. Laub, Berlin 1925, pp.23–4.

Was bedeutet rationale Wirtschaftsbetrachtung?, Einheitswissenschaft Heft 4, Verlag Gerold und Co., Vienna 1935.

International Picture Language, Kegan Paul, Trench, Trubner and Co., London 1936.

'Inventory of the Standard of Living', *Zeitschrift für Sozialforschung*, Jg. 6 (1937), pp. 140–51.

Modern Man in the Making, Secker and Warburg, London 1939.

Empiricism and Sociology, D. Reidel, Dordrecht 1973.

Nicklisch, H., *Allgemeine Kaufmännische Betriebslehre als Privatwirtschaftslehre des Handels und der Industrie* Bd. I, Verlag Carl Ernst Poeschel, Leipzig 1912.

'Betriebswirtschaftslehre. Was ist bei ihren Studium vor allem anderen zu beachten?', *Zeitschrift für Handelswissenschaft und Handelspraxis*, Jg. 14 (1921), pp. 97–101.

Wirtschaftliche Betriebslehre, 6th edn, C. E. Poeschel, Stuttgart 1922.

Notz, W., 'Frederick List in America', *American Economic Review*, vol. 16 (1926), pp. 249–65

O'Connor, M. J. L., *Origins of Academic Economics in the United States*, Columbia University Press, New York 1944.

Obst, G., 'Die deutschen Handelshochschulen', *Zeitschrift für Handelswissenschaft und Handelspolitik*, Bd. I, H. 6 (1908), pp. 192–6.

'Verhältnis der Privatwirtschaftlehre zur Volkswirtschaftslehre', *Zeitschrift für Handelswissenschaft und Praxis*, Jg. 5, H. 12 (1913), pp. 357–62.

'Die Reform des wirtschaftswissenschaftlichen Studiums', *Zeitschrift für Handelswissenschaft und Handelspraxis*, Jg. 13, H. 5 (1920), pp. 97–101.

Olshausen, H.-P., *Friedrich List und der deutsche Handels- und Gewerbsverein*, Gustav Fischer, Jena 1935.

Oncken, A., 'New Tendencies in German Economics', *Economic Journal*, vol. 9 (1899), pp. 462–9.

Osterloh, K.-H., *Joseph von Sonnenfels und die österreiche Reformbewegung im Zeitalter des aufgeklärten Absolutismus*, Matthiesen Verlag, Lübeck 1970.

Overy, R. J., 'Hitler's War and the German Economy: A Reinterpretation', *Economic History Review*, 2nd series, vol. 35 (1982), pp. 272–91.

Palyi, M., 'The Introduction of Adam Smith on the Continent', in *Adam Smith 1776–1926*, Augustus M. Kelley, New York 1966, pp. 180–233.

Pasquino, P., 'Introduction to Lorenz von Stein', *Economy and Society*, vol. 10 (1981), pp. 1–6.

Peacock, A., 'Recent German Contributions to Economics', *Economica*, NS, vol. 17 (1950), pp. 175–87.

Peacock, A. and Willgerodt, H., *Germany's Social Market Economy: Origins and Evolution*, Macmillan, London 1989.

Petzina, D., *Autarkiepolitik im Dritten Reich. Der nationalsozialistische Vierjahresplan*, Deutsche Verlags-Anstalt, Stuttgart 1968.

Pierson, N. G., 'The Problem of Value in the Socialist Society', in F. A. von Hayek (ed.), *Collectivist Economic Planning*, George Routledge, London 1935, pp. 41–85.

Pirou, G., 'Les Facultés de droit', in *L'Enseignement Economique en France et à l'étranger*, Special 50th Anniversary Issue of *Revue d'Economie Politique* (1937), pp. 1–21.

Pohle, L., 'Diplomprüfung für Volkswirte und staatswissenschaftliche Promotion', *Jahrbuch für Gesetzgebung, Verwaltung und Volkswirtschaft*, Jg. 46 (1922), pp. 861–74.

Pollock, F., *Die planwirtschaftlichen Versuche in der Sowjetunion 1917–1927*, Schriften des Instituts für Sozialforschung an der Universität Frankfurt a. M. Bd. 2, C. L. Hirschfeld, Leipzig 1929.

'Influences of Preparedness on Western European Economic Life', *American Economic Review, Papers and Proceedings*, Supplement, vol. 30 (1940), pp. 317–25.

'Staatskapitalismus' in H. Dubiel and A. Söllner (eds.), *Wirtschaft, Recht und Nationalsozialismus*, pp. 81–110.

Predöhl, A., 'Die angelsächsische Währungspläne und die europäische Währungsordnung', *Weltwirtschaftliches Archiv*, Jg. 58 (1943), pp. 1–26.

Price, A. H., *The Evolution of the Zollverein*, University of Michigan Press, Ann Arbor 1949.

Prion, W., 'Wissenschaftliche Privatwirtschaftslehre', Pt. 1 *Deutsche Wirtschafts-Zeitung*, Jg. 8 (1912), cols. 210–19, 396–402.

'Kaufmännische Betriebslehre', *Handels-Hochschul-Nachrichten*, (1913), pp. 61–7, 97–102, 133–8.

'Px', Review of Smith, *Untersuchung der Natur und Ursachen von Nationalreichthumern*, Bd. 1, *Allgemeine deutsche Bibliothek*, Bd. 31, 2. Th. (1777), pp. 586–9.

Rammstedt, O., *Deutsche Soziologie 1933–1945*, Suhrkamp Verlag, Frankfurt a. M. 1986.

Rathenau, E., *Autonome Wirtschaft*, Eugen Diederichs, Jena 1919.

Rau, K. H., Review of *Nationales System* in *Archiv der politischen Oekonomie und Polizeiwissenschaft*, Bd. 5 (1843), pp. 252–97, 349–412.

Raydt, H. (ed.), *Erster Jahresbericht der Handelshochschule zu Leipzig*, Max Hesse's Verlag, Leipzig 1899.

Raymond, D., *Thoughts on Political Economy*, Fielding Lucas Jun., Baltimore 1820.

The Elements of Political Economy, 2 vols., F. Lucas Jun. and E. J. Coale, Baltimore 1823.

Recker, M.-L., *Nationalsozialistische Sozialpolitik im zweiten Weltkrieg*, R. Oldenbourg Verlag, München 1985.

Ricardo, D., *Die Grundsätze der politischen Oekonomie*, Weimar 1821.

Grundsätze der Volkswirthschaft und der Besteuerung, Leipzig 1837.

On the Principles of Political Economy and Taxation, Works and Correspondence vol. 1, Cambridge University Press, Cambridge 1951.

Robertson, D., Review of Guillebaud, *Economic Journal*, vol. 49 (1939), pp. 305–8.

Röpke, W., *Die Lehre von der Wirtschaft*, Verlag von Julius Springer, Vienna 1937.

'Einführung' to F. A. Hayek, *Der Weg zur Knechtschaft*, Eugen Rentsch Verlag, Erlenbach-Zürich 1945.

Civitas humana, William Hodge, Edinburgh 1949.

The Social Crisis of our Time, William Hodge, Edinburgh 1950.

International Order and Economic Integration, Reidel, Dordrecht 1959.

Roscher, W., Review of List, *Das nationale System der politischen Ökonomie*, *Göttingische gelehrte Anzeigen*, Bd. 1 (1842), St. 118, pp. 1177–84; St. 119/ 120, pp. 1185–1200; St. 121, pp. 1201–16.

Grundriß zu Vorlesungen über die Staatswirthschaft. Nach geschichtlicher Methode, Dieterische Buchhandlung, Göttingen 1843.

'Der gegenwärtige Zustand der wissenschaftlichen Nationalökonomie', *Deutsche Vierteljahresschrift*, Bd. 1, H. 1 (1849), pp. 174–90.

System der Volkswirthschaft Bd. 1, J. G. Cotta, Stuttgart 1854.

'Die Ein- und Durchführung des Adam Smith'schen Systems in Deutschland,' *Berichte über die Verhandlungen der koniglich sächsischen Gesellschaft der Wissenschaften zu Leipzig*, Bd. 19 (1867), pp. 1–74.

'Die romantische Schule der Nationalökonomik in Deutschland', *Zeitschrift für die gesamte Staatswissenschaft*, Bd. 26 (1870), pp. 57–105.

Geschichte der National-Oekonomik in Deutschland, R. Oldenbourg, Munich 1874.

Roussakis, E. N., *Friedrich List, the Zollverein and the Uniting of Europe*, College of Europe, Bruges 1968.

Ruml, F., 'The Existing Curriculum and Offerings in Collegiate Education for Business', in L. C. Marshall (ed.), *The Collegiate School of Business*, University of Chicago Press, Chicago 1928, pp. 75–95.

Sartorius, G., *Handbuch der Staatswirthschaft zum Gebrauche bey akademischen Vorlesungen, nach Adam Smith's Grundsätzen ausgearbeitet*, Berlin 1796.

Sass, S. A., *The Pragmatic Imagination. A History of the Wharton School 1881–1981*, University of Pennsylvania Press, Philadelphia 1982.

Say, L., *Considérations sur l'industrie et la législation*, J.-P.Aillaud, Paris 1822.

Schäfer, G., 'Franz Neumanns *Behemoth* und die heutige Faschismusdiskus-

Bibliography 277

sion', Nachwort to *Behemoth*, Europäische Verlagsanstalt, Cologne 1977.
Schär, J. F., 'Das Verhältnis der Nationalökonomie zur Privatwirtschaftslehre im allgemeinen und zur Handelsbetriebslehre im besonderen', *Deutsche Wirtschafts-Zeitung*, Jg. 9 (1913), cols. 513–22.
Allgemeine Handelsbetriebslehre, 4th edn, G. A. Gloeckner, Leipzig 1921.
Schieder, T., 'Aufzeichnung über Siedlung und Volkstumsfragen in den wiedergewonnenen Ostprovinzen' dated 4–7 October 1939, reprinted in *1999*, Heft 1 (1992), pp. 85–91; with an introduction and commentary from A. Ebbinghaus and K. H. Roth, pp. 62–77.
Schiera, P., *Dall'Arte di Governo alle Scienze dello Stato*, Giuffrè, Milan 1968.
Schinzinger, F., 'German Historical School' in J. Eatwell, M. Milgate, and P. Newman (eds.), *The New Palgrave Dictionary of Economics*, vol. II, Macmillan Press, London 1987, pp. 516–18.
Schluchter, W., 'Wertfreiheit und Verantwortungsethik. Zum Verhältnis von Wissenschaft und Politik bei Max Weber', in his *Rationalismus der Weltbeherrschung*, Suhrkamp Verlag, Frankfurt a. M. 1980, pp. 41–74.
Schmalenbach, E., 'Theorie der Produktionskosten-Ermittelung', *Zeitschrift für Handelswissenschaftliche Forschung*, Jg. 3 (1908), pp. 41–65.
'Über Verrechnungspreise', *Zeitschrift für Handelswissenschftliche Forschung*, Jg. 3 (1909), pp. 165–85.
'Die Privatwirtschaftslehre als Kunstlehre', *Zeitschrift für Handelswissenschaftliche Forschung*, Jg. 6 (1911/12), pp. 304–16.
'Grundlagen dynamischer Bilanzlehre', *Zeitschrift für Handelswissenschaftliche Forschung*, Jg. 13 (1919), pp. 1–60, 65–101.
Schmidt, F., 'Die Zukunft der Betriebswirtschaftslehre', in Fs. Robert Stern, *Zur Entwicklung der Betriebswirtschaftslehre*, Berlin 1925, pp. 147–59.
Schmitt, C., *Der Hüter der Verfassung*, J. C. B. Mohr (Paul Siebeck), Tübingen 1931.
Der Begriff des Politischen, Duncker und Humblot, n.p., Berlin 1963 (reprint of 1932 edn).
'Weiterentwicklung des totalen Staats in Deutschland (Januar 1933)' in his *Positionen und Begriffe*, Hanseatische Verlagsanstalt, Hamburg 1940, pp. 185–90.
Political Theology, MIT Press, Cambridge, Mass. 1985.
Schmölders, G., 'In memoriam Jens Jessen (1895–1944)', *Schmollers Jahrbuch*, Bd. 69 (1949), pp. 9–10.
Schmoller, G., 'Zur Methodologie der Staats- und Sozial-Wissenschaften', *Jahrbuch für Gesetzgebung, Verwaltung und Volkswirtschaft* N. F. Jg. 7 (1883), pp. 975–94.
'Friedrich List', *Zur Litteraturgeschichte der Staats- und Sozialwissenschaften*, Duncker und Humblot, Leipzig 1888, pp. 102–6.
'Wilhelm Roscher (1888)', *Zur Litteraturgeschichte der Staats- und Sozialwissenschaften*, Duncker und Humblot, Leipzig 1888, pp. 147–71.
Schön, M., 'Gustav Schmoller and Max Weber' in W. J. Mommsen and J.

Osterhammel (eds.), *Max Weber and his Contemporaries*, Allen and Unwin, London 1987, pp. 59–70.

Schranz, A., 'Modern German Accountancy', *Accounting Review*, vol. 5 (1930), pp. 162–7.

Schröder, R., > ... *aber im Zivilrecht sind die Richter standhaft geblieben!* <, Nomos Verlagsgesellschaft, Baden-Baden 1988.

Schumpeter, J. A., *History of Economic Analysis*, Allen and Unwin, London 1954.

Schwab, G., *The Challenge of the Exception*, Duncker und Humblot, Berlin 1970.

Seager, H. R., 'Economics at Berlin and Vienna', *Journal of Political Economy*, vol. 1 (1893), pp. 236–62.

Seligman, E. R. A., 'Economics in the United States: An Historical Sketch', in his *Essays in Economics*, Macmillan, New York 1925, pp. 122–60.

Sheehan, J. J., *German Liberalism in the Nineteenth Century*, University of Chicago Press, Chicago 1978.

Simmel, G., 'Der Fall Jastrow', *Die Zukunft*, 10 October 1914, pp. 33–6.

Sincerus, A. [pseud. Christoph Heinrich Amthor], *Project der Oeconomie in Form einer Wissenschaft*, 2nd edn, Frankfurt 1717.

Small, A., *The Cameralists*, University of Chicago Press, Chicago 1909.

Sommer, A., 'Friedrich List und Adam Müller' *Weltwirtschaftliches Archiv*, Bd. 25, H. 2 (1927), pp. 345–76.

Spiegel, H. W., 'Wehrwirtschaft: Economics of the Military State', *American Economic Review*, vol. 30 (1940), pp. 713–23.

Stoltenberg, H. L., *Geschichte der deutschen Gruppwissenschaft (Soziologie)*, Hans Buske Verlag, Leipzig 1937.

Straub, E., 'Der Jurist im Zwielicht des Politischen', *Frankfurter Allgemeine Zeitung*, no. 163 (18 July 1981).

Stucken, R., 'Kriegsfinanzierung und Kreditausweitung', *Bank-Archiv*, (1940), pp. 323–5.

Sulzer, J. G., *Kurzer Begriff aller Wissenschaften*, 2nd edn, Leipzig 1759.

Taylor F., *On the Economic Theory of Socialism*, University of Minnesota Press, Minneapolis 1938.

Temin, P., 'Soviet and Nazi Economic Planning in the 1930s', *Economic History Review*, vol. 44 (1991), pp. 573–93.

Tenbruck, F. H., 'Abschied von *Wirtschaft und Gesellschaft*', *Zeitschrift für die gesamte Staatswissenschaft*, Bd. 133 (1977), pp. 702–35.

Terhalle F., 'Die deutsche Kriegsfinanzierung 1914–1918', *Bank-Archiv*, (1939), pp. 549–52.

'Die Aufbringung der Kriegskosten als volkswirtschaftlichen Aufgabe', *Bank-Archiv*, (1940), pp. 193–6.

'Staatsschulden – volkswirtschaftlich gesehen', *Bank-Archiv*, (1941), pp. 283–6.

Tims, R. W., *Germanising Prussian Poland. The H-K-T Society and the Struggle for the Eastern Marches in the German Empire, 1894–1919*, Faculty of Political Science, Columbia University, New York 1941.

Tomlinson, J., *Hayek and the Market*, Pluto Press, London 1990.

Tönnies, F., 'Preface' to Hobbes, *Behemoth or the Long Parliament*, Simpkin, Marshall and Co., London 1889.

Tribe, K., *Governing Economy. The Reformation of German Economic Discourse 1750–1840*, Cambridge University Press, Cambridge 1988.

'Prussian Agriculture – German Politics: Max Weber 1892–7' in K. Tribe (ed.), *Reading Weber*, Routledge, London 1989, pp. 85–130.

'The *Geschichtliche Grundbegriffe* Project: From History of Ideas to Conceptual History', *Comparative Studies in Society and History*, vol. 31 (1989), pp. 180–4.

'Mercantilism and the Economics of State Formation', in L. Magnusson (ed.), *Mercantilism*, Kluwer, Dordrecht 1993, pp. 175–86.

'Business Education at the Mannheim Handelshochschule, 1907–1933', *Minerva*, vol. 32 (1994), pp. 158–85.

Triffin, R., *Europe and the Money Muddle. From Bilateralism to Near-Convertibility, 1947–56*, Yale University Press, New Haven 1957.

Tufte, E. R., *The Visual Display of Quantitative Information*, Graphics Press, Cheshire, Conn. 1983.

van Eyll, K., 'Die Gedanke zur Gründung einer Universität oder einer Handelshochschule in Köln bei Gustav Mevissen', in F.-W. Henning (ed.), *Handelsakademie – Handelshochschule – Wirtschafts- und Sozialwissenschaftliche Fakultät*, Böhlau Verlag, Cologne 1990, pp. 21–38.

Veit, O., 'Geldüberschuß und Wirtschaftslenkung', *Weltwirtschaftliches Archiv*, Bd. 57 (1943), pp. 278–309.

Vierhaus, R., 'Liberalismus', in O. Brunner, W. Conze, and R. Koselleck (eds.), *Geschichtliche Grundbegriffe*, Bd. III, Klett-Cotta, Stuttgart 1982, pp. 760–2.

von Berg, G. H., *Handbuch des Teutschen Policeyrechts* Bd. I, 2nd edn, Gebrüder Hahn, Hanover 1802.

von Hayek, F. A., 'The Nature and History of the Problem', in his *Collectivist Economic Planning*, George Routledge, London 1935, pp. 1–40.

The Road to Serfdom, Routledge and Kegan Paul, London 1944.

von Justi, J. H. G., *Grundriß einer Guten Regierung*, Frankfurt 1759.

von Ludewig, J. P., *Die, von Sr. Königlichen Majestät, unserm allergnädigstem Könige/ auf Dero Universität Halle, am 14. Iulii 1727 Neu angerichtete Profession, in Oeconomie, Policey und Kammer-Sachen*, Halle 1727.

von Mises, L., 'Die Wirtschaftsrechnung im sozialistischen Gemeinwesen', *Archiv für Sozialwissenschaft und Sozialpolitik*, Bd. 47 (1920), pp. 86–121.

von Oppen, B. R. (ed.), *Documents on Germany under Occupation*, Oxford University Press, Oxford 1955.

von Rohr, J. B., *Compendieuse Haußhaltungs-Bibliothek*, Leipzig 1716.

Einleitung zur Staats-Klugheit, Leipzig, 1718.

von Schröder, W., *Fürstliche Schatz- und Rentkammer*, Königsberg 1752 (first published 1686).

von Seckendorff, V. L., *Teutscher Fürsten-Stat*, Frankfurt a. M., 1656.

von Sonnenfels, J., *Grundsätze der Polizey, Handlung, und Finanz*, 3 Bde., 5th edn, Vienna 1787.

von Stackelberg, H., 'Die Grundlagen der Nationalökonomie (Bemerkungen zu dem gleichnamigen Buch von Walter Eucken)', *Weltwirtschaftliches Archiv*, Bd. 51 (1940), pp. 245–81.

'Theorie und Systematik der Wirtschaftslenkung', *Ordo*, Bd. 2 (1949), pp. 193–205.

The Theory of the Market Economy, William Hodge, London 1952.

von Stein, L., *System der Staatswissenschaft*, 2 vols., J. G. Cotta, Stuttgart 1852, 1856.

Lehrbuch der Volkswirthschaft, Wilhelm Braumüller, Vienna 1858.

von Wieser, L., 'The Austrian School and the Theory of Value', *Economic Journal*, vol. 1 (1891), pp. 108–21.

Voss, H., 'Einleitung' to F. List, *Kräfte und Mächte*, Wilhelm Langewiesche-Brandt, Ebenhausen bei München 1942.

Walker, M., 'Rights and Functions: The Social Categories of Eighteenth-Century German Jurists and Cameralists,' *Journal of Modern History*, 50 (1978), pp. 234–51.

Walther, R., 'Exkurs: Wirtschaftlicher Liberalismus' in O. Brunner, W. Conze, and R. Koselleck (eds.), *Geschichtliche Grundbegriffe*, Bd. III, Klett-Cotta, Stuttgart 1982, pp. 787–815.

Weber, A., 'Das Diplomexamen für Volkswirte', *Jahrbücher für Nationalökonomie und Statistik*, III. Folge, Bd. 65 (1923), pp. 289–318.

Weber, F. B., *Systematisches Handbuch der Staatswirthschaft*, Bd. 1, Abt. I, Berlin 1804.

Weber, M., 'Die Ergebnisse der deutschen Börsenenquete', *Zeitschrift für das Gesaammte Handelsrecht*, 4 pts., Bd. 43 (1895), pp. 83–219, 457–514; Bd. 44 (1896), pp. 29–74; Bd. 45 (1896), pp. 69–156.

Landwirtschaft und Agrarpolitik, Berlin 1893.

'Germany as an Industrial State' in K. Tribe (ed.), *Reading Weber*, Routledge, London 1989, pp. 210–20.

Erstes Buch. Die begrifflichen Grundlagen der Volkswirtschaftslehre (1898, unpublished).

'Roscher und Knies und die logischen Probleme der historischen Nationalökonomie', in his *Gesammelte Aufsätze zur Wissenschaftslehre*, 5th edn, J. C. B. Mohr (Paul Siebeck) 1982, pp. 1–145.

'Politik als Beruf', *Gesammelte Politische Schriften*, Drei Masken Verlag, Munich 1921, pp. 396–450.

'Zeugenaussage im Prozeß gegen Otto Neurath', in W. J. Mommsen (ed.), *Zur Neuordnung Deutschlands*, Max Weber Gesamtausgabe I, Bd. 16, p. 495.

Wirtschaft und Gesellschaft, 5th edn, J. C. B. Mohr (Paul Siebeck), Tübingen 1972.

Weber, Marianne, *Max Weber. Ein Lebensbild*, J. C. B. Mohr (Paul Siebeck), Tübingen 1926.

Werner, F., 'Die Handelshochschule als Hochschule für die Verwaltung', in

C. Eckert (ed.), *Der Eintritt der erfahrungswissenschaftlichen Intelligenz in die Verwaltung*, Ferdinand Enke, Stuttgart 1919, pp. 109–28.

Wickett, S. J., 'Political Economy at German Universities', *Economic Journal*, vol. 8 (1898), pp. 146–50.

Wills, E. V., 'Political Economy in the Early American College Curriculum', *South Atlantic Quarterly*, vol. 24 (1925), pp. 131–53.

Wilson, T., *The Myriad Faces of War*, Polity Press, Cambridge 1988.

Wolf, H. C., 'The Lucky Miracle: Germany 1945–1951', in R. Dornbusch, W. Nölling, and R. Layard (eds.), *Postwar Economic Reconstruction and Lessons for the East Today*, MIT Press, Cambridge, Mass. 1993, pp. 29–56.

Yagi, K., 'Carl Menger after 1871', draft translation of his *Osutoria Keizai Shisoushi Kenkyu*, Chapter 2 (1988).

Zaliski, E., *Stalinist Planning for Economic Growth 1933–1952*, Macmillan Press, London 1980.

Zehnter, H., *Das Staatslexikon von Rotteck und Welcker*, Gustav Fischer, Jena 1929.

Zielenziger, K., *Die alten deutschen Kameralisten*, Gustav Fischer, Jena 1914.

Zitelmann, R., 'Die totalitäre Seite der Moderne', in M. Prinz and R. Zitelmann (eds.), *Nationalsozialismus und Modernisierung*, Wissenschaftliche Buchgesellschaft, Darmstadt, 1991 pp. 1–20.

Index

Ideas in Context

Edited by Quentin Skinner (general editor), Lorraine Daston, Wolf
Lepenies, Richard Rorty and J. B. Schneewind

Titles marked with an asterisk are also available in paperback